International economic policy coordination

Since this volume is a record of conference proceedings, it has been exempted from the rules governing critical review of manuscripts by the Board of Directors of the National Bureau (resolution adopted 8 June 1948, as revised 21 November 1949 and 20 April 1968).

4 October 1984

International economic policy coordination

Edited by

WILLEM H. BUITER

and

RICHARD C. MARSTON

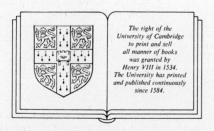

The right of the
University of Cambridge
to print and sell
all manner of books
was granted by
Henry VIII in 1534.
The University has printed
and published continuously
since 1584.

CAMBRIDGE UNIVERSITY PRESS

Cambridge
London   New York   New Rochelle
Melbourne   Sydney

Published by the Press Syndicate of the University of Cambridge
The Pitt Building, Trumpington Street, Cambridge CB2 1RP
32 East 57th Street, New York, NY 10022, USA
10 Stamford Road, Oakleigh, Melbourne 3166, Australia

First published 1985

Printed in Great Britain by the
University Press, Cambridge

Library of Congress catalogue card number: 84-29246

British Library cataloguing in publication data

International economic policy coordination.
1. International economic relations   2. World
politics – 1975–1985
I. Buiter, Willem H.   II. Marston, Richard C.
337   HF1411

ISBN 0 521 30554 3

UP

Contents

Tables

Figures

Preface

In this volume we are publishing the proceedings of the conference 'International Economic Policy Coordination', sponsored by the Centre for Economic Policy Research and the National Bureau of Economic Research, and held in London on June 28th–29th, 1984.

We would like to express our appreciation to the authors and discussants whose contributions are published here for their participation in the conference and readiness to help in the preparation of this volume. In addition to the authors and discussants, all those listed below also participated in the conference. Their great interest in the subject and lively contributions to the discussion added much to its value.

We would like to thank the Ford Foundation for providing financial support for the conference, and Thomas Bayard of the Foundation's staff for expressing interest in the project at an early stage in its planning. We are also grateful for financial support from the United Kingdom clearing banks and the Bank of England. The quality of this manuscript and the speed with which it was published owe much to the efforts of the technical editor, John Black of the University of Exeter. Stephen Yeo, Research and Publications Director of the CEPR, made sure that the authors, discussants and editors lived up to the commitments they had made at the conference. That the conference ran smoothly and efficiently was due in no small part to Monica Allen and Wendy Thompson of the CEPR, and we are most grateful to them. Finally, we would like to thank the Director of the CEPR, Richard Portes, and the Director of the International Studies Program of the NBER, William Branson, for first suggesting that a conference on international coordination should be coordinated internationally by the CEPR and NBER.

WILLEM H. BUITER
RICHARD C. MARSTON

Contributors

Editors

Willem H. Buiter *London School of Economics*
Richard C. Marston *The Wharton School, University of Pennsylvania*

Authors

W. Max Corden *Australian National University*
David Currie *Queen Mary College, London*
Barry Eichengreen *Harvard University*
Jacob A. Frenkel *University of Chicago*
Paul Levine *Polytechnic of the South Bank, London*
Marcus Miller *University of Warwick*
Patrick Minford *University of Liverpool*
Gilles Oudiz *Institut National de la Statistique et des Études Économiques*
Tommaso Padoa Schioppa *Banca d'Italia*
Assaf Razin *University of Tel Aviv*
Jeffrey Sachs *Harvard University*
Mark Salmon *University of Warwick*

Discussants

Michael J. Artis *University of Manchester*
David K. H. Begg *Worcester College, Oxford*
William H. Branson *Princeton University*
Ralph C. Bryant *The Brookings Institution*
Matthew B. Canzoneri *Federal Reserve System, Washington*
Richard N. Cooper *Harvard University*
Michael Emerson *Commission of the European Communities*
Jo Anna Gray *Washington State University*

Koichi Hamada *University of Tokyo*
Dale W. Henderson *Federal Reserve System, Washington and Georgetown University*
Louka T. Katseli *Centre of Planning and Economic Research, Athens*
Jorge Braga de Macedo *Princeton University*
Stephen Marris *Institute for International Economics, Washington*
Georges de Ménil *Ecole des Hautes Études en Sciences Sociales, Paris*
Kenneth Rogoff *Federal Reserve System, Washington*
Jeffrey R. Shafer *Organisation for Economic Cooperation and Development*
Stephen J. Turnovsky *University of Illinois*
David Vines *Department of Applied Economics, University of Cambridge*

Other participants

Charles Bean *London School of Economics*
Anthony Bottrill *HM Treasury*
Jeremy Bray *House of Commons*
Sam Brittan *The Financial Times*
Michael Calingaert *US Embassy, London*
Christopher Johnson *Lloyds Bank*
Geoffrey Maynard *The Chase Manhattan Bank*
Grayham Mizon *University of Southampton*
Joan Pearce *Royal Institute of International Affairs*
Richard Portes *Centre for Economic Policy Research and Birkbeck College*
Michael Wickens *University of Southampton*
Jackie Whitley *Lloyds Bank*
Charles Wyplosz *Institut Européen d'Administration des Affaires*

Introduction

WILLEM H. BUITER and
RICHARD C. MARSTON

In the postwar period, trading and financial ties have increased markedly among the industrial countries. Such ties ensure that one country's economic policies have spillover effects on other countries and that the domestic effects of these policies, in turn, are modified by the policies of other countries. Greater economic integration, therefore, has brought with it greater interdependence among national economic policies. Because of this interdependence, coordination of economic policy between countries is often vital, but successful coordination has been the exception rather than the rule.

Despite the importance of international coordination, the subject has not previously generated as much interest among economists as it deserves. Recently, however, a number of economists have begun to study coordination using a variety of innovative approaches. In June 1984, the Centre for Economic Policy Research and the National Bureau of Economic Research brought many of these economists together for a conference at Chatham House in London. The conference provided a unique opportunity for those studying coordination to assess the direction of current research on this important topic.

Economists have recently approached the subject of international coordination in several different ways. Some have studied in detail the international transmission process itself. Whether one country's expansionary policy is transmitted positively or negatively to another country depends on the strength of the real and financial links between the two economies. Particular patterns of transmission, in turn, may strengthen or weaken the case for the international coordination of policies. A simple example of this is the locomotive policy advocated in the mid 1970s. According to this policy, the locomotives (some of the main industrial countries) were to adopt expansionary policies which would, under the assumption of positive international transmission, pull all countries out of the recession. Negative transmission, in contrast, would call for very different policies.

Other studies analyze international coordination in strategic terms using game theory concepts drawn from the study of oligopoly. In these studies, unilateral national behavior is often modelled as Nash or Stackelberg non-cooperative behavior, with Stackelberg behavior occurring when one nation takes a leadership position vis-à-vis others. Such behavior is then contrasted with cooperative behavior and the incentives to violate cooperative agreements are studied. The advantages of one form of strategic behavior over another in many cases depend on the nature of the transmission mechanism, a dependence discussed at length in several of the papers. Strategic analysis can provide insight into one nation's interaction with another. As one panelist pointed out, for example, recent efforts at European cooperation can be interpreted as attempts to replace Stackelberg leadership by the United States with a more symmetric relationship between the United States and Europe (with the latter acting as a bloc rather than as a set of individual nations).

Where some studies depart radically from previous work is in the introduction of an intertemporal dimension to the analysis. Moving from a static to a dynamic analysis can make considerable difference to the analysis of coordination. As an example, Jeffrey Sachs was once asked to show if propositions involving beggar-thy-neighbor behavior developed in static models would continue to hold in multiperiod models where exchange rate changes could be reversed. The paper presented at the conference by Gilles Oudiz and Sachs succeeds in demonstrating that later adjustments of the exchange rate do significantly modify, though they do not reverse, the effects of current policy. In multiperiod models, moreover, current expectations about the future effects of a current policy may make that policy less effective. Government spending, for example, may be much less effective in a multiperiod model where the future effects of current financing are taken into account through intertemporal budget constraints. Furthermore, only in an intertemporal model do we find the problem of time consistency. This problem arises when governments have an incentive to renege on previously announced policies and when the private sector's expectations take such incentives into account. Policies that are coordinated may prove to be time consistent in circumstances where unilateral policies are inconsistent, since coordination may rule out certain actions by national governments.

All the papers in this volume emphasize one or more of these factors, some focusing more on transmission effects, others on strategic behavior, and still others on intertemporal considerations. The papers together reveal the high quality and wide range of recent research on international coordination.

In the first paper, Corden considers whether there is any basis for the popular argument that coordinated expansion would be easier to achieve than expansion by any individual country. Corden introduces a model of the real sectors of two economies in which international transmission occurs principally through the terms of trade. An economic expansion by one country improves the terms of trade of the other country, thus shifting the latter's Phillips curve in a favorable direction, and this in turn induces the latter country to pursue a more expansionary policy. The model illustrates clearly circumstances in which international cooperation which leads to coordinated expansion dominates non-cooperative behavior of either the Nash or Stackelberg variety. Later in the paper Corden qualifies his analysis by taking into account the future effects of current policy, including the possibility of future inflation inducing contraction by one country which hurts the other country.

Jacob Frenkel and Assaf Razin study international transmission effects in an intertemporal model, examining the effect of government expenditure on world rates of interest and spending. Their model assumes a two-country world within which capital markets are integrated, individuals behave rationally, and the behavior of individuals and governments is subject to temporal and intertemporal budget constraints. They show that a transitory rise in government spending raises interest rates and lowers domestic and foreign wealth while an expected future rise in government spending lowers interest rates, reduces the value of domestic wealth and raises the value of foreign wealth. Unlike in Corden's model, therefore, negative transmission can occur in some circumstances, with transmission occuring through world capital markets. The effect of a permanent rise in government spending on the rate of interest depends on whether the domestic economy is a net saver or dissaver in the world economy, i.e., whether it has a current account surplus or deficit. In general, the effects of government spending can be analyzed by reference to a multitude of 'transfer problem criteria' involving comparisons between marginal spending and saving propensities of governments and private sectors in the two economies.

The way in which national policies are transmitted from one country to another depends not only on the channels of transmission specified in a model, but also on the quantitative magnitude of key structural parameters. Patrick Minford uses a nine-country model he has estimated to investigate the transmission effects of US monetary and fiscal policy. The model exhibits many 'new classical' features including an aggregate supply curve based on a labor contract model and rational expectations.

Minford reports several policy simulations using this model, the most interesting of which is a simulation of US fiscal policy. According to this simulation, US deficits crowd out other US spending with the only stimulative effects being on the rest of the world (with a lag). The crowding out occurs because of strong wealth effects in the financial sector of his model. Monetary policy, in contrast, has very strong effects on output. Interpreting the results of his simulations, Minford suggests that the US monetary contraction in 1980–81 and expansion in late 1982 have been the major cause of the latest world business cycle.

Barry Eichengreen applies the strategic analysis characteristic of much recent work on international coordination to the financial history of the interwar period. Eichengreen develops an explicit two-country model of the interwar gold standard that shows clearly the advantages of coordinated action but also explains why cooperative solutions proved so difficult to achieve. The model features short run output variability, a money multiplier sensitive to bank rate, and perfect capital mobility. Eichengreen shows that cooperative behavior necessarily dominates Nash non-cooperative behavior, in the sense of more nearly achieving gold and price targets. Both countries, moreover, benefit if one country moves to a Stackelberg leadership position from the Nash equilibrium, but the country acting as the follower benefits more than the leader. Each country has an incentive, therefore, to engage in a game of 'chicken', attempting to force the other party to accept the role of leader. Eichengreen interprets this model in the light of interwar attempts at cooperation beginning with the Genoa Conference of 1922 and leading to the Tripartite Agreement concluded by Britain, France, and the United States in 1936.

The paper by Marcus Miller and Mark Salmon is one of several in the conference which address the problem of time consistency, which as discussed above arises when a government has an incentive to renege on previously announced policies. To ensure that policies are time consistent, Miller and Salmon assume that policy makers take the real exchange rate as given in setting current policy. This, according to the authors, is what will happen when the authorities have lost credibility so that the markets refuse to believe official pronouncements. Within this set of time consistent rules, they derive the optimal solutions for Nash open-loop games, where each nation takes the other's policy paths into account, and Nash closed-loop games, where policy rules are taken into account, and compare these with cooperative solutions.

Like Miller and Salmon, David Currie and Paul Levine examine the effects of policies in a dynamic model, in their case a model that features lags in both demand and supply behavior. They consider a variety of simple policy rules involving the money supply, nominal income, exchange rate, or price level. The price rule is found to perform significantly better than any other rule in a single economy, but when applied to all economies together it performs very poorly. This is because the price rule works through beggar-thy-neighbor variations in exchange rates that are not feasible if all countries follow the rule.

Gilles Oudiz and Jeffrey Sachs, as mentioned above, show that the payoffs to beggar-thy-neighbor policies look very different in one period and multiperiod contexts, because exchange rate changes in the current period are typically reversed in later periods. International coordination which avoids beggar-thy-neighbor actions, they find, is less desirable in a multiperiod model. They ask whether international coordination necessarily improves welfare if governments, as some have claimed, are more myopic than the private sector. Governments have a short run expansionary bias if policy can raise output today while increasing inflation only in the future. As long as policy is not coordinated, however, the fear of currency depreciation following a unilateral expansion keeps this bias in check, whereas coordination permits governments to expand together and avoid any depreciation. They also make several interesting points about time consistency. They show, for example, that international coordination can make policies time consistent in cases where unilateral policies are time inconsistent if the time inconsistency stems from the ability to manipulate the exchange rate.

In the final paper, Tommaso Padoa Schioppa analyzes whether the European Monetary System (EMS), the exchange rate system tying the mark, franc, lira and other European currencies together, can serve as a model for other efforts to coordinate economic policy. He contrasts 'institutional cooperation' through arrangements such as the EMS with 'ad-hoc cooperation', and argues that if institutions are strong enough, there is more scope for discretion in the management of international economic problems. He also considers the experience of multicountry monetary cooperation within the EMS and presents statistical evidence on the System's ability to achieve its objectives.

The conference concluded with a panel session, chaired by William Branson of the NBER and Princeton University, on prospects for international policy coordination. The last section of this volume presents the prepared remarks of the four panelists: Richard Cooper, Harvard University; Michael Emerson, Commission of the European Communities; Louka Katseli, Centre of Economic Planning and Research; and Stephen Marris, Institute for International Economics.

Richard Cooper cites a number of instances in which international cooperation was successful, either because public goods were involved (as in the establishment of Greenwich mean time or the metric system) or because there were significant externalities or spillovers (such as in the case of GATT or the non-proliferation treaty). Successful cooperation was achieved in such cases, according to Cooper, because the mutual benefits were both large in magnitude and apparent to those involved. Cooperation in the macroeconomic field, however, faces a number of obstacles including disagreements among governments on the outlook for economies at any given time, differences in objectives (e.g., inflation versus unemployment), and disputes over the distribution of gains. Even in instances where there are positive gains for all nations, the negotiations often bog down over how to divide those gains. Finally, there are considerable differences of opinion, even among experts, about how economies work. The variety of papers presented in this conference provide evidence to support this point.

In his remarks, Michael Emerson describes current US policy as that of limiting international cooperation to trade and LDC debt problems while ignoring macroeconomic coordination. He argues that if the failure to coordinate macro policies leads to a further deterioration of the world economy, this could jeopardize current trade agreements and make more difficult future cooperation in solving debt problems. Commenting on the prospects for European policy coordination, Emerson suggests that the first three years of the European monetary system had been disappointing, but that European policy was now better coordinated, albeit in a restrictive direction. Because policy is more credible than before, moreover, restrictive actions are less costly in terms of lost output and employment.

Louka Katseli focuses on the asymmetries which characterize the current international system and international decision-making. There are asymmetries in the origin of the shocks affecting different countries, as well as in the impacts of the shocks on various markets. In addition, there is an asymmetry in the monitoring of outcomes and performances of different countries; for example, there are rules which apply to the less-developed countries which seem not to apply to the United States, even when both are running deficits. Moreover, there is no monitoring of the position of creditor countries as there is for debtor countries. As far as coordination of policies is concerned, she suggests that more attention be paid to the structures of decision-making in international organizations, including how responsibilities for different economic problems are divided among various international agencies and meetings of national governments.

The last member of the panel, Stephen Marris, argues that a key lesson from the flexible rate period was not made clear by early advocates of flexible rates – that an expansion by one country might be precluded because of the effect of the ensuing depreciation on the domestic inflation rate. Because economic cooperation lifts the restraints imposed by the exchange rate, it might lead to more inflation than uncoordinated national policies. But such effects depend very much on events. Thus, at the time of the second oil shock, Marris suggests, governments were fortified in their deflationary policies by the knowledge that other governments were following similar strategies. Marris goes on to discuss the current policy problem – the divergence in policies between the United States and the rest of the world. He expresses the view that the gains from more coordination in fiscal and monetary policy are apparent to all in the present situation, despite the considerable divergence of views about the sign and magnitude of transmission effects in other more general circumstances.

The general discussion following the remarks by the panelists ranged over a number of issues. One question that continually arose concerned the direction that future research should take. Most participants agreed that recent work on international coordination, of which the papers in this volume are certainly representative, had succeeded in clarifying a number of issues of importance to the subject and in developing analytical approaches required to study them. There was disagreement, however, about whether future research should concentrate on further analytical work or should instead turn to empirical research which would attempt to quantify the gains from coordination. No resolution of this question was reached. We hope that this volume will serve as a basis for further research, both theoretical and empirical.

1   On transmission and coordination under flexible exchange rates*

W. MAX CORDEN

This paper considers the need for macroeconomic policy coordination under flexible exchange rates and the nature of the equilibria that may be reached in the absence of coordination. It was inspired by the extensive discussions that have taken place on the need for coordination, and especially by the so-called 'locomotive theory' of the late nineteen seventies, which suggested that coordinated expansion would be easier than expansion by any one country on its own. Essentially, the initial model presented here is a formalisation of popular arguments that lack of coordination of macroeconomic policies leads to more deflation than would an efficient or optimally coordinated set of policies. The model includes a short-term non-vertical Phillips curve – and hence assumes that macroeconomic management can affect employment and output.

The main model is presented in Part I. This is a condensation of Corden (1983b), where the model and its implications are spelt out in more detail. Part II analyses in detail a qualification that seems important, namely that one country needs to take into account the possible future adverse effects on itself of increased inflation in the other country. This qualification, which was only briefly discussed in Corden (1983b), involves intertemporal considerations that are ignored in the short-term (and short-sighted) approach of Part I. Finally, Part III both extends and qualifies the discussion. It is argued that the main model may be more relevant for a world of many countries, even though the formal model is a two-country model. On the other hand, the limitations of the whole short-term approach are also noted. In addition, the effects of introducing international capital movements are sketched out.[1]

I A two-country model of macroeconomic policy interaction

We now build a simple two-country model, beginning with one of the countries, Germany. The analysis will be completely symmetrical, so that

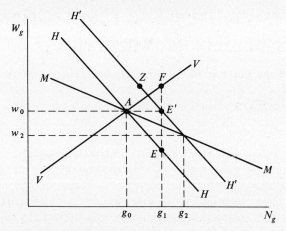

1.1 The effects on Germany of US expansion

the foundations also apply to the other country, the United States. The exchange rate floats and there are no international capital movements.[2]

The real wage, employment and the terms of trade

The German production function and capital stock are given. German employment, N_g varies so as to equate the marginal product of labor with the real wage in terms of Germany's own product, i.e. the *product real wage*, R_g. The German terms of trade are T, an increase being an improvement. The crucial distinction must then be made between the product real wage, R_g and the *income real wage*, W_g, where $W_g = W_g$ (R_g, T). The income real wage reflects the consumption basket of wage earners and is the nominal wage deflated by a price index of the home-produced and the imported good. For a given R_g, an improvement in the terms of trade would raise W_g.

Figure 1.1 shows the German income real wage, W_g on the vertical axis and German employment, N_g on the horizontal. MM is the marginal product of labor curve, drawn for constant terms of trade, T. A movement down the curve results from a fall in R_g, which (with T constant) causes W_g to fall. An improvement in the terms of trade would shift the curve upwards.

The curve HH is drawn for a constant level of United States output (and employment). It shows that, with US output given, an increase in German employment would involve a deterioration in the German terms of trade. The reason is that, with US output given, the US offer curve facing Germany is given, and the increase in German employment – which shifts the German offer curve outwards – will involve a movement along the US offer curve.

A rise in US output is represented by a shift of the HH curve to $H'H'$. If, at the same time, German employment expanded from g_0 to g_2 the terms of trade would stay constant and the German income real wage would fall from W_0 to W_2. This is the special case of a mutually *balanced expansion*. Another special case is where the German income real wage is rigid. An expansion of US output would then lead to a rise in German employment from g_0 to g_1.

We have assumed that a rise in US output improves the German terms of trade by shifting the US offer curve outwards, and that this, in turn raises the income real wage for given German employment. Hence the HH curve shifts to the right. This result follows from a model where each country is assumed to produce only one product (or, in a multi-product model, where the factor intensities do not differ much). It can be called the assumption of *positive transmission* and will be reconsidered at the end of Part II.

The real wage gap and the Phillips curve

The next step is to derive what is essentially a short-run non-vertical Phillips curve.

The curve VV traces out the target real wage at various levels of employment. For any given level of employment it shows the income real wage at which the labor market is in equilibrium in the special sense that the trade unions (or others who determine wages) are satisfied with the real wage at that level of employment, even though there are potential workers involuntarily unemployed. It represents the target of the unions, not of the government.

For any given level of employment there can be a *real wage gap*, namely a divergence between the target real wage and the actual real wage. The latter is assumed to determine the actual level of employment, the product market always being in equilibrium even though the labor market is not. At employment g_1 the real wage gap with the original level of US output is FE. The increase in US output lowers the real wage gap at that level of employment to FE'.

We now assume that the actual real wage can be brought below the target real wage (at least during the short period concerned) by continuous price inflation above the initial rate of inflation. Price inflation can bring about this real wage gap because of sluggishness of nominal wage adjustment, nominal wages lagging behind prices, the lag increasing with the rate of price inflation. The greater the required real wage gap, the greater price inflation needs to be. In turn, increased inflation is brought about by an

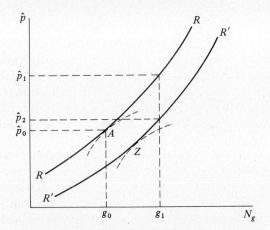

1.2 German policy choices when US expands

increase in the rate of growth of nominal demand (rate of growth of the money supply when velocity is constant).

Obviously this is a short-term analysis, subject to all the limitations of drawing a fixed non-vertical Phillips curve. Let $\hat{p}$ be the rate of German price inflation and $\hat{w}$ the rate of German nominal wage increase. The idea is that a rise in $\hat{p}$ over the period leads to a temporary rise of $\hat{p}$ over $\hat{w}$, so that W_g falls by a given amount over the period; this implies that by the end of the period $\hat{w}$ has caught up with $\hat{p}$.

Figure 1.2 shows the relationship between $\hat{p}$ and N_g. The curve RR is drawn for the initial level of US output. It is a kind of Phillips curve, showing how German employment rises as the rate of German price inflation rises during the period. Inflation $\hat{p}_1$, for example creates a real wage gap FE and so yields employment g_1. The initial rate of inflation $\hat{p}_0$ (perhaps determined by given expectations of nominal demand growth) yielded a zero real wage gap, and hence employment g_0. The rise in US output (and hence improvement in the German terms of trade for given German employment) shifts the RR curve to $R'R'$. German employment g_1 can now be sustained with a lower real wage gap FE' and hence lower rate of inflation $\hat{p}_2$. The next step is to introduce the usual social welfare contours allowing the selection of optimal points on the two 'Phillips curves'. If the original point A was an optimal point, the new one is likely to be south-east of A, say at Z, representing the idea that the gains from US expansion will be taken out in Germany partly by reduced inflation and partly by extra employment. Through this German policy reaction, an increase in US employment thus leads also to a rise in German employment.

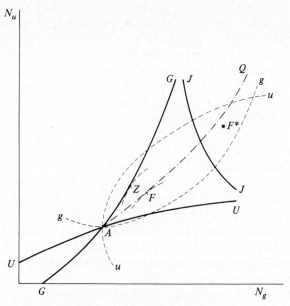

1.3 US and German policy reaction curves

The policy reaction curves

In Figure 1.3 GG is the German policy reaction curve. It shows the level of German employment, N_g brought about by nominal demand management in Germany for every given level of US employment, N_u. Every point on GG represents an optimal point (from the point of view of German policy-makers) on a German short-term Phillips curve. A movement upwards on GG (say from A to Z, equivalent to movements from A to Z in Figures 1.1 and 1.2) is associated with an improvement in the German terms of trade, a rise in the German income real wage, a fall in the German product real wage, and a fall in the German rate of inflation.

Following exactly the same principles, one can draw a US policy reaction curve UU, showing how US employment rises as German employment rises, each point on UU being an optimal point on a US Phillips curve, with German employment regarded as given.

Before making use of these reaction curves to analyse the two countries' policy interactions we might note that there are three distinct reasons why the German curve is steeper than the United States one – three factors that ensure (each factor on its own) stability and uniqueness of the Nash equilibrium to be discussed below: (1) diminishing physical returns to extra employment in each country owing to the fixity of the capital stocks, (2) an increase in the target real wage as employment increases, and (3) a reduction in the rate of price inflation as employment increases. In the absence of all three factors in both countries the two reaction curves would coincide with AQ, one country's expansion eliciting expansion by the other country along the *balanced expansion* (constant terms of trade) *path*. The presence of at least one of these factors in at least one country is sufficient for the analysis to follow.

Non-cooperative equilibria

If there were indeed non-cooperative behaviour based on the myopic assumption that the other country's output would stay fixed, the Nash equilibrium at A would be attained. The USA would always move vertically towards UU and Germany would move horizontally towards GG. Each country would have its target, UU and GG, and its proximate instrument, N_u and N_g – in turn determined by adjusting nominal demand via monetary and fiscal policies. The assignment of instrument to target would be stable.

The levels of social welfare attained are indicated by the two indifference curves through A, uu tracing out equal social welfare for the USA (any curve to the right representing an improvement), and gg tracing out constant social welfare for Germany, (higher curves representing an improvement). It is apparent that a move to any point on these curves up to C, or within the area enclosed by uu and gg, would be a Pareto-improvement. Thus, while the Nash equilibrium is stable, it is not Pareto efficient. The Nash equilibrium has a contractionary bias, in the sense that both countries could be better off if, within limits, they both expanded beyond that equilibrium.

Alternatively, a non-cooperative equilibrium might be attained through policy leadership by one country. Germany might react to US policy by taking US output as given, so staying on GG, while the United States adjusted its policy so as to attain the optimal point for it on GG. This would yield the Stackelberg equilibrium at Z. This is Pareto-superior to A, but still has some contractionary bias, because mutual expansion from Z could lead to Pareto-improvements.

Special note might be taken of the balanced expansion path AQ along which the terms of trade stay constant. Along this path neither country can be compensated by a terms of trade improvement for the adverse movement in its product real wage resulting from expansion, so that the two income real wages must fall. Along this path neither country is 'beggaring its neighbour' for the sake of restraining domestic price inflation. A non-cooperative equilibrium might be attained through policy leadership where the reactive country, Germany, aims to keep the terms of trade constant, while the USA chooses an optimal point given this reaction. *AQ* then becomes Germany's reaction curve and the USA will choose point *F*.

It cannot, of course, be assumed that non-cooperative behaviour would lead to any of the results just discussed. In particular, the Nash equilibrium implies myopia. The question then is whether there are any general rules to constrain non-cooperative behaviour that are likely to have favorable results. One might be called the *unilateral expansion rule* and seems, at first sight, plausible. Wherever countries find themselves initially, they may expand, but may not contract. The point is that one country's contraction always has an adverse effect on the other, so this rule ensures that any *voluntary* change is a Pareto improvement. A country will expand only if this would benefit itself, and such expansion must also benefit the other country. This rule would limit equilibria to somewhere on or within *the cone GAU* (above *A*). Such a rule might need to be supplemented by an agreement for coordinated contraction when both desire this.

Policy coordination

The scope for policy coordination is obvious. In Figure 1.3 *JJ* traces out points of tangency of the indifference curves. This is the *Pareto-efficiency locus*. It divides *the cone GAU* referred to above into an upper and a lower part. If the countries are not on this locus they can, by mutual arrangement, always achieve a Pareto-improvement. This could be brought about by both expanding (if they start in the lower part of the cone), both contracting (starting in the upper part), or one expanding and the other contracting (possibly required if starting outside the cone).

Starting at *A* it is apparent that there is much scope for a joint expansion that yields a Pareto improvement. In fact, a movement to any point enclosed by the two indifference curves through *A* will make them both better off. As long as they are not on *JJ* there is always scope for a Pareto-improvement.

Conceivably the starting point might be at a point such as *F**, a case of mutual over-expansion. Joint contraction can then bring about improvements for both. Contraction by one country will always have an adverse effect on the other country, but the losses for the other country are in this case outweighed by the gains from its own contraction. The common view, also stated earlier in this paper, that non-coordination is likely to lead to a contractionary bias, implies that coordination to obtain a Pareto-improvement calls for mutual expansion. The implicit assumption is that, in the absence of coordination, the Nash or Stackelberg equilibria would be reached. But once this assumption is removed, coordination to attain a Pareto improvement may require contraction by one or both countries.

II Intertemporal effects

It has been assumed that one country, say the USA, balances the favorable current output effects of an expansion against the unfavorable inflation effects. But the transmission to the other country, Germany, is purely through the output effect, which, if the transmission is positive, is favorable for Germany. US inflation has no effect on Germany, which can insulate itself from foreign inflation with a flexible exchange rate. Put another way, a US expansion has a favorable real and an unfavorable nominal effect, and only the real effect is transmitted to Germany. Thus it is in the interests of each country that the other country expands as much as possible irrespective of the inflationary effects in the other country, and, from a world point of view, each should expand more than if it considered only its own interest. This sums up the 'locomotive argument' for coordination, which has been formalised in this paper. But there is a difficulty in this approach.

Adverse future effects of foreign inflation

There is no reason why a country should regard an increase in its rate of inflation as adverse if this is never expected to have any real effects. Presumably an increase in current inflation (or in future inflation stimulated perhaps by an increase in inflationary expectations now) is thought adverse because it is expected to have adverse *real* effects of some kind. An increase in inflation may be thought to lead to accelerating inflationary expectations, requiring increased inflation to maintain employment; and increasing inflation may have adverse effects on productivity for given employment. In addition, to prevent inflation getting out of hand, employment may eventually have to be reduced for some time. But these *future* real effects in the USA of a rise in current US inflation would spill over to Germany in the usual way through the terms of trade. Hence, Germany should expect to lose later from current US expansion.

Current welfare and future welfare

It is thus necessary to introduce an explicitly intertemporal analysis. As before, we begin with the case of Germany, the analysis being completely symmetrical.

First we set out an equation for current German welfare, Z_c and then for expected future German welfare, Z_f. This refers to 'welfare' as perceived by the German authorities. We assume that Z_c depends not only on current German employment, N_g but also on the terms of trade for given employment, an improvement in the terms of trade raising German real incomes. An increase in US employment, N_u improves the German terms of trade (by shifting the US offer curve outwards), and so raises German welfare. Hence

$$Z_c = Z_c(N_g, N_u) \quad Z_{c1} > 0, Z_{c2} > 0 \tag{1}$$

Note that the current German rate of inflation does not have any direct effect on current German welfare. Furthermore, we are ruling out immiserizing growth. This would mean that an increase in German employment, and hence output, would worsen the terms of trade sufficiently for German welfare to decline.

Next, we set out an equation for expected future German welfare, Z_f. Firstly, it depends negatively on current German inflation $\hat{p}_g$. Secondly, it depends negatively on current US inflation, $\hat{p}_u$. The mechanism of the latter relationship is that current US inflation is expected to reduce US output and employment in the future, hence shift the US offer curve inwards, and so – assuming positive transmission – lower German welfare in the future.

$$Z_f = Z_f(\hat{p}_g, \hat{p}_u) \quad Z_{f1} < 0, Z_{f2} < 0 \tag{2}$$

The next step is to bring in the German Phillips curve equation. Current German employment, N_g is related positively to current German inflation, $\hat{p}_g$, an increase in both being brought about by nominal demand expansion, and to US employment (which determines the US offer curve). We no longer assume automatically that a rise in US employment must inevitably lead to a policy response in Germany that raises German employment. It will be shown below that a rational policy response could lead to negative employment transmission.

$$N_g = N_g(\hat{p}_g, N_u) \quad N_{g1} > 0, N_{g2} \gtreqless 0 \tag{3}$$

Finally, we bring in an equation for total welfare, Z which depends positively on the 'welfares' in the two periods.

$$Z = Z(Z_c, Z_f) \quad Z_1 > 0, Z_2 > 0 \tag{4}$$

How US expansion affects German welfare: positive and negative total transmission

Let us first represent the system for the special case of Part I of this paper where $Z_{f2} = 0$ (i.e. future German welfare does *not* depend on current US inflation).

In Figure 1.4 QQ is drawn for the initial level of US employment, N_u.

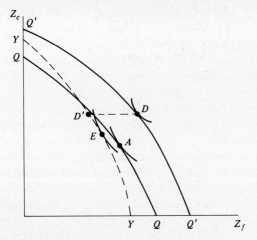

1.4 A case of negative total transmission

It represents the German Phillips curve, a movement along it to the left being brought about by nominal demand expansion in Germany which raises German employment (hence raising current welfare, Z_c) and raises German inflation (hence lowering future welfare, Z_f). The starting point is A, assumed to be the optimal point.

A rise in US employment, N_u, shifts the curve outwards to $Q'Q'$ by raising Z_c for any given Z_f (i.e. for any given $\hat{p}_g$). Assuming that the gain in welfare possibilities is taken out partly in the form of a rise in future welfare, $\hat{p}_g$ will have to fall (this being the only way in which future welfare can be raised at this stage) and equilibrium will be at a point such as D. At this stage there is clearly a rise in total welfare (move to a higher indifference curve) so we can say that there has been *positive total transmission* of US expansion.

The rise in US employment, N_u will be associated with a rise in US inflation, $\hat{p}_u$. We assume now that the USA has moved along its Phillips curve for given German employment, and we introduce the new element in the story: the rise in $\hat{p}_u$ has an adverse effect on expected future welfare in Germany, i.e. $Z_{f2} < 0$. This is represented by a movement to the left of the $Q'Q'$ curve to YY. For any given level of Z_c, there is a fall in Z_f.

If N_g and $\hat{p}_g$ stayed at the level that had yielded D, the point D' on YY would be reached (i.e. there would be no change in current welfare since N_g would not change). But the optimal point on YY could be above or below D'. This optimal point in Figure 1.4 is at E, and is the result of an income effect, which has reduced Z_c and Z_f below the level at D, and a substitution effect, which has shifted welfare towards Z_c. Compared with

D, Z_f must fall, while Z_c could rise or fall. Compared with A, the initial equilibrium, Z_c and Z_f could have risen or fallen.

The move from A to D raised total welfare, Z and the further move to E lowered it. In Figure 1.4 the net result has been to lower it (the indifference curve through E being below that through A), so that there is *negative total transmission*, in the sense that an increase in employment in the USA has lowered total welfare of Germany once the expected adverse effect on Germany of the rise in US inflation is taken into account. It is thus in Germany's interest to discourage US expansion.

There could, of course, be positive total transmission, and this seems much more probable. The less Germany expects her terms of trade to be affected by changes in future US productivity or employment, and the more Germany discounts the future, the more likely is positive total transmission.

Negative employment transmission

The effect of a rise in N_u on German welfare is distinct from the effect on German employment. It is just conceivable that German employment N_g declines when N_u rises. This is *negative employment transmission*. There are two reasons why this is possible.

(1) The rise in N_u raises current German welfare, Z_c for given German employment. While it also lowers $\hat{p}_g$ for given German employment, and so raises Z_f, it may be desired to shift more of the welfare gain into the future, so that there would be a movement along the Phillips curve designed to lower $\hat{p}_g$ further, and so lower German employment. Thus at D in Figure 1.4 N_g could have fallen relative to A.

(2) If the optimal point E on YY is below D' (as in Figure 1.4) the adverse future effect of the rise in $\hat{p}_u$ will have induced a movement along the German Phillips curve designed to shift some of this adverse effect into the present by lowering N_g and $\hat{p}_g$. The essential argument is that the expected future adverse effect of US inflation would be partially offset by a reduction in current German inflation, this bringing about a fall in German employment. Going right back to Figure 1.2, this means that the optimal point Z on the new Phillips curve $R'R'$ could be to the left of Ag_0.

Effects on two-country interaction

The question now is how these intertemporal considerations affect the two-country interaction model represented by Figure 1.3.

This model was based on two assumptions. (1) There was positive total transmission, expansion by one country always raising the welfare of the other, assuming the latter has made an optimal adjustment. This meant that welfare of both countries could be improved by movements upwards and to the right of A; in other words, a cooperative solution designed to yield a Pareto-improvement would involve mutual expansion relative to the Nash solution. (2) There was positive employment transmission, employment expansion by one country leading to employment expansion by the other along its reaction curve. Hence both reaction curves were positively sloped, and for reasons specified, the non-cooperative Nash solution was stable.

We have seen that, once intertemporal effects are introduced, there may still be both positive total transmission and positive employment transmission. In that case the interaction model of Part I, and with it Figure 1.3, are fully applicable.

It remains to allow for (1) negative total transmission and (2) negative employment transmission. We shall consider here only each on its own, always assuming the other is positive, and that negative transmission between countries goes in both directions. Mixed cases can be easily worked out.

(1) If there is negative total transmission the reaction curves will have the same slopes and characteristics as before (because employment transmission is still positive). But the indifference curves in Figure 1.3 will be bowed the opposite way and welfare will rise with movements *down GG* and *UU*. The Pareto-efficiency curve, JJ' will be below A, so that Pareto-improvements can result from mutual *contraction* when the Nash equilibrium is the starting point.

(2) If there is negative employment transmission the reaction curves will be negatively sloped. Furthermore, the Nash equilibrium could be unstable. But, given that positive total transmission remains, Pareto-improvements relative to the Nash equilibrium would still be obtainable from coordinated mutual *expansion*.

Positive and negative transmission again

At the beginning of this paper it was noted that the assumption of *positive transmission* was being made, namely that expansion by one country not only improved the other's terms of trade but also that this raised the other's income real wage for any given level of employment. This assumption was summed up in Figure 1.1 by the movement to the right of the HH curve (to $H'H'$) as a result of US expansion. We have also made the assumption that such positive transmission is expected to apply in the future – i.e. that a productivity decline in the USA would worsen Germany's terms of trade and shift its HH curve adversely.

Here two observations must be made. The first is that such positive transmission in each separate period can still be compatible both with negative *total* transmission and with negative *employment* transmission. In fact, in the cases that have just been discussed, this has been so. Positive transmission in the future has accounted for the inward movement of the YY curve in Figure 1.4 which – if it goes far enough (i.e. the adverse productivity effect of a rise in $\hat{p}_u$ is high and positive transmission is high) – may lead to negative total transmission. In addition, we have represented the case where more than the whole of a favourable effect from US expansion (movement to the right of the HH curve in Figure 1.1 or of RR in Figure 1.2) is taken out in lower inflation, with employment actually declining.

The second observation is that the assumption of positive transmission in each period cannot be taken for granted. It is conceivable that a US expansion shifts the HH curve in Figure 1.1 to the left. Such a possibility of *negative transmission* has been analysed in detail in Corden and Turnovsky (1983).

Either a US expansion might worsen the German terms of trade (if the US expansion is sufficiently anti-trade biased) or an improvement of the German terms of trade might shift the HH curve to the left because Germany exports products which are non-labor intensive. (A better example is an improvement in the Australian terms of trade, which raises food prices and so lowers the income real wage for given employment). In these cases the purely static model of Part I would yield negative employment transmission. On the other hand, if there is negative transmission in the future, then in the intertemporal model Germany would expect to gain in the future from a rise in current US inflation, provided the latter is expected to have an adverse effect on US productivity or employment.

III Beyond the model

Let us now briefly consider three matters that go beyond the particular short-term two-country model presented here.

A world of many countries

In a two-country setting, the Nash and Stackelberg equilibria imply either policy rigidities or some kind of myopia. The actual solutions must be regarded as indeterminate until further considerations from game theory are introduced. While presented here in a two-country framework, the analysis actually seems to be more relevant for a many-country model. The various countries must not be 'small' in the formal sense – i.e. they must be able to affect their terms of trade by their own economic expansion. But they must not be so large that they expect policy reactions from other countries. Such a world would then lead to a multi-country

Nash equilibrium. The Nash equilibrium is thus interesting because it may come close to describing the non-coordination outcome in a world of many countries. Alternatively, all countries other than the United States might be regarded as ignoring reactions, in which case the Stackelberg equilibrium is a reasonable representation of the non-coordination outcome.

Limitations of short-term approach

The short-term nature of the whole approach should not be forgotten. The Phillips curve is not vertical in the model, and it is not even expectations-augmented. Because the analysis is short-term – and seeks to represent ideas that have come from short-term macro-economic policy discussion – one may be justified in assuming that one country does not expect a reaction from the other country when making its own policy decisions. But probably one would not be justified in building a structure of sophisticated game theory on top of the simple model. In fact, it is to be questioned whether a time-consuming international coordination process could possibly be justified when the underlying variables – notably the Phillips curve – are likely to be rapidly shifting. Futhermore, these very shifts may be influenced by the extensive policy discussions which are bound to precede successful international co-operation.

At this point one should consider more precisely the implications of the Phillips curve gradually becoming vertical as expectations adjust – i.e. as nominal wages cease to lag behind prices. Macroeconomic demand policy will lose its efficacy, and unions will attain their target real wages (stay on VV in Figure 1.1). Assuming positive transmission through the terms of trade, in each country employment will increase when the other country expands (as a result of a fall in the target real wage or as a result of a productivity improvement). Thus there will still be two positively-sloped reaction curves in Figure 1.3, and the interaction between the trade unions in the two countries will establish the Nash equilibrium. But it will be beyond the power of governments, whether acting independently or in coordination, to alter this.

Capital market interaction

It is an obvious limitation of the model that it has ruled out any capital market interaction. I shall now spell out informally how this could be introduced. Let us assume that each country manages its aggregate demand policy in the light of the considerations discussed in the paper so far. But a given level of aggregate demand can be obtained by various mixes of monetary and fiscal policy. We shall now hold aggregate demand in each country for its domestic products constant, but vary the policy mix so as to attain various interest rate outcomes.

Since the interest rate will be determined in the world capital market, the effects of a change in the US policy mix will depend also on the German policy mix reaction. Hence a change in what will be called here an 'interest rate policy' in one country is really a change in its net demand for tradeable bonds – i.e. a shift in a net demand curve. Let us now suppose that the USA shifts the mix towards fiscal expansion (and hence monetary contraction, to maintain aggregate demand constant). This reduces its net demand for bonds (or raises its supply) and then brings about reactions in Germany both from the private sector and through a possible change in government policy. We can assume that each government has a reaction function of some kind. One might expect that an increase in the US supply of bonds (tending to raise the world interest rate with a given German budget deficit) would lead to a reduction in the German budget deficit as borrowing becomes more expensive (i.e. there is a movement down the German government's bond supply curve). In this way a non-coordination equilibrium could, in principle, be attained as each country makes some assumption about the other's policy, one case being the special assumption that the other's policy stays unchanged, leading to a Nash equilibrium.[3]

The next step is to look at the sign of *total transmission*. Does a shift to the right of the US supply curve of bonds (brought about, for example, by a US fiscal expansion) benefit or harm Germany? Suppose it is perceived to harm Germany. Then it will be in Germany's interest to induce the USA to engage in some fiscal contraction, always associated with monetary expansion. If it were true that each country is harmed by a policy shift in the other country that tends to raise the interest rate, then coordination designed to yield a Pareto improvement would involve both countries engaging in fiscal contraction and monetary expansion. The Nash equilibrium would yield too high a world interest rate from a world Pareto-efficiency point of view.

But this leaves open the question whether Germany is benefited or harmed by a high interest rate policy in the USA. The answer is not obvious. It must depend, among other things, on whether Germany is a net creditor or debtor. Yet the answer is crucial in determining the direction in which a Pareto-improving co-ordination arrangement would shift the system.

One aspect – but only one aspect – is the terms of trade effect. This must be superimposed on the terms of trade effects of changes in aggregate demand which are central to the main analysis in this paper. It is likely that a shift to a high interest rate policy in the USA would worsen the German terms of trade, at least for the period of time during which this policy gives rise to additional capital flows from Germany to the USA. This German terms of trade deterioration would be part of the mechanism by which a German current account surplus (equal to the capital account deficit) is generated. It is a cost of the 'transfer'.

In the main model of this paper the terms of trade were the only mechanism of transmission between countries. Any US policy that worsened the German terms of trade was then definitely adverse in its effect on German welfare. But, once capital flows and stocks of international debts are allowed for, this is no longer so. For example, if Germany is a net creditor at a floating interest rate, she will gain on that account from a US high interest rate policy.

NOTES

* This paper is closely related to a earlier paper, namely Corden (1983b). Part I is a summary of the earlier paper and some passages there and elsewhere are taken verbatim from this paper. The main addition here is the detailed argument of Part II. In the preparation of the earlier paper and revisions of it I have benefited from comments by John Black, Peter Kenen and Ben Smith.
1 There is a modest literature in this general area. All the interdependence issues are surveyed in Cooper (1984), which contains many references. On the international transmission process through the terms of trade under flexible exchange rates, see especially Hamada and Sakurai (1978), Mussa (1979) and Corden and Turnovsky (1983).
2 Canzoneri and Gray (1983), Sachs (1983) and Cooper (1984, sec. 5) deal with the flexible exchange rate two-country interaction case along somewhat similar lines as the present paper (as represented by Figures 1.3), though the microfoundations differ. Note that international capital movements are introduced in Part III of the present paper.
3 This type of argument, that there is an international laissez-faire system where governments are actors (and possibly are interest-rate responsive), and that variations in the interest rate help to attain equilibrium, is set out more fully in Corden (1983a).

REFERENCES

Canzoneri, Matthew B. and Jo Anna Gray (1983). 'Two Essays on Monetary Policy in an Interdependent World,' Federal Reserve Board, International Finance Discussion paper No. 219, Washington.

Cooper, Richard N. (1984). 'Economic Interdependence and Coordination of Economic Policies,' in R. Jones and P. B. Kenen (eds.), *Handbook in International Economics*, Vol. II, Amsterdam: North-Holland Publishing Co.

Corden, W. M. (1983a). 'The Logic of the International Monetary Non-System,' in F. Machlup et al. (eds.), *Reflections on a Troubled World Economy*, London: Macmillan.

Corden, W. M. (1983b). 'Macroeconomic Policy Interaction under Flexible Exchange Rates: a Two-Country Model,' Institute for International Economic

Studies, University of Stockholm, Seminar paper No. 264, Stockholm, forthcoming in *Economica*.

Corden, W. M. and Stephen Turnovsky (1983). 'Negative Transmission of Economic Expansion,' *European Economic Review*, **20**, 289–310.

Hamada, Koichi and M. Sakurai (1978). 'International Transmission of Stagflation under Fixed and Flexible Exchange Rates,' *Journal of Political Economy*, **86**, 877–95.

Mussa, Michael (1979). 'Macroeconomic Interdependence and the Exchange Rate Regime,' in R. Dornbusch and J. A. Frenkel (eds.), *International Economic Policy*, Baltimore: The Johns Hopkins Press.

Sachs, Jeffrey (1983). 'International Economic Policy Coordination in a Dynamic Macroeconomic Model,' National Bureau of Economic Research, Inc., Working Paper No. 1166, Cambridge.

COMMENT DALE W. HENDERSON

I Introduction

It is very appropriate to have Max Corden's paper as the first paper in the volume. First, Corden uses static game theory to analyze the strategy of macroeconomic policymaking in a two-country world economy under flexible exchange rates. His analysis is illustrative of the approach that has been adopted by several authors over the last fifteen years. Then, he introduces intertemporal effects into his analysis. By conveying to the reader the reasons for his obvious impatience with the limitations of static analysis, Corden sets the stage for the more elaborate dynamic analyses that appear later in the volume.

The remainder of this comment is divided into two parts. The first part is an attempt to formalize Corden's graphical analysis. The second contains some general comments on Corden's paper.

II A formalization of Corden's analysis

This part of the comment contains a mathematical analysis of macroeconomic policymaking in a two-country world economy that is very similar to Corden's graphical analysis. The two countries are called the home country and the foreign country. Variables with asterisks are foreign country variables.

Each country is specialized in producing one good. According to the production functions, (logarithms of) outputs (y, y^*) are increasing functions of (logarithms of) employments (n, n^*) and productivity disturbances (x, x^*):

$$y = k_1 + \alpha n + x \quad 0 < \alpha < 1 \tag{1}$$

$$y^* = k_1^* + \alpha^* n^* + x^* \quad 0 < \alpha^* < 1 \tag{2}$$

It is assumed that the productivity disturbances and the other disturbance terms introduced below have zero means and are identically and independently distributed.

Labor is employed up to the point at which (logarithms of) real wages are equal to (logarithms of) marginal products of labor:

$$w - s = k_2 - (1 - \alpha)n + x \tag{3}$$

$$w^* - s^* = k_2^* - (1 - \alpha^*)n^* + x^* \tag{4}$$

Real wages are equal to (logarithms of) nominal wages (w, w^*) minus (logarithms of) product prices (s, s^*). Marginal products are decreasing functions of employments and increasing functions of productivity disturbances.

Before markets meet each period, workers and firms enter into contracts that specify nominal wages and employment rules. Each period the monetary authorities announce (logarithms of) money supplies that they will make available if all disturbances are zero ($\bar{m}, \bar{m}^*$). Using this information, workers and firms set nominal wages at the values ($\bar{w}, \bar{w}^*$) that will be consistent with 'full employment' levels of employment ($\bar{n}, \bar{n}^*$) if all disturbances are zero:

$$w = \bar{w} \tag{5}$$

$$w^* = \bar{w}^* \tag{6}$$

Workers agree to supply whatever quantity of labor firms want at the realized real wage.

The market for home goods is in equilibrium when the supply of the home good is equal to world demand:

$$y = k_3 + \gamma y + \lambda y^* + \delta q + u \quad 0 < \gamma < 1 \tag{7}$$

World demand for the home good depends positively on home income, (the logarithm of) foreign income, (the logarithm of) the relative price of the foreign good (q), and a goods demand disturbance (u). The relative price of the foreign good (the terms of trade) is given by

$$q = e + s^* - s, \tag{8}$$

where e is (the logarithm of) the exchange rate expressed as the home currency price of foreign currency.

It is assumed that there is no capital mobility. Therefore, income must be identically equal to spending in each country, and world income must always be identical to world spending. Consequently, equilibrium in the home goods market implies equilibrium in the foreign goods market.

Consumer price indices or CPIs (p, p^*) are weighted averages of the prices of home and foreign goods:

$$\beta s+(1-\beta)(e+s^*) = p = s+(1-\beta)q \tag{9}$$

$$\beta^*(s-e)+(1-\beta^*)s^* = p^* = s^*-\beta^*q \tag{10}$$

The money market equilibrium conditions are simple quantity theory equations:

$$m+v = s+y \tag{11}$$

$$m^*+v^* = s^*+y^* \tag{12}$$

It is assumed that (logarithms of) velocities (v, v^*) are disturbance terms with the same properties as the other disturbance terms. Closing the model with equations (11) and (12) is in the spirit of Corden's analysis. He never mentions interest rates in the discussion based on his model.

It is convenient to express the model in terms of deviations of variables from their full-employment values which are also their expected values.[1] Variables with circumflexes over them stand for deviations. Mathematical representations of relationships similar to those graphed by Corden can be distilled from the model:

$$\hat{p} = (1-\alpha)\hat{n}+(1-\beta)\hat{q}-x, \tag{13}$$

$$\hat{p}^* = (1-\alpha^*)\hat{n}^*-\beta^*\hat{q}-x^* \tag{14}$$

$$0 = (\gamma-1)\alpha\hat{n}+\lambda\alpha^*\hat{n}^*+\delta\hat{q}+(\gamma-1)x+\lambda x^*+u \tag{15}$$

$$\hat{m}+v = \hat{n} \tag{16}$$

$$\hat{m}^*+v^* = \hat{n}^* \tag{17}$$

Equations (13) and (14) are 'Phillips curves.' Equation (13) can be obtained by combining equations (3), (5), and the right-hand equality of (9), all in deviation form; equation (14) can be obtained in an analogous way. With the terms of trade unchanged $(\hat{q} = 0)$, positive deviations in home employment $(\hat{n} > 0)$ must be accompanied by positive deviations in the home product price $(\hat{s} > 0)$ and, therefore, positive deviations in the home CPI $(\hat{p} > 0)$. With home employment and, therefore, the home product price unchanged, positive deviations in the terms of trade (relative price of the foreign good) cause positive deviations in the home CPI. Positive productivity disturbances generate negative CPI deviations. The Phillips curves of equations (13) and (14) relate CPI deviations to employment deviations. Given Corden's definition of $\hat{p}$ as the rate of inflation of the home CPI and his labeling of Figure 1.2, it might appear that he has a different kind of Phillips curve in mind. However, his verbal derivation of the Phillips curve is consistent with equations (13) and (14).

Equation (15) is the condition for equilibrium in the home goods market. It is obtained by combining equations (1), (2), and (7) in deviation form. Positive deviations in home employment and positive home productivity disturbances create excess supply; positive deviations in foreign employment and in the terms of trade as well as positive foreign productivity disturbances and goods demand disturbances create excess demand.

Equations (16) and (17) state that sums of money supply deviations and velocity disturbances determine employment deviations. Equation (16) can be obtained by combining equations (1), (3), and (11) in deviation form; equation (17) can be obtained in an analogous way. It is clear from equations (16) and (17) that fiscal policy changes cannot affect employment. The qualitative effects of balanced budget increases in home government spending would be identical to those of positive goods demand disturbances. Corden says that fiscal policy as well as monetary policy can be used to affect employment. He probably has in mind a model different from the one used here.

It is assumed that the monetary authorities act on the basis of full information about the disturbances. Under this assumption, the monetary authorities in each country can control the employment deviation in their country. Therefore, equations (16) and (17) can be dropped and employment deviations can be taken to be the instruments of the monetary authorities. Nothing is lost by ignoring velocity disturbances. The authorities in each country can offset the effect of these disturbances on employment in their country without affecting the CPI in their country or employment or the CPI in the other country.[2]

The utility functions of the monetary authorities are given by

$$U = -(1/2)(\hat{n}^2 + \sigma \hat{p}^2), \tag{18}$$

$$U^* = -(1/2)(\hat{n}^{*2} + \sigma^* \hat{p}^{*2}) \tag{19}$$

where σ and σ^* measure the costs of squared deviations in CPIs relative to squared deviations in employments. The monetary authorities in each country maximize their utility with respect to their own employment deviation taking the employment deviation of the monetary authorities in the other country as given.

In order to simplify the analysis it is assumed that the two countries are mirror images ($\bar{y} = \bar{q} + \bar{y}^*, \alpha = \alpha^*, 1 - \gamma = \lambda, 1 - \beta = \beta^*$) and that the productivity disturbances in the two countries are the same ($x = x^*$). Under these assumptions the reduced forms for the CPI deviations are

$$\hat{p} = [(1-\alpha)+\epsilon]\hat{n} - \epsilon\hat{n}^* - x - \psi u, \tag{20}$$

$$\hat{p}^* = -\epsilon\hat{n} + [(1-\alpha)+\epsilon]\hat{n}^* - x + \psi u, \tag{21}$$

where $\epsilon = \lambda\alpha\psi$ and $\psi = (1-\beta)/\delta$. Positive home employment deviations

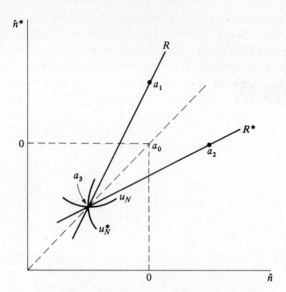

1A.1 Noncooperative equilibrium following a world productivity disturbance

lead to positive home CPI deviations both directly and indirectly through induced rises in q. Negative world productivity disturbances cause positive home CPI deviations directly. They have no indirect effects through q under the mirror image assumption. Negative foreign employment deviations and goods demand disturbances generate positive CPI deviations by raising q. The signs on the coefficients in equation (21) can be explained in an analogous way. It is also assumed that the monetary authorities in the two countries have identical tastes ($\sigma = \sigma^*$).

It is clear from inspection of equations (20) and (21) that if there are no disturbances, then there is no policy conflict. If $x = u = 0$, setting $\hat{n} = \hat{n}^* = 0$ yields $\hat{p} = \hat{p}^* = 0$, so both sets of monetary authorities can attain bliss. According to the model of this comment, a policy conflict of the kind depicted in Corden's Figure 1.3 would not arise unless the model were subjected to some kind of disturbance. Corden does not say what kind of disturbance if any is required to generate his policy conflict.

There is a disturbance that gives rise to a policy conflict like Corden's in the model of this comment. It is a negative world productivity disturbance ($\hat{x} < 0$). The effects of this disturbance are shown in Figure 1A.1. In the absence of the productivity disturbance, bliss for both sets of monetary authorities is at point a_0. Following a negative productivity disturbance, bliss for the home authorities is at point a_1. They still want a zero home employment deviation but now they want a positive foreign employment deviation. A positive foreign employment deviation would generate an appreciation of the home currency that would wipe out the positive CPI deviation caused by the productivity disturbance. For analogous reasons bliss for the foreign authorities is at point a_2.

The home (authorities') reaction function (R) passes through a_1, and the foreign (authorities') reaction function (R^*) passes through a_2. The reaction functions for the two sets of authorities are

$$\hat{n}^* = [(1+\sigma\mu^2)/\sigma\epsilon\mu]\,\hat{n} - (1/\epsilon)\,x - (\psi/\epsilon)\,u \qquad (22) \quad \text{(home)}$$

$$\hat{n}^* = [\sigma\epsilon\mu/(1+\sigma\mu^2)]\,\hat{n} + [\sigma\mu/(1+\sigma\mu^2)]\,x \\ - [\sigma\psi\mu/(1+\sigma\mu^2)]\,u \qquad (23) \quad \text{(foreign)}$$

where $\mu = [(1-\alpha)+\epsilon]$. Both reaction functions have positive slopes, and the slopes are the reciprocals of one another. The home reaction function has a slope greater than one since $\mu > \epsilon$. This result is intuitively appealing. Starting at the bliss point for the home authorities, a positive $\hat{n}^*$ lowers utility by creating a negative $\hat{p}$. The negative $\hat{p}$ could be wiped out by a positive $\hat{n}$ smaller than the original positive $\hat{n}^*$ because $\hat{n}$ has a bigger effect on $\hat{p}$. However, the home authorities would not increase $\hat{n}$ by enough to restore $\hat{p}$ to its bliss value because increasing $\hat{n}$ has negative direct effect on utility.

The noncooperative equilibrium is at point a_3 where R and R^* intersect. The noncooperative employment deviations $(\hat{n}_N, \hat{n}_N^*)$ are given by

$$\hat{n}_N = \hat{n}_N^* = (\sigma\mu x/\Delta)[(1+\sigma\mu^2)+\sigma\epsilon\mu] \qquad (24)$$

where $\Delta = (1+\sigma\mu^2)^2 - (\sigma\epsilon\mu)^2 > 0$. Therefore, the two identical employment deviations have the same sign as the productivity disturbance. Since the home reaction function was derived by setting the partial derivative of the home authorities' utility function with respect to the home employment deviation equal to zero $(\partial U/\partial\hat{n} = 0)$, it cuts home indifference curves at points at which their slopes are zero. The home indifference curve that passes through a_3 is U_N. By an analogous argument, the foreign reaction function cuts foreign indifference curves at points at which their slopes are infinite. The foreign indifference curve that passes through a_3 is U_N^*. It is apparent that the welfare of both countries would be improved if they both expanded. In mathematical terms, at a_3

$$\partial U/\partial\hat{n} = \partial U^*/\partial\hat{n}^* = 0 \qquad (26)$$

but
$$\partial U/\partial\hat{n}^* = \partial U^*/\partial\hat{n} = -(\sigma\epsilon x/\Delta)[\sigma\epsilon\mu+(1+\sigma\mu^2)],$$

which is opposite in sign to the productivity disturbance. Thus, in the case of a negative world productivity disturbance, the noncooperative solution has a contractionary bias just like the noncooperative solution to the policy conflict of Corden's Figure 1.3.

However, in the case of a positive goods demand disturbance the

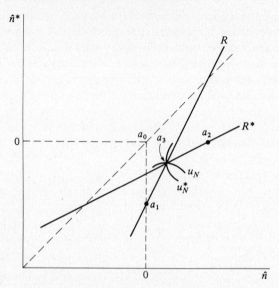

1A.2 Noncooperative equilibrium following a goods demand disturbance

situation is somewhat different as shown in Figure 1A.2. Following the disturbance, the bliss points for the home and foreign authorities are a_1 and a_2 respectively. The home authorities want a negative foreign employment deviation to prevent a negative home CPI deviation, and the foreign authorities want a positive home employment deviation to prevent a positive foreign CPI deviation. The noncooperative equilibrium is at point a_3. It is apparent that the welfare of both countries would be improved if the home authorities expanded and the foreign authorities contracted. Thus, in the case of a positive goods demand disturbance, the noncooperative solution has a contractionary bias for the home country and an expansionary bias for the foreign country. Whether or not the noncooperative solution has a contractionary bias for either or both of the two countries depends on the type of disturbance.

III Some general comments

In the model of this comment variations in today's money supply have no intertemporal effects because nominal wages are only fixed for one period, and all other variables are flexible. Of course, in a more complicated model, for example one with multiperiod contracts, today's policy actions would have intertemporal effects. Corden implements one possible approach to incorporating such effects. He assumes that some of today's target variables affect the utility that the authorities expect to experience tomorrow as well as the utility they experience today. This approach is certainly unconventional and is probably not the best way to proceed. The conventional approach is to specify the utility that the authorities experience in each period as a function of that period's target variables and to take account of intertemporal effects in the equations relating each period's target variables to current, past, and expected future instrument variables. Corden makes a number of interesting observations in implementing his approach. However, he offers no convincing reasons for using his approach instead of the more conventional one, which is employed in the other dynamic analyses in the volume.

Corden concedes that the assumption of zero capital mobility limits the applicability of his analysis. He then suggests a way of introducing capital mobility. His approach involves adding fiscal policy to the list of policy instruments. It is certainly possible to introduce capital mobility into the analysis of macroeconomic policymaking in interdependent economies without adding fiscal policy as shown by Canzoneri and Gray (1983). Introducing capital mobility complicates the analysis substantially. In the model of this comment, an increase in the home money supply has no effect on foreign employment and lowers the foreign CPI. In a model in which home currency and foreign currency securities are perfect substitutes, an increase in the home money supply may increase or decrease both foreign employment and the foreign CPI. Adding fiscal policy to a two-country model with capital mobility complicates the analysis further. Counting fiscal policy, each group of national authorities has two instruments. If each group of national authorities also has only two target variables, for example unemployment and inflation, it can use its two instruments to attain bliss. Policy conflicts can arise when each group of authorities has three target variables as shown by Sachs and Oudiz (1984), who assume that each group of authorities has as target variables unemployment, inflation, and the current account. Introducing capital mobility and adding fiscal policy are both worthwhile objectives, but there are advantages to pursuing them in sequence rather than simultaneously.

NOTES

1 The deviation forms of equations (1) through (12) are obtained by subtracting each equation with the disturbances set equal to zero from the same equation with the disturbances free to take on any value.
2 Rogoff (1983) points out this implication of the assumption that the monetary authorities have full information.

REFERENCES

Canzoneri, Matthew B. and Jo Anna Gray (1983). 'Two Essays on Monetary Policy in an Interdependent World,' International Finance Discussion Papers No. 219, Board of Governors of the Federal Reserve System, Washington, D.C.

Rogoff, Kenneth (1983). 'Productive and Counterproductive Cooperative Monetary Policies,' International Finance Discussion Papers No. 233, Board of Governors of the Federal Reserve System, Washington, D.C.

Sachs, Jeffrey and Gilles Oudiz (1984). 'Macroeconomic Policy Coordination among the Industrial Countries,' *Brookings Papers on Economic Activity*, 1–64.

COMMENT GEORGES DE MÉNIL

This is a very good paper with which to start this conference because it puts the basic issues on the table in a condensed and powerful way. My remarks will fall into three parts:

(1) a discussion of the basic framework of Corden's study.

(2) comments on the key points of his analysis and conclusions; and

(3) a remark on some of the interesting uses to which one might put this model.

I Framework

This is essentially a two-country model of the short-run determination of income and output in a world in which prices and particularly wages adjust with lags. Output is essentially demand determined, but supply considerations imply a short-run Phillips-like relationship in each country between employment and the rate of inflation. There are three transmission mechanisms operating between countries – the traditional Keynesian trade multiplier, 'relative price' effects on the trade balance, and inflation spillovers from one country to another. Corden's view of the effects that inflation in one country has on another are interesting and provocative, and I shall have something specifically to say about that. We are in a pure floating regime and trade is assumed to be in balance at all times. There are – and this is an important point – no capital flows between the two countries. Monetary and fiscal policy act on output and inflation in each country but interest rates are completely decoupled.

Corden presents this as a limitation of the analysis and discusses how the model can be extended to cover this lacuna. But I would like to turn this aspect of the model to good advantage by arguing that, as it stands, the model is a useful representation of the coordination problem in Europe, particularly on the Continent. As we know, extensive capital controls significantly limit capital flows in and out of France and Italy in the short run. In thinking of coordination between these two countries and the Deutsch Mark zone, it may be a useful first approximation to think of their interdependence as operating primarily through the trade account and inflation effects. In what follows, I shall therefore use Germany and France rather than Germany and the United States as prototypes of two countries exploring the possibility of economic cooperation.

II Analysis and Conclusions

Part I

I shall treat, in sucession, the first and second parts of the paper. Corden starts with a simple, short-run static model which was first presented as a seminar paper of the Stockholm Institute of International Economic Studies. In this first half of the paper, he carefully dissects the nature of the transmission mechanisms which operate through trade flows, paying particular attention to terms of trade effects. He argues that under normal conditions there will be a *positive transmission* of employment increases in one country to employment increases in another. The channel for this to which he pays the most attention operates in the following manner: expansion of employment and output in one country (say Germany) tends to improve the terms of trade in the other (say France) and thus, by raising real incomes, reduce the gap between the aspiration real wage of employees and the actual real wage. Reduction of this gap reduces inflationary pressures, and makes it possible for the French authorities to achieve any given level of employment at a lesser inflationary cost. The government actually takes the gains from this improvement in the short-run Phillips-like trade-off between inflation and unemployment partly in lower inflation and partly in more employment. Therefore employment rises in France. It is important to note, and Corden is the first to point this out, that it is not inevitable that expansion in Germany improve the terms of trade in France. In the presence of homothetic indifference curves, equiproportional expansion in the vector of outputs, would, for instance, leave the terms of trade unchanged. If the terms of trade go the other way, as they might but are unlikely to, that positive transmission mechanism would become a negative transmission mechanism.

It seems to me that, since Corden is not in a full employment world, he could also have appealed to the traditional international trade multiplier as an additional important factor tending to produce positive transmission.

Whether the transmission is positive or negative is, of course, extremely important. It determines the nature of the loss from uncooperative behavior and the qualitative direction of the action cooperation calls for. If transmission is positive in nature, if the structure presents what Canzoneri and Gray (1983) have earlier called a 'locomotive' configuration (Corden uses the same term), then uncooperative behavior will have a deflationary bias. If, on the other hand, the transmission is negative, or the structure is what Canzoneri and Gray have called 'beggar thy neighbor', then non-cooperative behavior can have an inflationary bias. In his conclusions to this section, Corden suggests some rules that could, short of full coordination, bring France and Germany closer to their contract curve. One of these is his interesting 'unilateral expansion rule'. It is fair to point out, that, if the transmission mechanism turned out to be negative, this rule would have an inflationary bias, and would thus *not* be a Pareto improvement.

Part II

Economists frequently include the rate of inflation in government preference functions without thinking twice about it. In this part of his paper, Corden addresses the relation between inflation and welfare in an interdependent world in a provocative way.

In part I, inflation played no direct role in the architecture of transmission, because flexible exchange rates and purchasing power parity were assumed to insulate Germany's inflation from France's inflation and vice versa.

In part II, Corden argues that inflation can only be a 'good' or 'bad' if it has real effects. If inflation is an argument of government welfare functions, it must be because governments believe that an increase in inflation today reduces output in the future. The link may operate through efficiency considerations, or through the unsustainability of high inflation, but, in either case, the argument is essentially an intertemporal one about the relationship between output and employment in the present and future.

Corden therefore proceeds to formulate the relation between present and future employment, and present and future welfare within each country. He demonstrates that this new intertemporal structure can generate negative transmission mechanisms.

Personally, I would rather put the rate of inflation directly in the government preference functions. Static models such as this one are simplified representations of the world of uncertainty in which we live. In this real world, an increase in the rate of inflation generates a degree of additional uncertainty about real incomes and their distribution which may weigh on welfare, and therefore be of concern to governments, independently of considerations of efficiency and loss of future output.

If one retains inflation in the government's preference function, and further drops the assumption of purchasing power parity, thus allowing for direct price effects, one obtains a price transmission mechanism similar to the one in Canzoneri and Gray and similar analyses. Such models can easily produce scenarios dominated by negative transmission. The 'beggar thy neighbor' aspects of real exchange rate appreciation in such models are well known.

In short, this complicated construct in the second part of Corden's paper is not required to produce Corden's result.

III Ramifications

Corden makes a number of thought provoking suggestions at the end of this paper about the broad implications of the model and possibilities for extending it. He observes that the Nash solution is particularly myopic when there are only two players. It is relatively simple in such circumstances for the players to improve on the outcome. The gains from cooperation are harder to achieve, and therefore more needing of analysis, in a multi-country context. Corden says that the relevance of his model lies, therefore, more in the light that it throws on the more complex question of multilateral cooperation than in its direct applicability to two-country relations. One example which comes to mind is that of the European Community and the continuing tensions within it over efforts to coalesce.

Corden also warns the reader about the hazards of fine-tuning. He suggests that if the Phillips curves become vertical, cooperation may be limited by the irreconcilable real wage claims of unions in the two countries.

In his discussion of possible further developments, Corden makes one surprising omission. The microeconomic structure which Corden has imbedded in his model is particularly suited for analysis of the inter-relationships between money and budgets, on the one hand, and trade and tariffs, on the other. In many instances, notably within the European Community, bargaining cuts across the boundaries between macroeconomic and microeconomic policies. A deficit country may, for instance, threaten trade obstructions in an effort to persuade a surplus partner to reflate. One can hope that in further work Corden will take advantage of the fertile ground that he has already prepared for exploring such trade-offs and bargains.

REFERENCE

Canzoneri, Matthew B. and Jo Anna Gray (1983). 'Two essays on Monetary Policy in an Interdependent World,' Federal Reserve Board, International Finance Discussion Paper No. 219, Washington.

2 Fiscal expenditures and international economic interdependence

JACOB A. FRENKEL AND ASSAF RAZIN*

I Introduction

One of the major sources of recent friction between Europeans and Americans has been the interpretation of the economic implications of US fiscal policies. Theorists and policymakers on both sides of the Atlantic have differed in the analysis of the role of budget deficits in affecting key macroeconomic aggregates. Specifically, some have argued that large budget deficits are responsible for the recently observed high real rates of interest while others have claimed that budget deficits cannot be blamed for these real rates. The latter group claimed that theory does not predict a clear-cut relation between budget deficits and rates of interest and that the empirical record itself is very weak.

The increased integration of the world economy resulted in increased concern in each country over policy measures taken in the rest of the world. The complex pattern of the economic linkages within the interdependent world economy resulted in a variety of models of the transmission mechanisms. These models include those that highlight the implications of foreign trade multipliers, e.g. LINK models which build on a Keynesian structure, as well as those that highlight the role of the terms of trade along the lines of the elasticity approach to the balance of payments.[1] In addition, some analyses have examined whether disturbances can be transmitted negatively to the rest of the world. For example, Laursen and Metzler have shown that in a model without capital flows, domestic autonomous government expenditures which raise domestic output, lower the level of output abroad, i.e. domestic spendings are transmitted negatively to the rest of the world.[2] Parallel to these developments there were examinations of the transmission mechanism along the lines of the Mundell-Fleming models.[3] These contributions were stimulated by the increased integration of world capital markets. They highlight the interdependence between the exchange-rate regime, the degree of capital mobility and the impact of

37

macroeconomic policies. Here, the key factor in the transmission mechanism has been the interaction between the rate of interest and the rate of exchange. Thus, it was shown that in a model with capital mobility and flexible exchange rates, an expansionary monetary policy is transmitted negatively to the rest of the world whereas fiscal policy is transmitted positively. More recently the large volatility of nominal exchange rates and the associated changes in real exchange rates have stimulated modelling of exchange-rate dynamics which has focused on the role of expectations. This line of modelling also relied on the real rate of interest as a key factor in the transmission mechanism, but the focus on expectations introduced an important dimension of dynamic considerations.[4]

These theoretical studies were based on the premise that world capital markets were indeed highly integrated. A separate branch of research has examined this premise. In this context one line of inquiry tested the implications of capital market integration for international equality of rates of return. These studies include tests of equality of real rates of interest as well as studies of covered interest arbitrage. By and large, the basic findings were favorable to the hypothesis that capital markets are integrated.[5] A second line of inquiry tested the implications of capital markets integration for the relation between national saving and national investment. These studies claimed that the positive correlation between national saving and investment suggests that the degree of capital market integration is somewhat limited.[6] While there may be some dispute over the exact degree of international capital mobility, there is no doubt that the mobility of capital serves an important role in linking world rates of interest and, thereby, in transmitting economic disturbances internationally.

In this paper we develop a model that is suitable for the analysis of (i) the linkage between fiscal spending and rates of interest, and (ii) the international transmission mechanism of fiscal policies. Our model is capable of generating a variety of patterns of links between fiscal spending and rates of interest, as well as a variety of patterns of international transmissions of fiscal policies.

The key characteristics of our model are: (i) A fully integrated world capital market; (ii) full rationality of all economic agents whose decisions are based on self fulfilling expectations and are subjected to temporal and intertemporal budget constraints, and (iii) government behavior that is constrained by an intertemporal solvency requirement. The model is of a general equilibrium nature and the various economies have access to, and are governed by, world markets. These markets determine both temporal prices (commodity terms of trade) and intertemporal prices (rates of interest).[7]

Some of the features of the model are (i) the prominent role that is being played by wealth (permanent income) and the minimal role that is being played by current income in determining the levels of private spending; (ii) the irrelevancy of the time pattern of taxes and government debt issue given the pattern of government spending and the requirement of intertemporal solvency;[8] (iii) the dependence of the current account of the balance of payments (and thereby the accumulation of national external debt) on the entire path of government spending rather than on the path of budget deficits. We show that the impact of fiscal spending and the dynamics of debt accumulation on the key macroeconomic aggregates at home and abroad depend on a comparison among various behavioral propensities. These comparisons generate a multitude of 'transfer problem criteria' that are familiar from the theory of transfers in international trade.[9] In the present context the relevant transfers are among private sectors and government sectors through current and future taxes and government spendings, as well as between the home and the foreign countries through the process of accumulation of external assets and debts. As a result of these transfers the key factors determining the impacts of policies are comparisons among (i) domestic and foreign patterns of private sectors' spending, (ii) domestic and foreign private sectors' saving propensities, and (iii) domestic and foreign patterns of governments' spending.

The focus on the entire path of the level and composition of government spending, also serves to highlight the importance of the distinction between permanent and transitory policies as well as between current and future policies. These distinctions along with the multitude of the 'transfer problem criteria' are shown to be critical in accounting for the apparent ambiguities in the effects of government spending on rates of interest and the related question of the nature of the international transmission of fiscal shocks. Our analysis attempts to isolate the roles of these critical factors in determining the outcomes of government expenditures.

In addition to providing a theoretical justification for the observed linkages, our model also has implications for the choice of relevant aggregate economic variables for empirical research. For example, our analysis has implications for the expected patterns of the dependence of the reduced form equations of each country's consumption function, on current and future fiscal spendings by the domestic as well as by the foreign governments. Similarly, our analysis has implications for the dependence of the reduced-form equations of world rates of interest and commodity prices on the paths of fiscal spendings.

Previous models of the international transmissions of fiscal policies share some of the features of our model. The novelty of the present analysis is the integration of these features into a consistent analytical framework.

This integration, however, has not been obtained without cost. At the present stage our analysis is limited in several important dimensions. The concluding section of the paper outlines some of the limitations and suggests possible extentions.

II One-commodity world

In this part of the paper we analyze a model of the world economy which produces and consumes a single composite commodity. We first outline the analytical framework which is then applied to the analysis of the effects of fiscal policies on interest rates and the nature of the international transmission mechanism.

II.1 The analytical framework

The analytical framework of the model contains the specification of production, consumption, the government and the foreign economy which interact to determine the equilibrium of the world economy.

II.1.1 *Production*

Consider two countries each producing the same good. Let the path of the supply of output in each country be fixed at its full employment level. Denote the supply of output at period t by Y_t and Y_t^*, respectively, where an asterisk designates variables pertaining to the foreign country.

II.1.2 *Consumption*

Assume that the home country's utility function is logarithmic as in equation (1)

$$U = \sum_{t=0}^{\infty} \delta^t \log c_t \tag{1}$$

where δ denotes the subjective discount factor and where c denotes the rate of consumption. The infinitely lived representative individual is assumed to maximize the utility function subject to the following set of budget constraints:

$$\begin{aligned}
c_0 &= Y_0 - T_0 - (1 + r_{-1}) B_{-1} + B_0 \\
c_1 &= Y_1 - T_1 - (1 + r_0) B_0 + B_1 \\
c_t &= Y_t - T_t - (1 + r_{t-1}) B_{t-1} + B_t
\end{aligned} \tag{2}$$

where T_t denotes taxes at period t, B_t denotes the one-period debt and r_t denotes the one-period market interest rate. In addition to the budget constraints in equation (2) there are two additional constraints which govern the maximization problem. The first states the initial conditions according to which the initial commitment of interest and amortization (B) is historically given as in equation (3)

$$B \equiv (1+r_{-1}) B_{-1} \tag{3}$$

The second is the solvency requirement according to which the present value of debt must approach zero in the limit:

$$\lim_{t \to \infty} \alpha_t B_t = 0 \tag{4}$$

where α_t denotes the present-value factor which is composed of one-period rates of interest compounded up to period t. Thus:

$$\alpha_t \equiv (1+r_0)^{-1} (1+r_1)^{-1} \ldots (1+r_{t-1})^{-1}$$

and obviously $\alpha_0 = 1$.

Consolidating the set of the budget constraints in (2) and using equations (3) and (4) yields

$$\sum_{t=0}^{\infty} \alpha_t c_t = \sum_{t=0}^{\infty} \alpha_t Y_t - \sum_{t=0}^{\infty} \alpha_t T_t - B \equiv W_0 \tag{5}$$

As can be seen, equation (5) is the present value constraint. It states that the sum of the present values of the rates of consumption in all periods must equal wealth (W_0), where the value of wealth consists of the sum of the present values of output streams (gross domestic products), minus the sum of the present values of taxes and the initial debt commitment. It is noteworthy that for the individual what matters is the present value of taxes rather than their precise distribution over time.

Maximizing the utility function (1) subject to the consolidated constraint (5), the competitive representative consumer is assumed to treat the market rates of interest (which determine α_t) as given. Further, since we assume full certainty and rational expectations, the future rates of interest as well as taxes and outputs are assumed to be known with perfect foresight.

The resultant consumption function is thus:

$$c_t = (1-\delta) W_t \tag{6}$$

where

$$W_t = \frac{\delta^t}{\alpha_t} W_0 \tag{7}$$

As is seen, the rate of consumption in period t is proportional to the value of wealth in that period with $(1-\delta)$ being the marginal (and the average) propensity to consume out of wealth. Thus, in this formulation, the subjective discount factor, δ, is also the marginal propensity to save out of wealth. In order to solve for the value of debt in each period and thereby gain some insight into the dynamics of debt accumulation, we use equations (6) and (7) in the budget constraints (2) and obtain

$$B_t = \frac{1-\delta^{t+1}}{\alpha_t} W_0 - \sum_{\tau=0}^{t} \frac{(Y_\tau - T_\tau)}{\alpha_t} \alpha_\tau + \frac{B}{\alpha_t} \tag{8}$$

Equation (8) states that the value of debt in period t must make up for the difference between the present values (as of period t) of consumption rates from period zero to period t, $[(T-\delta^{t+1})/\alpha_t] W_0$, and that of disposable incomes, $\sum_{\tau=0}^{t}(Y_\tau - T_\tau)\alpha_\tau/\alpha_t$; in addition, the current debt must also cover payments of the (current value of the) initial debt commitment, B/α_t.

II.1.3 *Government*
The government is assumed to spend at the rate G_t. Spending can be financed by taxes and debt issue at the market rate of interest. Government behavior, however, is constrained by the solvency requirement according to which the present value of spending must equal the present value of taxes:

$$\sum_{t=0}^{\infty} \alpha_t G_t = \sum_{t=0}^{\infty} \alpha_t T_t \tag{9}$$

By substituting equation (9) into the private sector's consolidated budget constraint we can express the value of wealth, W_0, as:

$$W_0 = \sum_{t=0}^{\infty} \alpha_t y_t - B \tag{10}$$

where
$$y_t \equiv Y_t - G_t.$$

In what follows we refer to y_t as output net of government spending.[10]

II.1.4 *The foreign economy*
Individuals in the foreign country are also assumed to have a logarithmic utility function

$$U^* = \sum_{t=0}^{\infty} \delta^{*t} \log c_t^* \tag{1'}$$

where an asterisk (*) designates variables pertaining to the foreign country. Individuals in the foreign country are assumed to operate in the same *world* capital market as those of the home country and thus they face the same set of rates of interest. Analogously to equation (5), the consolidated foreign budget constraint is

$$\sum_{t=0}^{\infty} \alpha_t c_t^* = W_0^* \tag{5'}$$

where
$$W_0^* = \sum_{t=0}^{\infty} \alpha_t y_t^* + B \qquad (10')$$

In equation $(10')$ $y_t^* \equiv Y_t^* - G_t^*$; i.e., it denotes the value of foreign output net of government spending. Finally, it is relevant to note that, in our two-country world, the home country's debt, B, appears as the foreign country's asset.

Maximization of the foreign utility function, $(1')$, subject to the constraint $(10')$ yields the foreign consumption function

$$c_t^* = (1 - \delta^*) W_t^* \qquad (6')$$

where
$$W_t^* = (\delta^{*t}/\alpha_t) W_0^* \qquad (7')$$

II.1.5 World equilibrium and debt

In our frictionless world, market clearing equilibrium requires that at *each* period of time world private sectors' demand for output equals the supply of world output net of government absorption. Using the consumption functions $(6)-(6')$ along with (7) and $(7')$ yields:

$$(1 - \delta)\frac{\delta^t}{\alpha_t} W_0 + (1 - \delta^*)\frac{\delta^{*t}}{\alpha_t} W_0^* = \bar{y}_t \qquad (11)$$

where
$$\bar{y}_t \equiv y_t + y_t^*$$

From this equilibrium condition we can express the equilibrium present-value factors, α_t, as

$$\alpha_t = \frac{(1 - \delta)\delta^t W_0 + (1 - \delta^*)\delta^{*t} W_0^*}{\bar{y}_t} \qquad (12)$$

Since $\alpha_0 = 1$ we can use (12) for $t = 0$ to obtain

$$(1 - \delta) W_0 + (1 - \delta^*) W_0^* = \bar{y}_0. \qquad (13)$$

To gain insight into the dynamics of the rates of interest we substitute for W_0 from equation (13) into equation (12) and after some manipulations we obtain:

$$\alpha_t = \delta^t + \frac{(1 - \delta^*)}{\bar{y}_t} W_0^*(\delta^{*t} - \delta^t) - g_t \delta^t \qquad (14)$$

where
$$g_t \equiv \frac{\bar{y}_t - \bar{y}_0}{\bar{y}_t}.$$

Likewise, we substitute for W_0^* from equation (13) into equation (12) to obtain:

$$\alpha_t = \delta^{*t} - \frac{(1-\delta)\,W_0}{\bar{y}_t}(\delta^{*t} - \delta^t) - g_t\,\delta^{*t}. \tag{14'}$$

Equations (14)–(14') show that the present-value factors, α_t, depend on three quantities: (i) the levels of the marginal propensities to save, δ and δ^*, (ii) the difference between these saving propensities, $\delta^* - \delta$; and (iii) the percentage growth of world output, g. As is seen, when the marginal propensities to save are equal to each other, $\alpha_t = \delta^t(1-g_t)$. In that case a rise in the saving propensity and a fall in the growth of output raise the present-value factors, i.e. lower the rates of interest since both changes raise world savings at the initial rates of interest. If world output is stationary, i.e. if $g_t = 0$, the magnitude of the present-value factors are bounded between δ^{*t} and δ^t. In that case the rates of interest are bounded between the two countries' subjective rates of discount.

The solution for W_0, W_0^* and the sequence of the present value factors, α_t, can be obtained from equations (12)–(13) and either (10) or (10'); this latter degree of freedom is due, of course, to Walras' Law.

Using (10'), (12) and (13) yields the solutions

$$W_0^* = \frac{\bar{y}_0 \sum_{t=0}^{\infty} \delta^t \lambda_t^* + B}{\varDelta} \tag{15}$$

$$W_0 = \frac{(1-\delta^*)\left[\bar{y}_0 \sum_{t=0}^{\infty} \delta^{*t} \lambda_t - B\right]}{(1-\delta)\varDelta} \tag{16}$$

$$\alpha_t = \frac{(1-\delta^*)\left\{\bar{y}_0\left[\delta^{*t} \sum_{\tau=0}^{\infty} \delta^\tau \lambda_\tau^* + \delta^t \sum_{\tau=0}^{\infty} \delta^{*\tau} \lambda_\tau\right] + (\delta^{*t} - \delta^t)\,B\right\}}{\bar{y}_t\,\varDelta} \tag{17}$$

where $\varDelta = \sum_{t=0}^{\infty} \delta^{*t} \lambda_t + \sum_{t=0}^{\infty} \delta^t \lambda_t^* > 0,$

and where λ_t^* denotes the share of foreign product net of government spending, i.e. $\lambda_t^* \equiv y_t^*/\bar{y}_t$; analogously λ_t denotes the corresponding share of the home country, i.e. $\lambda_t \equiv (y_t/\bar{y}_t) = 1 - \lambda_t^*$.

The requirement that the rates of consumption in both countries are positive imply that both W_0 and W_0^* are positive. Inspection of equations (15)–(16) reveals that these requirements imply restrictions on the initial debt position, B, as well as on the values of λ_t and λ_t^* which reflect the patterns of government spending. It may be seen that the maximal size of the initial value of debt in the system depends positively on the value of world output, and on the marginal propensities to save, and it also depends on the patterns of government spending.

The dynamics of the system is affected through changes in each country's debt position. The impact of these changes in debt positions can be analyzed and interpreted in terms of concepts familiar from the analysis of international transfers. To obtain insights into the economic factors governing the dynamics of the system we now turn to an examination of the effects of a redistribution of the world debt position.

Consider a transfer of assets from the home country to the foreign country. This transfer amounts to an increase in the value of B which measures the home country's debt. The impact of the transfer on each country's consumption and, thereby, on the process of further redistributions of debt through international transactions depends on its impact on both countries' wealth as well as on the path of world interest rates. Differentiation of equations (15)–(17) with some manipulations yields

$$\frac{dW_0^*}{dB} = \frac{1}{\varDelta} > 0 \tag{15'}$$

$$\frac{dW_0}{dB} = -\frac{1-\delta^*}{(1-\delta)\varDelta} < 0 \tag{16'}$$

$$\frac{d\alpha_t}{dB} = \frac{(1-\delta^*)(\delta^{*t}-\delta^t)}{\bar{y}_t \varDelta} \tag{17'}$$

We may conclude that, following a transfer from the home country, $dW_0^*/dB > 0$, $dW_0/dB < 0$, and sign $(d\alpha_t/dB) = $ sign $(\delta^*-\delta)$.

In interpreting these results consider the effect of the transfer on *world* savings at the initial rates of interest. The transfer raises foreign wealth by dB and lowers domestic wealth by the same amount. Consequently, at the prevailing rates of interest, world savings change by $(\delta^*-\delta)\,dB$. If $\delta^* > \delta$ the transfer induces positive world savings. Restoration of equilibrium with zero savings requires a fall in the rates of interest so as to discourage savings and stimulate current consumption through secondary changes in wealth. The secondary changes in wealth are brought about through the impact of the changes in the rates of interest on the valuation of wealth. When $\delta^* > \delta$ the rates of interest must fall, i.e., the values of α_t – the present-value factor – must rise as indicated by equation (17). The fall in the rates of interest raises each country's wealth. The secondary rise in wealth reinforces the initial effect of the transfer on foreign wealth whereas it mitigates the loss in wealth to the transferer. These mechanisms are illustrated by equations (15)–(17). As may be seen, when $\delta^* = \delta$, $dW_0^*/dB = -dW_0/dB = 1$ whereas when $\delta^* \gtrless \delta$, $dW_0^*/dB \gtrless 1$ and $-dW_0/dB \lessgtr 1$, respectively.

The preceding analysis of the effect of the transfer on the initial wealth positions and on the path of the rates of interest provides the ingredients of the effects of wealth reallocation that occur during the dynamic processes of the interdependent economies. Specifically, in our world with no investment, one country's savings must equal the other country's dissaving. And the analysis of transfers reveals that if the marginal saving propensity of the country which is a net accumulator of assets exceeds that of the other country, then the subsequent path will be characterized by lower interest rates (i.e., higher present-value factors), a higher value of the accumulator's wealth, a lower value of the decumulator's wealth and a higher value of world's wealth.

Before turning to various comparative statics it is already evident that in this model fiscal expenditures affect the equilibrium *only* through their impact on net disposable incomes, $y_t \equiv Y_t - G_t$ and $y_t^* \equiv Y_t^* - G_t^*$. Therefore, their impact is equivalent to that of an exogenous change in gross domestic product.

Since individuals are only concerned with the *present value* of taxes which in turn are equal to the present value of government spendings, it follows that the details of government finance through either taxes or debt issue do not affect the equilibrium of the system as long as the government solvency requirements are met. This is the Ricardian equivalence that is embedded in the present model.

II.2 The impact of fiscal expenditures

In this section we analyze the effects of fiscal spending in one country on world rates of interest and on the patterns of consumption in the rest of the world. The interdependence of private sectors' spending on foreign fiscal spending results from the impact of fiscal policies on the entire path of rates of interest which, in turn, are common to both countries. Thus, in this interdependent world fiscal spending in one country is 'financed' by crowding out of private spending in both countries.

Since private spending depends only on wealth position, it is important to examine the impact of government spending on wealth. That impact in turn depends on disposable incomes as well as on the time pattern of the rates of interest. Since that pattern depends on the precise timing of government spending, we will analyze in detail situations in which changes in government spending are transitory as well as those in which they are permanent. To avoid repetitive examples we focus in the subsequent analysis on the impact of fiscal expenditures in the home country on world interest rates and on private consumption at home and abroad.

II.2.1 *Transitory government spending*

Consider the effect of a transitory reduction in domestic fiscal spending in period s on the rates of interest and on foreign and domestic current spending. Since consumption is proportional to wealth, we will seek to determine the effects of fiscal spending on the levels of wealth. Suppose first that the change in fiscal spending is expected to take place in the future (i.e. $s \neq 0$). To solve for the effect of dy_s on the path of the present-value factors, α_t, we first differentiate equation (12) and use (13) to obtain:

$$\frac{d\alpha_t}{dy_s} = (1-\delta^*)\frac{\delta^{*t}-\delta^t}{\bar{y}_t}\frac{dW_0^*}{dy_s}-\gamma_{t,s}\frac{\alpha_t}{\bar{y}_t} \tag{18}$$

where

$$\gamma_{t,s} \equiv \begin{cases} 1 & \text{for } t = s \\ 0 & \text{for } t \neq s \end{cases}$$

We then differentiate the foreign wealth equation (10′), and obtain:

$$\frac{dW_0^*}{dy_s} = \sum_{t=0}^{\infty} y_t^* \frac{d\alpha_t}{dy_s} \tag{19}$$

Substituting (18) into (19) yields after some manipulations

$$\frac{dW_0^*}{dy_s} = -\frac{\alpha_s \lambda_s^*}{\varDelta} < 0 \tag{20}$$

Since $\bar{y}_0$ is given, domestic and foreign wealth must change in opposite directions so as to ensure an unchanged value of world consumption in period 0. Thus from (13) and (20) it follows that:

$$\frac{dW_0}{dy_s} = \frac{(1-\delta^*)\alpha_s\lambda_s^*}{(1-\delta)\varDelta} > 0 \tag{21}$$

Equations (20) and (21) imply therefore that a transitory future reduction in domestic fiscal spending raises current private consumption and lowers current foreign consumption. As shown in these equations, the magnitude of the change in current consumption depends on the timing of the given fiscal change, as well as on the relative size of the two economies. A given fiscal change that is expected to occur in the distant future will have a smaller impact on current consumption than a similar change that is expected to occur in the near future. This dependence is reflected in the value of α_s, the present value factor, which diminishes with the passage of time. Finally, it is noteworthy that the change in world wealth $[(dW_0 + dW_0^*)/dy_s]$ depends only on the difference between the two saving propensities; if $\delta = \delta^*$ world wealth remains unchanged.

The solution of the effect of the future transitory fiscal change on the path of the present-value factors is obtained by differentiating (17) with respect to y_s for $t = s \neq 0$:

$$\frac{d\alpha_t}{dy_s} = -\frac{\alpha_s(1-\delta^*)}{\bar{y}_s \Delta} \left[\frac{(1-\delta^{*s})}{1-\delta^*} + \sum_{t=s}^{\infty} \lambda_t \delta^{*t} + \sum_{t=s}^{\infty} \lambda_t^* \delta^t\right] < 0 \qquad (18')$$

and, for $t \neq s \neq 0$:

$$\frac{d\alpha_t}{dy_s} = \frac{\alpha_s \lambda_s^*(1-\delta^*)}{\bar{y}_t \Delta}(\delta^t - \delta^{*t}) \qquad (18'')$$

Equation (18') shows that a future transitory rise in net output occurring in period s, must lower the contemporaneous value of α_s which is the relative price of consumption in period s in terms of current consumption. This change in relative price is necessary to eliminate the incipient excess supply of goods in period s.

Equation (18'') shows that the effect of the future transitory rise in net output on the present-value factors in all other periods depends on the difference between the marginal propensities to save. The interpretation of this result can be given in terms of the previous analysis of debt transfer. Here, the rise in domestic wealth and the fall in foreign wealth (arising from the changes in y_s and α_s) imply that, at the prevailing present-value factors of all other periods ($t \neq s$) the difference between δ and δ^* determines whether world savings are positive or negative and, therefore, whether α_t must rise or fall.

To explore further the role of timing on the transitory shock suppose that the reduction in fiscal spending (or equivalently, the rise in net output) occurs at the present, i.e. $s = 0$. In that case, at the initial rates of interest, the rise in current domestic ouput raises domestic wealth by the same amount and, thereby, creates an excess supply of current goods. To restore equilibrium the relative prices of current consumption in terms of consumptions in all other periods (i.e., the rates of interest) must fall. Equivalently, the present-value factors, α_t, must rise. These changes imply that both domestic and foreign wealth must rise. Formally, using equations (12)–(13) and (19) we obtain:

$$\frac{dW_0^*}{dy_0} = \frac{\sum_{t=1}^{\infty} \delta^t \lambda_t^*}{\Delta} > 0 \qquad (20')$$

which, together with equation (13) implies that

$$\frac{dW_0}{dy_0} = 2 - \frac{(1-\delta^*)}{(1-\delta)}\frac{dW_0^*}{dy_0} = \frac{(1-\delta^*)\lambda_0}{\Delta} > 0 \qquad (21')$$

Equations (20')–(21') show that a transitory reduction in domestic current fiscal spending (i.e. a rise in y_0) raises the values of current wealth and thereby the values of private consumption in both countries.

To summarize, it was shown that a future transitory change in fiscal spending results in opposite changes in current domestic and foreign wealth. In general, for all periods during which the fiscal spending remains unchanged, market clearing requires that world private spending must also remain unchanged. Therefore, during those periods the fall in foreign wealth must be accompanied by a rise in domestic wealth. Whether the rates of interest linking the present period with other periods during which the fiscal spending remain unchanged, rise or fall, depends on whether the domestic propensity to save exceeds or falls short of the foreign savings propensity.

In contrast, during the period in which the fiscal change takes place, market clearing requires that the change in world private consumption must equal (with opposite sign) the change in government spending. The mechanism which brings about the necessary changes in private spending operates through changes in the rates of interest. For example a current transitory reduction in domestic fiscal spending creates, at prevailing interest rates, domestic (and therefore world) excess supply of present goods which is eliminated by a fall in interest rates linking the present period with the period during which the reduction in fiscal spending occurs. This fall in interest rates raises foreign and domestic wealth and serves to stimulate both domestic and foreign current private consumption. Thus, during the period in which the transitory fiscal changes occur, domestic and foreign wealth must move in the same direction. The complex changes in the paths of the rates of interest are reflected in complicated alterations of the term structure of interest rates.

II.2.2 *Permanent government spending*

Consider now the effects of a *permanent* reduction in domestic fiscal spending on foreign and domestic private consumption. The effects of the permanent change on the current value of wealth can be computed from the previous expressions. For example, the effect of a permanent change in fiscal spending (dy) on foreign wealth is equivalent to the sum of the effects of all current (dy_0) and future transitory changes (dy_s) of equal magnitudes. Thus, adding (20') to the sum of the expressions in (20) for $t = 1, 2, \ldots$, yields the effect of an equivalent permanent change, as in (22).

$$\frac{dW_0^*}{dy} \equiv \frac{dW_0^*}{dy_0} + \sum_{t-1}^{\infty} \frac{dW_0^*}{dy_t} = \frac{\sum\limits_{t=1}^{\infty} (\delta^t - \alpha_t) \lambda_t^*}{\Delta} \tag{22}$$

The sign of dW_0^*/dy depends on the relations between δ^t and α_t which, as shown by equation (14) depends on the relation between the two countries' saving propensities and on the rate of growth of world output net of government absorption. Specifically, for the stationary case with $g_t = 0$, δ^t exceeds α_t if δ exceeds δ^*. In that case a permanent rise in y raises the current value of foreign wealth, and vice versa. On the other hand, when the saving propensities are equal to each other (i.e., when $\delta^* = \delta$), the permanent change in y alters foreign wealth only if $g_t \neq 0$. Thus when $\delta^* = \delta$, dW_0^*/dy is positive if world output (net of government absorption) exhibits positive growth, and vice versa.

We now turn to examine the effect of the permanent change in domestic fiscal spending on the current value of domestic wealth. Differentiating equation (13) and using equation (22) yields

$$\frac{dW_0}{dy} = \frac{(1-\delta^*)\left[\sum\limits_{t=0}^{\infty} \delta^{*t}(1-\lambda_t^*) + \sum\limits_{t=0}^{\infty} \alpha_t \lambda_t^*\right]}{(1-\delta)\Delta} > 0 \tag{23}$$

Equation (23) demonstrates that a permanent fall in government spending (that is, a rise in y) must raise domestic wealth.

The effect of the permanent fall in domestic fiscal spending (i.e., a permanent rise in net output) on the rates of interest can be ascertained from the effect of this change on world savings at the prevailing rates of interest. The rise in net domestic output changes current domestic savings by $[dy_0 - (1-\delta) dW_0]$. In the stationary case, with the prevailing rates of interest, the percentage change in domestic output, $dy_0/y_0 \equiv \mu$, equals the percentage change in domestic wealth dW_0/W_0. In that case the incipient change in domestic savings is $\mu[y_0 - (1-\delta) W_0]$, where the term in the brackets measures the initial value of domestic savings. Clearly at the prevailing rates of interest, foreign savings do not change. As is evident, the initial value of domestic savings is positive if the domestic marginal propensity to save exceeds the foreign propensity, i.e. if $\delta > \delta^*$ (in that case equilibrium requires that initially foreign savings were negative). Conversely, if $\delta < \delta^*$, domestic savings were negative. Thus, the permanent fall in domestic fiscal spending (the rise in y), raises world savings and induces a fall in the rates of interest if $\delta > \delta^*$, and vice versa.[11]

III Two-commodity world

The analysis in Section II was confined to a world with a single composite commodity. In that world, therefore, the only relevant relative price was that of consumption in different periods, i.e. the rate of interest. In this section we extend the model so as to allow for two different commodities. Therefore, in addition to the intertemporal terms of trade, the extended model also incorporates the role of the more conventional terms of trade, i.e. the relative price of importables in terms of exportables.

III.1 The incorporation of the terms of trade and world equilibrium

Let the home country exportable good be denoted by x and its importable good by m. To simplify the analysis assume that each country is completely specialized in production. Thus good x is only produced in the home country at the level X and good m is only produced in the foreign country at the level M. Consumers on the other hand are assumed to consume both goods but since tastes may differ across countries, consumption patterns may differ. More formally, the expanded menu of goods is now incorporated into the utility function (1) by noting that c_t in (1) is a composite good which is defined as a Cobb-Douglas function of its components. Specifically

$$U = \sum_{t=0}^{\infty} \delta^t \log c_t \tag{1'}$$

where

$$\log c_t \equiv \beta \log c_{xt} + (1-\beta) \log c_{mt} - \gamma^{12}$$

In order to specify the budget constraint it is convenient to define current private expenditure by z_t where

$$z_t \equiv c_{xt} + p_t c_{mt}$$

thus, z_t measures private spending in units of good x in period t and p_t denotes the relative price of good m in terms of good x. Government spending also falls on both goods; G_{xt} denotes government spending on x and G_{mt} denotes government spending on m. Thus, the private sector's constraint, analogous to (5) becomes

$$\sum_{t=0}^{\infty} \alpha_t z_t = \sum_{t=0}^{\infty} \alpha_t [X_t - (G_{xt} + p_t G_{mt})] - B \tag{5'}$$

In equation (5'), the right hand side defines W_0, the value of wealth in period 0. Equation (5') also incorporates the government budget constraint according to which the present value of government spending equals the present value of taxes. In this specification B is denominated in units of x.

Maximization of the utility function (1′) subject to the budget constraint (5′) yields the spending function z_t which is analogous to the consumption function which was obtained in the one-good world:

$$z_t = (1-\delta)\, W_t \tag{6'}$$

and, as before,

$$W_t = (\delta^t/\alpha_t)\, W_0 \tag{7'}$$

Equations (6′)–(7′) determines the pattern of *intertemporal* spending. In the present two-good world, individuals also need to determine the *temporal* allocation of spending between the two goods. The solution of the maximization problem yields:

$$\begin{aligned} c_{xt} &\equiv \beta z_t \\ c_{mt} &= (1-\beta)\frac{z_t}{p_t} \end{aligned} \tag{25}$$

As usual, the marginal propensities to spend on each good, β and $1-\beta$ respectively, are the exponents of the Cobb-Douglas composite good c_t. Before turning to the analysis of equilibrium it is relevant to emphasize that δ measures the marginal propensity to save out of *wealth* whereas β measures the marginal propensity to consume good x out of *spending*. In this framework as in the previous section, behavior is governed by *permanent* income (wealth) and the effect of *current* income in governing current behavior is only indirect.

The foreign country is modelled in an analogous fashion. Output in the foreign country, is M_t, and the government is assumed to purchase G^*_{xt} of good x (which is imported from the home country) and G^*_{mt} of good m. The maximization problem is subjected to the private sector's initial wealth, W^*_0, and its solution yields the saving propensity, δ^*, and the marginal consumption propensities, β^* and $(1-\beta^*)$.

In order to facilitate the analysis of comparative statics we define henceforth x_t as domestic product net of the home country's government spending on domestic product, and m_t as the foreign product net of the foreign country's government spending on its product. Thus

$$x_t \equiv X_t - G_{xt}$$
$$m_t \equiv M_t - G^*_{mt}$$

The equilibrium conditions are analogous to those in Section II except that, in the present expanded framework, equilibrium requires that the world market for *each* good clears. Using the demand functions the equilibrium conditions for both goods are:

$$\beta(1-\delta)\frac{\delta^t}{\alpha_t}\,W_0+\beta^*(1-\delta^*)\frac{\delta^{*t}}{\alpha_t}\,W_0^* = x_t-G_{xt}^* \tag{26}$$

$$(1-\beta)(1-\delta)\frac{\delta^t}{\alpha_t p_t}\,W_0+(1-\beta^*)(1-\delta^*)\frac{\delta^{*t}}{\alpha_t p_t}\,W_0^* = m_t-G_{mt} \tag{27}$$

In period 0, $\alpha_0 = 1$, and therefore, the market clearing conditions for $t=0$ became

$$\beta(1-\delta)\,W_0+\beta^*(1-\delta^*)\,W_0^* = x_0-G_{x0}^* \tag{28}$$

$$(1-\beta)(1-\delta)\frac{W_0}{p_0}+(1-\beta^*)(1-\delta^*)\frac{W_0^*}{p_0} = m_0-G_{m0} \tag{29}$$

where the values of wealth are

$$W_0 = \sum_{t=0}^{\infty}\alpha_t x_t-\sum_{t=0}^{\infty}\alpha_t p_t\,G_{mt}-B \tag{30}$$

$$W_0^* = \sum_{t=0}^{\infty}\alpha_t p_t\,m_t-\sum_{t=0}^{\infty}\alpha_t\,G_{xt}^*+B \tag{31}$$

As before, by Walras' Law, we may ignore one of the equations in the system.

Inspection of the equilibrium conditions (26)–(31) reveals that the relevant exogenous variables are x_t, m_t, G_{xt}^* and G_{mt}; given the values of these variables the full solution can be obtained. This observation also suggests the particular channel through which government spending influences world equilibrium. Specifically, it is evident that government spending on goods produced in its own country exerts an identical effect on the equilibrium as an equivalent change in the level of domestic production of that good. Thus, a given rise in x_t yields the same effect whether it is caused by a rise in the level of production, X_t, or by a fall in government spending on that good G_{xt}. Further, in this two-good world the *composition* of government spending is crucial for the characteristics of world equilibrium. A given change in the total *level* of government spending affects world interest rates in a manner analogous to that of the one-good world. The key source for the interest-rate effect is that, in contrast with the government, which is essentially a zero saver, the private sector may either save or dissave parts of its income. Here, in addition to the interest rate effect, the composition of government spending also influences the relative price of the two goods since the pattern of government spending may differ from that of the private sector. Therefore, a given rise in G_{xt} may exert a different influence on world equilibrium than a rise in G_{mt} of equal value.

An explicit solution of the full system (26)–(31) is cumbersome. In order to highlight the key economic factors that affect the equilibrium, we now turn to a simplified version of the model. We assume that the paths of outputs and governments spending are stationary. Thus, let $x_t = x$, $m_t = m$, $G_{xt}^* = G_x^*$ and $G_{mt} = G_m$. By substituting these stationary values into equations (26)–(31) – as shown in Appendix I – we obtain the following solutions:

$$W_0^* = \frac{(x-G_x^*)\,[-\beta(xm-G_m\,G_x^*)+m(x-G_x^*)+\beta(I-\delta)\,(m-G_m)\,B]}{(x-G_x^*)\,[\beta^*(1-\delta^*)\,m-\beta(1-\delta)\,G_m]+\beta\beta^*(mx-G_x^*\,G_m)\,(\delta^*-\delta)} \tag{32}$$

$$W_0 = \frac{(x-G_x^*)\,[\beta^*(xm-G_m\,G_x^*)-G_m(x-G_x^*)-\beta^*(1-\delta^*)\,(m-G_m)\,B]}{(x-G_x^*)\,[\beta^*(1-\delta^*)\,m-\beta(1-\delta)\,G_m]+\beta\beta^*(mx-G_x^*\,G_m)\,(\delta^*-\delta)} \tag{33}$$

To solve for p_0 we first substitute equation (28) into (29) and obtain

$$p_0 = \frac{(1-\beta)\,(x-G_x^*)+(1-\delta^*)\,(\beta-\beta^*)\,W_0^*}{\beta(m-G_m)} \tag{34}$$

The explicit solution for p_0 can be obtained by substituting (33) for W_0^* into (34).

To gain insight into the determinants of p_0 we note that the equilibrium price must equate one country's trade balance surplus with the other's trade deficit or equivalently, the equilibrium price must ensure that the value of *world* spending on goods equals the value of *world* output. Thus, the equilibrium price p_0 must satisfy equation (35):

$$[(1-\delta)\,W_0+G_x+p_0\,G_m]-X = p_0\,M-[(1-\delta^*)\,W_0^*+G_x^*+p_0\,G_m^*] \tag{35}$$

where the left-hand-side of (35) measures the home country's trade balance deficit and the right-hand-side measures the foreign country's trade balance surplus. To ensure that the market for *each* good clears we use the market clearing condition for good x in period $t = 0$ (equation (28)) and substitute for W_0 into the trade balance condition (35); the solution for p_0 yields equation (34).

III.2 The impact of debt redistribution

The equilibrium of the system described in section III.1 was conditional on the prevailing allocation of debt, and, as before, the dynamics of the system is effected through changes in each country's debt position. Like in the one-good world, the dynamic process may be associated with changes in interest rates, depending on the effect of debt redistribution on world savings. In the two-goods world the dynamic process may also be associated with changes in relative prices, depending on the effect of debt redistribution on excess demands for goods. When such changes in relative prices occur the impact of changes in real rates of interest on wealth and thereby on consumption also depends on the path of relative prices. In this section we deal with these issues.

Consider first the impact of a transfer of assets from the home to the foreign country. From equations (32)–(33) we note that the rise in the value of B raises foreign wealth by a factor proportional to $\beta(1-\delta)(m-G_m)$ and lowers domestic wealth by a factor proportional to $\beta^*(1-\delta^*)(m-G_m)$. These changes in wealth alter the demand for goods, and, as seen from equations (32) and (34), induce a change in the relative price. The direction of the change in the relative price depends on the sign of $(\beta-\beta^*)$. Thus, conforming with the well-known transfer problem criterion, a redistribution of wealth towards the foreign country raises the relative price of foreign goods if $(1-\beta^*)$, the foreign marginal propensity to spend on these goods, exceeds $(1-\beta)$, the home country's marginal propensity to spend on foreign goods or, equivalently, if $\beta > \beta^*$.

To determine the effect of the transfer on *real* consumption in the presence of changes in relative prices we need to define a price index which will then be used for evaluating the real values of consumption and wealth, as well as in real rates of interest. We define the price index associated with one unit of the consumption bundle c_t as $p_t^{1-\beta}$ and, correspondingly, the foreign price index is defined as $p_t^{1-\beta^*}$. Formally, the domestic price index is obtained by minimizing the cost $c_{xt}+p_t c_{mt}$ associated with obtaining one unit of the consumption bundle $c_{xt}^\beta c_{mt}^{1-\beta}$; the resulting index is the (utility based) true consumer price index. Analogously, the foreign price index is obtained by minimizing the cost of obtaining one unit of the foreign consumption bundle.

Using the price index, the values of *real* consumption, c_t and c_t^* are related to private spendings, z_t and z_t^* according to $c_t = z_t/p_t^{-\beta}$ and $c_t^* = z_t^*/p_t^{1-\beta^*}$ which are also equal to $(1-\delta)W_t/p_t^{*-\beta}$, and to $(1-\delta^*)W_t^*/p_t^{1-\beta^*}$, respectively. Therefore, in order to evaluate the impact of debt transfer on real consumptions we need to evaluate its impact on the values of real wealth.[13] Since the value of real wealth depends on the paths of the present-value factors and prices, we first examine the impact of the transfer on the present value factor which expresses the rates of interest in terms of good x.

Using equations (26), (28) and (32) and assuming that initially government spendings are zero, the present-value factor measured in terms of good x can be written as:

$$\alpha_t = \delta^t + \frac{(1-\delta^*)[(1-\beta)x+(1-\delta)\beta B](\delta^{*t}-\delta^t)}{x[1-(1-\beta)\delta^*-\beta\delta]} \tag{36}$$

As may be seen, the effect of a transfer on α_t depends on the relation between δ and δ^*. A rise in B lowers α_t (i.e., raises the rate of interest in terms of good x) if $\delta > \delta^*$. In that case the interest rate effect of the transfer operates to lower the recipient country's wealth.

To compute the present value-factor in terms of good m we use equations (27), (32) and (33) and obtain:

$$\alpha_t p_t = \frac{\begin{array}{l}(1-\beta)x[\beta^*(1-\delta)\delta^t+(1-\beta^*)(1-\delta^*)\delta^{*t}] \\ \qquad +(1-\delta^*)(1-\delta)[\beta(1-\beta^*)(\delta^{*t})-\beta^*(1-\beta)\delta^t]B\end{array}}{\beta^*m[1-(1-\beta)\delta^*-\beta\delta]} \tag{36'}$$

As may be seen, the effect of a transfer on $\alpha_t p_t$ depends on the relation between the propensities to save, δ and δ^*, and the propensities governing the patterns of spending, β and β^*. As is evident, when $\beta = \beta^*$, the transfer does not alter the commodity terms of trade and the effects of the transfer depend only on the relation between the marginal propensities to save. In that case the present value factors in terms of x and m move in the same direction.

Having examined all the ingredients of the real values of wealth, we now turn to examine the effects of the transfer on the real values of consumption starting with the receiving country's consumption. Using equations (32) and (34) is it shown in Appendix II that around an initial equilibrium with zero government spendings and zero initial debt:

$$\frac{d\log c_0^*}{dB} = \frac{(1-\delta)}{(1-\beta)x}\left[\beta-(1-\beta^*)(1-\delta^*)\frac{(\beta-\beta^*)}{(1-(1-\beta^*)\delta^*-\beta^*\delta)}\right] > 0 \tag{37}$$

An examination of (37) reveals that when $\beta = \beta^*$, i.e., when a transfer does not alter the commodity terms of trade, then a receipt of a transfer must raise real consumption. In this case, all goods may be aggregated into a single composite commodity and the analysis reduces to that of the one-commodity world of Section II. Likewise, when $\delta = \delta^*$, i.e., when a transfer at the initial terms of trade does not alter world savings, then a receipt of a transfer will also necessitate a rise in real consumption. In this case expenditures must equal income in each country so as to eliminate intertemporal trade. Thus, this case corresponds to the traditional static transfer problem analysis where it is known that a receipt of a transfer must raise real consumption. In the general case both $\beta \neq \beta^*$ and $\delta \neq \delta^*$, and the transfer alters the commodity terms of trade – the temporal relative price of goods – and the rates of interest – the intertemporal terms of trade. It is noteworthy, however, that even in cases for which the transfer results in a higher consumer price index and in higher rates of interest (measured in terms of good x) the value of the receiving country's real wealth must rise along with the value of its real consumption.[14]

We now turn to examine the effect of the transfer on the value of the paying country's real consumption. Using equations (32)–(34) it is also shown in Appendix II that around the initial equilibrium with zero government spendings and zero initial debt:

$$\frac{d \log c_0}{dB} = -\frac{(1-\delta^*)}{x}\left[1 + \frac{(1-\delta)(\beta-\beta^*)}{(1-(1-\beta^*)\delta^* - \beta^*\delta)}\right] < 0 \qquad (38)$$

Equations (37)–(38) can be examined for special cases. When $\beta = \beta^*$, the transfer does not alter the commodity terms of trade and all goods may be aggregated into a single composite commodity as in Section II. When $\delta = \delta^*$ the transfer, at the initial terms of trade, does not alter world savings and expenditures must equal income in each country so as to eliminate intertemporal trade. In both of these cases it is obvious that the transfer raises foreign real consumption and lowers domestic real consumption. The same qualitative results remain in the general case (with $\beta \neq \beta^*$ and $\delta \neq \delta^*$) for which the transfer alters the temporal and the intertemporal terms of trade.

The preceding analysis determined the effect of a change in debt on the initial levels of real consumption in both countries (each in terms of its own price index). In that discussion the cause for the change in debt was an exogenous transfer. In general, however, the international reallocation of debt results from the dynamic processes which characterize each country's income-spending decisions and which are reconciled through the equilibrium condition that world savings must be zero. The expressions in equations (37) and (38) can also be used to determine at each point the impact of current account surpluses and deficits (i.e. of changes in debt holdings) on the current levels of real consumption. Since from (7') $W_t = (\delta^t/\alpha_t) W_0$ and $W_t^* = (\delta^{*t}/\alpha_t) W_0^*$, it follows that whether the home country accumulates or decumulates wealth, i.e. whether its debt falls or rises, depends on whether δ^t/α_t rises or falls with the passage of time. If $\delta^* > \delta$ it is seen from equation (36) that over time the home country's debt increases and its real consumption falls, while the foreign country's debt decreases and its real consumption rises. The opposite holds if $\delta^* < \delta$.

III.3 The effects of government spending

In this section we analyze the effects of fiscal spending on the patterns of consumption in the various countries. The two-good world contains additional channels of interdependence that were not present in the one-good world of Section II. Since the relative prices of goods reflect the pattern of spending in both countries, the analysis of fiscal policies needs to specify the spending patterns of the government. In general it will be seen that the impact of policies depends on relations between various behavioral propensities. Specifically, the key factors determining the outcomes of policies are differences among the spending patterns and the saving propensities of four groups: foreign and domestic private sectors as well as foreign and domestic governments. These differences govern the evolution of relative prices and rates of interest following fiscal changes.

In order to avoid tedious derivations we will focus in this section on the effects of permanent changes in the home country's government spending on domestic goods and those in which it falls on foreign goods. In these cases we will examine the effects of the policies on the values of real consumption at home and abroad which, to recall, are defined as:

$$c_t = (1-\delta) W_t/p_t^{1-\beta} \quad \text{and}$$

$$c_t^* = (1-\delta^*) W_t^*/p_t^{1-\beta*}$$

Using equations (32)–(34) it is shown in Appendix III that the logarithmic derivatives of real consumptions with respect to changes in government spending on domestic goods, G_x, and on foreign goods, G_m, evaluated around an initial equilibrium with zero government spendings and zero initial debt are:

$$\frac{d \log c_0^*}{dG_x} = -\frac{\beta^*}{x} < 0 \tag{39}$$

$$\frac{d \log c_0^*}{dG_m} = \frac{1}{m}\left[\frac{\beta(1-\delta)}{\beta^*Q} - (1-\beta^*)\frac{1+RS}{1+R}\right] \tag{40}$$

$$\frac{d \log c_0}{dG_x} = -\frac{\beta}{x} < 0 \tag{41}$$

$$\frac{d \log c_0}{dG_m} = \frac{1}{m}\left[\frac{\beta(1-\delta)-Q}{\beta^*Q} - (1-\beta)\frac{1+RS}{1+R}\right] \tag{42}$$

where

$$Q \equiv 1-(1-\beta)\delta^* - \beta\delta > 0$$

$$R \equiv \frac{(\beta - \beta^*)(1 - \delta^*)}{\beta^* Q}$$

$$S \equiv \frac{\beta(1 - \delta) - \beta^*(1 - \delta^*) - \beta\beta^*(\delta^* - \delta)}{\beta^* Q}$$

As may be seen, a rise in fiscal spending on *domestic* goods lowers the values of real consumption at home and abroad. The reduction in foreign consumption thus 'finances' part of the increased government spending. The proportional reduction in foreign real consumptions is β^*, i.e., the relative share of foreign spending on good x. Analogously, the proportional reduction in the home country's private sector's real consumption is β. Thus, when the home country's government increases spending on the domestic good the extent of the reduction in the values of real consumptions of the private sectors in both countries depends on the importance of that good in private sectors' budgets. The precise effects of a rise in government spending on *foreign* goods depends on the magnitudes of the various propensities as may be seen from equations (40) and (42).

In order to highlight the role of the government's spending propensities we define the government spending function G as:

$$G \equiv G_x + p G_m \tag{43}$$

and we assume that the government spending propensities are β_G on good x, and $(1 - \beta_G)$ on good m. Thus:

$$G_x = \beta_G G \quad \text{and} \quad p G_m = (1 - \beta_G) G,$$

which implies that, formally, G_m becomes a function of G_x, $G_m = G_m(G_x)$. It follows that around an initial equilibrium with zero government spending:

$$dG_m = \frac{\gamma}{p} dG_x \tag{44}$$

where $\gamma = (1 - \beta_G)/\beta_G$.

Using this specification of government spending we note that

$$\frac{d \log c_0^*}{dG} = \frac{\partial \log c_0^*}{\partial G_x} + \gamma \frac{\partial \log c_0^*}{p \partial G_m} \tag{45}$$

To obtain insights into the economic factors which are at play, we now turn to examine some special cases. These cases correspond to specific assumptions about some of the marginal propensities. We start with the case in which the domestic and foreign marginal propensities to save are the same, i.e., $\delta = \delta^*$. In that case using equations (39)–(40) and the specification of government spending which is embodied in (45) along with the solution for p_0 (from equation (A8) in Appendix II), we obtain:

$$\frac{d \log c_0^*}{dG} = \frac{\beta^*}{\beta_G \beta(1-\beta) x} [\beta(\beta - \beta_G) + 2(1-\beta^*)(1-\beta_G)(\beta - \beta^*)]$$

(46)

Equation (46) reveals that when $\delta = \delta^*$ the effect of domestic fiscal spending on foreign real consumption depends on differences among the patterns of spending of domestic private and public sectors, $\beta - \beta_G$, as well as between domestic and foreign private sectors, $\beta - \beta^*$. The economic interpretation of this result is as follows. When $\delta = \delta^*$ we know from equation (36) that in both countries the interest rate equals the subjective discount rate. Therefore, in each country savings are zero. In that case, neither the rates of interest, nor the total level of world spending are altered in response to government spending since the government, like the private sectors, is a zero saver. It follows that the potential effect of fiscal policies can only operate through changes in relative prices. In conformity with the standard analysis of economic transfers, such changes can occur only if the spending patterns differ among private and public sectors.

To demonstrate the role of the spending patterns consider the following special cases:

(i) When all spending patterns are identical, i.e., when $\beta = \beta^* = \beta_G$, we note from equation (46) that $d \log c_0^*/dG = 0$. Thus, in this special case, the effects of fiscal policy are not transmitted internationally and only the domestic private sector is crowded out. In that case aggregate behavior in the various markets are not affected by the fiscal policy and, therefore, there are no changes in relative prices.

(ii) When the spending patterns of the domestic and foreign private sectors are identical, i.e. when $\beta = \beta^*$, we note from equation (46) that the direction of the change in foreign real consumption following a rise in domestic fiscal spending depends only on the difference between β, the private sectors' spending pattern, and β_G, the corresponding government spending pattern. If $\beta > \beta_G$, a rise in government spending creates an excess supply of good x and an excess demand for good m at the initial relative price. Equilibrium is restored through a rise in p, the relative price of good m. This rise in p raises the real value of foreign wealth and, thereby, raises real consumption. The preceding discussion also implies that in the extreme case in which $\beta_G = 1$, i.e. when government spending falls entirely on good x, foreign real consumption must fall (as was already shown in equation (39)). At the other extreme, when $\beta_G = 0$, i.e., when government spending falls entirely on good m, (the case which corresponds to equation (40)), the value of foreign real consumption must rise. The effect of the rise in government spending on the home country's real consumption must always be negative independent of the patterns of government spending. Thus, in conformity with the traditional results of economic transfers, the secondary gain that might occur through an improvement of the terms of trade cannot offset the primary loss which in the present case is the tax levied to finance government spending.

The preceding analysis was confined to the case in which each country's income equaled its spending since δ was assumed to equal δ^*. As a result, the international transmission of fiscal policies operated entirely through the effects of these policies on the relative price of goods without any impact on the rates of interest. We turn now to examine the case in which the saving propensities differ, i.e. $\delta \neq \delta^*$. In order to isolate the effects of differences between private and public spending patterns we will assume that $\beta = \beta^*$. Analogously to the previous derivation it can be shown that if $(1-\delta)-(1-\beta)[1-(1-\beta)\delta^*-\beta] > 0$ then

$$\text{sign} \frac{d \log c_0^*}{dG} = \text{sign} \left\{ \frac{(1-\beta_G)}{\beta_G} - \frac{(1-\beta)[1-(1-\beta)\delta^*-\beta\delta]}{(1-\delta)-(1-\beta)[1-(1-\beta)\delta^*-\beta]} \right\}$$

(46′)

and vice versa. As may be seen, the sign in (46′) depends on the relation between the spending patterns of the private sectors and the government, β and β_G, as well as on the relation between the saving propensities δ and δ^*. In the special case for which $\beta = \beta_G$, equation (46′) becomes

$$\text{sign} \frac{d \log c_0^*}{dG} = \text{sign} (\delta^* - \delta)$$

(46″)

In that case the patterns of world spending on goods are independent of fiscal policies since $\beta = \beta^* = \beta_G$. Therefore the two goods can be aggregated into a composite commodity and the analysis reduces to that of the one-good world. And, as seen in equation (46″) the key factor determining the effect of fiscal spending on foreign real consumption is the relation between δ^* and δ. Analogously to the analysis of equation (22) (where we analyzed the effect of a rise in output net of government absorption), the interpretation of this result is in terms of the effect of government spending on the rate of interest. If $\delta^* > \delta$, the foreign country saves part of its income whereas the domestic economy dissaves; thus the domestic country's marginal propensity to save out of *income* is negative. In that case, a rise in the home country's government spending amounts to transferring income from a dissaver (the home country's private sector) to a zero saver (the government), thereby creating (at the prevailing rates of interest) excess world savings. To restore equilibrium the rates of interest must fall. The fall in the rates of interest raises foreign wealth and real consumption. The opposite occurs when $\delta^* < \delta$. In that case government spending lowers world savings and raises interest rates and, thereby, lowers foreign wealth and real consumption. In that case, the effect of government spending on the home country's real consumption is always negative and the analysis is analogous to that of the one-commodity world equation (24). As usual, the secondary gain arising from a fall in the rate of interest (that occurs when $\delta^* > \delta$) cannot outweigh the primary loss from the tax that is levied to finance government spending.

The preceding analysis focused on the nature of the international transmission of domestic fiscal spending. One of the central mechanisms through which the transmission is effected operates through the effects of fiscal spending on real rates of interest. In what follows we elaborate on the effects of fiscal spending on the real rates of interest.

The example underlying equation (46″) assumes that the patterns of spending are identical among domestic and foreign governments and private sectors. The assumption that $\beta = \beta^*$ implies that the real rates of interest are equal across countries. The additional assumption that $\beta = \beta_G$ implies that the effects of changes in fiscal spending on the real rates of interest depend only on the differences between the domestic and the foreign saving propensities.

The example underlying equation (46′), assumes that the spending patterns of the domestic and foreign private sectors differ from those of the government, i.e. that $\beta_G \neq \beta = \beta^*$. In that case real rates of interest are equal across the world but the impact on the real rates of government spending depend not only on the relation between the two countries' saving propensities but also on the relation between β and β_G. In the more general case for which all spending patterns differ, real rates of interest differ across countries and the effect of government spending on these rates is more complex.

To illustrate, consider the special case in which government spending falls entirely on the domestically produced good, i.e. $\beta_G = 1$. The effects of government spending on the real rates of interest can be computed from their effects on the present-value factors measured in terms of the consumption baskets. The domestic and foreign real present-value factors are $\alpha_t p_t^{1-\beta}$ and $\alpha_t p_t^{1-\beta*}$, respectively. It is shown in Appendix IV that:

$$\frac{d \log (\alpha_t p_t^{1-\beta})}{d \log x} = -(1-\beta) \tag{47}$$

and

$$\frac{d \log (\alpha_t p_t^{1-\beta*})}{d \log x} = -(1-\beta*) \tag{47'}$$

Thus, a reduction in government spending G_x (i.e. a rise in x) lowers the real present-value factors in both countries and raises the corresponding real rates of interest. In contrast with the case of equality among private and public spending patterns in which the direction of changes in real rates of interest depended on the relation between saving propensities, here these propensities play no role. In the present case with $\beta_G = 1$ domestic and foreign real rates of interest move in the same direction. The extent of their response to fiscal spending depends on the relative share of the good which is not consumed by the government (good m) in private sector's spending.

In the intermediate case for which government spending falls on both goods but the relative share β_G exceeds the corresponding shares of the private sectors, β and $\beta*$, the effect of government spending on the real rates of interest reflects the influence of both spending patterns and saving propensities. For example, if $\delta* > \delta$ a reduction in government spending lowers world savings (as shown in Section II) and thereby reinforces the effects embodied in equations (47)–(47'). On the other hand, if $\delta < \delta*$, the impact of government spending on world savings and, thereby, on the real rates of interest tends to mitigate and may reverse the effects operating via equations (47)–(47').

We have shown in this section that the effects of government spending on world rates of interest and the nature of the international transmission mechanism depend on the multitude of 'transfer problem criteria'. These include the relations between saving propensities and spending patterns of domestic and foreign governments and private sectors.

IV Concluding remarks

In this paper we analyzed the relation between government spending and real rates of interest as well as the international transmission of fiscal policies. Specifically, we examined the dependence of the patterns of consumption in one country on the level of government spending in the rest of the world. For this purpose we developed a general equilibrium model which was characterized by fully integrated world capital markets. Economic agents were assumed to behave rationally and government policies were constrained to obey the intertemporal solvency requirement.

It was shown that the effects of changes in countries' net debtor position as well as the effects of government spending can be analyzed by reference to a multitude of 'transfer problem criteria,' which are familiar from the theory of international economic transfers. In the present case the impact of policies depended on relations among the spending propensities of domestic and foreign private sectors and governments as well as on the difference between domestic and foreign saving propensities. For example, we showed that when spending patterns are similar across countries, the effect of a *permanent* rise in government spending on the rate of interest depends on whether the country in question is a saver or a dissaver in the world economy. If the country is a dissaver a rise in government spending lowers domestic consumption and rates of interest and induces a rise in foreign wealth and consumption. Thus, in that case, the international transmission is positive. The opposite holds when the country is a net saver. In the more general case the exact nature of the transmission and of the effect of government spending on interest rates depends also on comparisons among the various spending patterns which, in turn, determine the impact of fiscal policies on the terms of trade. The impact of permanent fiscal policies on the rates of interest and, thereby, on the nature of the transmission mechanism also depends on the percentage growth of world net output. Specifically, the rates of interest which result from expansionary fiscal policies tend to be higher, and the international transmission tends to be more negative, the faster is the percentage growth of world output.

Our analysis also drew a distinction between permanent and transitory policies as well as between current policies and expected future policies. It was shown that a *transitory current* fiscal spending, in addition to crowding out the domestic private sector, must also crowd out the foreign private sector and, thereby, result in a *negative* transmission. However, a *transitory future* rise in government spending must induce an immediate increase in foreign private sector's consumption and thereby result in a *positive* current transmission. In both cases, of course, domestic private sector's consumption must fall. These patterns of response reflect themselves in the current account of the balance of payments and in changes in the various countries' net debtor-creditor positions.

The distinction between permanent and transitory policies also reflects itself in complex changes in the patterns of interest rates. For example, a transitory future fiscal expansion lowers the rate of interest linking the present period with the period during which the transitory fiscal change occurs. The impact on the rates of interest linking the present period with all other periods depends on the difference between domestic and foreign marginal propensities to save. In contrast, a transitory current rise in fiscal spending must raise the rates of interest pertaining to all maturities. The rise in short-term rates of interest exceeds the rise in long-term rates and, thereby, the slope of the yield curve changes.

The analysis of the impact of government spending on real rates of interest revealed that even when capital markets are highly integrated, real rates of interest may differ if spending patterns differ across countries. With such differences in spending patterns, fiscal policies exert different quantitative effects on real rates of interest in the various countries. An implication of this analysis is that in the presence of non-traded goods, fiscal policies may also exert different qualitative effects on real rates of interest in different countries since, depending on the nature of the transmission mechanism and on the patterns of government and private sectors' spending, the relative prices of non-traded goods, and thereby the price indices, might be negatively correlated between countries.

The examination of the response to future changes is applicable to the analysis of the impact of the discovery of North Sea oil. That discovery changes current wealth, but its impact on the actual flow of oil is expected to occur only in the future. The rise in current wealth stimulates consumption and is transmitted internationally through a rise in world interest rates.

Our analysis is subject to several limitations which stem from some of the simplifying assumptions. We assumed that the output levels were given exogenously. An extension would allow for a process of investment which responds to rates of interest and which changes the paths of outputs. Such an extension would modify the pattern of the current account and debt accumulation.[15] The endogeneity of output could also be introduced through the incorporation of some Keynesian features such as price rigidities. Under such circumstances government spending would alter the level of economic activity and would be transmitted internationally through mechanisms similar to those of the foreign-trade multipliers.

Further extension would modify the assumption of full certainty. The incorporation of uncertainty might raise additional issues such as the role of bankruptcy and default. In that case, a relevant question would be the impact of fiscal policies on the likelihood of bankruptcies and defaults in the international capital markets.

One of the key features of our model has been the central role played by the path of government *spending* and the irrelevancy of the path of government deficits. Thus, the model conformed with the Ricardian proposition. One of the reasons responsible for this feature was the assumption that all taxes were of the non-distorting variety. As a result the time pattern of taxes and government debt issues was irrelevant once the pattern of government spending was given. An extension would allow for distorting effects of taxes.[16] Such distortions would introduce new considerations associated with the determination of the optimal paths of the various means of government finance.

Finally, our two-country world with exogenous government spendings enables exploitation of monopoly-monopsony powers in goods and capital markets. An extension would determine the optimal pattern of government spending along with the optimal trade-cum-capital-flows tax structure along the lines of the optimal tariff literature. Such a strategic behavior could then be incorporated into a more elaborate game-theoretic world equilibrium (see Hamada, 1984). In such a set-up, government spendings and its means of finance would become endogenous variables that are determined in the context of world equilibrium.

Appendix: The two-commodity stationary system

I The solution of the system
The solutions of the system for the stationary case can be obtained as follows. We first express the definitions of wealth in equations (30)–(31) as

$$W_0 = x \sum_{t=0}^{\infty} \alpha_t - G_m \sum_{t=0}^{\infty} \alpha_t p_t - B \tag{A1}$$

$$W_0^* = m \sum_{t=0}^{\infty} \alpha_t p_t - G_x^* \sum_{t=0}^{\infty} \alpha_t + B \tag{A2}$$

Substituting (A1)–(A2) into (28)–(29) yields:

$$\beta(1-\delta)\left[x \sum_{t=0}^{\infty} \alpha_t - G_m \sum_{t=0}^{\infty} \alpha_t p_t - B \right]$$
$$+ \beta^*(1-\delta^*)\left[m \sum_{t=0}^{\infty} \alpha_t p_t - G_x^* \sum_{t=0}^{\infty} \alpha_t + B \right] = x - G_x^* \tag{A3}$$

$$(1-\beta)(1-\delta)\left[x \sum_{t=0}^{\infty} \alpha_t - G_m \sum_{t=0}^{\infty} \alpha_t p_t - B \right]$$
$$+ (1-\beta^*)(1-\delta^*)\left[m \sum_{t=0}^{\infty} \alpha_t p_t - G_x^* \sum_{t=0}^{\infty} \alpha_t + B \right] = p_0(m - G_m) \tag{A4}$$

We then multiply both sides of (26) by α_t, sum both sides over all t (from 0 to ∞) and substitute (A1) and (A2) for W_0 and W_0^*. The resulting equation is then:

$$\beta\left[\sum_{t=0}^{\infty} \alpha_t - G_m \sum_{t=0}^{\infty} \alpha_t p_t - B \right]$$
$$+ \beta^*\left[m \sum_{t=0}^{\infty} \alpha_t p_t - G_x^* \sum_{t=0}^{\infty} \alpha_t + B \right] = (x - G_x^*) \sum_{t=0}^{\infty} \alpha_t \tag{A5}$$

Equation (A3), (A4) and (A5) constitute the relevant system for the case of stationary outputs and fiscal policies. The economic interpretation of the equation is as follows: Equations (A3) and (A4) describe the equilibrium in the markets for the two goods in period 0. It is evident that this is a rational expectations equilibrium since the demand functions are based on the fully expected realization of future values of rates of interest and prices. Equation (A5) requires that the sum of the present values of world demand for good x equal the corresponding sum of world supply. As may be noted we have used Walras Law to ignore the analogous requirement for good m.

Using this system we may solve for the three unknowns: The sum of the present value factors in terms of good $x - \Sigma_{t=0}^{\infty} \alpha_t$; the sum of the present value factors in terms of good $m - \Sigma_{t=0}^{\infty} \alpha_t p_t$; and the relative price of good m in terms of x in the first period $- p_0$. These solutions can then be used in (A1) and (A2) to obtain the values of W_0 and W_0^*. These are the solutions that are reported in the text.

II The effects of debt on real consumptions

In this part of the Appendix we derive the effects of debt transfers on the real values of domestic and foreign consumptions. These results are computed around an initial equilibrium with zero debt and zero government spendings. Around such an equilibrium, the values of W_0^*, W_0 and p_0 are (from (32)–(34)):

$$W_0^* = \frac{(1-\beta)x}{\beta^* D} \tag{A6}$$

$$W_0 = \frac{x}{D} \tag{A7}$$

$$p_0 = \frac{(1-\beta)x}{\beta^* m} \frac{[1-(1-\beta^*)\delta^* - \beta^*\delta]}{D} \tag{A8}$$

where

$$D = 1 - (1-\beta)\delta^* - \beta\delta > 0$$

From (32) we obtain

$$\frac{dW_0^*}{dB} = \frac{\beta(1-\delta)}{\beta^* D} \tag{A9}$$

which can be divided by (A6) to yield:

$$\frac{d \log W_0^*}{dB} = \frac{\beta(1-\delta)}{(1-\beta)x} \tag{A10}$$

Analogously, by differentiating (34) with respect to B and using (A9) we obtain:

$$\frac{dp_0}{dB} = \frac{(1-\delta^*)(1-\delta)(\beta-\beta^*)}{m\beta^* D} \tag{A11}$$

Dividing (A11) by p_0 from (A8) yields

$$\frac{d \log p_0}{dB} = \frac{(1-\delta^*)(1-\delta)(\beta-\beta^*)}{(1-\beta)x[1-(1-\beta^*)\delta^*-\beta^*\delta]} \tag{A12}$$

Recalling that:

$$d \log c_0^*/dB = d \log W_0^*/dB - (1-\beta^*) d \log p_0/dB$$

we may multiply (A12) by $(1-\beta^*)$ and use (A10) to obtain equation (37) in the text.

The effect of the transfer on domestic real consumption is obtained analogously. We first note that for equation (28):

$$dW_0 = -\frac{\beta^*(1-\delta^*)}{\beta(1-\delta)} dW_0^* \tag{A13}$$

and thus, by using (A9) and (A7) we get

$$\frac{d \log W_0}{dB} = -\frac{(1-\delta^*)}{x} \tag{A14}$$

Multiplying (A12) by $(1-\beta)$ and subtracting from (A14) yields equation (38) in the text.

III The effects of fiscal spending on real consumptions

In this part of the Appendix we derive the effects of fiscal policies on the real values of domestic and foreign consumptions. As before these results are computed around and initial equilibrium with zero debt and zero government spendings. From (32) we obtain

$$\frac{dW_0^*}{dx} = \frac{1-\beta}{\beta^*D} \tag{A15}$$

$$\frac{dW_0^*}{dG_m} = \frac{x}{m} \frac{\beta(1-\beta)(1-\delta)}{\beta^{*2}D^2} \tag{A16}$$

and from (A13) and (A15)–(A16) we obtain

$$\frac{dW_0}{dx} = \frac{1}{D} \tag{A17}$$

$$\frac{dW_0}{dG_m} = \frac{x[\beta(1-\delta)-D]}{\beta^*mD^2} \tag{A18}$$

Differentiating (34) with respect to x and using (A15) yields

$$\frac{dp_0}{dx} = \frac{(1-\beta)-(1-\delta^*)(\beta-\beta^*)\frac{(1-\beta)}{\beta^*D}}{\beta m} \tag{A19}$$

To convert (A19) into a logarithmic derivative we first substitute (A6) for W_0^* in equation (34) to obtain:

$$p_0 = \frac{(1-\beta)x}{\beta m}\left[1+\frac{(1-\delta^*)(\beta-\beta^*)}{\beta^*D}\right] \tag{A20}$$

and dividing (A19) by (A20) yields

$$\frac{d\log p_0}{dx} = \frac{1}{x} \tag{A21}$$

Multiplying (A21) by $(1-\beta^*)$ and subtracting from the logarithmic derivative of W_0^* with respect to x (obtained from (A15) and (A6)) we get $d\log c_0^*/dx$ which is equation (39) in the text, with a minus sign (since $dx = -dG_x$).

Analogously, dividing (A17) by (A7) yields the logarithmic derivative of W_0 with respect to x, from which we subtract the product of $(1-\beta)$ and (A20), to obtain $d\log c_0/dx$ which is equation (41) in the text (with a minus sign).

To compute the effects of changes in G_m on real consumptions we first note that from (34) and (A16):

$$\frac{dp_0}{dG_m} = \frac{(1-\beta)}{\beta}\frac{x}{m^2}\left\{1+\frac{(\beta-\beta^*)(1-\delta^*)}{\beta^{*2}D^2}[\beta(1-\delta)\right.$$
$$\left. -\beta^*(1-\delta^*)-\beta\beta^*(\delta^*-\delta)]\right\} \tag{A22}$$

and dividing by (A-21) yields

$$\frac{d\log p_0}{dG_m} = \frac{1}{m}\frac{1+RS}{1+R} \tag{A23}$$

where R and S are defined in equation (42) in the text. Multiplying (A23) by $(1-\beta^*)$ and subtracting from the ratio of (A16) and (A6) yields equation (40) in the text.

Analogously, dividing (A18) by (A17) and subtracting the product of $(1-\beta)$ and (A23) yields equation (42) in the text.

IV The effects of fiscal spending on real rates of interest

In this part of the Appendix we compute the effects of domestic permanent fiscal spending on domestic and foreign real rates of interest. For simplicity we focus on the case in which government spending falls entirely on good x, i.e. the case for which $\beta_G = 1$.

Equation (26) in text around an initial equilibrium with zero government spending and initial debt implies that

$$\alpha_t = 1/x[\beta(1-\delta)\,\delta^t W_0 + \beta^*(1-\delta^*)\,\delta^{*t} W_0^*] \tag{A24}$$

and its logarithmic derivative is:

$$\frac{d\log\alpha_t}{dx} = \theta\,\frac{d\log W_0}{dx} + (1-\theta)\,\frac{d\log W_0^*}{dx} - \frac{1}{x} \tag{A25}$$

where, using (A6)–(A7)

$$\theta = \frac{\beta(1-\delta)\,\delta^t}{\beta(1-\delta)\,\delta^t + (1-\beta)(1-\delta^*)\,\delta^{*t}}$$

Using (A17) and (A7) for $d\log W_0/dx$, and using (A15) and (A6) for $d\log W_0^*/dx$, we obtain

$$\frac{d\log\alpha_t}{dx} = 0 \tag{A25'}$$

Analogously, from equation (27) we obtain:

$$\frac{d\log p_t}{dx} = \tilde{\theta}\,\frac{d\log W_0}{dx} + (1-\tilde{\theta})\,\frac{d\log W_0^*}{dx} - \frac{d\log\alpha_t}{dx} \tag{A26}$$

where

$$\tilde{\theta} = \frac{\beta^*(1-\delta)\,\delta^t}{\beta^*(1-\delta)\,\delta^t + (1-\beta^*)(1-\delta^*)\,\delta^{*t}}$$

Using (A17) and (A7) for $d\log W_0/dx$, and using (A15) and (A6) for $d\log W_0^*/dx$, we obtain after subsituting (A25'):

$$\frac{d\log p_t}{dx} = \frac{1}{x} \tag{A26'}$$

As may be observed by comparing (A26') with (A21), the effect of x on the initial price p_0 is the same as its effect on the entire path of prices, p_t. This result reflects the finding in (A25') where it was shown that the change of x does not alter the entire path of interest rates.

Finally, logarithmic differentiation of the real present-value factors, $(\alpha_t p_t^{1-\beta})$ and $(\alpha_t p_t^{1-\beta*})$ with respect to x, and using (A25') and (A26'), yields equations (47)–(47') in the text.

NOTES

* Jacob A. Frenkel acknowledges support from the Sackler Institute of Advanced Studies at Tel-Aviv University, Israel, and Assaf Razin acknowledges support from the Ross Endowment. We wish to thank Itzhak Gilboa for assistance in the computations. In revising the paper we have benefited from useful comments by J. Aizenman, A. Dixit, E. Helpman, L. Svensson, and M. Obstfeld. The research reported here is part of the NBER's Research Program in International Studies and Economic Fluctuations. Any opinions are those of the authors and not of the National Bureau of Economic Research.

1 For surveys of some of this literature see Fair (1979) and Mussa (1979) and the references therein.

2 See Laursen and Metzler (1950) and Harberger (1950).

3 See contributions by Mundell (1968) and Fleming (1962).

4 See Dornbusch (1976) and Frenkel and Rodriguez (1982).

5 See, for example, Mishkin (1984), Huizinga and Mishkin (1983), Mark (1983) and Cumby and Obstfeld (1984) for studies of real interest rate equality. On covered interest arbitrage see Frenkel and Levich (1977).

6 For this hypothesis see Feldstein and Horioka (1980) and Feldstein (1983), and for some discussions see Harberger (1980) and Tobin (1983).

7 The basic model of these characteristics is developed in Helpman and Razin (1982) who study the implications of its monetary counterpart for the analysis of exchange rate dynamics.

8 On this see Barro (1974). In Frenkel and Razin (1984) we relax this assumption.

9 On the role of 'transfer problem criteria' see Mussa (1969).

10 In this formulation government spending reduces the resources available for private sector consumption without yielding utility services. The interaction between public and private goods in the utility function is a separate issue with which we do not deal in the present paper. An introduction of a 'useful' government as a *separable* argument in the utility function would not alter our results.

11 Formally, this effect can best be illustrated for the stationary case. In that case (with zero initial debt) the present value factor in (17) can be written as:

$$\alpha_t = \frac{(1-\delta^*)\lambda^*\delta^{*t} + (1-\delta)\lambda\delta^t}{(1-\delta^*)\lambda^* + (1-\delta)\lambda} \tag{24}$$

Differentiating (24) with respect to y and recalling that $r_{t-1} \equiv [(\alpha_{t-1}/\alpha_t) - 1]$, shows that sign $(dr_{t-1}/dy) = $ sign $(\delta^* - \delta)$.

12 The constant term $\gamma = \beta \log \beta + (1-\beta) \log (1-\beta)$ is chosen in order to simplify, without loss of generality, the subsequent expressions of real consumption.

13 In general, to determine the effect of a transfer on the real value of consumption in terms of the consumer price index, we need to determine the change in the real value of wealth as well as in the real interest rate (in terms of the consumer consumption bundle). In the present case, however, since we have used a logarithmic utility function, the marginal saving propensity is independent of the rate of interest and, therefore, the entire effect of transfers and other policies on real consumption operate through their effects on real wealth.

14 This result follows by noting that the denominator in equation (37) is positive, and the minimal value of the numerator cannot fall below a positive number.

15 For an analysis of the role of investment in determining the path of the current

account see Sachs (1981), and for an analysis of the effects of budget deficits on investment see Buiter (1984).
16 For an analysis of these effects see Barro (1979), Kydland and Prescott (1980) and Razin and Svensson (1983). In a related paper which was originally presented at the CEPR/NBER Conference on International Economic Policy Coordination (1984) we analyze the effects of budget deficits in a two-country model which departs from the Ricardian proposition due to differences between private and public discount rates. See Frenkel and Razin (1984).

REFERENCES

Barro, Robert J. (1974). 'Are Government Bonds Net Wealth?.' *Journal of Political Economy* **82**, 1095–1118.

Barro, Robert J. (1979). 'On the Determination of Public Debt.' *Journal of Political Economy*, **87**, 940–71.

Buiter, Willem H. (1984). 'Fiscal Policy in Open, Interdependent Economies.' National Bureau of Economic Research, Working Paper Series, No. 1428 (August).

Cumby, Robert and Maurice Obstfeld (1984). 'On the International Equality of Real Rates of Interest.' In J. Bilson and R. Marston (eds.), *Proceedings of the 1982 Bellagio Conference*, University of Chicago Press, Chicago, Illinois, forthcoming.

Dornbusch, Rudiger (1976). 'Expectations and Exchange Rate Dynamics.' *Journal of Political Economy* **84**, 1161–76.

Fair, Ray C. (1979). 'On Modeling the Economic Linkages Among Countries.' In R. Dornbusch and J. A. Frenkel (Eds.) *International Economic Policy: Theory and Evidence*, Johns Hopkins University Press, Baltimore.

Feldstein, Martin (1983). 'Domestic Savings and International Capital Movements in the Long Run and in the Short-Run.' *European Economic Review*, **21**, 129–51.

Feldstein, Martin and C. Horioka (1980). 'Domestic Savings and International Capital Flows.' *The Economic Journal*, **90**, 314–29.

Fleming, J. Marcus (1962). 'Domestic Financial Policies Under Fixed and Floating Exchange Rates.' *International Monetary Fund Staff Papers*, **9**, 369–379.

Frenkel, Jacob A. and Assaf Razin (1984). 'Budget Deficits and Rates of Interest in the World Economy.' National Bureau of Economic Research, Working Paper Series, No. 1354 (May).

Frenkel, Jacob A. and Carlos A. Rodriguez (1982). 'Exchange Rate Dynamics and the Overshooting Hypothesis.' *International Monetary Fund Staff Papers*, **29**, 1–30.

Frenkel, Jacob A. and Richard M. Levich (1977). 'Transactions Costs and Interest Arbitrage: Tranquil Versus Turbulent Periods.' *Journal of Political Economy*, **85**, 1209–26.

Hamada, Koichi (1984). 'Strategic Aspects of International Fiscal Interdependence.' Unpublished manuscript, Tokyo University.

Harberger, Arnold C. (1950). 'Currency Depreciation, Income, and the Balance of Payments.' *Journal of Political Economy*, **58**, 47–60.

Harberger, Arnold C. (1980). 'Vignettes on the World Capital Market.' *American Economic Review*, **70**, 331–37.

Helpman, Elhanan and Assaf Razin (1982). 'Dynamics of a Floating Exchange Rate Regime.' *Journal of Political Economy*, **90**, 728–54.

Huizinga John and Mishkin Frederick (1983). 'International Comparisons of Real Rates of Interest.' Unpublished manuscript, University of Chicago.

Kydland, Finn E. and Edward C. Prescott (1980). 'A Competitive Theory of Fluctuations and the Feasibility and Desirability of Stabilization Policy', in Fischer Stanley (ed.). *Rational Expectations and Economic Policy*, Chicago: University of Chicago Press.

Laursen, Svend and Lloyd A. Metzler (1950). 'Flexible Exchange Rates and The Theory of Employment.' *Review of Economic and Statistics*, **32**, 281–99.

Mark, Nelson C. (1983). *Aspects of International Economic Interdependence Under Flexible Exchange Rates.* Unpublished Ph.D. dissertation, The University of Chicago.

Mishkin, Frederic S. (1984). 'The Real Interest Rate: A Multi-Country Empirical Study.' *The Canadian Journal of Economics*, forthcoming.

Mundell, Robert (1968). *International Economics*, MacMillan, New York.

Mussa, Michael (1969). 'Three Times the Transfer Problem plus David Hume.' Unpublished manuscript, University of Chicago.

Mussa, Michael (1979). 'Macroeconomic Interdependence and the Exchange Rate Regime.' in R. Dornbusch and J. A. Frenkel (Eds.), *International Economic Policy: Theory and Evidence*, Johns Hopkins University, Baltimore.

Razin, Assaf and Lars E. O. Svensson (1983). 'The Current Account and the Optimal Government Debt.' *Journal of International Money and Finance*, **2**, 215–24.

Sachs, Jeffrey D. (1981). 'The Current account and Macroeconomic Adjustment in the 1970s.' *Brookings Papers on Economic Activity*, 201–18.

Tobin, James (1983). 'Comments on "Domestic Saving and International Capital Movements in the Long Run and in the Short Run" by M. Feldstein'. *European Economic Review*, **21**, 153–56.

COMMENT MATTHEW B. CANZONERI

Big US deficits and their implications for interest rates and aggregate demand, both at home and abroad, are certainly major issues of the day. Frenkel and Razin start from the reasonable position that the entire future paths of government spending and taxation matter, and that we require an intertemporal utility maximizing approach to analyze the problem. This position is logically quite reasonable, but it quickly forces the authors into analytically intractable structures. Consequently, they have to make many simplifying assumptions: output is exogenous; there are no informational difficulties or price rigidities, no money. Even so, their analysis deserves our serious attention, for I suspect that their basic results for interest rates and aggregate demand are robust. I might also add that these results are very difficult to derive, even with the simplifying assumptions. Indeed, one of the authors' major contributions here is to show us how to handle a very complicated intertemporal structure by aggregating future consumption into a composite good.

In an earlier paper, Frenkel and Razin postulated an even simpler Ricardian world where the timing of tax liabilities is irrelevant. An infinite lived citizen is both consumer and tax payer. This citizen faces the same borrowing costs as a consumer and as a tax payer. Thus, if the Government lowers current taxes and increases the present value of future tax liabilities correspondingly, the consumer's wealth or permanent income is unaffected; a temporary tax cut has no real effect. The simple Ricardian identification between consumers and tax payers yields an elegant and tractable intertemporal model of demand. Unfortunately, the Ricardian model is all too neat and clean if we think that deficits really do matter.

A major problem that Frenkel and Razin face in the present paper is that there is no consensus on how the Ricardian relationship between consumers and tax payers ought to be dirtied up; there appears to be no simple and appealing way of doing it. Here, the authors follow Yaari and Blanchard in assuming that the individual citizen has only a probability of surviving until the next period. Consequently, the individual citizen is required to buy life insurance to guarantee solvency when borrowing to finance consumption. The collective citizenry does not die, so the Government does not have to pay a life insurance premium when it borrows. The effect of these assumptions is that the individual citizen as consumer faces higher borrowing costs than the collective citizenry as tax payers. Now when the Government lowers current taxes and raises the present value of future tax liabilities correspondingly, wealth of the individual citizen-consumer goes up, because he discounts the future tax liabilities more heavily; deficits increase consumer demand.

Frenkel and Razin's results for an increase in the current deficit are straightforward, even if they are hard to derive. Consumption demand in the US depends upon US wealth; demand in Europe (here the 'other country') depends upon European wealth. Market supply is equal to the exogenous outputs minus the Government purchases. Interest rates work through wealth to bring demand in line with existing supplies in each period. If President Reagan succeeds in cutting US taxes temporarily (permanent cuts can not be analyzed in the Frenkel-Razin model unless growth is introduced), US wealth goes up for the reasons given above, and at prevailing interest rates the higher US consumption creates an excess demand for output. Interest rates rise to decrease wealth, both in the US and in Europe, and clear the market. The result is higher interest rates, higher US consumption and lower European consumption. US deficits are expansionary at home, but transmit negatively to Europe.

Elsewhere Jo Anna Gray and I have shown that much can be said about the direction to move in coordinating macroeconomic policies if only we can agree upon the sign and symmetry of the inter-country spillover effects of policy. Last summer at a similar conference on coordination issues I naively argued that this should not be too much to ask of the profession. Current or previous work by the people around this table illustrates the diversity of views that now exist. Frenkel and Razin's theoretical model implies negative spillover for fiscal policy. Minford's empirical model has strong wealth effects in money demand, so a bond financed increase in US Government spending has small negative effects on output at home and abroad. Oudiz and Sachs in a previous paper used the FRB's Multi-country Model and Japan's EPA Model to obtain strong positive effects both at home and abroad for an increase in US Government spending. Turning to monetary policy, Minford reports strong positive spillover effects while Oudiz and Sachs found a small negative transmission. I would suggest that the first order of business in policy coordination research is to achieve some sort of consensus on the sign and symmetry of policy spillover effects. I suspect that the assumptions made in this regard are far more important than distinctions between utility functions and game theoretic solution concepts that dominate much of our present discussion.

COMMENT DAVID VINES

I

Professors Frenkel and Razin produced a very useful paper for those who attended the conference. Unfortunately they have decided to shorten their paper, whereas in what follows I deal with the paper as actually presented at the Conference. This has advantages, for their full model has richer results than the one presented above.

The fundamental result of the Conference paper is well known. This is that an increased US budget deficit, resulting from lower US taxes, causes increased spending in the US, and crowds out spending in Europe by means of a rise in the world rate of interest. The novelty of the paper is that the authors produce this result in a model with well specified microfoundations. Two steps in the argument of the Conference paper are worth noting. First, there is a government which obeys a solvency constraint over time. Thus tax cuts in the present mean that taxes will have to be raised in the future. Second there are optimizing consumers, in perfect capital markets, who nevertheless do *not* obey Barro's neo-Ricardian theorem. Thus the present tax cuts and future tax increases in the US *do* cause increased US spending in the present. This contrasts with the model presented above in which the Barro theorem always holds.

The model is as follows. There are two countries (the US and Europe) and (in the simple version solved explicitly) only two time periods. There is also an integrated capital market with just one rate of interest: the relative price of present and future goods. 'Full employment' prevails: output is supply constrained and fixed.

Much of the paper is taken up with an exposition of the clever device, due to Blanchard, which enables the authors to escape from the results of the Barro theorem. The essential feature of this is that if a government cuts taxes now and plans to raise them in the future (in such a way as to remain solvent over time) then individuals know that there is a probability that they will not be alive in the future to pay the future taxes. Therefore the current reduction in taxes adds to present wealth, and this addition to wealth will add to present spending.

With this point established, the authors proceed as follows. In their one-commodity, two-country, two-time-period world, there are three endogenous variables: US wealth, European wealth, and the relative price of present and future goods. A present tax cut and a future tax rise in the US leads to an increase in consumption in the US in the present. The price of present goods rises i.e. the rate of interest rises. This rise in the rate of interest reduces the present value of European future income i.e. European wealth falls. European consumption thus falls. The US runs a balance of payments deficit and Europe runs a balance of payments surplus. The increase in US spending caused by the budget deficit has crowded out European spending by means of a rise in the world rate of interest.

It should be noted that there is nothing intrinsically *international* about all this. A similar result would be obtained upon analysing a single economy with an integrated capital market and two groups: one that pays a particular kind of tax and the other that does not. The analagous experiment would involve postponing the obligations of the first group to pay the tax.

In the paper included in this volume, Frenkel and Razin do add an extra international wrinkle to the analysis. In the present paper they treat US goods and European goods as less-than-perfect substitutes: a rise in spending in the US will not only raise the rate of interest, but will also raise the relative price of US goods (on plausible assumptions about home expenditures being biased towards home goods). This rise in the relative price of US goods causes a switching of expenditures towards European goods in both countries. This helps to relieve the excess demand in the US, and creates excess demand for European goods (which is what crowds out European spending). In the model complicated in this way these 'expenditure switching' effects work jointly with the 'expenditure changing' effects to establish the US current account deficit and European current account surplus. In the one good model of the Conference paper there are only 'expenditure changing' effects.

Frenkel and Razin also produced some new results at the Conference for the effects of a balanced budget increase in US government spending, and these results are new[1].

II

In this section I want to throw out a couple of new arguments of my own. My purpose is to relax two assumptions which underly the model of the Frenkel–Razin Conference paper. These are

(a) the full employment assumption for Europe
(b) the idea that the trade balance between the US and Europe adjusts instantly to changes in relative prices.

I share many of Frenkel's and Razin's assumptions, in particular that of an integrated world market. But for simplicity my analysis has no serious microfoundations, unlike that of Frenkel and Razin. There is no international budget constraint on the government, and no treatment of the Barro argument (indeed, no treatment of wealth effects at all).

Let us define the following variables and parameters. A star, *, denotes a European variable or parameter. Unstarred magnitudes refer to the US. All variables are defined as deviations from an initial equilibrium.

y, y^* output
g, g^* government spending
r, r^* rate of interest (real)
z US net exports (i.e. the US balance of trade surplus)
m^* European money supply (nominal)
e exchange rate (real), a rise in e denotes a real depreciation of the US currency
x expected rate of (real) depreciation of the US currency
$\bar{e}$ Long run equilibrium (real) exchange rate
$\alpha, \alpha^*, \beta, \beta^*, \gamma, \delta^*, \epsilon^*, h$, and θ are parameters, all positive

I make the following assumptions.

A. Output in the US is constant at a fixed full employment level; this is assured by wage and price flexibility

$$y = 0 \tag{1}$$

The US interest rate is a loanable funds phenomenon, unalterable by monetary policy, determined from the equation

$$y = \alpha(g+z) - \beta r \qquad (2)$$

where α is an expenditure multiplier and β depends upon the interest elasticities of private sector savings and investment.

In Europe wage and price stickiness and unemployment prevail. Output and the interest rate are determined in the normal manner[2]

$$m^* = \alpha^*(g^* - z) - \beta^* r^* \qquad (3)$$

$$y^* = \delta^*(g^* - z) - \epsilon^* r^* \qquad (4)$$

where $\alpha^*, \beta^*, \delta^*, \epsilon^*$, are reduced-form parameters from an IS-LM system.[3] Note that equation (3) determines r^* just as equation (2) determines r, but that α^* and β^* are amalgams of parameters different in kind from those making up α and β. This is because of the different assumptions about wage and price flexibility for the US, and for Europe.

B. I ignore the Barro theorem, ignore wealth effects, and subsume the consumption function in the parameters of the above equations.

C. I assume perfect international capital mobility and abstract from the need to model the effects of the intertemporal solvency constraints on government and nations. (I need, however, to assume that there is no fear of insolvency).[4] Thus

$$r = r^* + x \qquad (5)$$

D. Exchange rate expectations are regressive and consistent,

$$x = \theta(\bar{e} - e) \qquad (6)$$

Expectations will be rational for one and only one value of θ, but for ease of exposition we do not explicitly solve for, or require that θ takes, that value.

E. There is a lag in the response of the trade balance, z, to the real exchange rate, e

$$\dot{z} = h[\gamma e - z] \qquad (7)$$

We abstract for simplicity from the effect of changes in European output, y^*, upon the trade balance. Including this effect would not alter the basic picture.

These seven equations contain eight endogenous variables, y, y^*, r, r^*, x, e, $\bar{e}$, and z.

In *long run equilibrium* $e = \bar{e}$ and $\dot{z} = 0$. Thus from (7)

$$z = \gamma e \qquad (8)$$

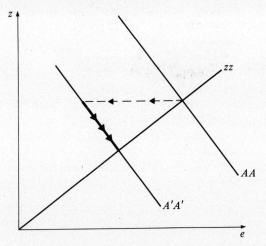

2A.1 Consequences of a rise in US government spending

This equation is plotted as the line, ZZ, in figure 2A.1. The line is upward sloping because in the long run, US net exports will be larger, the more competitive is the US economy.

In the *short run*, for given $\bar{e}$ and given z, we may solve the remaining six equations for the other six unknowns which include e. We obtain

$$e = \bar{e} + [\alpha^* \beta g^* - \alpha \beta^* g - (\alpha^* \beta + \alpha \beta^*) z]/(\beta \beta^* \theta) - m^*/(\beta^* \theta) \qquad (9)$$

This is the asset market equilibrium locus, AA, in figure 2A.1. A special case of this occurs when $\alpha = \alpha^*$ and $\beta = \beta^*$. (Such a special case is somewhat unlikely since, as noted above, the starred parameters represent amalgams of parameters different in kind from those making up α and β.[5]) This special case gives

$$e = \bar{e} + [\alpha(g^* - g - 2z) - m^*]/(\beta \theta) \qquad (9a)$$

This simplification makes clear the general idea underlying (9). Relatively higher government expenditure in the US, and a US trade surplus, and monetary expansion in Europe, all give rise to an appreciation of the US real exchange rate relative to long run equilibrium, because they all raise US interest rates relative to European interest rates.

Long run equilibrium exists at the point of intersection of the AA and ZZ lines in figure 2A.1.

Consider now the effects of an increase in US government spending, g. The AA locus shifts to the left. In the short run r^* is unaffected and US interest rates must rise enough to fully crowd out the increase in government expenditure. The exchange rate overshoots to give expectations of depreciation offsetting the increase in the US interest rate. Gradually the US trade balance worsens and so demands for European goods increase and European interest rates rise. Finally $r^* = r$ and we obtain the following equations for the long run equilibrium solutions.

$$e = \bar{e} = [\alpha^*\beta g^* - \alpha\beta^*g - \beta m^*]/\gamma(\alpha^*\beta + \alpha\beta^*) \tag{10}$$

$$r = r^* = [\alpha\alpha^*(g+g^*) - \alpha m^*]/(\alpha^*\beta + \alpha\beta^*) \tag{11}$$

The whole process is depicted in figure 2A.1.

We may thus draw from our analysis the following tentative conclusions about the effects of a US fiscal expansion.

(1) Initially there is a real exchange rate overshoot and the interest rate effects stay in the US. The US interest rate overshoots and European interest rates do not move.

(2) Gradually the real exchange rate returns part of the way to full equilibrium and an effect on the European interest rate comes about via the aggregate demand effect of the European balance of trade surplus. European output rises, to the extent permitted by the elasticity of demand for money in Europe. The deficit is 'paid for' partly by crowding out in the US, partly by the crowding out of interest-sensitive expenditures in Europe, and partly by the bringing into use of previously unemployed resources in Europe.

(3) Monetary expansion in Europe would alter this conclusion. A managed gradual expansion of the European money supply could, in principle, prevent European interest rates from ever rising. US interest rates would then have to eventually return to their original level. This would bring about, in the long run, a larger expansion in Europe, a larger European surplus and US deficit, and a larger appreciation of the dollar. There would then by no crowding out at all of interest-sensitive expenditures in Europe: saving out of the income earned by previously unemployed factors of production would entirely pay for the US fiscal expansion (and, because, of multiplier effects output would necessarily rise in Europe by more than the amount of this fiscal expansion). Of course this third conclusion would fail completely when full employment was regained in Europe. In that case assumption A* would break down.

III

What are the implications of the analysis in previous section for cooperation in economic management between the US and Europe? In order to isolate just one major implication, let us return to assumptions more nearly like those underlying the Frenkel and Razin Conference paper. First we now assume fixed full-employment output, with a loanable-funds theory of the interest rate, for Europe.[6] This replaces assumption A* with something identical to assumption A, so that the term m^* is set to zero in equations (3), (9), (9a), (10), and (11) and thus the interpretation of α^* and β^* becomes like that of α and β. Second we now assume instantaneous adjustment of net exports, so that $h \to \infty$ and equations (10) and (11) apply at all times.

The consequences of the change in US fiscal policy, analysed in the previous section, can be redescribed as follows under these new assumptions. The increase in government spending increases the use of US resources for consumption and reduces the use of them for investment. But with integrated capital markets, this change in the US output mix has implications for the rest of the world. In as much as the increase in US government spending raises the world rate of interest, it is 'paid for' not only by increased US saving and by reduced US investment, but also by a reduction in US exports relative to US imports. This is a running down of US foreign investment, or (what is the same thing) an increase in European foreign investment in the US. Europe must accept a reduction in interest sensitive investment in capital assets at home and accept instead an increase in its ownership of assets in the US.

There are reasons why, at the margin, Europe might prefer asset accumulation at home to asset accumulation in the US. These reasons rest on the possibility that investment at home, even if it provides a private return on capital no greater than that abroad, may increase the productivity and well being of the labour force at home and so bring a social return to the home economy greater than the private return on capital. It is interesting to note that these reasons are the very same as those put forward by Feldstein et. al. (1984, pp. 57 and 63) in order to explain why it may be desirable for the US that the fiscal expansion in the US be partly 'paid for' by Europe!

We have thus uncovered a situation in which there are two objectives of policy: the split in output between consumption and investment in the US and the analogous split in Europe. There are two instruments of policy: fiscal policy in the US and fiscal policy in Europe. But these two instruments are under the control of separate policy makers. And we have a situation in which each policy maker may wish to avoid lowering the investment share of output in his own country and to do this in such a way which would lower the investment share of output in the other country. This is the classic kind of case in which international cooperation could be beneficial.

It is possible that the outcome of any such cooperation should be close to the outcome which would be preferred by Europe rather than close to the outcome which would be preferred by the US. This conjecture could be supported by both income-maximising and income-distributional arguments. Europe is less capital-rich than the US. Thus a transfer of capital from the US to Europe would, ceteris paribus, increase world income *and* distribute it more equally.

NOTES

* I am indebted to Martin Weale for comments.
1 A present rise in government spending raises US demand for goods since consumption falls by less than the tax increase. This raises the rate of interest and depresses both US and European wealth. There is a US deficit and a European surplus. Not only the US private sector but also the Europeans are crowded out. By contrast, an expected *future* balanced budget increase in US government spending causes an increase in the future tax burden in the US: wealth and spending in the US fall. Frenkel and Razin also produced some further results about the effects of a future tax cut balanced by a tax rise even further into the future.
2 Note that the larger is the US trade surplus, z, the smaller is the demand for European goods.
3 Patrick Minford has pointed out to me that the outcome for European output and employment will differ according to exactly which wages and prices are assumed sticky in Europe. This is true. The equations in the text assume that all nominal wages and prices in Europe are exogenous, independent of both output and the real exchange rate.

   Money wage rigidity combined with effects on diminishing returns and with effects of the nominal exchange rate upon the price level would give a more complex system. But it would still be a system with the main features in the text, namely one for which European output would be positively affected by (1), a US trade deficit (2), higher European government spending, and (3) an increase in the nominal European money supply.

   But if *real* wages were completely rigid (or worse if they needed to rise with any increase in activity) then the point about unemployment being made in Section II would collapse. An increase in the European nominal money supply would not increase European output. And an increase in the US trade deficit would, if anything, be associated with a reduction in European output, since it is associated with a deterioration of the European terms of trade, and this would shift the European aggregate supply curve to the left. There is some evidence about the existence of such real wage resistance in Europe (Sachs, 1984, but see Layard et al., 1984).
4 Otherwise currency and default risk for the US will drive a wedge into equation (5). This may be a real possibility: US fiscal expansion *could* lead to a collapse of the US real exchange rate, rather than leading to the appreciation studied below. See Eaton and Turnovsky (1983).
5 It becomes more plausible if there is full employment in Europe (see section III).
6 We have entirely abstracted in our analysis from the case in which there is nominal wage stickiness in *both* the US and Europe. Meade (1984) argues that this calls for a cooperation in economic management between US and Europe

of a kind which would require fiscal management to bear a greater responsibility for domestic demand management than it does at present in the US. Monetary policy would then be freed to stabilise the real exchange rate. See also Vines, Maciejowski and Meade (1983).

REFERENCES

Blanchard, O. and R. Dornbusch (1984). 'US Deficits, the Dollar, and Europe.' Centre for European Policy Studies, CEPS Papers No. 6, Brussels, April.

Buiter, W. and M. Miller (1983). 'Changing the Rules: Economic Consequences of the Thatcher Regime.' *Brookings Papers on Economic Activity*, no. 2, pp. 305–365.

Eaton, J. and S. J. Turnovsky (1983). 'Covered Interest Parity, Uncovered Interest Parity and Exchange Rate Dynamics.' *Economic Journal*, vol. 93. pp. 555–75.

Frenkel, J. A. and A. Razin (1984a). 'Fiscal Expenditures and International Economic Interdependence.' This volume.

Frenkel, J. and A. Razin (1984b). 'Budget Deficits and Rates of Interest in the World Economy.' Paper actually presented at the CEPR Conference.

Feldstein, M., W. A. Niskanen and W. Poole (1984). *Annual Report of the Council of Economic Advisers*. Washington: US Government Printing Office.

Layard, R., G. Basevi, O. Blanchard, W. Buiter and R. Dornbusch (1984). 'Europe: the Case for Unsustainable Growth.' Centre for European Policy Studies, CEPS Papers No. 8, Brussels, May.

Meade, J. E. (1984). 'A New Keynesian Bretton Woods.' *Three Banks Review*, no. 142, pp. 8–25.

Vines, D., J. Maciejowski and J. E. Meade (1983). *Demand Management*. London: Allen and Unwin.

Sachs, J. D. (1983). Comment on Buiter and Miller (1983). *Brookings Papers on Economic Activity*, no. 2, pp. 366–72.

3 The effects of American policies – a new classical interpretation

PATRICK MINFORD*

I Introduction and summary

The object of this paper is to investigate the effects of US fiscal and monetary shocks on the world economy within a world macroeconomic model.

US policies over the past five years have been the object of admiration and vilification, exposition and caricature, both in the US itself and perhaps even more so in Europe. Some have argued that tight money and high deficits would not affect real interest rates or anything much except the rate of inflation and private saving. Others have argued that they would make recovery impossible by driving real interest rates to unheard-of levels. Yet others have argued that the high deficits have stimulated the world economy in a 'locomotive' manner. Established forecasters' reputations have been dented while some outsiders in the US forecasting game have scored hits (notably recently, monetarists and supply siders). Confusion reigns supreme, even over the ground rules of this discussion. The one common factor is the passionate intensity with which all views are held; the combination of Ronald Reagan and Paul Volcker has fired passions across the intellectual and political spectrum.

It is my contention that the effects of US policies cannot be understood in a US context alone; a closed-economy model will not do. I will be arguing that 'crowding out' is occurring on a *world* scale and that the 'injured parties' are outside the US in the main; furthermore, the scale of financing required for the US deficit has only been feasible through the *world* capital market.

This points to an understanding of a linked economic system. How could this be achieved? Some espouse vector-autoregressive methods to locate the sources of world business cycle shocks and the nature of their persistence – e.g. Saidi and Huber (1983). By its nature this work – while it has valuable uses – cannot identify structural relationships; therefore, one cannot easily interpret the results in terms of causal mechanisms.

One method of explanation appears to be available. One can set out a causal (or 'structural') system purporting to describe the linked economies; one can ask what effects this indicates for US policies and then check whether that set of effects appears broadly to have occurred in fact. This is the method I adopt in this paper.

In brief, I shall be using a description which relies importantly on two key features – rational expectations and wealth effects of government bonds. This description is parameterised, as best I have so far been able to achieve, using estimates of post-war behaviour (some estimates of our own, some a priori impositions, some previous work). The description yields a clear 'story' of the effects of monetary shocks and (bond-financed) fiscal shocks; this story is clear in spite of the 'largeness' of the model, because the model is constructed according to a very clear set of theoretical restrictions and it can therefore be simply understood – the number of equations is not a measure of intellectual complexity. Finally, I shall argue that the story fits the recent five-year episode rather plausibly, reconciling many of the details whose coincidence has appeared so baffling to different schools of interpretation.

Before going any further, a brief defence of the two main features would be wise. Rational expectations I regard as the analogue of routinely-assumed optimising behaviour in the information field, it is an 'as-if' assumption with the same status as the 'profit-maximising' or 'utility-maximising' assumptions we make about firms and consumers. It yields strong predictions and we have good reason to believe that competitive pressures exist in the real world driving people towards this norm of behaviour.

Wealth effects of government bonds have been carefully analysed by Barro (1974), to whom is due the revival among economists of the Ricardian equivalence theorem. As Barro notes, there are two main reasons why bonds could be net wealth to rational agents; the first occurs if the agent leaves no bequest. The second occurs if the income tax system is progressive, in effect insuring against income shocks; in this case higher future taxes will fall more on the lucky than on the unlucky and risk-averse agents will discount the tax stream to below the present value of the bonds. Empirical work to date has tended to support the view that bonds are net wealth (but not 100% net wealth) in line with these two aspects. These points are discussed further in Minford and Peel (1983, Chapter 9).

I now proceed to describe the model and so the nature of my explanation of recent events. Then I discuss the simulations of US policy. Finally, I review recent events and draw some tentative policy implications.

II The Liverpool international transmission model

The model is macroeconomic in the sense that it has no 'supply-side' at this stage; the equilibrium (or 'natural') values of output, real interest rates, real exchange rates, etc., are taken as exogenous.

The essence of our approach is fairly simple. We have linked together nine annual country models of identical structure, and added equations for the trade (only) of other countries, divided into three blocks. Hence the interesting detail relates primarily to the nine (major OECD) countries.

Each country model has the structure set out in Minford et al. (1984). (For detailed support of the following account, the reader is referred there). The model consists of:

(a) an inter-related set of private sector demands for stocks of money, government bonds (and net foreign assets), and durable goods, and for a flow of non-durable consumption goods; these demands depend on wealth and real returns.

(b) a government supply function of (narrow M1) money which together with the government and foreign sector budget constraints determines also the supply of bonds plus foreign assets.

(c) efficient financial markets in the operational sense that expected returns are equated across domestic and international financial assets.

(d) rational expectations which is implemented operationally by using the model's forecasts as the expectations.

(e) the supply of output is modelled via a price equation derived from an aggregate production function as a mark-up over costs which varies with the level of output.

(f) the labour market has a significantly large union sector; the non-union sector clears continuously (at levels heavily influenced by social security benefits). But the union's real wage target is seen as the outcome of intertemporal maximisation of their members' incomes and, given adjustment costs in firms' demand for labour, this gives rise to a union real wage which is a mark-up over expected non-union real wages and also dependent on lagged union real wages and firms' other cost factors. This real wage target is translated into a one year nominal wage contract on the basis of expected inflation. Aggregating together union and non-union wages and substituting out firms' demand for labour, we obtain a reduced form real wage equation positively related to output, lagged real wages and employer taxes on labour and negatively to unexpected inflation, benefits and employee taxes. Hence if there is unanticipated inflation, real wages fall, and so do output costs; the supply curve of output therefore shifts outwards temporarily.

In subsequent periods, real wages gradually return to equilibrium and output with it. This Lucas-type supply function is however derived by a rather different route from that chosen by Lucas and Rapping (1969).

(g) The current account external balance depends on the real exchange rate (defined as domestic relative to foreign consumer prices adjusted for the exchange rate) and domestic and foreign 'absorption' (total final expenditure).

Hence the model's features are predominantly 'New Classical'. These features distinguish it from available multi-country models such as Project Link, which tend to be very large, preserve a traditional Keynesian approach, and contain a large number of auxiliary hypotheses besides their Keynesian core. Variation in the auxiliary hypotheses makes it easy for these models to rationalise events ex post without jettisoning that core; but this procedure implies that little of any interest is being tested in prediction.

From an academic viewpoint our aim is to minimise the number of auxiliary hypotheses and so make it possible to test more effectively the core new classical hypotheses. Ideally, we would want to set up a 'Keynesian' alternative model with a minimum of auxiliary hypotheses, to compare with ours; however, at present this lies outside our capability.

The problem much stressed recently in model-building has been the 'Lucas critique' (Lucas, 1976); i.e. that model parameters may change when policies and other parameters of the exogenous environment change. *In principle* we can avoid this problem by specifying *all* expectations (and any relevant higher moments) explicitly. In practice, however, so many enter a model such as this that modelling economy enforces some choice of critical expectations to model explicitly, leaving others to be implicit and so vulnerable to the critique. Empirical trials should tell us how well our choices have been made and whether it would pay us to widen the choice, this is, however, in the nature of empirical work and does not pose a deep-seated challenge to our methods.

The model is based on preliminary econometric estimates using limited information methods; some parameters have been imposed on the basis of previous work, when satisfactory estimates could not be obtained. Full dynamic simulation tests have not yet been possible. Therefore, viewed empirically the model is as yet a tentative construct, far from fully tested. Nevertheless, in so far as its structure reflects a major strand of modern macroeconomic thinking and its parameters are related to available empirical work, its simulation properties are of interest.

III A simplified account of the model

A full listing of the model is provided in Appendix A. However, it may help understanding of the considerable mass of detail there to erect a stylised version, provided it is used with caution in interpreting the full model's simulation results. This version is taken from Minford, Ioannidis and Marwaha (1983). In this section we expound it briefly and relate it to some previous strands in the open economy literature.

For this version we assume two identical countries and adopt a loglinear form. Write the home country model as:

$$y = \delta_\theta \theta - \delta_r r - \delta_e e + \delta_F y_F + \delta_d d + \epsilon_\delta \qquad \text{(IS)} \, (\delta_F < 1) \qquad (1)$$

$$y = \sigma_p(p - \underset{-1}{E}p) + \sigma_e e + \epsilon_s \qquad\qquad\qquad \text{(PP)} \qquad (2)$$

$$m = \mu_y y + \mu_\theta \theta - \mu_\rho(\underset{-1}{E}p_{+1} - p + r) + p + \epsilon_\mu \quad \text{(LM)} \qquad (3)$$

$$\Delta m = \phi d + \epsilon_m \qquad\qquad\qquad \text{(Supply of money)} \quad (4)$$

$$\Delta d = \epsilon_d \qquad\qquad\qquad\qquad \text{(Deficit process)} \qquad (5)$$

$$x = -\beta_e e - \beta_y y + \beta_F y_F \qquad\qquad \text{(Current balance)} \quad (6)$$

$$\Delta\theta = \phi x \qquad\qquad\qquad\qquad \text{(Balance sheet} \qquad\quad (7)$$
$$\text{constraint)}$$

$$r = r_F - \underset{-1}{E}e_{+1} + e \qquad\qquad\qquad \text{(Efficient Market} \quad (8)$$
$$\text{condition)}$$

where y = output (log)

      θ = real value of financial wealth (log)

      p = prices (log)

     m = money supply (log)

      r = real interest rate (fraction per annum)

      e = real exchan͟. rate (fractional departure from equilibrium)

     d = government deficit, including interest payments (fraction of GDP)

     x = current account balance (fraction of GDP)

     $\underset{-i}{E}$ = rational expectation on data through $t-i$

     F subscript denotes 'foreign'.

All coefficients are positive. The ϵ_j are error terms, which may be

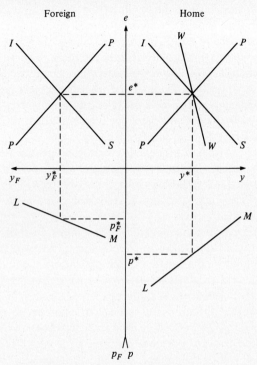

3.1 Full macroeconomic equilibrium in the world economy

autocorrelated. The constant terms have been set at zero implying that all real variables (y, e, θ, r) have equilibrium at zero.

Equations (1) and (3), IS and LM curves, come from the inter-related private sector demand for assets and non-durable consumption. The main point to note is the role of financial wealth, θ, in both goods and money demands.

Equation (2) is the PP, or Phillips, curve which relates output to unanticipated inflation and, the open economy aspects, the real exchange rate; the latter effect arises because as the terms of trade improve (the real exchange rate rises) the consumption real wage increases relative to the own-product real wage.

In equation (4), the money supply function, the assumption is that the government pursues monetary targets dictated by its expected equilibrium deficit, except for temporary spells (ϵ_m, which may be a process with autoregressive and moving average components) when it attempts exogenously to vary the fiscal/monetary mix. This long-run tendency to go for 'balanced' monetary financing is the result of the intertemporal budget constraint on government, which prevents permanent 'monetary' financing of a deficit. ϕ is the ratio of GDP to financial assets; hence ϕd is the expected rate of injection of financial assets into the economy arising from the government's deficit, and (4) states that this will normally be matched by the rate of monetary injection. Since both d, and such temporary spells, are assumed to be exogenous, the level of M at any time is exogenously determined (by the history of d and these spells). (3) and (4) give rise to the LM curve in the (p, y) domain in Figure 3.1.

Equation (5) is the postulated process driving the exogenous deficit (in the full model, the actual deficit is endogenous, while tax rates and government spending as a fraction of GDP are exogenous); it is treated as a random walk (as are tax rates and government spending in the full model).

(6) is a standard net exports (current balance) equation. (7) then equates changes in financial wealth with this current balance, the change in net foreign assets. This equation is a substantial simplification; the full change in financial wealth would be given by $\Delta\theta = \phi(x+d)-(\Delta p+k\Delta R)$ where the last bracketed term represents valuation effects. The simplification is effected by assuming that inflation and interest rates are in equilibrium where $\Delta p = \Delta m = \phi d$ and $\Delta R = 0$. (7) is used to construct the WW curve in Figure 3.1; this describes those combinations of e and y for which $\Delta\theta = 0$. To its right θ will be falling as x is negative, to its left θ is rising.

Equation (8) is the interest parity condition adjusted for expected exchange rate change, in terms of real interest and exchange rates. This is identically equivalent with the usual nominal formulation (as used, e.g., by Dornbusch, 1976). Note our definition of real interest rate uses the consumption deflator, p, and that of the real exchange rate uses the two countries' consumption deflators converted to a common currency. These deflators do of course include an effect of foreign prices through the prices of imports.

Substituting for r in terms of r_F, e and Ee_{+1} allows one to draw the IS and PP curves in the (e, y) domain as in Figure 3.1, in which we have now described all the elements going to make up a full equilibrium (the starred values are equilibrium ones) as illustrated, for the home economy.

The model for the other economy is a mirror image. We use the same coefficients, simply placing an F subscript on all 'home' variables including errors (and withdrawing it on all 'foreign' variables).

Notice however that $\theta_F = -\theta$, $x_F = -x$, and $e_F = -e$. Thus we have additionally for the foreign country:

$$y_F = \delta_\theta\theta-\delta_r r_F+\delta_e e+\delta_F y+\delta_d d_F+\epsilon_{\delta F} \qquad (9)$$

$$y_F = \sigma_p(p_F - \underset{-1}{E}p_F) - \sigma_e e + \epsilon_{sF} \tag{10}$$

$$m_F = \mu_y y_F - \mu_\theta \theta - \mu_\rho(\underset{-1}{E}p_{F+1} - p_F + r_F) + p_F + \epsilon_{\mu F} \tag{11}$$

$$\Delta m_F = \phi d_F + \epsilon m_F \tag{12}$$

$$\Delta d_F = \epsilon d_F \tag{13}$$

(1)–(13) comprise the full model.

Solution of this model can conveniently proceed in two steps. First, solve for the expectations, $\underset{-1}{E}p_{+1}$, $\underset{-1}{E}p$, and $\underset{-1}{E}e_{+1}$; these will emerge from the full solution conditional on information at $t-1(\Phi_{-1})$. Second, solve for the impact (first period) effect of the innovations or shocks at t, on all endogenous variables. The full solution for all endogenous variables can then be formed by adding these impact effects to the conditional solution. The first part of the solution gives the path by which the model converges to equilibrium in the absence of further shocks from initial values (as shocked) at $t-1$, the second part tells how shocks will change the initial values at t from those anticipated, to give rise to a new path with the same convergence properties. Our interest therefore segments respectively into convergence properties and impact effects.

The dynamic properties can be derived (for details see Minford et al., 1983) from the second-order difference equation governing the expected variables, which is:

$$\underset{-1}{E}Z_{+i+2} - 2\delta_r^{-1}\{\delta_r + \sigma_e(1+\delta_F)$$

$$+ \delta_e + \delta_\theta \phi(\beta_e + \beta_y \sigma_e + \beta_F \sigma_e)\} \underset{-1}{E}Z_{+i+1}$$

$$- \delta_r^{-1}\{\delta_r + 2\sigma_e(1+\delta_F) + 2\delta_e\} \underset{-1}{E}Z_{+1} = 0 \quad (i \geqslant 0) \tag{14}$$

If there is a saddle path, then there is one stable root, say λ. The form of the solution for the expected real exchange rate, for example, is:

$$\underset{-1}{E}e_{+i+1} = \lambda \underset{-1}{E}e_{+i} \quad (i \geqslant 0) \tag{15}$$

and for expected inflation in the home country:

$$\underset{-1}{E}\Delta p_{+i+1} = \phi d_{-1} + (1 + \mu_\rho(1-\lambda)^{-1})(K\lambda^i \underset{-1}{E}e) \tag{16}$$

where K is a combination of the model's parameters and ϕd_{-1} is the expected equilibrium inflation rate seen from $t-1$.

The impact of shocks can be evaluated on the simplifying assumption that θ moves little on impact, being the product of a gradual build-up via

Table 3.1. *Impact effects of home policy shocks*

	positive fiscal shock	positive monetary shock
p	?	+
p_F	+	?
e	+	−
r	+	−
r_F	+	?
y	+	+
y_F	?	?

the current balance. On this basis we may reduce our system to four equations:

an IS/PP locus at home and abroad (corresponding to the intersection in the upper quadrant of our diagrams)

and an LM locus at home and abroad (the lower quadrant solution).

We also use (8) to replace r in terms of r_F and e.

All variables are to be read as the 'unexpected components' of the solution; e.g. 'r' = $r - Er$. The system is then:

$$
\begin{bmatrix}
-\{\delta_r + \delta_e + \sigma_e(1+\delta_F)\} & -\delta_r & -\sigma_p & \delta_F\sigma_p \\
\mu_y\sigma_e - \mu_\rho & -\mu_\rho & 1+\mu_\rho+\mu_y\sigma_p & 0 \\
\phi_e(1+\delta_F)+\delta_e & -\delta_r & \delta_F\sigma_p & -\sigma_p \\
-\mu_y\sigma_e & -\mu_\rho & 0 & 1+\mu_\rho+\mu_y\sigma_p
\end{bmatrix}
\begin{bmatrix} e \\ r_F \\ p \\ p_F \end{bmatrix}
=
\begin{bmatrix} 0 & -\delta_d \\ 1 & 0 \\ 0 & 0 \\ 0 & 0 \end{bmatrix}
\begin{bmatrix} \epsilon_m \\ \epsilon_d \end{bmatrix}
$$

where we have omitted all shocks other than domestic monetary and fiscal. The effects of foreign monetary and fiscal shocks are symmetric; and those of other shocks are left to the interested reader.

It can readily be established that the determinant is negative. We can then sign the effects of a positive domestic shock as in Table 3.1.

The fiscal shock raises real interest rates worldwide, but *more* domestically, also raising the real exchange rate. There is a rise in domestic output (maybe a rise in home prices); the higher exchange rate raises foreign prices, and the effects on foreign output are ambiguous. Thus expansionary fiscal policy is in this world not clearly a 'friendly' act (not a surprising finding in the light of recent attacks from Europe on President Reagan's budget deficits). Figure 3.2 illustrates the impact effects. The IS curve shifts to the right in the home country along the PP curve. The rise in interest rates shifts the LM curve outwards. The effect on prices is ambiguous.

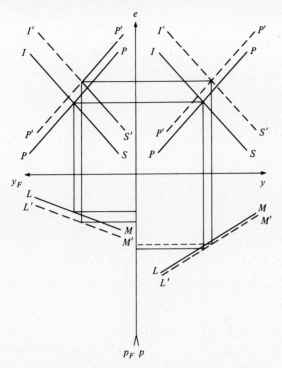

3.2 Temporary fiscal expansion in the home country – stylised model

(Figure 3.2 shows them as falling slightly, so that the PP curve shifts to
the left.)

In the foreign country there are two responses. First the rise in y shifts
the IS curve to the left (expansionary), second the rise in world real interest
rates shifts the IS to the right (contractionary). It also shifts the LM curve
outwards which raises prices for given y and so shifts the PP curve
outwards.

The balance of these forces causes an intersection of IS and PP at lower
foreign y_F, corresponding to the higher e.

Monetary expansion has familiar effects at home, lowering interest rates
and the exchange rate, and raising prices and output. Foreign interest rates,
however, will not necessarily fall, while foreign output and prices may not
rise; the exchange rate depreciation (an appreciation from the foreign
country's viewpoint) may act to offset the expansionary effects of domestic
monetary expansion on the foreign country.

Figure 3.3 illustrates the possible impact effect of a monetary expansion
in the home country. At home the LM curve shifts outward. This raises

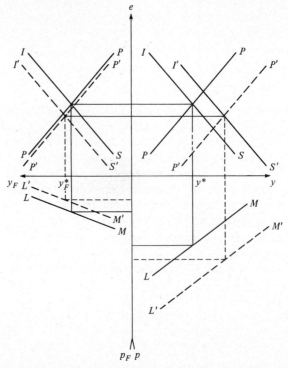

3.3 Temporary money supply growth in the home economy – stylised model

the price level unexpectedly, therefore the PP curve shifts outwards. The rise in output at home will raise output abroad and the reflected impact back home is to shift the IS curve outwards. The new IS/PP intersection is at a higher output level, and a lower real exchange rate. The nominal exchange rate falls more sharply than the real exchange rate.

Abroad, the fall in the home exchange rate implies generally rising nominal exchange rates. Typically, the real exchange rate rises, prices fall, the PP curve shifts inwards. The rise in home output shifts the IS outwards. The new IS/PP intersection is at a higher output level and a higher real exchange rate.

IV The model in the context of previous work

Before we proceed to summarise the full model, we highlight in this section the major ways in which previous work has differed in its theoretical assumptions and indicate the effects on these properties such differences would appear to make.

The major ways appear to be:

(a) Rational expectations
(b) Wealth effects
(c) Specification of 'wage/price' equations
(d) Degree of capital mobility

(a) If we substitute adaptive (AE) for rational expectations (RE) the effect familiarly will be to impart much longer lags, probably cycles, to the dynamics and possibly instability. This tedious exercise for our simple model is left to the reader. As for impact effects, those of temporary unexpected changes may well be similar because they have little effect on future expectations (in our simple model they would be identical for all shocks under RE and AE because expectations are dated at $t-1$). But this will not be true of permanent unexpected changes, for here the forward expectation has a powerful impact on current interest rates which strongly influence current demand and output. The 'paradoxical' impact effects of our model (see next section) in this case would thus be lost.

(b) The role of wealth (or 'portfolio balance') effects is clearly crucial to our model. It both affects the impact and the subsequent dynamic effects. It is the wealth variables interacting with future expectations that moderate (and can more than offset) the initial expansionary effect of 'locomotive' policies, that impart the oscillations (the 'inventory cycle' effect) and that subsequently provide an engine to drive the model back towards stock equilibrium. Clearly, in this respect the model belongs to the family of work emphasising stock/flow interactions, such as the work of Branson and Teigen (1976) and Kouri (1976) in the external sector, and it embraces the work on the government budget constraint in closed economy models.

We can illustrate the dynamic behaviour without wealth in our simple model, by setting $\delta_\theta = \mu_\theta = 0$. We may derive the expected final form for e as:

$$Ee_{+1} = \left\{1 + \frac{2\sigma_e(1+\delta_F)}{\delta_r}\right\} Ee + \frac{\delta_d}{\delta_r} d_{F-1} - \frac{\delta_d}{\delta_r} d_{-1} \qquad (18)$$

Imposing boundary conditions, this implies that:

$$Ee_{+i} = e^* = \frac{\delta_d d_{-1} - \delta_d d_{F-1}}{2\sigma_e(1+\delta_F)} \quad (i \geqslant 0) \qquad (19)$$

The removal of wealth implies the real exchange rate is expected to 'jump' to its new equilibrium, which in turn depends on fiscal policy; in our model it gradually returns to an equilibrium which is independent of fiscal policy. There are of course other ways than through wealth effects to supply both the missing dynamics (e.g. adjustment costs) and to force the equilibrium to that at which there is current account balance (e.g. by letting fiscal policy react to foreign indebtedness, a wealth effect on the government). In our full model, adjustment costs supply further dynamics, but wealth alone enforces the appropriate equilibrium, and indeed this latter process is entirely classical, for it is impossible for rational consumers to spend at rates indefinitely unaltered by foreign debt.

(c) Our wage/price equations give rise to a supply curve similar to the Lucas type; output rises with unanticipated inflation and with a rise in the real exchange rate (the real wage and profits; this parallels the intertemporal substitution element in Lucas). The derivation however appears to be 'Keynesian' in the sense that 'contracts' are emphasised (for a part of the unionised sector) as in Taylor's work (e.g. Taylor, 1979). Clearly therefore it fits uneasily into any 'camp'; in this annual model it behaves like a Lucas equation, in a quarterly model it would behave more like a Taylor equation. Perhaps this illustrates a point; that there is not such a big difference in practice between these two types of model. It seems that the model simulation properties would not be seriously affected by switches of specification within these two families.

Nor is there a qualitative difference in behaviour of the model if we assume non-clearing markets, with some slow 'tatonnement' process towards clearing market equilibrium. If we take for example a standard 'Lipsey-Phillips curve' (Lipsey, 1960) set-up where there is variable (with excess demand) mark-up pricing and the rate of wage change depends on expected inflation and excess demand, i.e.:

$$\Delta p = \alpha \Delta w + (1-\alpha)(\Delta p_F - \Delta s) + \beta y \tag{20}$$

$$\Delta w = E_{-1}\Delta p + \gamma y \tag{21}$$

Where w = nominal wages, s = nominal exchange rate ($+$ is appreciation), both in logs. Now substitute for Δw into (20) and subtract Δp from both sides to get ($e = p + s - p_F$):

$$0 = -\alpha(p - E_{-1}p) - (1-\alpha)(\Delta e) + (\beta + \alpha\gamma)y \tag{22}$$

So that

$$y = \frac{\alpha}{b + \alpha\gamma}(p - E_{-1}p) + \left(\frac{1-\alpha}{\beta + \alpha\gamma}\right)\Delta e = \sigma_p(p - E_{-1}p) + \sigma_e \Delta e \tag{23}$$

This is identical to (2) and (10), except that first the σ_p, σ_e here in this Keynesian sticky-price setting may be expected to be larger than those in (2) and (10) ($\beta + \alpha\gamma$ is smaller, or supply is more elastic in the short run) and secondly e enters in first difference form. The last change raises the order of the final form difference equation in expected e to 3rd order; there will now be two stable roots, one unstable for a normal solution, but the resulting change in the dynamic properties cannot be evaluated a priori.

A special case of the non-market clearing set-up is the 'rigid real wage-price mark-up' model beloved of English Keynesians; the source of the rigidity is usually specified as being exogenous, sociological perhaps. Rewrite (20) and (21) as:

$$p = \alpha w + (1-\alpha)(p_F - s) \tag{24}$$

$$\Delta w = \underset{-1}{E\Delta p} - \lambda (w-p)_{-1} \tag{25}$$

i.e. real wages tend to some fixed target. From (24) $(w-p)_{-1} = (1-\alpha/\alpha)e_{-1}$. Differencing (24), and substituting for Δw and $(w-p)_{-1}$, gives:

$$\alpha\Delta p = \alpha \underset{-1}{E\Delta p} - \lambda(1-\alpha)e_{-1} - (1-\alpha)\Delta e$$

or $\qquad \Delta e = -\dfrac{\alpha}{1-\alpha}(p - \underset{-1}{Ep}) - \lambda e_{-1} \tag{26}$

This model is one in which the real exchange rate is rigid apart from price shocks from which it gradually recovers at the rate λ. The equilibrium domestic *output* level is now forced to be that at which the current account is balanced at *this* rigid real exchange rate. Thus the PP curve in our diagram is horizontal.

It is worth noting that *both* countries could not behave in this way, because the model solution for real variables would then either be indeterminate or non-existent, equations (2) and (10) would in the first case both yield the same, and in the second yield different solutions for e.[1]

This special case does not in fact yield qualitatively different properties from our model. The final form equation for expected e now simply has the root $(1-\lambda)$. Expected inflation solves as before. The impact effects are altered in detail by $\sigma_e \rightarrow \infty$ in an obvious enough manner.

The interesting and perhaps surprising result of this analysis is that the behaviour of the model is qualitatively robust in respect of non-market-clearing 'Keynesian' wage/price structures as such. This is *not* a crucial element (unless quite absurd constraints are put on the model – e.g. see footnote 1).

(d) The tight link between real interest rate differentials and the real exchange rate (the real wage) arises from the efficient market assumption (which is equivalent in our model to 'perfect capital mobility'). There seems no point in speculating on the effects of *zero* capital mobility, since under floating rates this would imply that current accounts had to be in permanent balance, a condition which would impose great strains on the model (let alone the 'real world').

To analyse imperfect capital mobility, we may replace in our stylised model (8) $(r = r_F + e - \underset{-1}{Ee_{+1}})$. We now have a capital flow equation:

$$\Delta K = k'\Delta(r - r_F + \underset{-1}{Ee_{+1}} - e) \tag{27}$$

where for simplicity we leave out the small 'continuing flow' effect of the level of real interest differential (adjusted for expected change in the real exchange rate). Equilibrium in the floating exchange rate market occurs when:

$$x + \Delta K = 0 \tag{28}$$

so that

$$x = -k'\Delta(r - r_F + \underset{-1}{Ee_{+1}} - e) \tag{29}$$

Since

$$x = \frac{1}{\phi}\Delta\theta \quad \text{we have that:}$$

$$r - r_F + \underset{-1}{Ee_{+1}} - e = -\frac{\theta}{k} \tag{30}$$

which replaces (8) accordingly; $k = k'\phi$ (we set the constant of integration at zero).

The effect of (30) on the dynamics of the model is qualitatively unimportant. All that happens is that $\delta_\theta + k^{-1}\delta_r$ replaces δ_θ in (14). The stable root will change, but the effect cannot be established a priori; though, if it was positive and remains so, it will be smaller than before (if so imperfect capital mobility is *stabilising* on the rate of convergence).

The impact effects are more complicated however. Suppose we write (30) for this purpose as:

$$r = r_F - \underset{-1}{Ee_{+1}} + e - k^{-1}x - k^{-1}\theta_{-1}.$$

We can now reconstruct the impact system as:

$$\begin{bmatrix} 1 & \beta_e + (\beta_y + \beta_F)\sigma_e & 0 & \beta_y\sigma_p & -\beta_F\sigma_p \\ k^{-1}\delta_r & -\delta_r - \delta_e - (1+\delta_F)\sigma_e & -\delta_r & -\sigma_p & \delta_F\sigma_p \\ k^{-1}\mu_\rho & \mu_y\sigma_e - \mu_\rho & -\mu_\rho & 1+\mu_\rho+\mu_y\sigma_p & 0 \\ 0 & \sigma_e(1+\delta_F)+\delta_e & -\delta_r & \delta_F\sigma_p & -\sigma_p \\ 0 & -\mu_y\sigma_e & -\mu_\rho & 0 & 1+\mu_\rho+\mu_y\sigma_p \end{bmatrix} \begin{bmatrix} x \\ e \\ r_F \\ p \\ p_F \end{bmatrix} = \begin{bmatrix} 0 \\ -\delta_d\epsilon \\ \epsilon_m \\ 0 \\ 0 \end{bmatrix}$$

$$\tag{31}$$

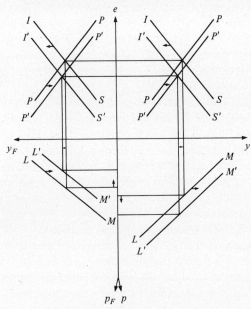

Arrows indicate effects of imperfect
capital mobility (i.e. of x deteriorating)

3.4 The effects of imperfect capital mobility under fiscal or monetary
expansion

where the dashed lines enclose the previous system. It can be seen that the
effects on the determinant are now to render it strictly ambiguous in sign,
because of the terms in $k^{-1}\mu_p$ (the terms in $k^{-1}\delta_r$ unambiguously make
the determinant more negative); this is analogous to the effect of wealth
on an IS/LM set up where powerful wealth effects on *money* demand can
move output perversely.

We can however handle this ambiguity by noting that (30) has introduced
a new shift factor, x, into the home IS and LM curves in our diagram;
a fall in x shifts the home IS to the left and the home LM to the right (it
has no direct effect on the foreign IS and LM curves, or on either of the
PP or WW curves). Therfore we can argue that the solution would be the
same except for this effect of x.

Since it is reasonable to suppose that fiscal and monetary expansion
shocks cause x to deteriorate (the normal case), the effect of imperfect
capital mobility can be investigated using this assumption.

The own country direct effects of lower x (r_F, y_F constant) are to raise
prices, p, lower the real exchange rate, e, and raise interest rates, r; the
effects on output, y, are ambiguous. In the rest of the world r_F has to move

so as to accommodate; assuming that direct foreign output effects because of changing home output are small, this will require a fall in r_F which will shift the foreign IS outwards, LM inwards and PP inwards (another way of looking at this is that the appreciation abroad lowers prices and so, via the Phillips curve, raises output, while lowering the demand for money). This situation is illustrated in Figure 3.4.

Since fiscal expansion had an ambiguous effect – under perfect capital mobility – on prices and raised the real exchange rate, it is not possible to say how imperfect capital mobility will leave the overall effect on them; both prices and the real exchange rate may now fall or rise. However, interest rates will rise, more than under perfect mobility. Further, monetary expansion will under imperfect capital mobility still raise prices (more so than under perfect mobility) and cause the real exchange rate to fall (further than under perfect mobility – the contrary of Bhandari, 1981); interest rates will fall but less than under perfect mobility.

Provided capital is reasonably mobile (as the evidence indicates, as a minimum) it would seem therefore that assuming perfect capital mobility may not seriously distort the picture, at least for monetary shocks; and we also have some idea of the direction of what distortion there is.

In sum, if one had to name the features that are most important to our results that follow, these would be rational expectations and wealth effects; in our context at least non-market clearing and capital mobility, though much has been made of both in the literature, would probably not change the basic picture.

V The full model

As a preliminary to considering the full model, we now examine the principal simplifications of it in our earlier stylised version. First, the impact effects of wealth were neglected. If this assumption is dropped, the analysis becomes generally ambiguous. As is by now familiar from the wealth literature, it is possible for fiscal expansion to be deflationary on output at home on impact, because it provokes a 'financial crisis' effect via wealth; the same applies to monetary expansion (examples are Minford (1980) and Blanchard (1981)). The full model has such wealth effects, though the elasticities on wealth are small (typically 0–0.4). Therefore this is one major way in which the full model differs from the simplified version.

The second major simplification lies in the dating of expected inflation in the real interest rate definition. In the full model this is dated $\underset{t}{E}_{t+1}$, on the grounds that this will in an annual context be a better approximation than $\underset{t-1}{E} p_{t+1}$; the best approximation would be a partial information solution (e.g. Barro, 1981) but we cannot implement that at this stage. The result is that the effect of future events previously unanticipated will have a current impact through nominal interest rates.

Thirdly, financial wealth itself in the full model depends on the current price level and on current interest rates because of their valuation effects; this interaction is omitted in the simplified version.

These three differences can produce 'paradoxical' impact effects. Though the wealth effects in the full model are small, a shock which permanently alters the environment (e.g. a permanent fiscal and monetary expansion) will exert harsh leverage through these three interactions; expected inflation will shift sharply, so altering financial values sharply, which applied to even small wealth coefficients implies a large impact effect, swamping conventional responses.

If we turn last and briefly to the dynamics of the full model, first this has lagged adjustment terms in the IS, LM and PP curves and expected future output enters the PP curve (because of union bargaining), which adds further roots to the characteristic equation. Second, a moving average process is introduced by stock-adjustment in the IS function; investment responds to the rate of change of financial assets, of the real interest rate and of expected output. This 'accelerator' mechanism imparts a short moving average process to the path of the model after impact, resembling an inventory cycle. When financial conditions are changed substantially (e.g. by permanent shifts in the environment), then this inventory cycle becomes a prominent short-run feature.

To introduce these features into the analytic version would have made it unduly complicated for a 'classroom model'. We therefore leave them at this descriptive account and proceed to examine the behaviour of the full model.

This is a very large model for rational expectations solution. There are 160 equations and 45 expectational variables. Experience of estimating and solving the UK model, which is just over one tenth the size but is by now fully operative in forecasting and policy analysis, has taught us that the coefficients used must be tightly circumscribed by prior restrictions if the model is to be capable of generating a 'proper' solution – i.e. one that lies within a plausible distance from the equilibrium path. The coefficients that give most trouble in this respect are the wealth coefficients; at this stage we have been unable to find a specification within which free estimation of these gives proper solutions. The reason seems to be that *total* wealth (w) is highly collinear with time and its coefficient correspondingly hard to identify, while financial wealth (θ) is extremely dependent on the volatile valuation effect which we have had great difficulty in estimating (revalued series do not appear to exist for most OECD countries). These coefficients

Table 3.2. *Impact effects of US fiscal and monetary shocks*

	fiscal expansion shock		monetary expansion shock	
	2-country model	full model	2-country model	full model
p	?	−	+	+
p_F	+	+	?	+
e	+	+	−	−
r	+	+	−	−
r_F	+	+	?	−
y	+	0	+	+
y_F	?	−	?	+

are largely imposed therefore in the current version, at values that imply small impact effects (as assumed in our previous formal discussion).

The annual data, at the level of aggregation we were using failed also to generate sensible current account balance equations. The coefficients of these have accordingly been taken from Beenstock and Minford (1976), who estimated a comprehensive set of trade elasticities of plausible size on a consistent basis. The long-run elasticities on 'competitiveness', which were estimated via polynomial distributed lags of long duration (up to six years) have been applied here to the *expected* deviation from purchasing power parity over the five years ahead, rather than the lagged values of this deviation.

The other coefficients are generally freely estimated subject to these imposed values.

VI US policy simulations with the full model

A once-for-all rise in the US money supply

We begin with that simulation standby – a monetary shock, i.e. an unanticipated once-for-all rise in the money supply. Table 3.2 compares the signs of the full model impact effect with those of the stylised model; they are different only in pinning down ambiguous signs, in a plausible enough manner (as foreign income and prices *rise*, foreign real interest rates *fall*).

Figure 3.5 illustrates the model's behaviour for a two-country world. There is a powerful real interest rate effect in the model. As world real interest rates fall, the US 'IS' curve shifts to the right; this shift is less than that of the PP curve so the real exchange rate falls. In the rest of the

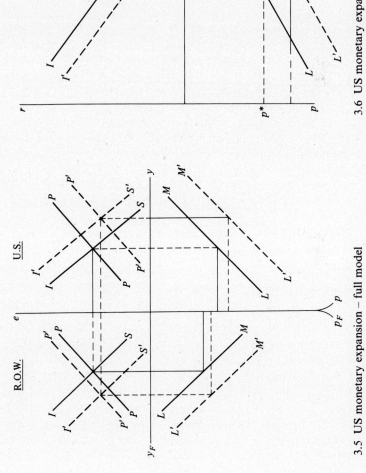

3.5 US monetary expansion – full model

3.6 US monetary expansion – world effects – full model

Effect on level of output (%)

United States

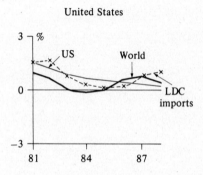

United Kingdom

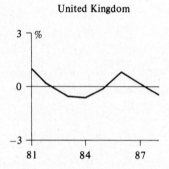

West Germany

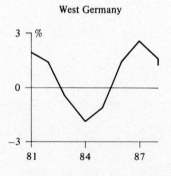

Japan

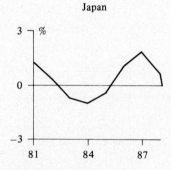

3.7 Rise in US money supply by 2% (once for all from 1981)

Effect on level of output (%)

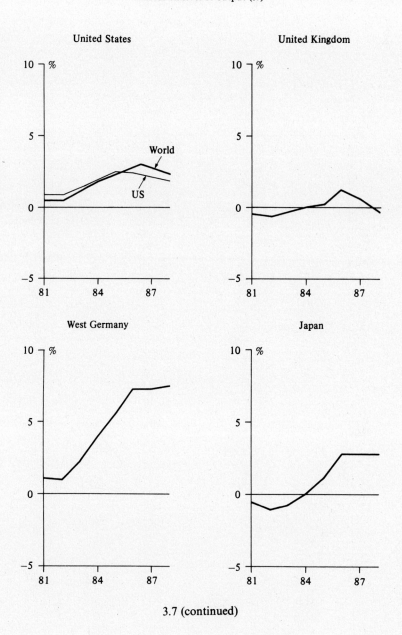

3.7 (continued)

Effect on 5-year real interest rate (% p.a.)

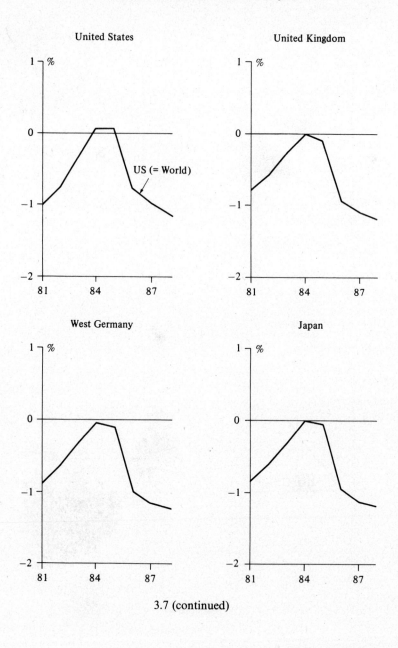

3.7 (continued)

Effect on real exchange rate (% of equilibrium)

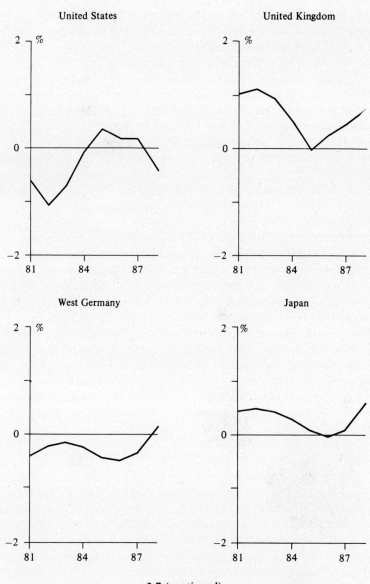

3.7 (continued)

world, wealth falls as prices rise causing the LM curve to shift out. This is the principal difference from the stylised model, shown in Figure 3.3 (even though real interest rates fall, causing the LM curve to shift *in*, this shift is more than offset). As prices rise, the PP curve shifts out in turn. The world real interest rate effect on the IS curve is sufficiently large for the shift to dominate the PP curve's.

At the world level, the simulation offers no real puzzles. Figure 3.6 illustrates the aggregate world picture. At the world level, the Phillips curve is vertical, because we have no intertemporal substitution built into supply (at least at present; this may well have resulted from an admitted failure to investigate this so far). When US (and so world) money supply rises, the LM curve shifts out; this shift out is dampened by the fall in world interest rates (rising money demand) and exaggerated by the fall in world real bonds (lowering it), but the overall effect of outward shift is not altered. The consequent rise in prices shifts the Phillips curve outwards along the IS curve; real interest rates fall and output rises.

We now turn to the numbers produced by a 2% once-for-all money supply increase. Figure 3.7 shows effects for selected countries on output, real interest rates, prices and the real exchange rates. The basic flavour of the simulation is given by this diagram. World output rises by 1.3% (US by 1.8%) on impact – a large effect for only a 2% money supply increase. World (and US) real interest rates fall 1%. World and US prices rise, as does the US real exchange rate (while others fall on average).

These are the impact effects, already discussed qualitatively. Figure 3.7 also shows the dynamic path back to equilibrium. This turns out (rather unusually among the model's simulations) to have a strong cyclical component; the result is that it moves fairly rapidly back to equilibrium (in about 3 years) but then begins to depart again. More typical model dynamics are the monotonic convergence at about 25% per year exhibited in the fiscal simulation, to which we now turn.

US fiscal expansion

We study next a temporary rise (for one year only) in the US budget deficit – financed by bonds (i.e. the money supply is held constant).

Referring to Table 3.2, we can see that the impact effects in the full model tally closely with those of the stylised model, with one exception; output in the US is unaffected (crowding out is 100%). Output abroad *falls* instead of rising as conventional theories would indicate; this settles an ambiguous result in the stylised model. US prices also fall in the full model, while they may go either way in the stylised version.

These output effects can be explained using Figure 3.8 which shows the

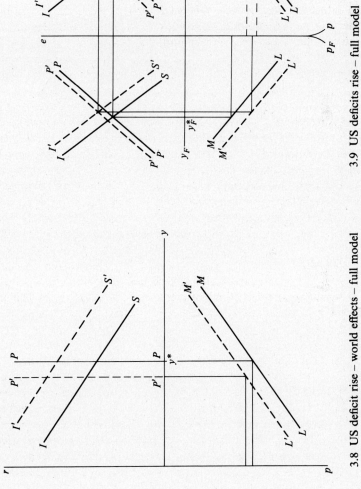

3.8 US deficit rise – world effects – full model

3.9 US deficits rise – full model

Effect on level of output (%)

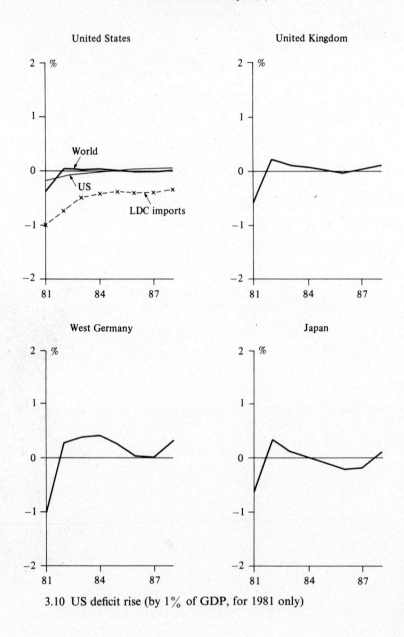

3.10 US deficit rise (by 1% of GDP, for 1981 only)

Effect on price level (%)

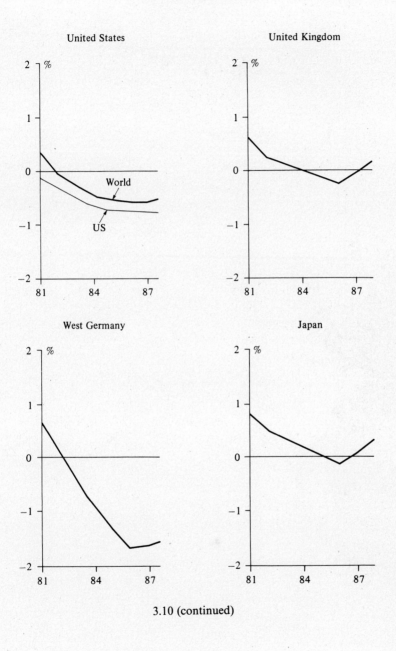

3.10 (continued)

Effect on 5-year real interest rate (% p.a.)

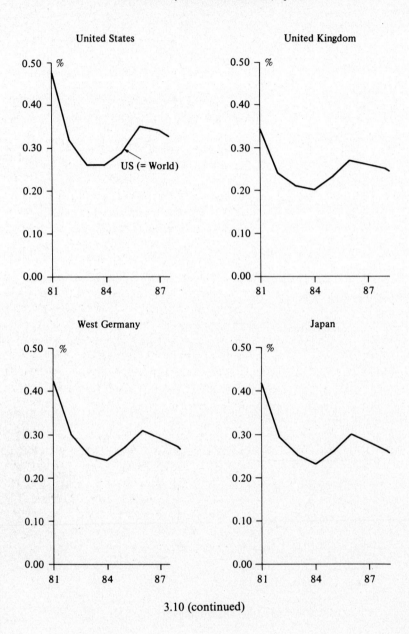

3.10 (continued)

Effect on real exchange rate % of equilibrium)

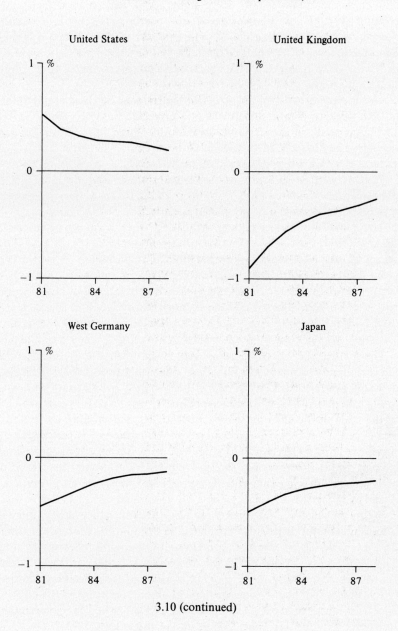

3.10 (continued)

world picture. The fiscal expansion raises real interest rates, conventionally enough as the IS curve shifts to the right; this lowers demand for money shifting the LM curve outwards but the rise in bonds (and so wealth) associated with the higher deficit more than offsets this effect, on money demand, so that the net effect is for the LM curve to shift inwards, lowering prices for given output. The PP curve therefore shifts to the *left*, and output falls.

This is none other than the result first introduced by Blinder and Solow (1973), whereby wealth effects of bond financing may be greater on the LM curve than on the IS curve, so that more than 100% crowding out occurs. (They associated this result with instability, but that does not in general occur in a rational expectations context).

The two-country effect in the simulation is illustrated in Figure 3.9. It resembles the earlier diagram (Figure 3.2) except that now the rise in world real interest rates has a bigger negative impact on both IS curves.

The actual numbers are illustrated for the same variables as before in Figure 3.10, for a 1-year rise in the US deficit of about 1% of US GDP. It can be seen that there is a contraction on impact both on world and (very slight) US GDP. There is also a sizeable contraction (1%) in LDC's import volumes because of the effect on their debt interest of higher world real interest rates. These real rates in turn rise by 0.5% at the long end (and 1.1% at the short end). This is a substantial effect and it can be seen that *international* crowding out (especially the LDC's) is fairly significant.

The US real exchange rate appreciates by 0.5%, about the same as the US real long rate of interest. When one reflects that the actual US budget deficit has risen from 1% of GDP in 1979 to $2\frac{1}{2}$% in 1980 and 1981, 4% in 1982 and 6% in 1983, and that at present there is no viable plan to reduce it, the scale of the effect on world real interest rates and on the US real exchange rate of recent US fiscal policies is suggested – approximately 6 times the impact effects of this stimulation. Being a longer-lasting fiscal change, these effects would last correspondingly longer – in fact in a simulation of the same shock lasting 5 years, real world interest rates stayed over 1% higher for 9 years.

When we turn to the dynamic path on this temporary shock, there is little cyclical component. Convergence is monotonic and proceeds at about 25% per year. The recovery of non-US output in year 2 reflects the strong stock-adjustment effect of higher real interest rates; in year 2 this 'unwinds' giving rise to the moving average process discussed earlier. (From the output supply side, this unwinding is permitted by the positive effects on supply of expected future output and of the lagged real exchange rate – see equation 15, Table 3A.1a, in Appendix 3A.)

To sum up, this fiscal simulation indicates that US fiscal expansion does

Table 3.3. *Recent world events (% or % p.a.)*

	1978	1979	1980	1981	1982	1983
Growth in GDP						
US	4.7	2.4	−0.3	3.0	−1.7	3.4
OECD	3.9	3.2	1.2	2.0	−0.5	2.2
Inflation (CPI)						
US	7.6	11.3	13.5	10.4	6.2	3.2
Industrial Countries	7.2	9.1	11.9	9.9	7.5	5.1
Real Short-Term *						
Interest Rates						
US	−0.4	−1.3	−1.9	3.7	4.5	5.4
Fiscal and Monetary						
Policies						
US Federal Deficit (calendar year) as % of US GNP	2.0	1.1	2.6	2.5	4.3	5.8
US growth in M1**	7.3	7.6	9.1	5.1	4.8	9.0
Industrial Countries growth in M1**	10.8	9.6	6.6	6.0	6.7	9.5

* Treasury Bill Rate (3 months) minus average inflation rate (this assumes that over such a short-time horizon expected and actual inflation are equal, probably not a bad approximation).
** IFS definition.

not 'stimulate' the world or the US economy but mainly causes higher world real interest rates and a US real appreciation. The crowding-out that results from higher real interest rates has a particular impact on LDC's and other major debtors.

Some notes on recent events and policy implications

Based on these simulations, we can hazard an outline of the reasons for the 1980–2 world recession and the 1983 recovery; we have not yet been able to use the model formally to track these events but an informal discussion is possible.

The salient features of the world economy since 1978 can be crudely summarised. World output fell between 1979 and 1982 in a prolonged 'double-bottomed' recession. It then began – at the end of 1982 – a fairly normal recovery, rapid (as typically occurs) in the US and sluggish elsewhere (except for the UK whose recovery began, like its recession, earlier than most and had gathered some strength by end 1982). World real interest rates, having been very low for most of the 1970s, rose sharply in 1980 and have remained high ever since. Inflation rose to a peak in 1980 of over 10% and has since then fallen rapidly, reaching 3% in the US in 1983 and 5% in the world.

On the policy side, the US deficit has grown substantially as a fraction of GDP; allowing for plausible 'cyclical adjustment' does not change that picture. If one takes at face value the determination of the Federal Reserve Board to hold inflation at 3% or so, then given that the deficit is being financed by nominal bonds of average maturity, '(prospective) inflation accounting' does not change the picture significantly either. From the rational expectations viewpoint, we need to know how much of this deficit change was unanticipated; my suggestion would be that it was unanticipated in 1979 but that by the end of 1980 the expectation of sustained high deficits under Reagan's policies had become dominant.

US monetary growth, which is essentially independent of the President in the USA, began to be curbed in 1980 when it reached 9.1%; this has to be seen against a rise in inflation to 13.5% (we can think of inflation as reflecting largely the *expected* monetary growth in the previous year). It would have been reasonable to expect the Fed to allow much faster M1 growth given the 'needs of trade'. Hence I would suggest that there was a substantial unexpected fall in M1 growth. In 1981, M1 growth fell sharply to 5.1%; again inflation at 10.4% in 1981 suggests that much of this fall was unanticipated. The same but to a lesser extent was true of 1982 (the low average M1 figure conceals a very low figure early in the year but a much higher figure in the second half). Thus there may have been three successive negative monetary shocks in a row. The 1983 figure by contrast indicates a strong positive monetary shock; M1 grew by 9% against inflation of 3%.

According to this interpretation, the rise in world real interest rates in 1980 was the result of the rise in the US deficit *and* the unexpected fall in US M1 growth. That world real rates have *stayed* so high and appear set to continue that way is due to the *sustained* high deficits (for negative monetary shocks gave way to a positive shock in 1983).

The pattern of growth is to be explained not at all by *fiscal* shifts; these were positive in 1980 (and again in 1982) but did not prevent recession in 1980 and continued recession in 1982. Indeed according to the model they may have somewhat *worsened* the recession (partly by precipitating the LDC debt crisis).

Rather, the recession, its 'double-bottom' and long duration, are plainly due to the succession of negative monetary shocks, inspired in turn by the Fed's determination to get inflation back down to rates last seen in the 1960s. The recovery process would have occurred anyway in 1983 according to the model, provided there was no *further* negative shock then. It has however been speeded up by a fairly strong positive monetary shock (related, it seems, to the Fed's fears for the collapse of the international monetary system under a major default).

Last, the inflation story can be interpreted as the successive downgearing of expected monetary growth, as the Fed's determination and stamina progressively became apparent. In the US there were no announcements of long-term targets, only one year ones; this lack of long-term commitments was encouraged by the political system – for example, mid-term elections to Congress and the Fed Chairman, Paul Volcker's own reappointment date in 1983 – but it no doubt partly contributed to the downward-ratchet pattern of expectations. A 'sharp enduring shock' administered in 1980 and backed by a complete political commitment would, if possible, have – according to the model – precipitated a bigger recession in 1980 (it was actually quite mild) but one that would have ended more quickly and brought inflation down more rapidly.

In view of the propensity for many economists to cite 'oil factors' as major causal agents over this period, I should stress that it enters the story here not at all. Oil is 'just another input commodity' in this model; its price is a relative price and energy technology is just one source of technological change. Clearly, shocks to tastes and technology matter at the micro level and if sufficiently correlated across industries *may* matter at the business cycle level. I feel free to refer to such correlated shocks as sources of macro shock (this would undoubtedly be the case for the 1973 oil shock); but in this recent episode there is no compelling reason to do so.

The role of non-US policies in this account has similarly been neglected. However, there is clear evidence (in industrial countries' M1 growth for example) of these reacting to US monetary policies in an imitative manner; to account for and allow for this part of the story is however beyond the scope of this paper. It does not appear to alter its basic outlines.

Should US fiscal policy have moved 'in line' with tight money? This has been the main flashpoint of recent US-rest of world policy interchange. The rest of the world has not welcomed the effect of US government borrowing in pushing up real interest rates worldwide. (The logic of tight money has separately been accepted as necessary for anti-inflation policy). This complaint, in the light of the model's interpretation, has two dimensions. First, there is the dislike of shocks in themselves; uncertainty is increased – a stable fiscal policy is to be preferred to an unstable. Second, in so far as the rest of the world is a net debtor to the US (which it is),[2] it suffers a rise in its real debt burden; there is therefore a transfer effect.

Shocks are as unwelcome in the US as elsewhere; the fact that a new government felt it necessary to impose one reveals its judgement that the need offset the unwelcome effects. Governments, like private agents, optimise in response to changed circumstances. One can only speculate on whether it was truly in the US interest for taxes to be deferred in this way; the optimal tax pattern over time is discussed in Barro (1974), who argues from the transactions costs of changing tax rates that they should be constant. If this is so, then the issue revolves around whether government spending projections are for such falls that future tax rates will *fall*, making it optimal to *lower* them now.

As far as transfer effects are concerned, such possibilities are inherent in the signing of debt with short-term maturities; the debt was voluntary so no complaint is possible. Nevertheless, a severe transfer effect on LDCs has turned out to be particularly disruptive – and *did* force a shift in US monetary policy in 1982 (to avoid monetary collapse). In its own interest, the US needs to take these effects into account, legitimate as it is to cause them.

A few things the model does imply are:

(a) the more *predictability* in government policy the better; shocks and uncertainty cause costs. Therefore, if the US shift to higher deficits was *not* internally justified, it imposed costs on the world by disturbing plans and in particular raised the variance of output.
(b) planned 'reflation' or 'locomotive' policies will have their principal effects on inflation and, if fiscal and bond-financed, on real interest rates; they will not speed up recovery or end recession.
(c) there are a number of ways in which international feed-back rules for monetary and fiscal policy could 'work' to reduce the variance of world output (as discussed by Minford and Peel, 1983, chapter 3); but it is not at all obvious what *values* should be given to the feedback coefficients to improve the stability of the model relative to its present tolerable rate of convergence.
(d) governments also can optimise individually with respect to world capital market conditions by borrowing less at times of high real interest rates; if they do, the response of world real rates to higher US borrowing would of course be smaller and so too would the disturbance to world output.

To sum up, with respect to US policies, the rest of the world does not appear to have a case for them to change, other than to point out the *effects* which the US authorities may not have taken into account in designing them. A world government might take a different view of what US policy should be; but then we do not have one – and if we did, the rest of the world would not be free either!

Table 3A.1a. *Structure of the non-US country models*

(Equation listed with ' $\equiv$ ' are identities or approximations to them)

(1) $\log m/\theta = a_1 + a_2 \cdot R_s + a_3 \log w + a_4(PEXPL - R_L) + a_5 T$
$\qquad + a_6 \log (M/\theta)_{-1} + a_{36} PEXPL^2$

(2) $\log g/\theta = a_7 + a_8(PEXPL - R_L) + a_9 \log w + a_{10} T$
$\qquad + a_{11} \log (g/\theta)_{-1} + a_{37} PEXPL^2$

(3) $\log c = a_{12} + a_{14}(PEXPL - R_L) + a_{15} \log w + a_{16} T$
$\qquad + a_{17} \log (y/y^*) + a_{18} \log c_{-1} + a_{38} PEXPL^2$

(4) $y \equiv c + \Delta g + eg + x \, \text{vol} + a_{13} \cdot g_{-1}$

(5) $w \equiv \theta + g$

(6) $\theta \equiv eg - ty + x \, \text{val} + \theta_{-1} \left[1 + a_{40} \cdot \left(R_L - a_{41} \dfrac{\Delta R_L}{R_{L_{-1}}} \right) - \Delta P/P_{-1} \right]$

(7) $x \, \text{vol}/y^* = a_{26}(a_{20} ERXRL + a_{21} \log WT + a_{22} \log WBC$
$\qquad + a_{23} \log y + a_{24} \log y^* + a_{25})$

(8) $\dfrac{x \, \text{val}}{y^*} = \dfrac{x \, \text{vol}}{y^*} + a_{26} a_{27} RXR + Z$

(9) $r_L = (RXR - ERXRL)/5 + r_{FL}$

(10) $r_S = (RXR - ERXR) + r_{FS}$

(11) $R_S \equiv r_S + PEXP$

(12) $R_L \equiv r_L + PEXPL$

(13) $\log M = a_{30} \Delta \log M_{-1} + a_{31} \log (y/y^*)_{-1} + a_{32} \Delta \log P$
$\qquad + a_{33} DMT + \log M_{-1}$

(14) $\log P \equiv \log P_{-1} + \Delta \log M - \Delta \log m$

(15) $RXR = a_{28} RXR_{-1} - [DA - Z + a_{28} Z_{-1} - a_{34}(\log (y/y^*)$
$\qquad - a_{28} QEXPL_{-1})]/a_{29}$

(16) $r_{FL_i} = (r_{WL} - c_1 c_{i+1} r_{Li})/(1 - c_1 c_{i+1}) \quad i = 2, 9$

(17) $r_{FS_i} = (r_{WS} - c_1 c_{i+1} r_{S_i})/(1 - c_1 c_{i+1}) \quad i = 2, 9$

Appendix A. Listing of the Liverpool multilateral macroeconomic model
PIERRE-RICHARD AGÉNOR

The Liverpool multilateral macro-model is a large, non-linear rational expectations model linking together the nine major OECD countries.[3] Each country model has a structure resembling the Liverpool Model of the UK economy, described in Minford et al. (1984). The model is closed by trade and price equations for the rest of the world, divided into three blocks: other industrial, oil-producing, and non-oil developing countries. In this appendix, we briefly summarise the model's main features and provide a complete listing of the equations and coefficients currently in use.

Table 3A.1b. *Structure of the US model*

(1) $\log m = a_1 + a_2 r_S + a_3 \log(y/y^*) + a_4 \log\theta + a_5 T + a_6 \log m_{-1}$

(2) $g = y - c - eg - x\,\text{vol} + (1 - a_{13})g_{-1}$

(3) $\log c = a_{12} + a_{14}\log(PEXPL - R_L) + a_{15}\log(w)$
$\qquad + a_{16}T + a_{17}\log(y/y^*) + a_{18}\log c_{-1}$

(4) $\log y = \log y^* + a_{28}(RXR - a_{29} + a_{34}T) + a_{36}\log(y/y^*)_{-1}$

(5) $w \equiv \theta + g$

(6) $\theta \equiv eg - t\cdot y + x\,\text{val} + \theta_{-1}\left[1 + a_{40}\left(R_L - a_{41}\dfrac{\Delta R_L}{R_{L_{-1}}} - \dfrac{\Delta P}{P_{-1}}\right)\right]$

(7) $\dfrac{x\,\text{vol}}{y^*} = \left[\dfrac{x\,\text{val}}{y^*} - a_{26}\,a_{27}\,RXR - Z\right]$

(8) $\dfrac{x\,\text{val}}{y^*} = -\left[a_{37}\displaystyle\sum_{i-2}^{9} c_{i+1}\dfrac{x\,\text{val}_i}{y_i^*} + a_{38}\displaystyle\sum_{i-10}^{12} c_{i+1}\dfrac{x\,\text{val}_i}{x\,\text{vol}_i}\right]$

(9) $r_L = \left(r_S + \displaystyle\sum_{i-1}^{4} Er_{S+1}\right)\Big/5$

(10) $r_S = (1/a_8)[a_7 + a_9\log w + a_{10}T + a_{11}\log(g/\theta_{-1}) - \log(g/\theta)]$

(11) $R_S \equiv r_S + PEXP$

(12) $R_L \equiv r_L + PEXPL$

(13) $\log M = a_{30}\Delta\log M_{-1} + a_{31}\log(y/y^*)_{-1}$
$\qquad + a_{32}\Delta\log P + a_{33}DMT + \log M_{-1}$

(14) $\log P \equiv \log P_{-1} + \Delta\log M - \Delta\log m$

(15) $RXR = -\dfrac{1}{1-c_2}\displaystyle\sum_{i-2}^{9} c_{i+1}RXR_i$

The basic structure for each non-US country model is set out in table 3A.1a; variables definitions appear in table 3A.3.

Equations (1) and (2) consist of an inter-related set of private sector portfolio demands for stocks of money, government bonds (inclusive of net foreign assets) and durable goods. In equation (1), the demand for real money balances is related to the stock of financial assets, short-term nominal interest rates, total wealth, long-term real interest rates and the variance of inflation forecasting errors (measured as the squared value of the long-run expected inflation rate). Equation (2) relates the stock of goods demanded (including fixed capital, consumer durables, and inventories) to the stock of financial assets, long-term real interest rates, total wealth and price variability, which is now a proximate determinant of the risk on goods. Equation (3) relates non-durable consumption to total wealth, real long-term interest rates and price variability, a proxy for real wage risk. Equation (4) is the GDP identity. Equation (5) defines total wealth as the sum of goods and financial assets. Equation (6) defines the

Table 3A.1c. *Equations for the rest of the world and the common bloc*

Rest of the world

(1) $\log x \text{ vol} = b_1 \log WT$

(2) $\log P = \sum\limits_{i=0}^{4} b_{2+i} \log WBC_{-i} + \log PI + b_{13}$

(INDBLOC and OILBLOC)

(3a) $\log IMP = \sum\limits_{i=0}^{4} b_{7+i} \log (x \text{ vol}_{-i} P_{-i}) - \log PW$

(LDCBLOC)

(3b) $\log IMP = \sum\limits_{i=0}^{4} b_{7+i}[\log (x \text{ vol}_{-i} P_{-i}) - DEF_{-i} r_{WL_{-i}}] - \log PW$

(4) $x \text{ val} = b_{12}(P . x \text{ vol} - PW . IMP)/P$

Common bloc

(5) $\log WT = c_1 \left(\sum\limits_{i=1}^{9} c_{1+i} . \log(y_i) \right) + \sum\limits_{i=10}^{12} c_{1+i} \log(x \text{ vol}_i) + V$

(6) $\log WBC = \sum\limits_{i=1}^{9} c_{1+i} . \log(y_i/y_i^*)$

(7) $r_{WL} = r_{USL}$

(8) $r_{WS} = r_{USS}$

(9) $\log PI = \sum\limits_{i=1}^{9} c_{1+i} \log(P_i)$

(10) $\log PW = \sum\limits_{i=10}^{12} c_{1+i} \log(P_i) + c_{14} \log PI$

change in private sector financial wealth as equal to changes in its counter-parts, public sector debt and net foreign assets (via the budget deficit and the current balance in volume terms), plus valuation effects due to changes in prices and interest rates. Equation (7) relates the current account in volume terms (excluding terms of trade effects) to the expected (5 years ahead) 'real exchange rate' (defined as the domestic price level relative to the foreign price level converted into domestic currency), world trade, the world business cycle and the deviation of output from its trend; terms of trade effects are included in equation (8). Equations (9) and (10) describe the term structure of interest rates, in an open economy under perfect capital mobility and 'efficient' financial markets; the (real) exchange rate and (real) interest rates are supposed to move until the expected return on foreign and domestic bonds is the same. In equations (11) and (12), real and nominal interest rates are forced into consistency by the Fisher identities. Equation (13) is the nominal money supply equation. Equation (14) determines the inflation rate through the nominal-real money identity.

Table 3A.2a. *Country coefficients*

Parameters (a_i)	US	Canada	Japan	Germany	France	Italy	Belgium	Holland	UK
1	1.6867	8.0655	19.66	-4.5361	6.1758	45.5831	-0.67	-3.775	12.02
2	0.0	-0.75	-1.5	-1.5	-1.5	-1.8523	0.0	-1.968	-1.32
3	0.6826	-1.8	-2.0	1.5	-2.2	-5.0604	0.004	0.0	-1.41
4	0.1	0.0	0.0	0.0	0.0	0.0	0.0	0.0	0.0
5	0.0009	0.1564	0.091	-0.0956	0.175	0.213	0.0062	0.052	0.0425
6	0.5869	0.7771	0.615	0.5177	0.2415	0.3719	0.5	0.201	0.0
7	6.1063	7.4895	23.439	0.3912	7.4552	41.7192	1.8068	5.855	11.46
8	0.5	1.5	1.5	2.5	2.5	3.435	0.690	0.6942	1.04
9	-1.0	-2.5	-2.5	0.5	-2.0	-4.175	-0.2839	-1.0	-1.2
10	0.0362	0.1425	0.2052	-0.04	0.147	0.159	0.025	0.017	0.0456
11	0.6793	0.6281	0.6103	0.5325	0.4275	0.603	0.3476	0.352	0.46
12	0.0	-0.132	0.0	0.0	-1.255	-0.54	-0.4	0.0	0.0
13	0.074	0.068	0.0901	0.071	0.071	0.0581	0.045	0.05	0.084
14	0.5	0.75	0.8	1.1984	1.0	0.15	0.69	0.3	0.0
15	0.35	0.3167	0.4093	0.5421	0.7045	0.28	0.1212	0.883	0.38
16	0.0	0.0	0.0	0.0	0.0	0.0	0.0	0.0	0.0
17	0.424	0.0	0.3364	0.2979	0.0	0.0	0.2068	0.473	0.18
18	0.64	0.6354	0.5453	0.2854	0.35	0.76	0.7878	0.312	0.53
19	0.95	0.95	0.95	0.95	0.95	0.95	0.95	0.95	0.95
20	-2.8	-1.5	-4.5	-2.6	-2.9	-2.8	-3.7	-2.1	-2.6
21	1.15	0.73	0.2	1.07	1.02	1.3	0.83	0.93	1.2
22	0.0	0.0	0.0	0.0	0.0	0.0	0.0	0.0	0.0

23	−0.94	−1.68	−1.65	−1.06	0.64	−1.91	−1.5	−1.25	−3.1
24	0.0	0.79	0.71	−0.56	0.95	0.24	0.2	−0.07	0.0
25	0.0	0.0	0.08	0.0	0.0	0.0	0.029	0.0	0.0
26	2.2831	0.29	0.17	0.281	0.2	0.21	0.53	0.56	0.27
27	0.976	0.25	0.0	1.0	0.0	0.0	0.0	0.0	0.7
28	0.0965	0.88	0.88	0.88	0.88	0.528	0.9861	0.9	0.88
29	1.8566	0.2845	1.8571	1.8571	1.4783	0.4144	1.2188	0.6863	1.0
30	0.0	0.0	0.0	0.0	0.0	0.0	0.0	0.0	0.0
31	0.0	0.0	0.0	0.0	0.0	0.0	0.0	0.0	0.0
32	0.0	0.0	0.0	0.0	0.0	0.0	0.0	0.0	0.0
33	1.0	1.0	1.0	1.0	1.0	1.0	1.0	1.0	1.0
34	0.0238	0.9725	0.2	0.1539	0.2515	1.9112	0.0	0.3022	0.4
35	0.5	0.5	0.5	0.5	0.5	0.5	0.5	0.5	0.5
36	0.7759	0.0	0.0	0.0	0.0	0.0	0.0	0.0	6.1
37	2.2831	0.0	0.0	0.0	0.0	0.0	0.0	0.0	2.85
38	0.9776	0.0	0.0	0.0	0.0	0.0	0.0	0.0	−0.33
39	2.95	6.66	10.8	8.67	6.66	2.48	1.71	2.49	2.2
40	0.95	0.95	0.9	0.95	0.95	0.95	0.95	0.95	0.95
41	0.32	0.32	0.32	0.32	0.32	0.32	0.32	0.32	0.5
42	2.95	6.66	10.8	8.67	6.66	2.48	1.71	2.49	2.2
43	−0.0336	−0.0942	−0.0845	−0.1625	−0.0942	−0.0149	−0.0607	−0.045	0.0075

Table 3A.2b. *Coefficients for the rest of the world*

Parameters	INDBLOC b_i	OILBLOC b_i	LDCBLOC b_i	COMMON BLOC c_i
1	0.403	0.428	0.39	0.616
2	0.0	0.0	0.37	0.438
3	0.0	0.0	0.44	0.047
4	0.0	0.0	0.42	0.141
5	0.0	0.0	0.44	0.12
6	0.0	0.0	0.31	0.096
7	0.3	0.1	0.5	0.05
8	0.4	0.2	0.3	0.018
9	0.3	0.3	0.2	0.024
10	0.0	0.2	0.0	0.066
11	0.0	0.2	0.0	0.128
12	0.029	0.029	0.029	0.137
13	1.4402	0.4774	3.7945	0.119
14	—	—	—	0.616
15	—	—	—	1.5818

Equation (15) relates real exchange rate changes to actual and one year ahead expected deviation of output from its trend. Finally, equations (16) and (17) relate foreign interest rates to (country-adjusted) world interest rates.

The US model, described in table 3A.1b, is specified in a slightly different way, in order to capture the role of this country in the world economy and to ensure consistency of exchange rate and trade relationships. Equations (1), (3), (5), (6), (11), (12), (13) and (14) are unchanged. The stock of goods demanded (equation 2) is now determined through the GDP identity. Real output (equation 4) depends on the real exchange rate and the lagged (one period) value of output deviation from its trend. The US trade balance (including terms of trade, equation 8) is inversely related to a weighted measure of the rest of the world trade balances. Equation (8) in table 3A.1a is now inverted to determine the trade balance excluding terms of trade adjustments. The US short-term real interest rate (equation 10) is determined by inverting the goods equation. The long-term real interest rate is calculated as the average value of the current and four-years ahead expected short-term interest rate (equation 9). Finally, the US real exchange rate (equation 15) is inversely related to a weighted measure of other main industrial countries' real exchange rates.

Equations for the rest of the world (other industrial, 'INDBLOC', oil-producing, 'OILBLOC', and non-oil developing countries, 'LDCBLOC')

Table 3A.3. *World model definitions*

log	natural logarithm.
*	long-run value of variable.
$E_{-j}(X_{+i})$	rational expectation formed at time $t-j$ on information available, of X at time $t+i$.
T	time (years).
R_L, r_L	nominal, real long-run interest rate.
R_S, r_S	nominal, real short-run interest rate.
W	total private sector wealth (1975 prices).
θ	financial assets (1975 prices).
g	goods (1975 prices).
m	money (1975 prices).
M	nominal money supply.
eg	government spending (1975 prices).
P	price level of domestic goods (1975 = 100).
PI	price index, industrialized countries (1975 = 100).
PW	price index, world.
x val	trade balance including terms of trade effects (1975 prices).
x vol	trade balance excluding terms of trade effects (1975 prices); exports volume for the rest of the world.
c	non-durable consumption (1975 prices).
RXR	real exchange rate (log deviation from 1975 = 100).
y	gross domestic product, average estimate (1975 prices).
(y/y^*)	output deviation from trend.
WT	volume of world trade.
WBC	world business cycle.
r_{FS}	foreign real short-run interest rate.
r_{FL}	foreign real long-run interest rate.
r_{WS}	world real short-run interest rate.
r_{WL}	world real long-run interest rate.
t	overall tax rate.
DMT	(expected) long-run growth rate of nominal money supply.
$QEXP$	$E[(y/y^*)_{+1}]$
$QEXPL$	$E[(y/y^*)_{+2}]$
$PEXP$	$E\Delta \log P_{+1}$
$PEXPL$	$E\left[\left(\sum_{i=1}^{5} \Delta \log P_{+i}\right)\Big/5\right]$
$ERXR$	$E[RXR_{+1}]$
$ERXRL$	$E[RXR_{+5}]$
IMP	imports volume (1975 prices).
DA, Z	dummy variables.
DEF	foreign debt, non-oil developing countries

are given in the upper part of table 3A.1c. Export volumes (equation 1) are related to world trade. Equation (2) relates price changes to world economic activity and inflation in industrialized countries. Imports volume for INDBLOC and OILBLOC countries (equation 3a) depends on export capacity and world prices; for non-oil developing countries, export capacity is defined net of interest payments on foreign debt (equation 3b). Equation (4) defines the trade balance, in volume terms.

In the 'COMMON' bloc (lower part of table 3A.1c) indices of world trade and world economic activity are defined as weighted measures of output and exports in the industrialized countries (equations 5 and 6). World interest rates, defined in equations (7) and (8), are set equal to US interest rates. Finally, equations (9) and (10) define the industrialized and world price indices.

The country coefficients currently in use are given in table 3A.2a and the coefficients for the rest of the world and common bloc equations are given in table 3A.2b. Some of these parameters are based on preliminary econometric estimates using limited information methods, some have been imposed on the basis of previous work when satisfactory estimates could not be obtained. Efforts continue to improve the quality of parameter estimates.

Appendix B. The solution and simulation of the model
SATWANT MARWAHA

1. Introduction
This note outlines the basic approach used for solution of a large-scale Rational Expectation model, and is an extension of the methodology in Matthews et al. (1981). The extension is just a complement to the above and makes the solution techniques more efficient computationally. The extension has involved two additions, which are: (1) Instead of solving the complete model simultaneously, we solve it in country blocks, i.e. imposing a 'block diagonal' structure; this is basically taking advantage of the fact that the interdependence between the country models is not great, except indirectly. (2) Two more model solution techniques have been introduced, namely modified Powell Hybrid method (see Garbow et al., 1980, Powell, 1970, and Walsh, 1975) and a modified Levenberg-Marquardt (see More, 1977, Powell, 1970 and Walsh, 1975). These techniques both involve the calculation of a Jacobian, hence the use of (1) lets these be implemented without being too costly.

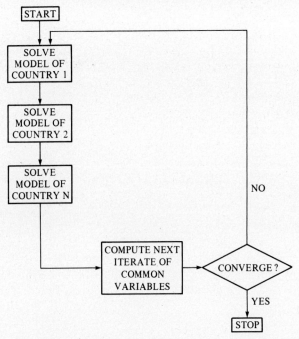

3.11 Iteration structure for period 1, given expectational variable iterate

2. The rational expectation solution

This has been described in Matthews et al. (1981) and as can be seen in Figure 3.12, this arrangement is a Jacobi type iteration for the solution of expectational variables, given that the complete model has been solved, using earlier iterates. The terminal is chosen to be greater than the expectational horizon (and as a guide the terminal is twice the expectational horizon).

3. The complete model solution

This solution is illustrated in Figure 3.11. There are two levels of solution, the first being the solution of the country model and the second being the solution of the common variables. The solution techniques for the country model are described below, and it can be seen that the second level of solution is similar to one described in (2); that it is a Jacobi type iteration of blocks of equations.

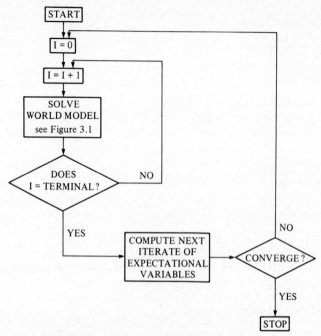

3.12 Iteration structure for expectational variables

4. Solution of non-linear set of equations

The technique of Gauss-Seidel (GS) is usually used for solution of most econometric models.

The advantage of GS is its simplicity and cheapness in terms of time, but GS is unreliable in the presence of strong non-linearities, hence the following two techniques can be employed.

The first is the modified Powell Hybrid method; its main characteristics involve the change in the model iterate being the convex combination of the Newton and scaled gradients, and the updating of the Jacobian by rank-1 method of Broyden. The Jacobian is approximated by forward differences at the initial point, and is not recalculated until rank-1 method fails to converge.

The second is the modified Levenberg-Marquardt and its main characteristics are the use of implicitly scaled variables and an optimal choice of the change in the model iterate.

The above two techniques give a good performance in finding solutions, and are not too costly, as is usually feared with such techniques which calculate Jacobians.

5. Conclusion

The solution techniques for a large model described above are the ones currently used in RATEXP mark 4, and as can be seen from Figures 3.11 and 3.12, other techniques can be used to achieve the same results or even improve on the current version; for example, the solution of the country models in Figure 3.1 could be rational solution, and then the common iterates be performed.

NOTES

* I am grateful to the ESRC for the financial support of this paper under Grant B 00220004. The current paper draws on Minford et al. (1983); my debt to my previous co-authors, Chris Ioannidis and Satwant Marwaha (who wrote Appendix B), is considerable. Eric Nowell carried out the simulations reported here; Richard Agénor has assisted recently in model development and wrote Appendix A, the model listing. I am grateful for helpful comments to Willem Buiter, Matthew Canzoneri, Michael Emerson, Richard Marston and Jeffrey Sachs, as well as to a number of other participants at this conference.
1 Some English Keynesians (such as the Cambridge Economic Policy Group) however would argue that this behaviour was general; international co-ordination of real wages would be needed to resolve inconsistency, and controls could be introduced to fix one variable and so resolve indeterminacy. Finally, co-ordinated demand expansion (locomotive policies) could then be used to raise world output, given no supply constraints.
2 Net overseas assets of the US banking system at end-1981 were about £138 billion.
3 The United States, Canada, Japan, Germany, France, Italy, Belgium, the Netherlands, and the United Kingdom.

REFERENCES

Barro, R. J. (1974). 'Are government bonds net wealth?'. *Journal of Political Economy*.
Barro, R. J. (1980). 'A capital market in a Equilibrium Business Cycle Model'. *Econometrica*.
Beenstock, M. and P. Minford (1976). 'A quarterly econometric model of world trade and prices, 1955–71' in *Inflation in Open Economies*, (eds. M. Parkin and G. Zis). Manchester University Press.
Bhandari, J. S. (1981). 'Exchange rate overshooting revisited'. *Manchester School*.
Blanchard, O. J. (1981). 'Output, The Stock Market and Interest Rates'. *American Economic Review*.
Blinder, A. S. and R. M. Solow (1973). 'Does fiscal policy matter?'. *Journal of Public Economics*, 2.

Branson, W. H. and R. L. Teigen (1976). 'Flow and stock equilibrium in a dynamic Metzler model'. *Journal of Finance.*

Dornbusch, R. (1976). 'Expectations and Exchange Rate Dynamics'. *Journal of Political Economy.*

Garbow, B., K. Hillstraum and J. More (1980). 'Documentation for Minpack'. Argonne National Laboratory.

Kouri, P. J. K. (1976). 'The exchange rates and the balance of payments in the short and in the long run: a monetary approach'. *Scandinavian Journal of Economics.*

Lipsey, R. G. (1960). 'The relationship between unemployment and the rate of change of money wage rates in the U.K., 1862–1957: a further analysis'. *Economica.*

Lucas, R. E. Jr. (1976). 'Econometric policy evaluation: A critique', in K. Brunner and A. H. Meltzer (eds.), *The Phillips Curve and Labour Markets*, Carnegie Rochester Conference Series on Public Policy No. 1, Supplement to the *Journal of Monetary Economics.*

Lucas, R. and L. Rapping (1969). 'Real wages, employment and inflation'. *Journal of Political Economy.*

Matthews, K. G. P., S. Marwaha and R. Pierse (1981). 'RATEXP MK2', ESRC Working Paper No. 8102, Department of Economic and Business Studies, The University of Liverpool.

Minford, A. P. L. (1980): 'A rational expectations model of the United Kingdom under Fixed and Floating Exchange Rates', in K. Brunner and A. H. Meltzer (eds.), *On the State of Macroeconomics*, Carnegie Rochester Conference Series on Public Policy No. 12, Supplement to *Journal of Monetary Economics.*

Minford, A. P. L., C. Ioannidis and S. Marwaha (1983). 'Rational Expectations in a Multilateral Macro-Model', in P. de Grauwe and T. Peeters (eds.), Macmillan.

Minford, A. P. L., S. Marwaha, K. G. P. Matthews and A. Sprague (1984). 'The Liverpool Macro-Economic Model of the United Kingdom'. *Economic Modelling*, January.

Minford, A. P. L. and D. A. Peel (1983). *Rational Expectations and the New Macroeconomics*, Martin Robertson.

More, J. (1977), 'The Levernberg-Marquardt Algorithm implementation and theory'. *Numerical Analysis*, Watson, G. A. (ed.). Lecture Notes in Mathematics 630, Springer-Verlag.

Powell, M. C. D. (1970). 'A hybrid method for non-linear equations', in *Numerical Methods for Non-Linear Equations*, P. Rabinowitz (ed.), Gordon and Breach.

Saidi, N. and G. Huber (1983). 'Postwar Business Cycles and Exchange Rate Regimes: Issues and Evidence', mimeo, University of Geneva, paper presented to 1983 Konstanz Seminar on Monetary Theory and Monetary Policy.

Taylor, J. B. (1979). 'Estimation and Control of a Macroeconomic Model with Rational Expectations'. *Econometrica.*

Walsh, G. R. (1975). *Methods of Optimization.* Wiley.

COMMENT MICHAEL EMERSON

I much appreciate Patrick Minford's fearless contributions to economic policy debate, especially in some of the no-go areas where many dare not tread. Passing on from macro financial policy in the UK, the micro-economics of unemployment and, recently I believe, the organisation of local government services in the city of Liverpool, Professor Minford here has a go at the major issues of macro financial policy at the world level. In all these fields Professor Minford widens the range of debate among economists and politicians – certainly in the UK. This means that he will not always be carrying everyone's agreement before him, but that is hardly surprising in the circumstances.

Professor Minford's paper is divided into three main parts, and I will comment on each in turn:

– design of the author's multi-country model
– results offered by the model
– some less formal interpretation of recent events in the world economy.

A limitation in the paper is that the links between these three parts are none too strong. The applied model is only partly estimated econometrically and not fully tested – as the author himself clearly says. So the link between the theory and the results is not fully supported. In addition the model could not be used to simulate recent experience, which breaks the link between the model and the author's comments on recent events.

Design of the Minford model

Setting aside for the moment the author's choice of a monetarist, rational expectations and neo-classical form to his model, there is a general question of multi-country model design posed here. Can compact models do better than the juggernaut multi-country models which have been built elsewhere – for example the LINK project, and the somewhat smaller Japanese EPA and US Federal Reserve Board MCM models?

In principle I think we should be rather sympathetic to multi-country modelling that gives priority to stripping the individual country models down to essentials, and exploring the uncertain international properties of a system of national economies which themselves on their own have familiar characteristics. In particular, valuable perspective may be gained by consolidating various regional or sectoral economies, for example Western Europe, and primary commodity producing countries. This may help better see the wood for the trees.

As regards the behavioural properties of the Minford model in comparison with its opposite Keynesian counterpart, I was rather puzzled by the author's plea for the opposition to stand up and show the colour of its money. Examples of multi-country models with a Keynesian income-expenditure structure exist, for example the 1980 vintage of the OECD Interlink model. In this particular model a US fiscal expansion of 1% of GDP would have an output impact multiplier of about 2 on the US in the second year, and of about 0.35 on the rest of the OECD area. The impact on inflation would be small. Monetary policy shocks would typically not give plausible results or indeed be feasible for the model system. Real balance and wealth effects would be largely absent, and the exchange rate would not be endogenised.

In relation to all this, then, Minford is staking out the ground at the opposite end of the spectrum. Fiscal policy generates 100% crowding-out, but monetary policy is very potent.

Results

For a more detailed presentation of his model the author refers us to his 1983 source, which is the proceedings of the 1981 Leuven conference on multi-country exchange rate modelling.[1] The disclaimers in the present paper – about the imposition of some parameters and the experimental stage of the project – also appear in the Leuven paper. A question therefore is how far this project is really advancing in proving its viability in terms of standard econometric tests?

As regards the model's main properties, I shall comment in turn on its response to monetary and fiscal shocks.

US monetary expansion. A 2% increase in US money supply gives a massive, almost equivalent impact of US output in year 1: Even more striking is its $1\frac{1}{2}$% impact on world output. For the US the impact on output remains substantially positive for 5 to 6 years, whereas for inflation the impact gradually builds up, especially over 3 to 4 years. For the rest of the world the impact on the price level is eventually $+4$%, against $+2$% for US. I find the higher inflationary impact on the rest of the world odd.

I have looked for some other evidence worth citing. The Japanese EPA model, in a simulation under flexible exchange rates, suggests an impact on the US's own GDP about $\frac{1}{4}$ as powerful as Minford in years 1 and 2. For the rest of the world (Europe in particular) the output impact is very small indeed, indeed negative for Germany to read from Oudiz & Sachs' paper; this is because the exchange rate impact is to appreciate the DM.

Another source is Michael Bruno's[2] reduced-form analysis which for Europe offers a little encouragement for Minford, with US money supply appearing with a coefficient of 0.2 (with weak statistical significance) in explaining European output fluctuations. But by comparison Minford's monetary policy results remain very strong indeed.

US fiscal expansion. Minford argues that the US fiscal stimulation does not stimulate the US or the world. The mechanisms that gives this result are as follows:

Step 1, the US fiscal shock pushes out the IS curve, giving higher output and a higher interest rate; so far so good.

Step 2, this lifts the US real exchange rate, cuts US prices and so pushes the supply curve inwards to the left, so we ride up the IS curve, back to a lower level of output more than offsetting the initial stimulus.

This is where the acid tests arise for the Minford model. All depends upon:

– the amplitude of the interest rate's reaction to the output increase,
– the amplitude of the exchange rate reaction to the interest rate rise,
– the extent to which domestic prices also will be pushed upwards, especially in non-tradeable sectors, with the initial upturn of activity, perhaps offsetting the exchange rate effect on prices and therefore activity,
– or, if prices are reduced, the amplitude of the positive wealth effect as a result of this disinflation.

These are the places in the argument where the size of key parameter values determine the sign of the outcome. These key parameters are given in an Annex to the paper, but without indication of how they score on the usual tests of empirical significance. I feel that the conclusion that a US fiscal policy has a perverse impact on the US itself in the first year after the shock implausible. Since Minford's parameters, we know, are not fully estimated and rest in some degree on a priori assumptions, we are entitled to express such views.

Observations on recent events

Minford argues that the fiscal shift in US did not do anything for the current US expansion – it was all money. The 1983 recovery would have happened anyway with just the monetary boost. I believe that this is an implausible extreme interpretation. In my view fiscal policy did contribute to the US expansion. Without it in the US the expansion would have been slower. However, for the rest of the world the US fiscal deficit has had serious adverse effects. The 1982 cyclical relapse in Europe can be traced to the collapse of world trade that year, in turn substantially but not exclusively linked to the debt crisis in Latin America, in turn substantially accounted for by US fiscal policy.

More generally the US financial policy mix (monetary, exchange rate, budgetary) has temporarily redistributed world output (+ in US, – in Europe) and world inflation (– in US, + in Europe), and this has kept European policy on the defensive. If US policies had been less distorted, European policies would have been different, and OECD output would have been more evenly distributed. OECD output (according to the OECD Economic Outlook of June 1984) is expected to rise at an annual average rate of about 3% in 1983–85, with the US at 4% and Europe at 2%. With a less eccentric US policy it might have been the same with a more even distribution, or possibly a bit higher in total, say with the US at $3\frac{1}{2}$% and Europe at 3%. Thus I am quite sympathetic to Minford's conclusions along these lines.

Finally, there are a few pieces of surrealism in the author's conclusions. On oil shocks, Minford feels 'no compelling reason to refer to them as a macro shock'. On US policies, because they are chosen constitutionally by the powers that be, they are necessarily optimal, and 'the rest of the world does not appear to have a case for them to change'. On LDC debt, this was taken on voluntarily and so 'no complaint is possible'.

I imagine Minford says these things with tongue in the cheek. I think I am familiar with the reasoning that leads him to these conclusions. I won't argue about this. I completely disagree, and also feel that their gratuitous delivery at the end of the paper will lead readers not to take the author's overall arguments are seriously as he would like.

NOTES

1 Minford, A. P. L., C. Ioannidis and S. Marwaha (1983). 'Rational Expectations in a Multilateral Macro-Model', in P. de Grauwe and T. Peeters (eds.), *Exchange Rates in Multicountry Econometric Models*. Macmillan.

2 Paper in M. Emerson (ed.), *Europe's Stagflation*. Oxford University Press, 1984.

COMMENT RICHARD C. MARSTON

Minford offers what he terms a 'new classical interpretation' of the effects of monetary and fiscal policy in a multicountry setting. His interpretation includes several provocative conclusions which will be examined below.

Before doing so, I should point out that Minford deserves considerable credit for estimating such a large and sophisticated econometric model on which his analysis is based. Estimation of a model for nine countries is too large a task for most individual researchers, and simulation of such a large model under rational expectations has generally been beyond the capability of even large organizations.

Minford's model contains three features which distinguish it from many, though not all, large-scale econometric models. First, aggregate supply is a function of price surprises so that changes in the money supply, for example, have only transitory effects. The specification of aggregate supply is not based on a Lucas-type confusion between local and general prices, but instead on a contract lag in the labor market, although (as explained later) the contract model is different from those found in the open economy literature. The second distinguishing feature of the model is rational expectations. Expectations of inflation and the depreciation of the currency are generated rationally by the rest of the model. With uncovered interest parity also assumed, the path of future inflation and real depreciation are tied together because UIP links real interest rates and the expected depreciation of the real exchange rate. The third feature of the model is the presence of relatively large wealth effects on the aggregate demand or IS equation and in the demand for money equation.

Given a model with these three features, Minford has generated a set of simulations with surprising results, the most surprising of which is the following: a temporary debt-financed increase in government spending in the United States actually lowers output in the United States and raises output (at least in some later periods) in Germany, the United Kingdom and Japan. This is 'crowding out' with a vengeance.

What I would like to do is to focus on aspects of the model that lead to some of these results. The first two features of the model, the aggregate supply function and rational expectations, are by now almost standard in *non*-empirical work, at least, on the open economy. Models with aggregate supply based on contract lags and with rational expectations, in fact, exhibit behavior very similar to that found in a textbook Keynesian model, at least in response to the temporary, unanticipated shocks considered in this paper.

The actual specification of aggregate supply used in the paper, however, includes a lagged dependent variable. In the simulations, this variable appears to be very important. The monetary simulation illustrated in Figure 3.7 suggests that a once-for-all increase in the money supply has output effects seven years and beyond. That's an implausibly long lag for a model based on labor contracts, and is certainly not in the spirit of the 'new classical' literature. The source of the long lag can be traced, I believe, to the large coefficient of lagged output in the US aggregate supply equation (see equation 4 of table 1b in Appendix 3A), although there may be other factors in this complex model helping to account for such prolonged effects.

While discussing the supply equation, I would also like to question the way in which external influences are modelled. In any model used to study international transmission effects, the modelling of the real exchange rate is obviously important. In equation (2) and Figure 3.1, aggregate supply is a function of the current real exchange rate, but not the lagged real exchange rate or the unanticipated change in that exchange rate. The exchange rate enters because imported materials are a second variable input (besides labor) in the production process. This specification of aggregate supply neglects a second channel for real exchange rates to influence aggregate supply. If domestic products are distinct from foreign products, as they are in Minford's model, then producers will respond to a different real wage than will labor. Labor will respond to a real wage deflated by a general price level based on foreign as well as domestic goods. Because of this interplay between the two real wages, aggregate supply is a function of the real exchange rate just as in Minford's specification. However, in a contract model, the real exchange rate enters not currently, but with a lag. Or, if there is wide indexation, the real exchange rate enters as a price surprise. (See Marston, 1984). Since indexation varies widely across countries, the way in which the real exchange rate enters the aggregate supply equation will also vary across countries. And perhaps in no country will the real exchange rate enter exclusively, or even primarily, as a current variable.

I can be a little more specific about the aggregate supply curve in the present context. It's probable that the aggregate supply curve for the United States is close to being vertical (in real exchange rate/output space), while it is negatively sloped (as shown in Figure 3.1) for the rest of the world. It may be close to vertical for the United States for two reasons: (1) The most important imported material, oil, is priced in dollars rather than in foreign currency (as specified in the model). The dollar price isn't exactly constant, but it is much less sensitive to the exchange rate than the franc or mark price, for example. (2) Wages are not highly indexed in the United States, nor is the US consumer price index very sensitive to the exchange rate. So aggregate supply should not be very sensitive to unanticipated changes in foreign prices or the real exchange rate. In contrast, the rest of the world must face oil priced in dollars and, in some European countries at least, wages are highly indexed. (See Branson and Rotemberg (1980)). So we should see a considerable asymmetry in aggregate supply behavior, part of which cannot be captured by the current empirical specification of the model.

Let me turn now to the crowding out effect. The feature which so distinguishes Minford's model from many others, and which to a large extent accounts for his striking results, is the role of wealth in the aggregate demand and money demand equations. Friedman (1972) argued that government spending financed with government debt would be powerless to raise output. Indeed, a rise in government spending might actually lower output. This could occur because the issue of debt raises private wealth, and so raises the demand for money, shifting the LM curve (in interest rate, output space) to the left. That same issue of debt also raises aggregate demand, shifting the IS curve to the right (thus adding to the stimulative effect of higher government spending). If the wealth effect on the demand for money is strong enough, then output can actually fall. (Blinder and Solow (1973), showed that this case of falling output was unstable, but it is not clear whether or not their results would remain the same under rational expectations).

Critics of Friedman's position might take two alternative approaches. Some economists, of whom Barro (1974) is perhaps the most influential, would argue in terms of Ricardian equivalence. The debt issue should have no effect on private wealth since individuals would anticipate the future taxes needed to service the debt. Other economists would take a different tack. They would accept the argument that government debt adds to wealth, as Minford does, but argue that changes in wealth have little effect on the demand for money. According to this view, money is a dominated asset in portfolios, held strictly for transactions purposes. A rise in wealth, if the level of transactions is constant, has no effect on money demand. This latter view is quite persuasive if by money we mean currency and checkable deposits, especially if those deposits pay non-market rates of interest (as they do in many countries). There are near-monies such as Eurocurrency deposits which clearly dominate money holdings for purposes of short term investment. Having phrased the argument that way, it should be clear that the influence of wealth on the demand for money should depend upon the institutional and legal constraints on the banking system, and thus should vary widely from country to country.

According to Minford, the effect of wealth on the demand for money is extremely difficult to estimate. In his model for the United Kingdom (reported in Minford (1984)), the wealth parameters in both the aggregate demand and money demand equations were quite unstable, and were sensitive to the statistical technique used to estimate them. Evidently the same thing is true of the multicountry model, since in this model the wealth parameters were ultimately imposed rather than estimated. But since the parameters were not estimated, it is hard to assess the reliability of the stimulation results. What we need is a sensitivity analysis which would indicate how the crowding out (and other results) are affected when the wealth elasticities are varied around their present values.

There is one final point that I would like to raise about wealth effects. Not only should the wealth elasticities differ across countries, but so also should the sensitivity of changes in wealth to changes in exchange rates. The currency composition of wealth can vary substantially from country to country. So also can the sensitivity of the national price levels used to deflate wealth. The net effect of a change in the exchange rate on real wealth depends upon the balance between these two forces, asset denomination and price sensitivity. Minford's model doesn't seem to take the currency composition into account at all. Given the importance of the wealth effects, it is clearly essential to do so.

REFERENCES

Barro, Robert J. (1974). 'Are government bonds net wealth?' *Journal of Political Economy* **82**, 1095–1117.

Blinder, Allan S. and Robert M. Solow (1973). 'Does fiscal policy matter?' *Journal of Public Economics* **2**, 319–37.

Branson, William H. and Julio Rotemberg (1980). 'International adjustment with wage rigidity.' *European Economic Review* **13**, 309–41.

Friedman, Milton (1972). 'Comments on the critics.' *Journal of Political Economy* **80**, 906–50.

Marston, Richard C. (1984). 'Real wages and the terms of trade: alternative indexation rules for an open economy.' *Journal of Money, Credit and Banking* **16**, 285–301.

Minford, Patrick C., Satwant Marwaha, Kent Matthews and Alison Sprague (1984). 'A rational expectations model of the UK under fixed and floating exchange rates.' *Economic Modelling* (January), 24–62.

4 International policy coordination in historical perspective: a view from the interwar years

BARRY EICHENGREEN*

'Measures of currency reform will be facilitated if the practice of continuous cooperation among central banks of issue, or banks regulating credit policy in the several countries can be developed. Such cooperation of central banks, not necessarily confined to Europe, would provide opportunities of coordinating their policy, without hampering the freedom of the several banks.'

> (From Resolution 3 of the Report of the Financial Commission of the Genoa Conference, 1922.)

In the days of the gold standard, it is sometimes said, international policy coordination was a moot point.[1] Popular accounts based more on caricature than on careful historical analysis portray the gold standard as a remarkably efficient mechanism for coordinating the actions of national authorities. Policies were so easily reconciled, it is argued, because those responsible for their formulation, regardless of nationality, shared a belief in balanced budgets and a common overriding objective: pegging the domestic currency price of gold. When central banks intervened in financial markets, it is suggested, they did so mechanically, obeying 'rules of the game' which dictated that they only reinforce the impact on domestic money and credit markets of balance of payments conditions. For example, a central bank losing reserves would raise its discount rate while the central bank gaining reserves would lower its discount rate, thereby reinforcing one another's efforts to restore external balance. Hence monetary policy under the gold standard is a favorite example of those who argue that international policy coordination is most readily achieved under a rules-based regime rather than one that depends on discretion.

This naive vision of the days of the gold standard as a simpler, more harmonious era is at best partial and at worst misleading. The very actions of central banks suggest that their objectives were not in fact so easily reconciled by the operation of gold standard constraints. Discount rates

139

tended to move together, not inversely as the 'rules of the game' would suggest.[2] Central banks sterilized international gold flows more often than they intervened to reinforce their impact on domestic markets.[3] These and other actions resemble the outcome of a noncooperative game, in which the participants act to neutralize rather than accommodate the efforts of their counterparts. Yet on occasion central banks and governments managed to achieve cooperative solutions to their problems, such as when they negotiated swap arrangements, earmarked gold, or extended international loans.[4] Both central banks and governments clearly recognized their interdependence, if they did not always succeed in coordinating their actions.

Still, it is fair to say that the interwar period opened the modern era of interdependence. In the 1920s questions of policy coordination and central bank cooperation acquired a new tone of urgency. In part this reflected greater opportunities for coordinating policies in a world with a Bank for International Settlements, an international telegraph, and a trans-Atlantic telephone.[5] In part it reflected the higher costs of ignoring interdependence in a world of rapid communication, integrated markets and volatile capital flows. Above all it reflected the widening scope for conflict as governments attached growing importance to domestic economic objectives and put less weight on balance of payments targets.

The interwar period provides examples of various forms of successful collaboration. The League of Nations provided stabilization loans to countries experiencing hyperinflation in return for their accession to protocols which precluded their central banks from monetizing budget deficits and committed them to return to gold. International conferences held at Brussels in 1920 and Genoa in 1922 laid the basis for reconstructing the international monetary system. The United States saw Britain's return to gold as the linchpin upon which the gold standard's resurrection depended, and it provided credits of $300 million to facilitate Britain's restoration of the prewar sterling parity.[6] These efforts were fully successful in reconstructing the international system: once its renewal had been signaled by Britain's return to gold, some fifty nations joined the US and the UK as participants in the interwar gold standard.

Yet the interwar period provides equally dramatic illustrations of failures of cooperation and their costs. The brief duration and early demise of the interwar gold standard is taken to indicate the inability of major participants to effectively coordinate their actions. A prime example is the failure of the countries at the center to harmonize their choice of parities. The important cases are Great Britain, where overvaluation of sterling was associated with unprecedented levels of unemployment and depression in the export trades; and France, where undervaluation of the franc was associated with sustained economic growth and until 1931 insulation from the worst effects of the Great Depression. One corollary of this competitive imbalance was an uneven international distribution of gold. Nations such as the United States and France whose international competitive positions were relatively strong acquired and retained a large portion of the world's monetary gold, leaving others such as Britain to defend the convertibility of their currencies on the basis of slender reserves. Another indication of this inability to coordinate policies was the widespread failure to play by the rules of the gold standard game; instead central banks sterilized international reserve flows and hesitated to adjust their discount rates in response to external pressures.

This paper takes a new look at the financial history of the interwar period to see what light this experience sheds on current concerns over international policy coordination. After a review of the literature and the historical preconditions, it tells a story in three parts. The first part examines the role for policy coordination as envisaged by contemporaries at the start of the period. It takes as a case study the Genoa Economic and Financial Conference of 1922. We will argue that the advantages of policy coordination were in fact well understood in the twenties but that political disagreements impeded efforts to establish a mechanism for cooperative action. Instead, policymakers ultimately pursued noncooperative strategies within the framework of the international gold standard.

The second part considers the effects of noncooperative behavior once the gold standard was again in operation. Identifying these effects requires an explicit model. Yet the idea of strategic behavior by national authorities is wholly incompatible with standard models of the gold standard's operation. The analysis therefore requires the development of an alternative model of the interwar gold standard. While the model developed below bears little resemblance to previous frameworks used to analyze gold standard adjustment, it indicates clearly not only the advantages of coordinated action but suggests why cooperative solutions proved so difficult to achieve.

The final part concerns the question of what the principal participants learned from their pursuit of noncooperative strategies. The lessons of the interwar gold standard as they were understood by contemporaries found reflection in the next attempt to reconstruct the international monetary order: the Tripartite Monetary Agreement concluded by Britain, France and the United States in the autumn of 1936.[7] The terms of the Tripartite Agreement were remarkably similar to the Genoa Resolutions of 1922. Where they differed was in the absence of favorable references to fixed parities and to the gold-exchange standard. They differed as well by more tightly circumscribing the range of issues subject to collaboration. This along with the decline of political obstacles to cooperation permitted the noble sentiments of the Tripartite Agreement to be implemented. Thus, the history of international financial collaboration in the interwar period sheds light not only on the rationale for policy coordination but also on the circumstances conducive to its practice.

I. Leadership and cooperation under a gold standard regime

In theoretical treatments of the gold standard's operation, there is no scope for policy coordination. The adjustment process works automatically, affecting surplus and deficit countries alike. The price-specie-flow variant of the adjustment mechanism emphasizes the role of relative prices in restoring external balance. A gold outflow leads to monetary deflation and falling prices until the international competitiveness of the goods produced by the deficit country is enhanced sufficiently to restore equilibrium to the external accounts. The monetary variant of the adjustment mechanism stresses the role of wealth and real balance effects. A gold outflow reduces absorption through the real balance effect on consumption until the equality of income and expenditure is restored. In each case, the surplus country is affected symmetrically. Beyond standing ready to buy and sell gold at the official price, the only role for central banks is to mechanically reinforce the impact on domestic money and credit markets of incipient gold flows.

Strikingly, these theoretical treatments bear little resemblance to historical analyses of the gold standard's operation either at the end of the 19th century or between the wars. Where theoretical models describe central banks as mechanically reinforcing one another's actions, historical accounts emphasize instead the potential for conflict between national authorities and their strategic interaction. Yet in none of these accounts is the scope for conflict adequately defined, leaving unclear the advantages of leadership and cooperation.

Historical descriptions of the classical gold standard place great weight on asymmetries in the system's operation. Great Britain in particular is seen as possessing unrivaled abilities to manipulate the process of adjustment. Britain's market power is attributed to her position as the world's foremost trading and lending nation. British exports, which had already quadrupled between 1800 and 1850, increased eightfold between 1850 and 1913, and on the eve of the first World War Britain accounted for 14 per cent of world exports, a figure far exceeding her share of world production or income. The world's principal organized commodity markets all were centered in England. Not the least of these was the London gold market, which regularly received the bulk of South Africa's gold production. In addition, Britain had no close competitor as the world's preeminent international lender. By 1913, British overseas investments amounted to nearly 45 per cent of the external investments of the major creditor countries of the West. Britain's annual capital export was nearly five times that of France, her nearest rival. Never before or since have a nation's overseas investments been such a large share of national income.[8]

Britain's commercial and financial preeminence had profound implications for the international role of sterling, which had implications in turn for the operation of the adjustment mechanism. Sterling was the world's leading vehicle currency in international transactions. Trade that neither touched British shores nor passed through the hands of British merchants overseas might nonetheless be invoiced in sterling. Transactions the world over were settled with the transfer of sterling balances between foreign accounts maintained in London. Securities denominated in sterling were the most popular form of international reserves with which central banks might supplement their stocks of gold.[9]

Under these circumstances, it is argued, the Bank of England exercised powerful leverage over international flows of commodities, capital and gold – leverage it could employ to manipulate the process of adjustment by which external balance was restored. Changes in Bank Rate (the rate charged by the Bank of England for loans to discount houses and other dealers in Treasury and commercial bills) exerted an influence not shared by foreign discount rates and to a large extent determined credit conditions not merely at home but abroad.[10] A rise in Bank Rate is typically thought to have forced up the required rate of return on Treasury and commercial bills, and by rendering these assets more attractive increased the opportunity cost to the banking sector of extending loans and overdrafts to borrowers. Given the share of sterling loans and advances in international markets for short-term capital, rates of return on foreign-currency-denominated assets that were substitutes for sterling were forced up as well. Moreover, because the world's most important gold market also was located in London, the Bank of England by altering the cost and availability of short-term credit directly influenced the tendency of non-residents to purchase and ship abroad gold newly delivered to market.

To paraphrase Walter Bagehot's famous aphorism, raising Bank Rate to a sufficiently high level would succeed in drawing gold from the moon. This leverage over capital flows followed from the fact that no foreign power could match the Bank of England's influence in international financial markets. The United States, without even a central bank, lacked the resources and the expertise to rival Britain in the market. The Bank of France's sphere of influence was limited to Russia and France's colonial possessions. Foreign authorities possessed no feasible alternative but to respond to Bank of England initiatives, as the British understood. Hence, the Bank of England could anticipate with considerable accuracy the response of foreign authorities to a change in Bank Rate in London, and it could frame its policy accordingly. To the Deputy Governor of the Bank of England Keynes described the reaction of foreign governments in the following way: 'In prewar days it used to be maintained – I think truly – that to a large extent we led the world; that is to say, if we reduced Bank rate it probably brought about a corresponding reduction in the rates in other countries.'[11] As he framed the argument when helping to draft the report of the Macmillan Committee, Britain could 'by the operation of her Bank Rate almost immediately adjust her reserve position. Other countries had, therefore, in the main, to adjust their conditions to hers.'[12]

There is little agreement on the costs and benefits of the Bank of England's exercise of leadership. The benign view of the prewar arrangement is that it operated to the benefit of both the leader and her followers by permitting the participants in the gold standard system to economize in their use of gold. The Bank of England could maintain a slender gold reserve because she had the power to reverse a gold outflow through unilateral initiative. Other central banks, such as those of France, Germany, Austria-Hungary and Russia, has less leverage over financial flows and were therefore forced to hold larger reserves in order to accommodate wider swings in their reserve positions. But due to the Bank of England's capacity to operate with relatively slender reserves, the gold backing of the world's monetary base could be efficiently reduced. Since the Bank of England's leverage over international capital flows erased any lingering doubts about the convertibility of sterling, other countries were encouraged to supplement their holdings of gold with this key currency, further augmenting international reserves to the benefit of all concerned.

A less sanguine view is that through her exercise of market power Britain was capable of shifting the burden of adjustment abroad. Triffin has argued that, due to London's singular importance as a source of credit for financing international transactions in foodstuffs and raw materials, Britain was through the impact of Bank Rate overseas more than compensated for the economic costs of stringent credit conditions.[13] The argument is that a temporary credit stringency swung the terms of trade in Britain's favor by increasing the cost to foreign producers of carrying stocks of primary products. Given the higher cost of holding inventories, stocks of foodstuffs and raw materials were dumped onto world markets, reducing the cost of British imports. Obviously, carrying costs were important as well to British producers of manufactured exports, who had the same incentive as producers of primary commodities to liquidate stocks in the face of tighter credit conditions. Assuming however that the market for primary products was characterized by exceptionally low price elasticities of demand, Britain's international terms of trade would still have improved on balance.[14]

By the interwar period, it is frequently suggested, circumstances had been transformed. Britain no longer possessed unparalleled influence over the international adjustment mechanism. Other nations had acquired sufficient leverage to formulate if not independent then at least distinctive national policies, leaving the Bank of England in no better position than its rivals to ignore developments abroad. In particular, the interwar period has been characterized as the era when London declined to the benefit of New York.[15] The war and its aftermath had transformed the United States from a net debtor to a net creditor, and she suddenly found herself in possession of a large share of the world's monetary gold. When Britain returned to gold in 1925, US gold reserves were roughly six times those of the Bank of England. The British government owed the US $4.7 billion in war debts, although their ultimate magnitude and the schedule by to which they might be repaid remained very much in doubt. Moreover, Washington was newly equipped with a Federal Reserve Board and New York with a Federal Reserve Bank to direct and carry out financial market intervention.

Through the first part of the twenties New York surpassed London as a source of funds invested abroad. The UK's share of world export value declined from 14 per cent in 1913 to barely 12 per cent in 1925 and little more than 11 per cent in 1928. Before the war, Britain had consistently run current account surpluses; in the century ending in 1913 there had been but two years of deficit. The situation was different between the wars; in the short span from 1925 to 1931 there were already two years of current account deficit.[16] Bankers and merchants, finding themselves to be dealing with both financial centers and running down the balances on sterling accounts maintained in London, increasingly held diversified portfolios of the two key currencies.

The British position was not eased by concurrent developments in France. Unlike Britain, France's share of world trade was stable after 1913. Following de facto stabilization in 1926 at a rate which undervalued the franc, France's external position remained strong until Britain's devaluation in 1931. In 1928, when de jure convertibility of the franc was restored, the Bank of France's holdings of liquid sterling assets roughly matched in value the Bank of England's entire gold reserve. Over the next four years, the Bank of France engaged in a persistent effort to convert these balances into gold as part of a conscious policy of elevating Paris to the stature of a first-rank financial center.[17]

The British authorities recognized their heightened interdependence

with foreign nations. In particular, the Bank of England found it impossible
to neglect the reaction of foreign central banks to a prospective change
in Bank Rate. Were the Bank of England to disregard foreign reactions
when setting its discount rate, it would 'render itself liable to be flooded
with, or depleted of, gold, as the case may be.' As high an official as the
Deputy Governor of the Bank of England admitted that 'such leadership
as we possessed has certainly been affected by the position which America
has gained.'[18]

While policymakers clearly recognized their heightened interdependence,
the implications of this recognition remain somewhat unclear. One
literature attempts to document the stimulus this recognition of interdependence provided for cooperative action. For example, Clarke (1967)
describes instances where central banks extended to one another routine
clearing services, shared privileged information, and arranged international stabilization loans. Another literature emphasizes the inability of
policy-makers to coordinate their actions despite this recognition of
interdependence. Thus, Viner (1932, p. 28) and Gayer (1937, p. 29) describe
London, Paris and New York as having worked at 'cross-purposes.' Yet
it is not easy to extract from their analyses a sense of how working at
cross-purposes affected the operation of the monetary system. In part this
is due to the tendency of these authors to argue by analogy rather than
specifying the economic model they have in mind. Nevin (1955, p. 12) is
typical of this mode when, likening the international monetary system to
an automobile, he characterizes Britain and the United States as 'two quite
excellent drivers... perpetually fighting to gain control of the vehicle.' A
system influenced by the actions of two financial centers, like a car with
two drivers, will function only if those centers are capable of cooperating
and acting consistently. But, he goes on, 'in the real world, this seldom
happens, and the existence of more than one centre with powers of control
leads to the existence of more than one policy.' What we would like to know
is whether the presence of two chauffeurs causes the car to be driven too
fast, too slowly, or too erratically, and what the implications of the
chauffeurs' behavior are for the welfare of the passengers.

Arguments by analogy, however appealing, provide no answer to these
questions. The historian's instinct is to turn to the documents for guidance.
The economist's is to construct a model. We consider these approaches
in turn.

II. The Genoa conference of 1922 and the role for cooperation

When the Genoa Economic and Financial Conference convened in April 1922, European exchange and trade relations were in disarray. Physical devastation in the main theaters of the war created persistent excess demands for foodstuffs and raw materials, particularly in Central and Eastern Europe. Capital goods imports were needed to replace plant and equipment destroyed in the course of the war. Yet the nations of Continental Europe possessed limited resources out of which to finance the required imports. Industrial and agricultural production remained well below 1913 levels.[19] The United States curtailed and quickly eliminated official lending to its European allies, insisted on prompt repayment of its war loans, and constrained Europe's capacity to earn foreign exchange by sharply raising tariff rates. Europe therefore turned to deficit spending to finance economic reconstruction.[20] Some such as the French proceeded on the premise that Reparations payments would eventually permit any new debt to be retired and prewar monetary arrangements to be restored. Others such as the Germans were preoccupied almost entirely by the immediate problem of reconstruction. By the summer of 1920 the mark had already begun its descent; the franc, in contrast, fluctuated uneasily in response to new information about prospects for Reparations.

In Western Europe and the United States, the Armistice had been followed by a sudden and dramatic boom. Consumers finally were permitted to vent demands that had been pent up during the war, and producers took the opportunity to replenish their stocks. In Britain the pressure of demand led to an inflation of prices unprecedented in peacetime. Employment expanded rapidly, and wages rose in response. In light of these inflationary pressures, the Bank of England raised its discount rate in November 1919 and April 1920. Almost simultaneously, industrial production turned down, and unemployment among trade union members rose from 1.4 to 16.7 per cent within a year. Wholesale prices fell by nearly 50 per cent between the spring of 1920 and the beginning of 1922. In France wholesale prices turned down in May, falling by 41 per cent within a year, while the index of industrial production fell by eight per cent between 1920 and 1921. In the United States fluctuations in industrial production, while not as pronounced as in Britain, followed basically the same pattern, while wholesale prices fell by 46 per cent in the 10 months following their May 1920 peak.[21]

As in the 1970s, financial instability impeded efforts to liberalize international trade. Since the major belligerents had all imposed trade controls in the course of the war, they had in place the administrative machinery needed to administer import licensing and quota schemes.

While some such as Britain rapidly moved to dismantle wartime controls, others such as France, which initially emulated the British example, turned back to tariff protection once their currencies began to depreciate. Trade with central Europe was further depressed by the slow recovery of these economies. Together with the embargo on Russian trade, the prospects for an export-led recovery appeared dim.

The Reparations question cast a shadow over attempts at monetary reconstruction and impeded efforts to arrange cooperative solutions to Europe's financial problems. The provisions of the Treaty of Versailles designed to provide a mechanism by which realistic Reparations claims might be negotiated were disabled by the refusal of the US Congress to ratify the Treaty. The Treaty itself deferred final determination of the amount of Reparations but required an initial payment of 200,000 million gold marks, the first installment falling due in May 1921.[22] When the Reparations Commission, staffed not by financial experts but by politicians taking instructions from their governments, finally determined the value of Reparations in April 1921, the amount was fixed at $32 billion, three times the sum recommended by the economic experts at Versailles and a much larger amount than the Germans anticipated. In principle, the transfer might be made by payment in gold, payment in services, or payment in commodities. Yet the Reichsbank's gold reserve barely amounted to one semi-annual Reparations payment. German guest workers would scarcely be welcomed in neighboring countries already experiencing high unemployment. Thus, Germany had no alternative but to attempt to finance its transfer through an export surplus. The value of the transfer Germany might have accomplished given the impact of the surplus on her terms of trade has been debated ever since.[23] The only certainty from the point of view of financial market participants was that the magnitude and timing of Reparations payments would remain uncertain, with unknown implications for the public finances of the major creditor countries.

This was the background against which the Genoa Conference of 1922 was convened. Genoa was only one in a series of international monetary and financial conferences held in the 1920s, and negotiations there were not unrelated to previous meetings at Brussels in 1920 and at Cannes in January 1922. For example, the participants in the Brussels Conference has issued declarations which resembled in general terms the resolutions subsequently adopted at Genoa. However, only at Genoa were the particulars of these proposals specified and methods for implementing them through the international coordination of policies given explicit consideration.

The countries with greatest influence over the proceedings at Genoa were the United States, France and Britain. The three nations approached the Conference with very different objectives. Despite other differences the Americans and the British shared a common interest in rebuilding the international economy. The leaders of both nations agreed that recovery required the revitalization of foreign trade, for which reconstruction of the gold standard was a necessary prerequisite. Beyond these general goals, however, the two sets of policymakers had little in common. The British were willing to go considerably further than the Americans to promote the expansion of trade. They hoped that diplomatic and commercial relations with the Soviet government could be established and that Reparations could be reduced. To facilitate the renegotiation of Reparations, they suggested that the United States forgive at least a portion of its war debt claims. With this groundwork laid, they hoped that the creditor countries would be encouraged to extend loans to the European debtors, promoting economic recovery on the Continent and stimulating international trade.

While restoring sterling's prewar parity was seen as an essential element of monetary reconstruction, the British were wary of the economic costs that the deflation associated with restoration might entail. From their perspective the preferred solution was inflation abroad rather than deflation at home – in particular, inflation in the United States. The British contemplated various schemes to encourage the Americans to inflate, ranging from subtle diplomatic pressure to a far-fetched plan to immediately pay in gold a large share of Britain's war debt in order to drastically expand the American monetary base.[24] This last scheme was dismissed due to the likelihood of American sterilization and its impact on the Bank of England's reserve position. It would be preferable for monetary expansion to be initiated abroad and backed as necessary by reserves of foreign exchange. That a significant portion of foreign exchange reserves would be held in the form of sterling undoubtedly figured in British calculations.[25]

Although the Americans shared Britain's interest in promoting the expansion of world trade, from their vantage point the problem was less pressing. They were willing to participate in discussions of international economic policy only as part of a general settlement. While Herbert Hoover and his Secretary of State, Charles E. Hughes, expressed an interest in convening in what the President termed a 'real honest-to-God economic conference' designed to reestablish fixed exchange rates, international convertibility and free international movement of commodities and gold, they evinced little enthusiasm for meetings like those at Genoa which seemed likely to concentrate on stop-gap measures to be adopted in lieu of balanced budgets or Reparations settlements, and whose success appeared to hinge on American concessions regarding war debts.[26] In the end, Hughes agreed only to send to the Conference as an unofficial observer the American Ambassador to Rome, Richard Washburn Child.

In contrast to the Americans, the French sought to define the agenda for Genoa as narrowly as possible. The French opposed British proposals for universal adoption of nondiscrimination in trade and the most-favored-nation clause, so they sought to discourage discussion of a general convention on trade policy. In contrast they pressed for discussion of sanctions against the Soviet Government on the question of prewar debts.[27] This dispute intensified after January 1922, when Briand's relatively moderate government was replaced by a more nationalistic administration headed by Poincaré, who commenced almost immediately to spar over these issues and Reparations with the equally combative Lloyd George. Poincaré was skeptical about the usefulness of multilateral negotiations and agreed to participate in the conference only on British assurances that France's position on Reparations, the terms of the Treaty of Versailles, and the Russian Imperial Government's debt to France would not be questioned.[28]

The monetary proposals discussed at Genoa originated with the British delegation. In drafting their proposals the British could draw on the First Interim Report of the Cunliffe Committee and on the considerable talents of their monetary specialists, notably Ralph G. Hawtrey, since 1919 Director of Financial Enquires at H.M. Treasury.[29] A number of Britain's Genoa proposals resembled the Cunliffe Committee's recommendations, including the argument that a credible commitment to financial stability required a return to gold.[30] Resurrecting the gold standard, it was stated, required balancing government budgets, insulating central banks from pressure to extend credit to government agencies, and consolidating national debts. Little was novel in these ideas. More novel were the measures first proposed by the Cunliffe Committee and incorporated into the British proposals to economize on the demand for monetary gold: these included eliminating internal circulation of gold coin, concentrating gold reserves at the central bank, and permitting domestic residents to acquire coin and bullion for export only from the authorities. By limiting the use of gold to international settlements, the Cunliffe Committee and the British delegates at Genoa sought to minimize competing demands for reserves.

The British draft was circulated among foreign authorities in February 1922, and in March experts from Belgium, France, Italy and Japan met with British representatives in London to undertake revisions. These proposals were adopted with only slight modification by the Financial Committee at the Genoa Conference in April and by the Conference itself in May.[31]

The Genoa resolutions contained a number of provisions designed to ease the transition to gold. These included the recommendation, ultimately adopted, that governments with significantly depreciated currencies consider stabilizing at a lower rate of exchange. While accepting the argument that prewar parities provided the ideal basis for stabilization, the experts suggested that countries which had experienced sustained inflation might be well advised to avoid the output costs associated with restoring the prewar level of prices. Moreover, they observed that governments would be seriously burdened by the increased real value of internal debt which would result from a substantial reduction in prices.[32] Policymakers were therefore encouraged to stabilize at rates not far distant from those currently prevailing. Significantly for the operation of the interwar gold standard, no sanctions were included to discourage governments from engaging in competitive depreciation.

The Genoa resolutions also contained proposals to economize on the use of gold. The measures proposed by the Cunliffe Committee were altered to meet what the British experts regarded as mounting deflationary pressures. Resolution 9 on currency adopted by the Financial Commission urged governments to establish a mechanism to minimize the need for gold by 'maintaining reserves in the form of foreign balances, such as the gold exchange standard, or an international clearing system.'

It was in this connection that the issue of policy coordination was raised. Monetary authorities were encouraged to coordinate their demands for gold and to avoid the wide fluctuations in internal prices that would otherwise result from the 'simultaneous and competitive efforts of a number of countries to secure metallic reserves.'[33] Thus, central banks were for the first time explicitly urged to desist from the competitive struggle for gold. These proposals for international cooperation were predicated upon the establishment of central banks where they did not exist and on their insulation from political influence or control. Thus, at Genoa countries with relatively stable currencies were therefore urged to adopt institutional arrangements similar to those imposed by the League of Nations upon countries undergoing hyperinflation.

The only resolution on international policy coordination acceptable to all the participating countries was one couched in general terms. While consultation and collaboration were encouraged, no formal mechanism for their practice was specified. Instead, the Bank of England was requested to call an early meeting of central bankers to prepare a convention to implement these measures. An accompanying resolution warned that the success of any such plan was contingent upon the participation of the United States. In the words of the Financial Commission, no scheme for stabilizing prices 'can be fully effective without coordination of policy between Europe and the United States, whose cooperation therefore should be invited.'[34]

There is no question that the economic costs of noncooperative behaviour were clearly understood in 1922. Permitting central banks to engage in a competitive struggle for gold was seen as threatening to transmit deflationary pressures to the world economy and delaying recovery from the War. Multilateral negotiations were seen as the most effective technique for achieving agreement on an acceptable international distribution of reserves. Yet it was far from apparent how agreement on this matter might be reconciled with national autonomy on the question of the level at which to stabilize exchange rates, or how these noble sentiments might be institutionalized. But if the participants in the Genoa Conference lacked a coherent view of how policy coordination might be practiced, they agreed on the principle of responding cooperatively to international financial problems.

Ultimately, even this modest attempt to provide a framework for cooperation proved to be overly ambitious. To the surprise of the participants, the next step in the process, namely the proposed meeting of central banks, was never held. The Bank of England took the initiative of discussing the proposed meeting with the Federal Reserve, whose participation was endorsed by the US State Department. Once the Bank of England's Committee of Treasury approved the tentative invitation drafted by Norman and Benjamin Strong, a meeting seemed imminent.[35] However, efforts to convene the meeting met with political obstacles, and the prospective conference was soon reduced to a mere bargaining chip to be used in disputes over these other concerns. The French ruled out their participation unless Reparations were again excluded from the agenda. The Americans objected that meaningful progress could not be made unless the Reparations question was reopened. In the autumn of 1922 Britain sent a delegation to Washington to discuss funding the British war debt, and the Bank of England's involvement in these negotiations again postponed the meeting of central bankers. France's occupation of the Ruhr in 1923 cast doubt on German participation, and the financial difficulties of Austria and Hungary were the occasion for further delay. By the summer of 1923, enthusiasm for a general convention of central banks had dissipated. This was not to mark the end of financial collaboration, but subsequent exchanges between central banks took place primarily on a bilateral basis.[36]

With the failure of the Genoa Conference to yield even a general framework for international policy coordination, many of the dangers cited by the financial experts quickly came to pass. There were no sanctions to discourage governments from stabilizing at parities which yielded a system of misaligned exchange rates. There was no mechanism for reconciling the competing objectives of national monetary authorities nor to prevent central banks from engaging in what was characterized as a competitive scramble for gold. The implications of noncooperative behavior within the framework of the interwar gold standard would become evident soon enough.

III. Leadership and Cooperation Under the Interwar Gold Standard

A. Motivation

Establishing a basis for cooperation among central banks was clearly one of the principal goals of the policymakers who attempted to lay the foundation for the gold standard's resurrection. Yet the gold standard is typically portrayed as a self-equilibrating mechanism under which external balance is restored to deficit and surplus countries alike through the smooth operation of an anonymously functioning international adjustment mechanism. The very concept of conflicting objectives, much less strategies such as leadership and cooperation, are wholly incompatible with familiar attempts to model the gold standard's operation. These familiar models are simply incapable of addressing the questions at hand.

The purpose of this section is therefore to develop an alternative model of the gold standard with which the issues of leadership and cooperation can be addressed. No attempt is made to capture the operation of the international gold standard in all its complexity, for this is not the model's purpose. Its purpose is rather to provide a simple macroeconomic framework which highlights the channels through which the actions of one country's central bank impinge upon the internal and external position of another and the incentives that these repercussion effects provide the second country to respond to the actions of the first. It strips away complications in order to lay bare the dynamics of strategic interaction and to explore the implications of long-standing arguments about the benefits of leadership and cooperation during the interwar period.

The model is based on the notion that the interwar gold standard can be viewed as an 'international struggle for gold.'[37] Simply put, central banks in our model desire incompatibly large shares of the world's gold reserves. This provides the basis for conflicting objectives and for strategic interaction.

Despite its simplicity, the model generates several useful insights. As in any strategic game in which the players hold conflicting objectives, noncooperative behavior has economic costs compared with cooperative solutions.[38] In our model, central banks incapable of coordinating their policies set their discount rates at undesirably high levels, putting downward pressure on the level of prices and depressing incomes at home and abroad. For example, this is the result at the Nash solution to this noncooperative game. While central bank policy was but one factor at work in the world economy in the 1920s, this result is suggestive when applied to a period marked by historically high discount rates, conflicts among central banks, and steady deflation culminating in a Great Depression.

The Stackelberg leader-follower solution to the two-country model provides a halfway point between the Nash and cooperative equilibria. Compared to the Nash solution, the leader-follower solution is less deflationary and yields higher incomes both at home and abroad. Barring cooperation, the exercise of leadership clearly is in the interest of both players; the question is whether either player will choose to exercise it. In fact, there is an incentive for both players to resist the leadership role. It is a standard (and perfectly intuitive) property of models of symmetrical countries that both players prefer to adopt the same strategy. We show below that the same holds true in a model of asymmetric countries, where one central bank has exceptional power to influence the direction of international capital flows.

In structure the model has much in common with previous analyses of policy coordination (see for example Hamada, 1976 and 1979). It incorporates the assumption that each central bank has more targets than instruments, forcing it to confront the tradeoff between its objectives. This is the assumption of instrument scarcity in whose absence problems of strategy vanish. In addition, it incorporates the assumption that each domestic target variable is affected by the actions of the foreign central bank. This is the assumption of interdependence.

There exists scope for strategic interaction in a model of the gold standard only if central banks can exercise discretion. We will assume that central banks are able to engage in discretionary initiatives to alter the composition of the monetary base through open market operations or changes in fiduciary circulation and to affect the size of the money multiplier through changes in discount rates. While the idea that changes in central bank discount rates affect the relationship between the gold reserve and the money supply is a departure from textbook treatments of the gold standard, it captures the fact that the authorities were capable in the short run of either reinforcing the impact of incipient gold flows on domestic financial markets or neutralizing them through sterilization. In fact, under the gold standard there were important sources of slack in the connection between gold reserves and broadly defined monetary aggregates. Central banks could hold gold in excess of that required to back notes in circulation, enabling them to intervene in financial markets with purchases of bonds and bills and to alter the monetary base without any accompanying change in reserves. Only the need to maintain confidence in the convertibility of the currency placed limits on their discretionary actions. Similarly, commercial banks, even if free of statutory reserve requirements, had an incentive to hold precautionary reserves to guard against unanticipated withdrawals. The size of such precautionary reserves was determined in part by the cost of feasible alternatives, including discounting (in the British case, via discount houses) at the central bank. Under the British banking system, there was a conventional ratio between a bank's cash and its liabilities which was basically the same whether those liabilities were demand or time deposits. Nonetheless, the authorities could influence this ratio and hence affect broadly defined monetary aggregates through changes in the deposit multiplier.[39] This was even more true of the countries of the Continent, where there was typically no conventional or legal relation between reserve assets and deposits.

Each central bank in our model minimizes a quadratic loss function defined over gold reserves and domestic prices. Although the historical record suggests that central bankers followed rules of thumb when setting discount rates, we adopt the assumption of optimizing behavior as a simplifying device. The assumption that each bank has an optimal gold reserve is motivated by the observation that, while a central bank could feel more confident of its ability to defend the convertibility of the currency with a larger gold reserve on hand, it was less profitable to hold barren metal than interest-bearing financial assets.[40]

The idea that central banks maintained a target level for prices is another simplifying assumption. Occasionally it is argued that central banks were concerned ultimately with the domestic currency price of gold and that they desired only to prevent such fluctuations in prices and economic activity as might threaten convertibility. By this interpretation, the price level is properly viewed not as an independent goal of policy but as an intermediate target whose achievement was helpful for attaining the ultimate objective: maintaining convertibility. Yet central banks were under pressure throughout the interwar years to respond actively to internal conditions. The British case provides an illustration of the pressures brought to bear. British central bankers were publicly cautious when relating their policy to the state of the domestic economy. According to Montagu Norman, the Bank of England's interwar Governor, the ill effects of a high Bank Rate on domestic industry and trade were greatly exaggerated and 'more psychological than real.'[41] Of course, by 1930, when this statement was made, the Bank has been subjected to Treasury criticism for more than half a decade; in 1924, a more relaxed time, Norman has expressed concern for the impact of monetary deflation on the state of the economy.[42] The caution that characterized the Bank's public pronouncements by the end of the decade can be seen as a response to the criticism to which it was subjected. Keynes' articles on monetary policy are the best-known examples of the genre.[43] Surely, however, the Bank of England was more profoundly affected by criticism emanating from H.M. Treasury. The principal goals of Treasury policy in the twenties were to retire outstanding debt and to reduce the burden of debt service charges through conversion of the five per cent government loans of 1917 at low interest rates. Debt service had risen from 11 per cent of central government spending in 1913 to 24 per cent in 1920 and more than 40 per cent by the end of the decade.[44] Hence between 1925 and 1929 the Treasury consistently objected to Bank of England initiatives which raised the price and reduced the availability of credit. These objections were often communicated to the Bank directly. For example:

> The Governor of the Bank called at the Treasury on the 2nd December [1925] about 7:15 pm, and informed me that there was every probability that the Bank Rate would be increased...I reported this to the Chancellor on the following morning and he at once telephoned to the Governor that if the rate was raised, he would have to inform the House that it had been done without his being consulted and against his wishes. It was not fair to the Exchequer that action should be taken which affected all its affairs without an opportunity being given to him to consider it. He expressed an earnest request that action should be deferred at any rate for a week, to enable this to be done.[45]

Whatever the central bankers' beliefs about the effects of monetary policy, it is difficult to dispute that such pressures would have encouraged them to act as if they were concerned about the state of industry and trade. In fact, Bank of England reaction functions for the period 1925–31 indicate some sensitivity of discount rate policy to the state of the domestic economy.[46] In what follows, the target of a stable price level can be thought of as shorthand for stable prices, output and employment and, depending on the reader's interpretation of the historical literature, different weights can be attached to internal and external targets without greatly affecting the results.

B. Specification

Consider a world of two identical countries, home and foreign.[47] We log-linearize all relationships and use lower case letters to denote the logs of the variables represented by the corresponding upper case letters, except for interest rates which are always measured in levels. Each country has a model supply M, which can be thought of as an $M1$ or $M2$ measure. This aggregate is the product of the monetary base and the money multiplier V. The base is made up of domestic credit and the central bank's gold reserves. The domestic credit component of the base can be positive or negative, depending on whether central banks hold excess gold reserves or there is a fiduciary issue outstanding. However, to simplify the model we abstract entirely from the domestic credit component of the base.[48]

We assume that a rise in the discount rate, by increasing the cost of rediscounting at the central bank, induces the consolidated banking sector to hold a larger ratio of precautionary reserves to liabilities. Hence the money multiplier depends negatively on the central bank discount rate. Using asterisks to indicate foreign variables, we have:

$$\left.\begin{array}{l} m = -vr + h\bar{g} \\ m^* = -vr^* + (1-h)\bar{g} \end{array}\right\} \tag{1}$$

where v is the elasticity of the money supply with respect to the discount rate r. $\bar{g}$ denotes the log of the world stock of monetary gold, of which shares h and $(1-h)$ are held by the domestic and foreign countries. The demand for real balances is a function of output Y and the market interest rate i:

$$\left.\begin{array}{l} m - p = \phi y - \lambda i \\ m^* - p^* = \phi y^* - \lambda i^* \end{array}\right\} \tag{2}$$

where p and p^* denote logs of domestic and foreign prices respectively. Only mathematical complexity is added by assuming that nominal balances are deflated by a consumer price index comprised of domestic and foreign prices.

Aggregate supply in each country is an increasing function of producer prices:

$$\left.\begin{array}{l} y = y(p) = \gamma p \\ y^* = y^*(p^*) = \gamma^* p^* \end{array} \quad \gamma, \gamma^* > 0 \right\} \tag{3}$$

where for convenience we assume constant elasticities of supply (γ and γ^*) and standardize the normal level of output to unity. These functions can be thought of as the short-run supply curves of an aggregation of profit-maximizing firms confronting predetermined wages or material costs. Rather than introducing costs explicitly, we simply note that the classical full employment model ($\gamma = \gamma^* = 0$) and the Keynesian income-expenditure model ($\gamma = \gamma^* \to \infty$) can be treated as special cases. The short-run focus of the model should be borne in mind in the discussion that follows.

Aggregate demand depends positively on the relative price of imports and negatively on the interest rate. The exchange rate is normalized to unity and suppressed.

$$d = \delta(p^* - p) - Bi$$
$$d^* = -\delta(p^* - p) - Bi^*$$

$$\left.\right\} \tag{4}$$

We close the model with the open interest parity condition on the assumption that nonmonetary assets denominated in the two currencies are perfect substitutes and capital is perfectly mobile.

$$i = i^* \tag{5}$$

The omission of gold production, wealth effects and dynamics of adjustment, to mention but a few complications, is obvious. Many of these complications could be appended to the model. However, our intent here is not to build a complete model but to present a simple analytical framework containing the essential ingredients for the study of a particular historical episode.

We now posit an objective function for each country of the form:

$$U = -[(p - \bar{p})^2 + \omega(h - \bar{h})^2] \tag{6}$$

where ω is the weight attached to gold reserves relative to prices, output and employment.[49] We assume $\bar{h} > \frac{1}{2}$ to capture the idea that the two countries prefer incompatibly large shares of the (log of the) world's stock of monetary reserves – in other words, that the gold standard can be characterized as a competitive struggle for gold. It will be convenient to normalize $\bar{p}$ to zero.

To derive a semi-reduced form expression for h, we set each country's money supply equal to its money demand and take the difference of these two relations.

$$h = 1/(2\bar{g})[\bar{g} + v(r - r^*) + (1 + \phi\gamma)(p - p^*)] \tag{7}$$

Setting aggregate supply (3) equal to aggregate demand (4) and substituting each country's money supply and money demand equations [(1) and (2)] into its goods market clearing condition yields a semi-reduced form for p:

$$p = \Omega[v/2(r + r^*) - \bar{g}/2] \tag{8}$$

where

$$\Omega = \frac{-1}{y + \lambda/B(1 + \phi\gamma)} \quad \Omega < 0$$

It is evident that this model provides the minimal ingredients for a study of interdependence. The first element we require for an analysis of interdependence is that each central bank faces a tradeoff between its target variables. From (7) and (8):

$$\frac{\partial h}{\partial r} = \frac{v}{2} > 0 \quad \frac{\partial p}{\partial r} = \Omega\frac{v}{2} < 0 \tag{9}$$

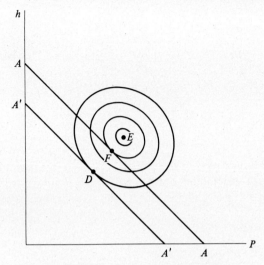

4.1 The home country's objective function

and similarly for the foreign country. A rise in the domestic discount rate decreases the domestic money multiplier, putting downward pressure on the price level, and by reducing domestic money supply relative to domestic money demand attracts gold from the foreign country.

The second element we require is that the target variables in the home country are affected by the actions of the foreign central bank. Again from (7) and (8):

$$\frac{\partial h}{\partial r^*} = \frac{-v}{2} < 0 \quad \frac{\partial p}{\partial r^*} = \Omega\frac{v}{2} < 0 \tag{10}$$

An increase in the foreign discount rate reduces the foreign money multiplier and the foreign money supply, attracting gold from the home country and depressing the world price level. Analogous results hold for the foreign country.

It is worth noting we have here a case of positive international transmission. Initiating an expansionary policy in one country leads to expansion in the other. This result contrasts with the assumption often made about international transmission between the wars: that policy was 'beggar-thy-neighbor' in the sense that expansion in one country caused contraction in the other. The contrast is due to the way we model the international monetary regime: in this model of the 1920s with fixed exchange rates international transmission is positive, while in a comparable model of the 1930s with flexible rates, transmission might well be negative.

The choices confronting central banks can be illustrated with two

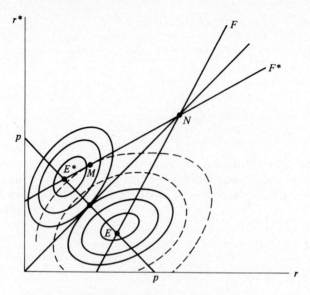

4.2 Home and foreign policy reaction curves

familiar diagrams. From (9), we know that, given r^*, the domestic central
bank can vary r to attain different combinations of h and p. In Figure 4.1,
the frontier of feasible combinations is labelled AA. The optimal setting
for r is one which achieves an $h-p$ combination tangent to an indifference
curve at the point labelled F.

Consider now a rise in r^*. This shifts the AA frontier inward to $A'A'$.
The home country's central bank, faced with a smaller world money
supply, is forced to accept lower prices, smaller gold reserves, or a
combination of the two. As drawn, it moves to a point such as D tangent
to a less desirable indifference curve where both prices and reserves have
fallen.

The same exercises can be conducted for the foreign central bank. The
analysis becomes interesting once we combine the two banks' problems and
consider their interaction. This can be done by transposing the indifference
curves to $r-r^*$ space as in Figure 4.2. We read off from Figure 4.1 the
home country's rankings of different combinations of the two discount
rates. Thus, point E in Figure 4.2 at the center of the home country's solid
indifference curves corresponds to point E in Figure 4.1. The fact that the
foreign central bank's indifference curves lie to the northwest of the home
central bank's indifference curves reflects the assumption that the two
central banks ideally wish to hold incompatibly large shares of the world's

gold stock. This is accomplished when each bank's discount rate is high relative to that of its rival.

The downward sloping pp locus depicts combinations of r and r^* for which a price level $\bar{p}$ obtains. Along parallel lines below and to the left of pp, prices are higher, while above and to the right, prices are lower. With symmetry, the two central banks share a common rank ordering over prices and the pp line has a slope of -45 degrees.

The F and F^* curves in Figure 4.2 are the reaction functions of the two central banks. The F curve, representing loss-minimizing discount rates for the home central bank given the foreign discount rate, is the locus of points where the tangent to the home indifference curve is horizontal. Similarly, the F^* curve is the locus of points where the tangent to a foreign indifference curve is vertical. The reaction functions may be positively sloped, as in Figure 4.2, or negatively sloped. The slopes can be derived by substituting the semi-reduced forms for h and p into the objective function, differentiating with respect to each discount rate and setting the solutions to zero:

$$\left.\frac{\delta r^*}{\delta r}\right|_{F^*=0} = \frac{\omega + \Omega^2}{\omega - \Omega^2} \tag{11}$$

$$\left.\frac{\partial r^*}{\partial r}\right|_{F=0} = \frac{\omega - \Omega^2}{\omega + \Omega^2} \tag{12}$$

Both reaction functions will be positively sloped when the weight attached to gold reserves ω is large relative to that placed on prices. Then each central bank responds to a foreign discount rate increase by raising its own rate, attempting to stem the loss of gold reserves at the cost of still lower prices. Conversely, both reaction functions will be negatively sloped when the weight put on gold reserves is relatively small. In this case, each country responds to a discount rate increase abroad by lowering its discount rate, attempting to reduce the fall in prices at the cost of still lower gold reserves. So long as stability is maintained (as can be shown to obtain under symmetry and under other cases considered below), the analysis is essentially the same.

The discussion to follow will concentrate on the configuration depicted in Figure 4.2. The case of upward-sloping reaction functions, in which each country is inclined to respond to a change in the foreign discount rate in the same direction, appears to be the historically relevant case for the 1920s.

C. Solutions

We can now determine the equilibrium values of r and r^* under different solution concepts. After discussing the outcome under different assumptions, we will ask the question of which solution is likely to obtain.

First, we consider the model's Nash solution at the intersection of the reaction functions. Note that in the symmetrical model the two discount rates are identical at the Nash solution, so the level of prices and reserves will be the same in each country. In particular, since $p = p^*$ at the Nash solution, we can cancel the second additive term in equation (9) when solving for its characteristics. Differentiating the objective function with respect to each discount rate under the assumption that the other discount rate is invariant, setting each solution to zero and equating them yields:

$$r_N = r_N^* = \frac{1}{v}\left[\tfrac{1}{2}\bar{g} + \frac{\omega}{\Omega^2}(\bar{h} - \tfrac{1}{2}) \right] \tag{13}$$

where the N subscript denotes the Nash solution.

Second, we consider the cooperative solution. Under symmetry, each country holds exactly half the world's monetary gold, and prices are again identical in the two countries. The best they can then do is to set their discount rate equal to one another at the level consistent with $p = 0$. Setting (9) equal to zero yields:

$$r_C = r_C^* = \frac{1}{2v}\bar{g} \tag{14}$$

where the C subscript denotes the cooperative solution. From (13) and (14), $r_N > r_C$ so long as $\bar{h} > \tfrac{1}{2}$.

Under symmetry, the Nash and cooperative solutions yield identical distributions of gold. However, under the assumption of Nash behavior, the desire of rival banks to possess incompatibly large shares of the world's gold stock causes both banks to elevate their discount rates above the level consistent with price level $\bar{p}$. Each is subject to the misapprehension that a marginal increase in its discount rate will secure it larger gold reserves at the cost of a relatively small decline in prices. In fact, each discount rate increase elicits an increase in the foreign discount rate, yielding the initiating bank no additional gold reserves but resulting in still lower prices. Thus, the strategic interaction of central banks imparts a deflationary bias to the world economy, given only the assumption that $\bar{h} > \tfrac{1}{2}$.

Finally, we consider the case where the home country acts as Stackelberg leader and the foreign country follows. Substituting the foreign country's reaction function into the home country's objective function and minimizing the loss yields the solution depicted at point M in Figure 4.2, where a home indifference curve is tangent to the foreign reaction function. The home country's central bank recognizes that if it lowers its discount rate the foreign central bank will respond in kind. Hence, it is aware that the loss of gold reserves brought about by its discount rate reduction will be partially offset by the reduction in the foreign discount rate, and that the response of the foreign central bank will yield further benefits by reinforcing the tendency of lower discount rates to raise the world money supply and price level. The leader-follower strategy yields a lower domestic discount rate than the Nash solution, resulting in a higher level of utility for the domestic country, whose loss of gold is more than offset by higher prices, output and employment. The foreign central bank benefits on both counts, since prices are higher and it now obtains a larger share of the world's gold stock.[50]

In this model, the strategic interaction of central banks imparts a deflationary bias to the world economy, assuming only that at the optimum they desire incompatibly large shares of the world's gold stock. Leadership has advantages over other noncooperative strategies: a country which takes its foreign rival's reaction into account can initiate a reduction in discount rates, raising prices and stimulating activity at home and abroad. Cooperation has further advantages over leadership: through cooperation both discount rates can be lowered and the deflationary bias in monetary policy can be eliminated.

D. Sustainable Strategies

To this point we have not addressed the question of which solution is likely to obtain. In this section we first consider this question using the symmetrical model of previous sections which is intended to represent the strategic interaction of two or more comparable financial centers during the interwar years. We then extend the analysis to a simple assymmetrical case intended to capture aspects of the prewar situation.

Assuming that cooperative strategies are not feasible, is the Nash solution or the Stackelberg leader-follower solution likely to obtain? We have noted that both countries benefit with movement from the Nash solution to the leader-follower solution. It is clear also that with upward-sloping reaction functions the follower reaps the greater gains: while both countries benefit from higher prices, only the follower benefits from a larger gold reserve. In Figure 4.2, the gains from discount rate reductions are evenly distributed among countries as they move down the 45 degree line toward the origin. Since the leader-follower solution is on the follower's side of that line, the leader reaps the smaller benefits. As Cooper (1984) suggests, the fact that the follower reaps the larger benefits encourages both parties to engage in a game of 'chicken,' each attempting to force the other to accept the role of leader. There may be extended periods when the Nash solution is observed as this game of 'chicken' is being played out. Clearly this is one way to interpret statements to the effect that the interwar monetary system was characterized by the absence of leadership.

We might attempt to capture the change in structure of international financial markets between the end of the 19th century and the interwar period by adding to the model an asymmetry in the ability of discount rates to influence international capital flows. Assume that the discount rate of the domestic central bank (which might be thought of as the Bank of England) has a larger impact than the foreign discount rate on the domestic money supply (i.e., that $v^* = \theta v$ where $0 < \theta < 1$). In all other respects, including objective functions, the two countries remain the same. Since from (9) and (10) $dh_i/dr_i = -v_i/2$, the domestic discount rate has a larger impact than the foreign discount rate on the international distribution of gold.

Strikingly, introducing this asymmetry into the model does not alter the fact that, in the case of positively-sloped reaction functions, each country prefers its foreign counterpart to play the Stackelberg leader. The intuition is straightforward. For simplicity of exposition, consider the case where v is unchanged from sub-sections B and C above but v^* is now smaller. Since $v^* = \theta v$, we can rewrite equation (1) for the foreign country as:

$$m^* = -v\theta r^* + (1-h)\bar{g} \tag{1'}$$

and leave the rest of the model unchanged. In this case, the model and its solutions are the same, except we can think of the foreign central bank as setting and the domestic central bank as reacting to θr^* rather than r^*. At each solution, the domestic discount rate is the same as in the symmetrical case, while the foreign discount rate is simply θ times its value in the symmetric model. In $r - \theta r^*$ space, the various solutions could be depicted by the symmetrical diagram of Figure 4.2. In $r - r^*$ space, the slope of each reaction function would have to be multiplied by $1/\theta$. All of the conclusions from the symmetric model concerning the gains to Stackelberg leaders and followers continue to hold.

The simple asymmetrical model suggests, therefore, that to the extent that the Bank of England had more power than its foreign counterparts over the direction of gold flows, this would not have encouraged it to exercise leadership in the Stackelberg sense. If asymmetries in economic structure are to provide an explanation for the Bank of England's leadership role, they must be more subtle than the simple asymmetry considered here.

IV The tripartite monetary agreement of 1936 and the role for cooperation

The devaluation of sterling in 1931 marked the end of the truly international gold standard of the interwar years. The Bank of England had succeeded in holding sterling between the gold points during the period 1925–1930 only under considerable duress. The onset of the Great Depression then placed a downward pressure on prices, pushed the government budget into deficit and by the summer of 1931 raised unemployment rates to 20 per cent of the insured labor force. Following financial crises in Austria and Germany and with the Labour and National Government's inability to take convincing steps either to balance the budget or to initiate economic recovery, defense of the sterling parity was abandoned in September. Against the dollar and the currencies of other countries that continued to peg to gold, the pound depreciated by 25 per cent, from $4.86 to $3.75 at the end of the first week of floating.

More than two dozen countries allowed their currencies to depreciate with sterling, among them most of the Empire, Scandinavia, and Eastern Europe.[51] Germany for its part adopted draconian exchange controls and moved increasingly toward a system of bilateral clearing arrangements with its Eastern European trading partners.

The United States broke with gold in 1933. In March, Roosevelt restricted foreign exchange dealings and gold and currency movements, and in April he issued an executive order requiring individuals to deliver their gold coin, bullion and certificates to Federal Reserve Banks. At this point, the dollar began to float. By setting a series of progressively higher dollar prices for gold, the Administration engineered a significant devaluation. The dollar was finally stabilized in January 1934 at $35 an ounce, 59 per cent of its former gold content. The only major currencies that remained freely convertible were those of the Gold Bloc countries: France, Belgium, Holland, Italy, Poland and Switzerland. These countries were willing to go to great lengths to defend their established parities.

Thus, the international monetary system of the mid-1930s was a hybrid of different regimes. Britain was engaged in a managed float administered by the Exchange Equalization Account (EEA). The United States in January 1934 pegged the dollar to gold at the new $35 price but extended convertibility only to countries on the gold standard. France, under the provisions of the monetary law of 1928, was fully on the gold standard and obligated to buy and sell gold without limit at the prevailing price.

As late as the summer of 1936 the official goal of French policy was to defend and maintain the franc Poincaré. Despite the depth of the Depression, the Bank of France continued to respond to gold losses by raising its discount rate. Belgium's devaluation in 1935 served to signal the extent of the franc's overvaluation, and confidence was further undermined by political developments abroad, including Italy's invasion of Ethiopia, Germany's occupation of the Rhineland, and the outbreak of the Spanish Civil War. With the formation of Leon Blum's Popular Front Government in April 1936, pressure on the franc intensified. Blum was pledged to stimulate domestic activity while at the same time maintaining the gold standard parity.[52] Market participants were aware of the incompatibility of these objectives. Blum's proposals had included public works and public employment, a reduction in the length of the work week, paid holidays, universal collective bargaining, and public control of heavy industry and finance. French labor initiated sit-down strikes soon after the election to induce speedy implementation of these measures, and the Bank of France's gold reserves plummeted as a result of capital outflows. The Bank responded by raising its discount rate to 6 per cent, three times the Bank of England's rate. Discreet consideration began to be given to the possibility of devaluation.

As devaluation of the franc came to be seen as probable, French policymakers considered how to capitalize on the situation and foreign policymakers how to minimize the damage. Yet the French position was not without difficulties. One French objective was to devalue by a margin adequate to secure a competitive advantage – in other words, devaluation on the 1920s model. At the same time, they were constrained by the necessity of not arousing the indignation of the electorate or their trading partners. Since the Popular Front had come to power committed to the gold standard, it was desirable that devaluation occur as part of a multilateral system of exchange rate adjustments which laid the basis for a general return to gold. Moreover, given the spectre of 1923 and 1926, the French were concerned that a substantial devaluation might cast doubt on the credibility of any fixed parity and set off a vicious spiral of depreciation. To allay speculation the French therefore proposed that realignment be followed by the establishment of new, more realistic gold standard parities by the Bank of England, Bank of France and Federal Reserve.

In addition to the domestic political situation, the Popular Front had reason to worry about foreign retaliation. Earlier in the decade, France had imposed new commercial restrictions in response to foreign devaluation, leaving her little diplomatic defense against the adoption of comparable measures by the US and UK. Equally worrisome was the danger of competitive devaluation. There was no international code of conduct governing the management of exchange rates. The British EEA could intervene with sales of sterling to push the pound down along with the franc, and if 1933 was any indication the American response might be a further devaluation of the dollar. Hence from the French perspective it was essential before proceeding with devaluation to secure an agreement on acceptable margins of adjustment.

For the British and Americans, the danger attached to a French devaluation was that it was beggar-thy-neighbor policy. To the extent that London and Washington viewed one another as inclined to retaliate against a French devaluation, each feared that its own competitive position would be seriously eroded. Moreover, competitive devaluation would only exacerbate exchange-rate instability and uncertainty, with a depressing impact on trade. For the British, the spectre of a French devaluation raised the further possibility that London's complete control over the foreign exchange value of sterling would be compromised by French intervention directed at other targets.

The US and UK engaged in sporadic negotiations in the spring of 1935, but to little effect since the Americans were primarily concerned to avoid another round of competitive devaluation while the British were primarily concerned to retain their freedom of action. Following the triumph of the Popular Front in 1936, channels of communication between the governments were reopened. The US continued to press for multilateral negotiations over acceptable margins of adjustment, while the UK was willing to go no further than to express its hope that the dollar-pound rate could be held steady so long as devaluation of the franc was moderate.[53] Blum and his ministers couched any discussion of devaluation in terms of a fundamental restructuring of the international monetary order. In early September the French proposed an agreement among the three governments which would specify new bands for the franc, dollar and pound, commit the three governments to collaborative efforts to maintain those rates, bind them not to devalue except by mutual agreement or under exceptional and unforeseen circumstances, and compel them to return to gold convertibility once stability was restored.[54]

The ambitious French proposal was coolly received in London and Washington. The Americans were unwilling to commit to an eventual return to gold or to stabilizing the dollar within a fixed band. Treasury Secretary Morgenthau favored only a mechanism for collaboration among the exchange equalization funds of the three countries and working agreements about the management of rates. The British opposed even more strongly any scheme which threatened to limit their freedom of action.[55] British officials hoped only that Blum and his Minister of Finance Vincent Auriol would devalue the franc in a convincing yet moderate manner, by a margin large enough to induce foreign capital inflows and permit stabilization but small enough to leave unaffected relations between London and Washington.[56]

The French response to these objections was to drop their proposal for fixed bands but to continue advocating an eventual return to gold.[57] However, the Americans and British continued to object to any mention of the gold standard. By the middle of September the French had begun to recognize that the only agreement which might prove acceptable to both London and Washington was one couched in very general terms.[58] Auriol's next proposal was for a single declaration by the three governments pledging to avoid unilateral changes in exchange rates and unnecessary trade restrictions.[59] The Treasuries and central banks of the three countries were to agree to cooperate in managing the exchange markets either through bilateral consultations or multilateral negotiations. This proved an acceptable formula. However, to hasten their appearance, Morgenthau suggested substituting for a document signed by the three governments the simultaneous issuing of separate statements once reference to the particularly contentious issues had been removed.

With all reference to the gold standard and fixed parities eliminated, the Tripartite Declarations, much like the resolutions adopted at Genoa in 1922, amounted basically to three simultaneous statements of willingness to engage in consultations among Treasuries and central banks.[60] No formal mechanism for actually coordinating policies was specified in the documents. Nevertheless, these declarations were seen as essential to insure that the new level for the French franc would be defensible. Otherwise, competitive devaluations would be anticipated by the market and create anticipations of a further devaluation of the franc. In return for extending this expression of cooperation so desired by the French, the Americans and British hoped that they might be able to influence France's choice of parity and prevent an excessive devaluation.

Immediately upon the French devaluation of slightly more than 25 per cent and release of the declarations, continuous cooperation among the exchange equalization funds and central banks of the three countries commenced. Belgium embraced the principles of the agreement one day later, and the Dutch and Swiss governments joined within a month. The agreement was hailed by the press. As the *New York Times* put it, 'A streak of sunlight had broken through the dark clouds of nationalism; International cooperation was still possible.'[61]

In contrast to the aftermath of the Genoa Conference, specific arrangements for day-to-day collaboration followed within a month. Under the provisions of the Gold Agreement Act of October 1936, exchange rates were agreed to daily and the three exchange funds cooperated in market intervention, deciding on a common currency to be bought or sold and settling accounts daily in gold.[62] In this respect, the contrast with 1922 was striking. Part of the explanation for the successful implementation of the

Tripartite Agreement lies in the fact that by 1936 the major political obstacles to collaboration – notably Reparations and war debts – had largely receded from view. At least as important, however, was explicit recognition that the range of issues subject to collaboration would be circumscribed and that nothing in the agreement threatened to undermine each government's independence to formulate domestic policy.

The Tripartite Declarations had warned that although 'in their policy toward international monetary relations [governments] must take into full account the requirements of internal prosperity, the constant object of their policy is to maintain the greatest possible equilibrium in the system of international exchange and avoid to the utmost extent the creation of any disturbance by domestic monetary action.'[63] From this statement it might appear that priority was attached to international policy coordination. In fact, however, internal balance was explicitly recognized as the paramount goal of policy, and the maintenance of international stability was basically a useful ancillary target. As Beyen (1949, p. 112) suggests, policy coordination was seen not as a positive objective of policy but as a negative promise not to indulge in initiatives that might be overly disruptive to the international monetary system.

The international monetary order that emerged from the Tripartite Agreement placed great emphasis on consultation, but beyond efforts to coordinate day-to-day management of the markets placed few restraints on independent action. It provided no mechanism for the formal coordination of monetary or fiscal policies. Nothing in either agreement bound the participating countries to set their exchange rates at current levels. However, under the new arrangement the dollar began to emerge as the link between gold and other currencies, a position it was to hold for more than two decades following the Second World War. The US was by no means bound to stabilize its currency at $35 to an ounce of gold, a price which could be changed on 24 hours notice. But with the passage of time the Administration grew increasingly attached to this rate. With the dollar fixed but adjustable in terms of gold and other currencies adjustable at the beginning of each day in terms of the dollar, the system resembled a hybrid of Bretton Woods (in terms of the relation between gold and the dollar) and a crawling peg (in terms of the relationship between the dollar and other currencies).

By the end of 1936, many of the recommendations put forward at Genoa in 1922 had been implemented but, ironically, at the expense of exchange rate stability. Consultation among governments and central banks, so strongly recommended at Genoa, had been institutionalized under the provisions of the Gold Agreement Act of October. Consultation extended however only to day-to-day management of exchange markets, national governments retaining complete discretion to set their external rates. The dollar-sterling rate was effectively pegged within a narrow band from the French devaluation in 1936 until the second half of 1939, but the French engaged in several substantial devaluations in the second half of 1937 and again in 1938. The gold economy measures urged at Genoa appeared in the form of restrictions on the internal circulation of gold coin and bullion and measures to limit international flows to transactions between central banks and stabilization funds. With the emergence of currency areas centered upon New York, London and, to a lesser extent, Paris, the reserve currency arrangement proposed at Genoa increasingly became a reality. Indeed, to the extent that the dollar was the currency most tightly linked to gold, it began to exhibit features of the unique role as an international reserve currency it was to take on after World War II. The role for policy coordination lay in lending a semblance of order to the currency markets, insuring that retention of a link for gold was consistent with an adequate level of reserves, and discouraging beggar-thy-neighbor policy. The role for exchange rate flexibility was to provide governments with independence of action. We will never know how long this system would have succeeded in reconciling these objectives.

V   Conclusion

The interwar period witnessed experiments with every modern international monetary arrangement: clean floating in the first half of the twenties and a gold exchange standard in the second, managed floating in the early 1930s, and after 1936 the reintroduction of a link with gold and a form of adjustable peg. Whether the regime was based loosely on a system of rules, as in the case of the gold standard, or placed few limits on the discretion of the authorities, as in the case of floating exchange rates, policymakers harbored no illusions that the international monetary arrangement alleviated the problem of interdependence. In each instance they sought to insure exchange-rate and balance-of-payments stability by establishing a framework conducive to international policy coordination.

   A desire for policy coordination is by itself insufficient to insure successful collaboration. The aftermath of the Genoa Conference, when political obstacles impeded efforts to arrange a convention of central banks, illustrates the pitfalls to successful implementation. Ultimately, governments turned to noncooperative strategies within the framework of the gold-exchange standard. The competitive struggle for gold and the deflationary pressures that resulted indicated clearly the advantages of cooperation. Therefore, when France's devaluation in 1936 erased the last vestiges of the interwar gold standard, policymakers once more attempted to establish a framework for coordinated action. On this occasion, not only was the political situation opportune, but in contrast to earlier efforts the negotiators carefully circumscribed the range of issues subject to collaboration and placed relatively few restrictions on each government' s freedom of action. Hence the successful conclusions of the Tripartite Agreement and the Gold Agreement Act.

What emerges clearly from this analysis of the interwar period is the tension which pervades all efforts to coordinate economic policies – a tension which is certainly evident also in the 1980s. Then as now the problem for monetary coordination was how to reconcile the need for freedom of action with the desire for order in foreign exchange markets and with the recognition that national policies have international repercussions. Then as now the institutional response was a hybrid international monetary system combining arrangements for exchange market management with autonomy of national policy, and placing a premium on international policy coordination without providing a mechanism for bringing it about.

NOTES

* This paper was written during visits to Stanford University and INSEE. I am grateful to Paul David and Jacques Melitz for helpful discussions, and to the French Ministry of Foreign Affairs, the French Ministry of Finance and the Controller of H.M. Stationery Office for permission to refer to the Public Records. The French Ministry of External Affairs provided financial support.
1 For example, according to Beyen (1949, p. 28), 'Under a fully automatic standard,' by which he means the prewar gold standard, 'the need for consultation between central banks was, of course, limited.' He tells a story which illustrates central bankers' attitudes toward policy coordination and consultation. It seems to have been the tradition at the Netherlands Bank for the President and the Directors to personally count the bank notes withdrawn from circulation at a meeting held directly after lunch. One day in 1912 or 1913 two Directors of the Reichsbank paid a visit to Amsterdam, and the President of the Bank had the novel idea of taking them to lunch. The conversation was 'highly interesting,' and the President arrived at the bank note meeting fifteen minutes late with what he thought was an adequate excuse. The oldest of the Directors was unappeased and commented, 'Your work is here, not in coffeehouses.'
2 Of course, parallel movements in discount rates could be consistent with the rules of the game if all of the countries considered are either gaining or losing gold to some other country not included in the discount rate comparison. See the discussions in Bloomfield (1959), Morgenstern (1959) and Triffin (1964).
3 For the period of the classical gold standard (1880–1914), Bloomfield (1959) calculates that central banks complied with the rules of the game only 34 per cent of the time. Even the Bank of England, thought to be invested with special

responsibility for managing the system, adhered to the rules only 47 per cent of the time.

4 For example, see the discussions of Bank of England – Bank of France loans in Clapham (1944), volume 2, pp. 329–92 and Sayers (1936), Ch. 5.

5 The trans-Atlantic telephone was still used sparingly between the Wars. The 1936 interchange between Morgenthau and Cochran reported by Clarke (1977) shows that the reason why the Transatlantic telephone was sparingly used was that it was difficult to hear.

6 Moggridge (1972), Ch. 3. Thus, for example, in November 1921 the three Scandinavian central banks informed the Bank of England that, however desirous they were of returning to gold, they felt unable to commit to a parity against gold and the dollar unless the UK did so first. The Americans were aware of the problem; since Montagu Norman immediately sent a copy of the confidential Scandinavian memorandum to Benjamin Strong, Governor of the Federal Reserve Bank of New York. It is not surprising, then, that New York saw Britain's return to gold as a joint operation. Clay (1957), pp. 141–2.

7 A comprehensive analysis would consider also the World Economic Conference held in London in 1933. See Traynor (1949).

8 United Nations (1949), p. 2. International comparisons are provided by Edelstein (1981).

9 On the composition of international reserves before 1914, see Lindert (1969).

10 A typical statement of this conventional wisdom can be found in Cleveland (1976), p. 17. As Keynes nostalgically described the prewar system from his vantage point in 1930: 'In the latter half of the 19th century, the influence of London on credit conditions throughout the world was so predominant that the Bank of England could almost have claimed to be the conductor of the international orchestra. By modifying the terms on which she was prepared to lend...she could to a large extent determine the credit conditions prevailing elsewhere.' Keynes (1930), p. 274.

11 Macmillan Committee evidence of Sir Ernest Harvey, Question 7515, 2 July 1930, reprinted in Sayers (1976), volume 3, p. 205.

12 Committee of Finance and Industry (1931), p. 125.

13 See especially Triffin (1964) and the sympathetic discussion in Ford (1962).

14 It has proven difficult to extract from the historical record convincing evidence in support of this theory. Attempts to plot the UK's terms of trade against levels or first differences in Bank Rate have generally proven inconclusive. See Moggridge (1972), pp. 12–13; Kenen (1960), p. 60; Lindert (1969), p. 44. Moreover, a number of observers of the London money market (Moggridge, 1972; Brown, 1940) have argued that the volume of commercial bills discounted to finance inventory carrying costs was insensitive to interest rate movements. Hence we make no attempt to incorporate this potential asymmetry into the model developed below.

15 Costigniola (1977), p. 1914 and passim; see also Parrini (1969).

16 Trade statistics can be found in Loveday (1931), p. 153. Current account estimates are by the Bank of England from Sayers (1976), vol. 3, pp. 312–3.

17 Bouvier (1981), pp. 5–6.

18 Keynes (1931), p. 211; Macmillan Committee evidence of Sir Ernest Harvey, Question 7515, 2 July 1930, reprinted in Sayers (1976), volume 3, p. 205.

19 League of Nations (1931), p. 17; Svennilson (1954), pp. 233–46.

20 Moulton and Pasvolsky (1932), p. 431.
21 For monthly statistics, see International Conference of Economic Services (1934).
22 For details, see Bergmann (1927).
23 The classic references are of course Keynes (1931) and Ohlin (1929). Recent discussions include Maier (1976) and Silverman (1982).
24 Public Record Office (PRO) T160/5, 'Export of Gold to America,' by R. G. Hawtrey, 5 March 1923.
25 Certain accounts attribute great foresight to the British, suggesting that their enthusiasm for the gold-exchange standard was part of a conscious strategy of relaxing Britain's balance of payments constraint, rejuvenating the City of London, and enhancing the Bank of England's control over international markets. See Costigniola (1977), p. 917.
26 Costigniola (1977), p. 916, Traynor (1949), p. 72.
27 Archives of the French Ministry of Foreign Affairs (Min. Aff. Etr.) B82/112, 'Reunion Interministrielle au sujet de L'Equitable Traitement du Commerce,' 28 January 1922.
28 See the interchange of memoranda between the French and British governments in United Kingdom (1922).
29 PRO T160/5, 'The Genoa Currency Resolutions,' by R. G. Hawtrey, 4 February 1922. See also Hawtrey (1923).
30 See First Interim Report of Committee on Currency and Foreign Exchanges After the War (1918).
31 The various drafts can be found in United Kingdom (1924), p. 59–63. The resolution of the Financial Commission and the Experts' Report appear in Mills (1923).
32 To quote the Report of the Committee of Experts, 'The question of devaluation is one which must be decided upon by each country according to its view of its own special requirements. We think it important however to draw attention to some of the considerations which will necessarily weigh with any country in coming to a decision on this question. There is a prevalent belief that a return to pre-war gold parity is necessary or desirable for its own sake. There are undoubtedly advantages to be obtained by such a return, but we desire to point out that for countries where currency has fallen very far below the pre-war parity, a return to it must involve social and economic dislocation attendant upon continuing readjustment of money-wages and prices, and a continual increase in the burden of international debt. Regard being had to the very large debts which have been incurred since the Armistice by many of the countries concerned, we are inclined to think that a return to the old gold parity involves too heavy a strain upon production. We repeat that the decision must be left in each case to the country concerned...' Mills (1923), p. 369. The French were less enthusiastic than the British about endorsing the option of devaluation, perhaps due to the franc's weakness and the impact of such a position on confidence. They supported devaluation only for cases where it was demonstrably 'impossible' to return to the prewar parity. Min. Fin. Etr. B 82-16/121, Conference Financière, 11 April 1922.
33 Resolution 9, reprinted in Mills (1923), p. 369.
34 *Ibid*, Resolution 10.
35 Clay (1957), p. 158.

36 There were notable exceptions to this rule, such as the meeting held on Long Island in 1927 among representatives of four major central banks. See Eichengreen (1984).

37 The phrase comes from the interchange between Keynes and Norman before the Macmillan Committee. See Question 3490, reprinted in Sayers (1976), volume 3, p. 185. This idea was then adopted in much of the subsequent literature. For example, Cassel (1936, p. 13) remarks 'usually, however, the central banks themselves are responsible for the injurious increase in the demand for gold insofar as they compete with one another in their endeavors to strengthen their reserve.'

38 This ranking necessarily holds only when all the players contribute to the cooperative solution. Thus, for example, cooperation between governments can be welfare reducing in the absence of cooperation between a government and the private sector. Rogoff (1983) provides an example of such an outcome.

39 British conventions regarding reserve ratios are discussed by Beyen (1949), pp. 62–3. See also Balogh (1947). Cairncross and Eichengreen (1983) provide evidence for Britain on the links between the discount rate and the money multiplier. See especially Table A3.1.

40 The Bank of England and the Bank of France remained privately held institutions influenced still by the desire to pay customary dividends to shareholders. While the extent to which the profit motive and public service figured in the authorities' calculations remains difficult to discern, incorporating the profit motive into models of central bank behavior is a step in the direction of realism.

41 See Norman's Macmillan Committee evidence: Committee on Finance and Industry (1931), Questions 3328–3517, 26 March 1930, reprinted in Sayers (1976), volume 3, pp. 12–253.

42 For example, see Norman's statements to the Chamberlain-Bradbury Committee in the summer of 1924, cited in Moggridge (1969), Ch. 2.

43 Formal statements for Keynes' view of the relationship of monetary policy to the state of trade appear in Keynes (1930), while his efforts at pamphleteering are collected in Keynes (1931). Keynes' most accessible account of the channels of transmission came in his private evidence to the Macmillan Committee. See Keynes (1981).

44 See Eichengreen and Giavazzi (1984).

45 PRO T176/13, Leith-Ross Memorandum, 3 December 1925.

46 See Eichengreen, Watson and Grossman (1985).

47 Extending the model to more than two countries adds generality but alters none of the conclusions presented below. See Eichengreen (1984), Appendix B, where a simple three-country model is analyzed. Note also that some implications of relaxing the assumption of identical countries are explored below.

48 The model is readily adapted to the analysis of open market operations, and many of the same conclusions follow. Again, see Eichengreen (1984). An advantage of adding the domestic credit component of the monetary base to the model is that it would permit domestic assets denominated in one country's currency to be held as international reserves by the other. Again, this adds realism to the model but alters none of the conclusions presented below.

49 This formulation, which places the stock of reserves in the authorities' objective function, is in contrast to most previous specifications of policy coordination problems, which typically assume that the authorities have a target balance of payments surplus (i.e., a target for the flow change in reserves). As Niehans

(1968) points out, the specification here would appear to make more sense in a utility-maximizing framework.

50 In the case of negatively sloped reaction functions, the details and implications differ. The domestic central bank realizes that a rise in its discount rate will elicit a reduction in the foreign discount rate, since the foreign country attaches great weight to the stability of prices. The home country's gain from increased reserves more than offsets any loss due to lower prices. In contrast, the foreign country is worse off and unwilling to play the follower. Since both countries prefer to lead, the configuration will be unstable.

51 Hence the movement of the effective exchange rate was somewhat less pronounced; see Redmond (1980).

52 Opposition on the Left to the option of devaluation was based on a recognition that devaluation would only work by reducing real wages, a result which was viewed as unacceptable. Sauvy (1984), volume 1, p. 246.

53 On the reopening of negotiations, see Sauvy (1984), vol. 1, p. 270. On the different national objectives, see Clarke (1977), p. 25.

54 Clarke (1977), p. 34.

55 This is precisely the way they put it to the French. Archives of the French Ministry of Finance (Min. Fin.) B32325, Letter from the Chancellor of the Exchequer, 14 September 1936. Another British concern, sometimes now heard in connection with the European Monetary System, was that the establishment of fixed bands for exchange rates would strengthen the position of speculators by increasing the likelihood of adjustments in one direction, and thereby increase rather than diminish speculative pressures. See Clarke (1977), p. 36.

56 Drummond (1979), p. 9.

57 Min. Fin. B32325, 'Projet des note aux gouvernements Americain et Britannique,' 8 September 1936.

58 PRO T177/31 'Sir Warren Fisher for Mr. Morgenthau,' 14 September 1936, in Telegraphic Correspondence Respecting the Devaluation of the Franc. Printed for the Foreign Office, September 1936.

59 'Secretary of State to Chancellor of the Exchequer,' 20 September 1936, in *ibid.*

60 For the text of the three declarations, see Bank for International Settlements (1937).

61 'Restoring Monetary Order,' *New York Times*, 4 October 1936.

62 The exchange funds informed one another each morning of the currency in which they proposed to deal. If the other parties agreed to the currency and the rates, a gold price was specified at which each central bank would exchange foreign currency for gold at the close of the business day. This price was subject to change at the beginning of the next trading day. See PRO T177/33, 'Cypher Telegram to Mr. Mallet (Washington),' 7 October 1936.

63 See Bank for International Settlements (1937).

REFERENCES

Balogh, Thomas (1947). *Studies in Financial Organization*. Cambridge: National Institute of Economic and Social Research.

Bank for International Settlements (1937). *The Tripartite Agreement of September 25, 1936 and Subsequent Monetary Arrangements*. Basel: BIS.

Bergmann, Carl (1927). *The History of Reparations*. Boston: Houghton Mifflin.

Beyen, J. W. (1949). *Money in a Maelstrom*. London: Macmillan.

Bloomfield, Arthur (1959). *Monetary Policy Under the International Gold Standard, 1880–1914*. New York: Federal Reserve Bank of New York.

Bouvier, Jean (1981). 'A Propos de la Strategie D'Encaisse (or et devises) de la Banque de France de 1928 à 1932.' University of Paris-I, unpublished.

Brown, W. A. (1940). *The International Gold Standard Reinterpreted*. New York: National Bureau of Economic Research.

Cairncross, Alec and Barry Eichengreen (1983). *Sterling in Decline: The Devaluations of 1931, 1949 and 1967*. Oxford: Basil Blackwell.

Clapham, J. A. (1941). *The Bank of England.* Cambridge, Cambridge University Press.

Clarke, S. V. O. (1967). *Central Bank Cooperation, 1924–1931*. New York: Federal Reserve Bank of New York.

(1973). 'The Reconstruction of the International Monetary System: The Attempts of 1922 and 1933.' *Princeton Studies in International Finance* No. 33.

(1977). 'Exchange-Rate Stabilization in the Mid-1930s: Negotiating the Tripartite Agreement.' *Princeton Studies in International Finance* No. 41.

Clay, Henry (1957). *Lord Norman*. London: Macmillan.

Cleveland, Harold van B. (1976). 'The International Monetary System in the Interwar Period,' in Benjamin Rowland (Ed.). *Balance of Power or Hegemony: The Interwar Monetary System*. New York: New York University Press.

Committee on Currency and Foreign Exchanges After the War (1918). *First Interim Report*. Cd. 9182, London: HMSO.

Committee on Finance and Industry (1931). *Report*, Cmd. 3897. London: HMSO.

Cooper, Richard N. (1984). 'Economic Interdependence and the Coordination of Economic Policies.' Harvard Institute of Economic Research Discussion Paper, forthcoming in Peter B. Kenen (ed.). *Handbook of International Economics*. Amsterdam: North Holland.

Costigniola, Frank (1977). 'Anglo-American Financial Rivalry in the 1920s.' *Journal of Economic History*, **37**, pp. 911–34.

Eichengreen, Barry (1981). 'Sterling and the Tariff, 1929–32.' *Princeton Studies in International Finance* No. 48.

(1984). 'Central Bank Cooperation Under the Interwar Gold Standard.' *Explorations in Economic History*, **21**, 64–87.

Eichengreen, Barry and Francesco Giavazzi (1984). 'Inflation, Consolidation or Capital Levy? European Debt Management in the 1920s.' Harvard University and University of Venice, unpublished.

Eichengreen, Barry, Mark W. Watson and Richard Grossman (1985). 'Bank Rate Policy Under the Interwar Gold Standard: A Dynamic Probit Model,' (forthcoming).

Ford, Alec (1962). *The Gold Standard: Britain and Argentina*. Oxford: Clarendon Press.

Gayer, A. D. (1937). *Monetary Policy and Economic Stabilization*. London: Black.

Hamada, K. (1976). 'A Strategic Analysis of Monetary Interdependence.' *Journal of Political Economy*, **84**, pp. 677–700.

(1979). 'Macroeconomic Coordination and Strategy Under Alternative Exchange Rates.' In Rudiger Dornbusch and Jacob A. Frankel (Eds.), *International Economic Policy: Theory and Evidence*. Baltimore: Johns Hopkins University Press.

Hawtrey, Ralph G. (1923). Monetary Reconstruction. London: Longmans, Green.

International Conference of Economic Services (1934). *International Abstract of Economic Statistics*. The Hague: ICES.

Kenen, Peter B. (1960). *British Monetary Policy and the Balance of Payments*. Cambridge, Massachusetts: Harvard University Press.

Keynes, John Maynard (1930). *A Treatise on Money*. London: Macmillan.

(1931). *Essays in Persuasion*. London: Macmillan.

(1981). *Activities, 1929–1931: Rethinking Employment and Unemployment Policies*. In Donald Moggridge (Ed.), *The Collected Writings of John Maynard Keynes*, Vol XX, Cambridge: Macmillan and Cambridge University Press for the Royal Economic Soceity.

League of Nations (1931). *Course and Phases of the World Economic Depression*, Geneva: League of Nations.

Lindert, Peter (1969). 'Key Currencies and Gold, 1900–1913.' *Princeton Studies In International Finance* No. 24.

Loveday, A. (1931). *Britain and World Trade*. London: Longmans, Green.

Maier, Charles (1976). *Recasting Bourgeois Europe*. Princeton: Princeton University Press.

Mills, J. Saxon (1922). *The Genoa Conference*. New York: Dutton.

Moggridge, Donald E. (1969). *The Return to Gold, 1925*. Cambridge: Cambridge University Press.

Moggridge, Donald E. (1972). *British Monetary Policy, 1924–1931*. Cambridge: Cambridge University Press.

Morgenstern, Oskar (1959). *International Financial Transactions and Business Cycles*. Princeton: Princeton University Press.

Moulton, H. G. and Leo Pasvolsky (1932). *War Debts and World Prosperity*. Washington, D.C.: The Brookings Institution.

Nevin, Edward (1955). *The Mechanism of Cheap Money*. Cardiff: University of Wales Press.

Niehans, Jurg (1968). 'Monetary and Fiscal Policies in Open Economies Under Fixed Exchange Rates: An Optimizing Approach.' *Journal of Political Economy*, **76**, pp. 893–920.

Ohlin, Bertil (1929). 'The Reparation Problem: A Discussion.' *Economic Journal*, **39**, pp. 172–8.

Parrini, Carl P. (1969). *Heir to Empire: United States Economic Diplomacy, 1916–1923*. Pittsburgh: University of Pittsburgh Press.

Redmond, John (1980). 'An Indicator of the Effective Exchange Rate of the Pound in the 1930's.' *Economic History Review*, pp. 83–91.

Rogoff, K. (1983). 'Productive and Counterproductive Monetary Policies.' International Finance Discussion Paper 223 (Board of Governors of the Federal Reserve System). December.

Sauvy, Alfred (1984). *Histoire Economique de la France entre les Deux Guerres*, Paris: Economica (second edition).

Sayers, Richard S. (1936). *Bank of England Operations, 1890–1914*. London, P. S. King.

Sayers, Richard S. (1976). *The Bank of England 1891–1944*. Cambridge: Cambridge University Press.

Silverman, Dan P. (1982). *Reconstructing Europe After the Great War*, Cambridge, Massachusetts: Harvard University Press.

Svennilson, I. (1954). *Growth and Stagnation in the European Economy*. Geneva: United Nations.

Traynor, Dean E. (1949). *International Monetary and Financial Conferences in the Interwar Period*. Washington, D.C.: Catholic University of America Press.

Triffin, Robert (1964). 'The Myth and Realities of the So-Called Gold Standard.' In *The Evaluation of the International Monetary System: Historical Reappraisal and Future Perspectives*. Princeton: Princeton University Press.

United Kingdom (1922). *Correspondence between His Majesty's Government and the French Government Respecting the Genoa Conference*. Cmd. 1742. London: HMSO.

     (1924). *Papers Relating to International Economic Conference, Genoa, April–May 1922*. Cmd. 1667, London: HMSO.

United Nations (1949). *International Capital Movements During the Inter-War Period*. New York: United Nations.

Viner, Jacob (1932). 'International Aspects of the Gold Standard.' In Quincy Wright (Ed.), *Gold and Monetary Stabilization*, Chicago: University of Chicago Press.

COMMENT WILLEM H. BUITER

This paper represents a very successful attempt to apply the perspectives of two distinct disciplines – history and economics – to the problem of international macroeconomic policy co-ordination. The period that is studied, the years between the two world wars, is a very eventful one, and Professor Eichengreen's historical narrative alone makes this a worthwhile paper. What stands out, however, is the careful and well-motivated attempt to use simple formal economic theory and game theory to bring out systematic features of the interwar experience and to draw conclusions for international policy coordination now and in the future.

One may disagree with the details of Eichengreen's attempt to model the stylized facts of the interwar policy game. It must surely be agreed, however, that unlike many attempts at an inter-disciplinary or multi-disciplinary approach, where the whole turned out to be less than any single constituent component, the contribution of the present paper is more than the sum of its historical and economic parts.

The paper starts with a useful reminder that even during the 'classical' gold standard years (1880–1913) the world was never blessed with an efficient, quasi-automatic mechanism for coordinating the actions of national monetary authorities. There is ample anecdotal evidence and quite a bit of supporting statistical material on discount rate movements to support the view that the rules of the gold standard game were frequently flouted by central banks intent on neutralizing rather than accommodating or reinforcing the effects of their counterparts.

The formal modelling exercise in Section IIIB, is intended to apply only to the gold exchange standard in the second half of the twenties and possibly to the pre-1913 gold standard. It is not applicable to the fairly free float of the early twenties and the managed floating of the early thirties.

A properly functioning gold standard corresponds to the Stackelberg leader-follower solution in Eichengreen's model while the Pareto-inferior Nash-Cournot equilibrium characterizes the competitive struggle for gold of the interwar gold exchange standard. Even the Stackelberg solution has a deflationary or contractionary bias (relative to the cooperative solution) as the two players boost their discount rates to attract a larger share of the given world stock of gold. I like the outcome a bit better than the inputs, but as there are certain to be many ways of generating the same kinds of reaction functions and similar relationships between the Nash, Stackelberg and cooperative equilibria, this need not be a very serious criticism.

Eichengreen uses a static, deterministic, linear-quadratic two player game. The economic environment of the players is a two-country, 'Keynesian' IS-LM-aggregate supply curve model with a fixed exchange rate and perfect capital mobility. Each country's monetary authority has a 'domestic' target price level and a 'external' target share of the fixed world stock of reserves. Having the price *level* rather than the rate of inflation as a target is necessitated by the static nature of the approach. The choice of the price level rather than the level of output or employment as the domestic target seems potentially misleading. Depending on the source of the shock, the pursuit of price level stability through monetary policy may increase output instability (the case of a supply shock) or reduce it (the case of demand shock). I am also a bit worried about the authorities' apparent ability to keep their discount rates systematically below or above the market-determined interest rate.

When Eichengreen considers the asymmetric leader-follower game, the assumption is maintained that only gold functions as an international reserve asset. The role of Sterling as a supplementary reserve asset for the 'follower' countries before World War I and the role of the US dollar after World War II suggests a way of introducing asymmetries into the behavioural equations of the model that may be superior to the differential impacts of discount rates on money supplies considered by Eichengreen.

At the very beginning of the paper, reference is made to the view that '...international policy coordination is most readily achieved under a rules-based regime rather than one that depends on discretion.' The words 'rules' and 'discretion' have been used and interpreted in many different ways. In the context of dynamic game theory, policy behaviour is said to be governed by rules if credible, binding commitments can be made today concerning future moves or actions. The future move in question need not be an unconditional one, but could be a contingent response to exogenous events (states of nature) or to actions by other players. Discretion applies when a sequence of policy actions is constrained by the inability to make credible, binding commitments.

While effective cooperation and international policy coordination clearly presuppose behavior governed by rules, not all behavior governed by rules need be cooperative or desirable. Also, the characterization of the (ideal) gold standard as 'based loosely on a system of rules' and of a floating exchange rate regime as placing 'few limits on the discretion of the authorities' seems incorrect. Clearly, the behavior of national money stocks or of discount rates could be governed by a set of rules while the exchange rate floats freely. Whether these rules are specified in terms of prices, of quantities or of some function of prices and quantities is a separate issue altogether. The IMF's 'exchange rate surveillance' since the advent of floating in the early seventies, represents an attempt to impose rules of good neighborly behavior on the international community when major currencies float more or less freely.

A further relevant issue not addressed by the paper concerns the magnitude of the gain from leadership or cooperation. The unambiguous rank ordering of Nash, Stackelberg and cooperative equilibria doesn't add up to a strong case for policy coordination until the likely empirical magnitude of the gains has been quantified. The important task of measuring the gains from internalizing the macroeconomic policy externalities in the interwar period still remains to be done.

The interwar policy makers and advisors clearly recognized the monetary and fiscal prerequisites for a successful operation of the gold standard. First, monetary policy must be directed to the maintenance or restoration of 'fundamental' equilibrium in the balance of payments. This requires that monetary policy not be subject to short-term political pressures, i.e. a *de facto* independent Central Bank. Such independence is not credible if the outstanding debt-output ratio is high and current and prospective public sector deficits are so large that further borrowing is impossible or prohibitively costly. The pressure to monetize the deficit would become irresistible. Balanced budget fiscal policy is a simple, if crude, way to rule out unsustainable deficits and the threat of future monetization. While it is possible, in principle, to design more flexible, contingent monetary and budgetary policy rules that permit survival of the fixed exchange rate regime while retaining the capacity for appropriate stabilizing fiscal and monetary responses to internal or external shocks, the historical record of attempts at 'firm but flexible' policy design is not too encouraging. It is to be hoped that our attempts to sail between this Scylla and Charybdis will be more successful than those in the twenties and thirties.

COMMENT JO ANNA GRAY

In his paper on policy coordination, Barry Eichengreen reviews and analyzes the international financial history of the late 1900s and the interwar years, with emphasis on the later period. The objective of this analysis is '...to see what light this experience sheds on current concerns over international policy coordination.' In discussing the interwar period, Eichengreen draws an analogy (attributed to Edward Nevin) between the international financial system of that time and '...a car with two drivers...' – the two drivers being, in this case, Britain and the United States. He goes on to say that 'What we would like to know is whether the presence of two chauffeurs causes the car to be driven too fast, too slowly, or too erratically, and what the implications of the chauffeur's behavior is for the welfare of passengers.'

This discussion begins by summarizing Eichengreen's analysis of the interwar period and his conclusions concerning the deflationary bias of that period. Using Eichengreen's model, we then offer an explanation – different from Eichengreen's – for the fact that discount rates over this period frequently moved together rather than in opposite directions. And, finally, we turn to the question of what helpful lessons policy makers today may draw from the analysis of this paper.

The theoretical core of Eichengreen's paper is a two-country model that is designed to illustrate the consequences of the conflicting objectives of central banks during the late 1920s. The model assumes a fixed exchange rate and a gold standard. Domestic monetary authorities manipulate money supplies (through the central bank discount rate) in order to stabilize price levels and achieve target levels of gold stocks. The inefficiencies associated with non-cooperative behavior in this model have two sources. First, each country's monetary policy affects the price level and gold stock of the other country; that is, there are externalities associated with the use of each country's policy tool. Second, the gold stock targets of the two countries sum to more than the available stock of gold; the countries' objectives are inconsistent.

The question of whether the non-cooperative Nash solution to Eichengreen's model is too inflationary or too deflationary – that is, whether the car is driven too fast or too slowly – has an unambiguous answer in this model. The car is driven too slowly. This conclusion may be demonstrated with the following reasoning: A Pareto-efficient solution to this problem is one in which each country achieves its desired price level, but in which the two countries split evenly the available gold stock – each obtaining less than its target amount of gold. This solution can be reached through cooperation, but is not easily sustained since each country has an incentive to raise its discount rate above the level consistent with this solution in an effort to obtain more gold. A rise in either country's discount rate imposes negative externalities on the other country (a lower gold stock and a lower price level), necessarily lowering the other country's welfare. The Nash solution is reached when the negative price level effects associated with additional unilateral increases in discount rates outweigh the (ultimately unrealized) benefits associated with increased gold-reserves. Clearly, then, the Nash solution is 'too' contractionary since it involves higher discount rates for both countries than would be obtained under cooperation.

More formally, the deflationary bias inherent in the Nash solution to Eichengreen's model is illustrated in his figure 4.3. There, the Nash solution is given by the intersection of the two countries' reaction functions, F and F^*. The cooperative solution discussed above lies midway between the two bliss points, E and E^*, along the pp locus. It is evident from the diagram that the Nash solution produces lower levels of utility for policy makers in both countries than does the cooperative solution.

Figure 4.2 also provides us with a convenient vehicle for evaluating one of the paper's major themes: The fact that discount rates frequently moved in the same direction during the interwar period is taken throughout the paper as evidence of lack of cooperation between central banks. While this conclusion may follow in more traditional analyses of the gold standard, it does not necessarily follow in the game theoretic framework adopted by Eichengreen. In fact, his model can be used to show that discount rates may covary positively across countries, *regardless of whether policy makers cooperate or not*.

To see this, consider a stochastic version of Eichengreen's model in which each country's money and goods markets are subject to random disturbances. These disturbances may be global in nature (affecting both countries in the same way) or country-specific (directly affecting only one of the two countries). Thus, for example, the money demand functions for the two countries might be respecified as follows:

$$\left. \begin{array}{l} m-p = \phi y - \lambda i + \alpha + \mu \\ m^* - p^* = \phi y^* - \lambda i^* + \alpha + \eta \end{array} \right\} \qquad (2')$$

Here α is the global disturbance and μ and η are uncorrelated country-specific disturbances. It can be shown that the r-intercept of the home country's reaction function F is a decreasing function of α and μ and that the r^*-intercept of the foreign country's reaction function F^* is a decreasing function of α and η. Consequently, individual realizations of these disturbances will produce equilibrium movements of r and r^* in the same direction. This will be true regardless of whether the equilibrium concept employed is the Nash solution or the cooperative solution[1] to the model. Thus, the stochastic version of Eichengreen's model does not necessarily lead one to conclude that a positive covariance of central bank discount rates is evidence of non-cooperative behavior.

To conclude this discussion, we turn briefly to the question of the relevance of Eichengreen's analysis the 1980s. As his paper demonstrates, explicitly modelling the game aspects of international policy coordination can provide fresh insights into the issues involved. This is likely to be as true when considering the 1980s as when considering the interwar years. The applicability of this paper to the current situation is, however, considerably limited by both the special nature of the model employed and by the substantial differences in circumstance prevailing during these two periods of time.

Eichengreen's model takes as given the 'rules of the game'. Those rules include not only fixed exchange rates but a gold standard. The situation today is one in which policy makers appear to be searching for Pareto-improving rules of the game. Recent work in this area suggests that two important determinants of the choice of rules are (i) the economic structures of the countries under consideration and (ii) the objectives of policy makers. Eichengreen does not explore in any detail the economic structure of the world economy during the interwar period. However, it is unlikely that further effort along these lines would produce considerably greater understanding of the today's situation. The structure of labor, goods, and capital markets have changed considerably over the past fifty years. It is also the case that policy makers' objectives differ a great deal from what they appear to have been in the 1920s; targeting levels of gold reserves is no longer an important objective for most countries. These dissimilarities in structure and objectives are likely to severely limit the useful information that can be gleaned from the experience of the 1920s concerning the optimal choice of policy regimes today.

NOTE

1 There are of course an infinite number of Pareto-efficient cooperative solutions to this model. They compose the contract curve. In this discussion, 'the' cooperative solution refers to that point on the contract curve at which the gains from cooperation are equally divided between the two countries.

5   Policy coordination and dynamic games

MARCUS MILLER AND MARK SALMON*

Introduction

The conventional theory of economic policy has been revised to take account of forward-looking expectations formed in the private sector and John Driffill (1982) has shown how 'rational' expectations in the foreign exchange market affect optimal monetary policy in a small open economy. For large open economies with substantial spillover effects, policy may need to take into account overseas reactions. National policy makers may thus find themselves in a strategic relationship with each other as well as with private market speculators.

In a number of papers Koichi Hamada analysed the relations between national economic policy makers as a static game, contrasting non-cooperative Nash or Stackelberg outcomes with those which might be achieved by co-operation, see Hamada (1979) and references therein. Recently, Oudiz and Sachs (1984) have made a bold attempt to estimate the potential benefits of international policy co-ordination, treating policy formation as a static game.

The dynamic aspects of economic interdependence emphasised by Hamada and Sakurai (1978) have invited the application of dynamic game theory, where policy makers minimise costs over an extended period of time. The papers by Sachs (1983) and Turner (1984) effectively complement the work of Hamada and Sakurai by treating the policy variables as the instruments in a Nash dynamic game.

While it is true that these models include dynamic elements, they exclude strategic 'asymmetries': no country acts as a Stackelberg leader, and there are no forward-looking elements in private sector behaviour to take account of in designing policy. (The exchange rate is determined only by the current account, assuming zero capital mobility.) In an earlier paper, Miller and Salmon (1983), methods for solving dynamic games with both of these characteristics were described, with particular emphasis on the analogy between a Stackelberg leader in an open loop dynamic game and a government announcing policy to a market with forward looking expectations. It was noted that such 'asymmetries' lead to the *time inconsistency* of optimal policy – the temptation for a leader to depart from previously announced plans when the announcement effects of policy upon 'forward looking' followers have been achieved.

In the absence of precommitment, however, such time inconsistent optimal policy lacks credibility. In this paper, therefore, we focus on how various *time consistent* solutions may be obtained and computed for situations involving both strategic asymmetry and forward-looking expectations.

To characterise the relations between policy makers, we examine first the symmetric equilibria of Nash differential games, both open and closed loop. We then consider the open and closed loop Stackelberg equilibria arising when one of the players is elevated to the status of leader, but constrained to implement time consistent policies. As between the governments and forward looking markets (here the foreign exchange market) two alternatives are considered. Either policy makers treat the path of the exchange rate as given in determining their policy, or the exchange rate is taken to be a given linear function of the state of the system.

A general description of the various solutions obtained in this way is provided in Section 1 with technical details available in the Annex. In the following section a two-country version of the model proposed in Buiter and Miller (1982) is introduced and a number of these equilibria computed and compared given fairly standard objectives with respect to the control of inflation and output. This relatively unfavourable performance of co-ordinated policy in this application doubtless reflects the absence of any long run 'conflict of objectives', a point to which we return in conclusion.[1]

I Time consistent equilibria

After a brief account of the linear dynamic system and the quadratic costs to be minimised, we describe a number of time consistent equilibria, which follow from varying both relationships prevailing between the policy makers themselves as well as those prevailing between the policy makers and private markets. Technical details are available in the Annex.

(a) Linear dynamics and quadratic costs

Throughout this paper we assume a constant parameter linear differential equation system of the form

$$Dx(t) = Ax(t) + B_1 u(t) + B_2 v(t) \qquad (1)$$

where $x(t)$ is a vector of 'state' variables

$u(t)$ is the vector of 'control' variables associated with player 1

$v(t)$ is the vector of 'control' variables associated with player 2

D is the differential operator, $Dx \equiv \dfrac{d}{dt}(x)$.

The state vector $x(t)$ is partitioned between those variables $x_1(t)$ which are predetermined at time t, and those $x_2(t)$ which are not. The latter represent forward-looking asset prices which discount expected future events and move flexibly as 'news' about such events arrives. (Time subscripts may be omitted from the vector notation where convenient.)

Each of two policy makers ('players') minimises a quadratic cost function over an infinite horizon, viz.

$$V_i(t_0) = \int_t^\infty [x^T(s)\, u^T(s)\, v^T(s)]\, Q_i \begin{bmatrix} x(s) \\ u(s) \\ v(s) \end{bmatrix} ds \quad i = 1, 2 \qquad (2)$$

where Q_i is positive semi definite, $i = 1, 2$

Q_{1uu}, Q_{2vv} positive definite

and the integral is assumed to converge without discounting.

(b) Strategic relations between policy makers

To focus upon the relationships between policy makers, we first describe open and closed loop Nash and Stackelberg differential games on the assumption that the entire state vector is predetermined.

The Nash equilibria are familiar, see Basar and Olsder (1982), and can be briefly described. The first occurs when each player takes the entire future path of the other's controls as given when computing his or her own controls. Thus in choosing $u(t)$, $t \geqslant t_0$ to minimise $V_1(t_0)$ subject to the dynamics of the system described by equation (1) player one takes $x(t_0)$ and $v(t)$, $t \geqslant t_0$ as given; while player two in minimising $V_2(t_0)$ takes as given the path for $u(t)$, $t \geqslant t_0$. The *Open Loop Nash* equilibrium is defined by the requirement that the control path which each player takes as predetermined should match what the other player chooses as optimal.

The second form of Nash equilibrium which we compute occurs when each player responds to the current state of the system and recognises that the other player is responding likewise. Specifically player 1 minimises V_1 by choosing a closed loop or feedback rule for u on the hypothesis that player two operates a linear rule $v = R_2 x$, while player 2 minimises V_2 assuming $u = R_1 x$. The *Closed Loop Nash* equilibrium is defined by the requirement that the feedback rule either player assumes for the other should in fact be the optimal current state feedback rule for that other player. While it is straightforward to compute the open loop Nash solution for a linear quadratic game, the feedback rules required for the closed loop solution have to be found iteratively. The procedure used in this paper is to compute optimal rules $\hat{R}_1$, $\hat{R}_2$ for players one and two conditional on some arbitrary initial values for R_1 and R_2 (typically zero). These optimal rules replace the initial estimates, and this procedure is repeated until convergence is achieved.

So far both players have been treated symmetrically but we now consider the consequences of one player acting as a Stackelberg leader. One immediate consequence is that if player 1 is in the position of announcing at t_0 a path for his controls $u(t)$, $t \geqslant t_0$, conditional upon which player 2 will choose $v(t)$, $t \geqslant t_0$, the optimal path for u is *time inconsistent*; so that recalculating an optimal plan at a later date $t_1 > t_0$ will not produce a continuation of the chosen path for u.

Simaan and Cruz (1973), who used the maximum principle to compute the time inconsistent optimal solution for the linear quadratic Stackelberg differential game, argued that *time consistent* optimal plans could be obtained by using dynamic programming methods (cf. also Cruz (1975) for a general discussion of the class of Stackelberg equilibria generated in this way).

However, Cohen and Michel (1984) have recently shown that the maximum principle may also be used to obtain the time consistent solution for the *Open Loop Stackelberg* game by imposing an appropriate constraint on the leader's optimisation. Thus while choosing u to minimize $V_1(t_0)$ subject to

$$Dx = Ax + B_1 u + B_2 v \tag{3}$$

given $x(t_0)$ and the follower's first order conditions, namely

$$\partial H^2/\partial v = 0 \rightarrow v = R_{vx} x + R_{vu} u + R_{vp_2} p_2 \tag{4}$$

$$Dp_2 = \partial H^2/\partial x \tag{5}$$

where p_2 are the follower's costate variables and

$$H^2 = [x^T u^T v^T] Q_2 \begin{bmatrix} x \\ u \\ v \end{bmatrix} + p_2^T Dx$$

is the follower's Hamiltonian generates the time inconsistent solution, they argue that the optimal time consistent solution can be obtained by choosing u to minimise $V_1(t_0)$ given $x(t_0)$ subject to (3), (4) and the constraint that

$$p_2 = \theta x \tag{6}$$

where θ is chosen so that the solution also satisfies equation (5).

Table 5.1. *Varieties of non-cooperative behavior*

| Objectives[1] (Value functionals to be minimised) | Strategic constraints[2] | | | |
| | Symmetric Games | | Asymmetric Games[3] | |
	Open Loop Nash	Closed Loop Nash	Open Loop Stackelberg	Feedback Stackelberg
Player 1 $\min_u V_1(t_0) = \int_{t_0}^{\infty} [x^T u^T v^T] Q_1 \begin{bmatrix} x \\ u \\ v \end{bmatrix}$	path for $v(t), t \geqslant t_0$ treated as open loop	$\left.\dfrac{\partial v}{\partial u}\right|_x = 0$ $v = R_2 x$	$v = [R_{vu}\, R_{vx}\, R_{vp_2}] \begin{bmatrix} u \\ x \\ p_1 \end{bmatrix}$ $p_2 = \theta x$	$v = [R_{vu}\, R_{vx}\, R_{vp_2}] \begin{bmatrix} u \\ x \\ p_2 \end{bmatrix}$ $v = R_2 x$
Player 2 $\min_v V_2(t_0) = \int_{t_0}^{\infty} [x^T u^T v^T] Q_2 \begin{bmatrix} x \\ u \\ v \end{bmatrix}$	path for $u(t), t \geqslant t_0$ treated as open loop	$\left.\dfrac{\partial u}{\partial v}\right|_x = 0$ $u = R_1 x$	path for $u(t), t \geqslant 0$, treated as open loop	$\left.\dfrac{\partial u}{\partial v}\right|_x = 0$ $u = R_1 x$

Notes: [1] The symmetric matrices Q_1, Q_2 are subject to positive definiteness conditions
[2] Other non-strategic constraints include the state equation and the initial conditions
[3] Player 1 acting as leader

It is clear that the result is time consistent, since substitution of (4) and (6) into (3) implies that the leader faces an orthodox single controller problem. The remarkable feature of Cohen and Michel's procedure is that it generates the 'dynamic programming' solution, because the constraint on p_2 reflects the restriction on the leader's choice of controls imposed by Bellman's principle of optimality. (The calculation of the appropriate value for θ may be achieved by using the iterative procedures already mentioned.)

The last time consistent equilibrium to be described is for a Stackelberg game where each player is aware of the other's feedback rule, but the leader is, in addition, able to exploit the follower's reaction function, see Basar and Haurie (1982). It is the leader's ability, by his current choice of u, to affect the follower's choice of v that makes the game asymmetric and distinguishes it from the closed loop Nash equilibrium. Thus while player 2 minimises V_2 subject to $u = R_1 x$, the leader minimises V_1 subject to both $v = R_2 x$ and (4), the follower's reaction function. The *Feedback Stackelberg* equilibrium is defined by the requirement that the feedback rules assumed for the other player are optimal for that player.

In table 5.1 we summarise the strategic constraints which these four relationships impose on the optimisation problem facing each player, in addition to the state equation (3) and the initial value $x(t_0)$ common to both players. The conditions which must be satisfied in equilibrium by the feedback rules, R_1, R_2, and the time consistency constraint, θ, appearing in the Table are spelt out in Annex 1.

(c) Policy co-operation with market anticipations

In this section we consider co-operative equilibria calculated by postulating a single 'policy-coordinator' who minimises the weighted sum of V_1 and V_2 given a state vector which contains 'forward-looking' asset prices, x_2, as well as predetermined variables, x_1.

If the policy co-ordinator, starting at time t_0 and acting as a Stackelberg leader *vis-à-vis* private markets, were to choose paths $u(t), v(t), t \geqslant t_0$ so as to minimise the weighted sum of $V_1(t_0)$ and $V_2(t_0)$ subject to all of the state equations

$$Dx_1 = A_{11} x_1 + A_{12} x_2 + B_{11} u + B_{12} v \tag{3a}$$

$$Dx_2 = A_{21} x_1 + A_{22} x_2 + B_{21} u + B_{22} v \tag{3b}$$

given $x_1(t_0)$, with $x_2(t_0)$ responding to the announced policy, then the resulting plan would be time inconsistent in the absence of precommitments. So we seek time consistent alternatives.

One is the 'loss of leadership' solution proposed by Buiter (1983) where the policy coordinator treats the path of asset prices as predetermined when designing policy. Specifically the weighted sum of $V_1(t_0)$ and $V_2(t_0)$ is minimised subject to (3a) (the state equations for x_1), but given $x_1(t_0)$ and $x_2(t)$, $t \geqslant t_0$. Equilibrium is defined by the requirement that the assumed path of asset prices be a correct discounting of the chosen policy, so that the remaining state equations for x_2 will also be satisfied. As the label suggests, this approach achieved time consistency by denying the leader the asymmetric position initially assumed, and postulating instead a type of Nash equilibrium.

Time consistent policy which is compatible with strategic asymmetry may, however, be determined by applying Bellman's principle of optimality. Proceeding by analogy with Cohen and Michel (1984), we assume that co-operative policy will, in this infinite horizon linear-quadratic context, be constrained to a fixed linear feedback rule, which may be found by replacing the state equations (3b) in the time inconsistent solution by an appropriate constraint of the form

$$x_2 = \theta_0 x_1 \tag{7}$$

so co-operative policy will minimise the weighted sum of $V_1(t_0)$ and $V_2(t_0)$ subject to (3a) and (7), given $x_1(t_0)$. As for the analogous open loop Stackelberg constraint, equation (7) must in equilibrium generate values for x_2 which correctly discount the optimal policy, so that the remaining state equations are satisfied. The calculation of θ_0 is discussed further below and in Miller and Salmon (1985).

(d) Non-cooperative policy with market anticipations – a summary

Finally we consider the nature of the time consistent equilibria which arise from various forms of non-cooperative behaviour in a dynamic setting with forward-looking financial markets. A summary is presented in Table 5.2, which indicates the constraints on optimisation.

The derivatives appearing in the first two rows come from the strategic constraints shown in Table 1 above. Thus the entries in the top of column (1) indicate that, for the Open Loop Nash game where player one takes the other's control $v(t)$, $t \geqslant t_0$ as predetermined, both $\partial v/\partial u$ and $\partial v/\partial x_1$ are assumed to be zero by player one. In columns (2) and (4) we show the feedback coefficients assumed by each player to characterise the behaviour of the other in closed loop equilibrium.

Where player one acts as a Stackelberg leader, he or she can exploit the reaction function of the follower, namely

$$v = R_{vu} u + R_{vx} x + R_{vp_2} p_2$$

so that the term $\partial v/\partial u$ is no longer zero in columns (3) and (4). In the open

Table 5.2. *Non-cooperative time-consistent solutions*

		Relation between policy makers			
		Symmetric		Asymmetric[b]	
Strategic Constraints on Optimisation[a]		(1) Open Loop Nash	(2) Closed Loop Nash	(3) Open Loop Stackelberg	(4) Feedback Stackelberg
On Player One	$\left.\dfrac{\partial v}{\partial u}\right|_{x_1}$	0	0	R_{vu}	R_{vu}
	$\dfrac{\partial v}{\partial x_1}$	0	R_2	R	R_2
On Player Two	$\left.\dfrac{\partial u}{\partial v}\right|_{x_1}$	0	0	0	0
	$\dfrac{\partial u}{\partial x_1}$	0	R_1	0	R_1
On Both Players[c]	$\dfrac{\partial x_2}{\partial x_1}$	$0/\theta_0$	$0/\theta_0$	$0/\theta_0$	$0/\theta_0$

Notes: [a] x_1 denotes predetermined state variables, x_2 'asset prices'
[b] Player one acting as leader
[c] Arising from alternative assumptions as to the relationship between policy makers and forward looking asset prices.

loop Stackelberg case, the leader uses this reaction function together with the constraint that

$$p_2 = \theta x$$

in calculating the feedback rule for the follower.

It is important to note that the relevant state vector for all the feedback rules is only x_1. As we indicate symbolically in the last line the variables x_2 are *either* treated as predetermined *or* as linear functions of x_1, given by

$$x_2 = \theta_0 x_1$$

as discussed in the preceding section.

II Anti-inflationary monetary policy in a two-country setting

The notion that a floating exchange rate would ensure that money was neutral in its effects was challenged by Dornbusch (1976) who, in a model with floating rates and perfect capital mobility, showed that temporarily rigid ('sticky') goods and/or factor prices were enough to ensure substantial non-neutrality in the short run. Hamada and Sakurai (1978), in a two-country model with the same short run stickiness of nominal factor prices but with zero capital mobility, showed how domestic monetary policies could generate spillover effects overseas despite freely floating rates.

It is naturally a matter of some interest to see what such interdependence implies for the design of policy in general and for the gains to policy co-ordination in particular. While non-cooperative commercial policy can evidently inflict considerable welfare losses, recent analysis using the Hamada/Sakurai framework (of countries linked *only* by trade in goods) suggests that this may not carry over to macroeconomic policy coordination, see Paul Turner (1984). In this paper, therefore, we investigate some implications of policy interdependence on an environment where two countries (with a floating exchange rate but sticky factor/goods prices) are linked by both trade and capital flows – indeed capital is assumed to be perfectly mobile.

The structure used is that developed for one country in Buiter and Miller (1982), to which the reader is referred for more complete discussion. Briefly, there is a 'Keynesian' determination of aggregate production, an augmented Phillips curve governing inflation, and perfect capital mobility with forward looking expectations in the foreign exchange market. (The design of time inconsistent optimal policy in a single open economy of this sort has already been comprehensively analysed by Driffill (1982)).

(a) Economic model and policy objectives

Definition of variables, and of notation used

i rate of change of consumer price index
π 'core' inflation
y output (in logs), measured from 'natural rate'
z integral of past output
c 'competitiveness' for home country (in logs), i.e. real price of foreign goods
r real consumption rate of interest
p_s costate (for state variable s)
H Hamiltonian

Table 5.3. *Economic model and policy objectives*

Home Country	Overseas Country
Model Structure	
Static Equations	
Aggregate Demand[a]	
$y = -\gamma r + \delta c + \eta y^*$	$y^* = -\gamma r - \delta c + \eta y$
Phillips Curve	
$i = \phi y + \sigma Dc + \pi$	$i^* = \phi y^* - \sigma Dc + \pi^*$
Core Inflation	
$\pi = \xi\phi z + \xi\sigma c$	$\pi^* = \xi\phi z^* - \xi\sigma c$
Dynamic Equations	
Accumulation $Dz = y$	$Dz^* = y$
Arbitrage $E[Dc] = r - r^*$	
Economic Policy	
Loss Function	
$\min_{r} V \equiv \dfrac{1}{2}\displaystyle\int_{t}^{\infty} \beta\pi^2 + y^2$	$\min_{r^*} V^* \equiv \dfrac{1}{2}\displaystyle\int_{t}^{\infty} \beta\pi^{*2} + y^{*2}$
Hamiltonian	
$H = \dfrac{\beta\pi^2 + y^2}{2} + p_z\,Dz + p_{z^*}\,Dz^*$	$H^* = \dfrac{\beta\pi^{*} + y^{*2}}{2} + p_{z^*}^{*}\,Dz^* + p_z^{*}\,Dz$

Note: [a] By substitution $y = -\kappa\gamma r - \kappa\eta\gamma r^* + \kappa(1-\eta)\,\delta c$, $y^* = -\kappa\gamma r^* - \kappa\eta\gamma r$ $-\kappa(1-\eta)\,\delta c$ where $\kappa \equiv (1-\eta^2)^{-1}$

V Loss function, integral of costs
D differential operator, $Dx = dx/dt$
E expectations operator

subscript a denotes average
subscript d denotes difference
superscript * denotes variable pertaining to foreign country

The equations of the model are listed in Table 5.3. The first pair of equations show local output being 'demand determined' where demand depends on the real consumption rate of interest, on the real exchange rate and on the level of real output overseas. (This is something of a 'reduced form' where the dependence of demand on local output has been solved out.) The next pair of equations show that the rate of change of the consumer price index in each country depends on demand pressure, on 'core' inflation and on the change in the real exchange rate (where σ represents the share of imports in the price index).

Core inflation is itself determined as the weighted sum of two components:

a backward looking integral of past output and the current level of the real exchange rate. The latter is in turn a 'forward looking' integral of expected international real interest rate differentials, as implied by the arbitrage condition.

We characterise the stance of domestic monetary policy simply by the level of the domestic real interest rate, and it is assumed that policy makers aim to minimise the undiscounted integral of a quadratic function of output and core inflation. Although no direct 'costs' are attached to the level of the real interest rates, the structure of the model implies that welfare in each country depends on domestic and overseas interest rates, in addition to the 'state variables' z, z^* and c.

(b) Co-ordinated Policy

It is easiest to begin the study of policy design with cooperative behaviour for, as we have seen, this can be treated as a single-controller problem by the convenient fiction that a 'policy co-ordinator' chooses r and r^* to minimise the weighted average of national welfare costs, V and V^*.

The necessary conditions for such a coordinator minimising an equally weighted sum are shown in Table 5.4, for the time-inconsistent optimal policy on the right and for time consistent policy on the left. Note that time consistency has been achieved by simply dropping p_c, the costate variable for the real exchange rate, and replacing this by the assumption that the latter is a stable function of the state variables, i.e.

$$c = \theta_1 z + \theta_2 z^*$$

(The appropriate choice of θ_1, θ_2 to ensure that Bellman's principle is satisfied are discussed below). For the 'Nash' time consistent alternative, where the policy co-ordinator treats the real exchange rate as completely predetermined independently of his actions and of the state variables, the necessary conditions are obtained by setting θ_1 and θ_2 to zero, in Table 5.4.

The numerical results[2] produced by the choice of an arbitrary, but plausible, set of parameter values namely

$$\beta = \phi = \xi = 1, \gamma = \delta = \tfrac{1}{2}, \eta = \tfrac{1}{3}, \sigma = \tfrac{1}{10},$$

are shown in Table 5.5. While all three policies possess a stable root of unity, time inconsistent policy has two others larger in absolute size. Each of the two time consistent policies has only one other stable root, less than unity in absolute size in both cases.

The Riccati coefficients in the table describe how the real exchange rate is related to the state variables along the stable path associated with these roots, and the so-called reaction coefficients provide the same information

Table 5.4. *Coordinated policy*

Time consistent	Time inconsistent

Hamiltonian

$$H = \frac{1}{2}\left(\frac{\beta^2 + y^2}{z}\right) + \frac{1}{2}\left(\frac{\beta\Pi^{*2} + y^{*2}}{z}\right)$$
$$+ p_z y + p_{z*} y^*$$

$$H = \frac{1}{2}\left(\frac{\beta^2 + y^2}{z}\right) + \frac{1}{2}\left(\frac{\beta\Pi^{*2} + y^{*2}}{z}\right)$$
$$+ p_z y + p_{z*} y^* + p_c c$$

First order conditions

$$\frac{\partial H}{\partial r} = -\kappa\gamma(\tfrac{1}{2}y + p_z)$$
$$-\kappa\eta\gamma(\tfrac{1}{2}y^* + p_{z*}) = 0$$

$$\frac{\partial H}{\partial r} = -\kappa\gamma(\tfrac{1}{2}y + p_z)$$
$$-\kappa\eta\gamma(\tfrac{1}{2}y^* + p_{z*}) + p_c = 0$$

$$\frac{\partial H}{\partial r^*} = -\kappa\gamma(\tfrac{1}{2}y + p_{z*})$$
$$-\kappa\eta\gamma(\tfrac{1}{2}y + p_z) = 0$$

$$\frac{\partial H}{\partial r^*} = -\kappa\gamma(\tfrac{1}{2}y^* + p_{z*})$$
$$-\kappa\eta\gamma(\tfrac{1}{2}y + p_z) - p_c = 0$$

$$-Dp_z = \tfrac{1}{2}\beta\xi\phi\pi + \theta_1 H_c$$

$$-Dp_z = \frac{\partial H}{\partial z} = \tfrac{1}{2}\beta\xi\theta\pi$$

$$-Dp_{z*} = \tfrac{1}{2}\beta\xi\phi\pi^* + \theta_2 H_c$$

$$-Dp_{z*} = \frac{\partial H}{\partial z^*} = \tfrac{1}{2}\beta\xi\phi\pi$$

where

$$H_c \equiv \frac{\partial H}{\partial c} = \tfrac{1}{2}\beta\xi\sigma(\pi - \pi^*)$$
$$+ \kappa\delta(1-\eta)\left(\frac{y + y^*}{2} + p_z - p_{z*}\right)$$

$$-Dp_c = \frac{\partial H}{\partial c} = \tfrac{1}{2}\beta\xi\sigma(\pi - \pi^*)$$
$$+ \kappa\delta(1-\eta)\left(\frac{y + y^*}{2} + p_z - p_{z*}\right)$$

Notes: State variables z, z^*, c
Costate variables p_z, p_{z*}
In equilibrium $c = \theta_1 z + \theta_2 z^*$

State variables z, z^*, c
Costate variables p_z, p_{z*}, p_c

for the real interest rates. Thus for the 'Nash' equilibrium tabulated in column (a) we found

$$\begin{bmatrix} c \\ r \\ r^* \end{bmatrix} = \begin{bmatrix} -0.835 & 0.835 \\ 1.048 & 0.285 \\ 0.285 & 1.048 \end{bmatrix} \begin{bmatrix} z \\ z^* \end{bmatrix}$$

As might be expected from the symmetry of the two economies, for all three solutions we find z and z^* have Riccati coefficients which are equal but of opposite sign and possess symmetric reaction coefficients.

These coefficients are used to calculate the initial values shown in the lower half of the table, assuming an inherited rate of core inflation of 10% in the home country and zero overseas. All three policies respond with real interest rates of about 10% at home and 3% overseas, which implies an initial loss of competitiveness of about 8% for the inflationary economy.

From the last line of the table is is apparent that there is little difference

Table 5.5. *Coordinated policy*

	Time consistent		Time inconsistent optimal policy
	(a)	(b)	
Roots			
Averages	-1.0	-1.0	-1.0
Differences	-0.913	-0.842	$-1.200, -1.667$
Ricatti Coefficients			
$\theta_1, \theta_2, (\theta_3)$	-0.835, 0.835	-0.790, 0.790	-0.833, 0.833, 3.333
Reaction Coefficients			
$\rho_1, \rho_{12}, (\rho_{13})$	1.048, 0.285	0.999, 0.334	0.994, 0.388, -6.444
$\rho_{21}, \rho_{22}, (\rho_{23})$	0.285, 1.048	0.334, 0.999	0.388, 0.944, 6.444
Initial Value			
$z, z^*, (p_c)$	10, 0	0, 0	10, 0, 0
c	-8.36	-7.90	-8.33
r, r^*	10.48, 2.85	9.99, 3.34	9.44, 3.89
y, y^*	-9.56, -0.44	-9.21, -0.79	-9.17, -0.83
π, π^*	9.16, 0.84	9.21, 0.79	9.17, 0.83
Welfare Costs			
Average of V and V^*	22.96	23.03	22.92

Notes: (a) Path of real exchange rate assumed to be exogenously given in designing policy. (b) Path of real exchange rate assumed to be a linear function of stable state variables.

Table 5.6. *Time consistent coordinated policy*

Averages	Differences
Model Properties	*Model Properties*
$\pi_a = \xi\phi z_a$	$\pi_a = \xi\phi z_a + 2\xi\sigma c$
$Dz_a = y_a$	$Dz_a = y_a$
	$Dc = r_d = \dfrac{2\sigma c}{g} - \dfrac{(1+\eta)}{\delta}\,y_a$
First Order Conditions	*First Order Conditions*
$y_a = -2p_c$	$y_a = -2p_d$
$-Dp_a = \tfrac{1}{2}\beta\xi\phi\pi_a$	$-Dp_d = \tfrac{1}{2}\beta\xi\phi\pi_a + 2\theta_1 H_c$
	$H_c = \tfrac{1}{2}\beta\xi\sigma\pi_a + \dfrac{(1+\eta)}{\delta}\left(\tfrac{1}{2}y_a + p_d\right)$
Adjoint Equations	*Adjoint Equations*
$\begin{bmatrix} Dz_a \\ Dp_a \end{bmatrix} = \begin{bmatrix} 0 & -2 \\ -\tfrac{1}{2}\beta^3\xi^2\phi^2 & 0 \end{bmatrix}\begin{bmatrix} z_a \\ p_a \end{bmatrix}$	$\begin{bmatrix} Dz_a \\ D_c \\ -Dp_d \\ 0 \end{bmatrix} = \begin{bmatrix} 0 & 0 & 0 & -2 \\ 0 & 2\delta/\gamma & 3(1+\eta) & 0 \\ \tfrac{1}{2}\beta\xi^2\phi^2 & \beta\xi^2\phi\sigma & 0 & 2\theta_1 \\ \tfrac{1}{2}\xi\sigma\phi & \beta\xi^2\sigma^2 & 0 & -1 \end{bmatrix}\begin{bmatrix} z_a \\ c \\ p_d \\ H_c \end{bmatrix}$
so $\lambda_a = -\sqrt{/\beta\xi\phi^2}$	
Stable roots	*Stable roots*
(see text for parameter values)	
$\lambda_a = -1$	$\begin{cases}\lambda_a = -0.913 \text{ where } \theta_1 = 0 \\ \lambda_a = -0.842 \text{ where } \theta_1 = C_{21}\,C_{11}^{-1} = -0.79\end{cases}$

between the welfare costs arising under these policies. That the time inconsistent policy should generate the least cost is only to be expected. What is of more interest is that the time consistent 'Stackelberg' equilibrium is dominated by the 'Nash' equilibrium in this case.

The distinction between these last two policies can best be seen by a transformation of variables.[3] By forming 'averages', so $y_a = \frac{1}{2}(y+y^*)$, and 'differences', $y_d = y-y^*$, and assuming $\theta_1 = -\theta_2$, the system under control is decomposed into two separate blocs each involving but a single stable root, as shown in Table 5.6.

The system of averages with its root of unity is common to both time consistent solutions. Since the stable eigenvector is $\begin{bmatrix} 1 \\ \frac{1}{2} \end{bmatrix}$ this implies that $y_a = -z_a$; so the world average recession is equal in percentage terms to world average inflation, both declining with a unit root. Where the policies are distinct, of course, is in connection with the exchange rate which enters the other sub-system. To obtain the 'Nash' equilibrium, the parameter θ_1 in Table 5.6 is set equal to zero, which generates a root of -0.913, as we have seen, and a Riccati coefficient of -0.835, as $c = -0.835$ $(z-z^*) = -0.835\, z_d$ along the stable path. If one constrains the value of $\theta_1\ (=-\theta_2)$ assumed by the policy co-ordinator to match the Riccati coefficient of the system, one obtains the root of -0.842 and the Riccati coefficient of -0.79 which characterise the time consistent Stackelberg equilibrium.

(c) Non-cooperative policy

The solutions which emerge when the national policy makers set real rates in a non-cooperative fashion are examined in this section and provide some surprises.

Where the two monetary authorities are on an equal strategic footing the necessary conditions for optimisation for the resulting Nash games are given in Table 5.7. For the *Closed Loop Nash* equilibrium the overseas authority acts as if $r = \rho_{11}z + \rho_{12}z^*$ and the home government acts as if $r^* = \rho_{21}z + \rho_{22}z^*$, where these feedback coefficients satisfy constraints discussed in the Annex. For the *Open Loop Nash* game, of course, these feedback coefficients are omitted.

As before, two variants of the perceived relationship between policy makers and the foreign exchange market may be considered. If the monetary authorities take the exchange rate as predetermined in designing interest rate policy (so θ_1 and θ_2 are zero in Table 5.7), the result of decentralising policy is easy to describe. It has no effect! Both non-cooperative Nash equilibria will be the same as that shown for co-ordinated policy in the first column of Table 5.5. The reason for this is

Table 5.7. *Time consistent symmetric (Nash) game*[a]

Home Country	Overseas Country
First Order Conditions (10 equations)	

$$\frac{\partial H}{\partial r} = -\kappa\gamma(y+p_z)$$
$$-\kappa\eta\gamma p_{z*} = 0$$

$$-Dp_z = \beta\xi\phi\pi + \theta_1 H_c$$
$$+\rho_{21} H_{r*}$$

$$-Dp_{z*} = \theta_2 H_c + \rho_{22} H_{r*}$$

where
$$H_{r*} \equiv \kappa\eta\gamma(y+p_z) - \kappa\gamma p_{z*}$$
$$H_c \equiv \beta\xi\sigma\pi$$
$$+\delta(1+\eta)^{-1}(y+p_z-p_{z*})$$

$$\frac{\partial H^*}{\partial r^*} = -k\gamma(y^*+p_{z*}^*)$$
$$-\kappa\eta\gamma p_z^* = 0$$

$$-Dp_{z*}^* = \beta\xi\phi\pi^* + \theta_2 H_c^*$$
$$+\rho_{12} H_r^*$$

$$-Dp_z^* = \theta_1 H_c^* + \rho_{11} H_r^*$$

where
$$H_r^* \equiv \kappa\eta\gamma(y^*+p_{z*}^*) - \kappa\gamma p_z^*$$
$$H_c^* = -\beta\xi\sigma\pi^*$$
$$-\delta(1+\eta)^{-1}(y^*+p_{z*}^*-p_z^*)$$

Model Structure
(7 equations)
(IS)[b] $y = -\gamma r + \delta c + \eta y^*$
(CI) $\pi = \xi\phi z + \xi\sigma c$
(Accumulation $Dz = y$)
(Arbitrage) $Dc = r - r^*$

$y^* = -\gamma r^* - \delta c + \eta y$
$\pi^* = \xi\phi z^* - \xi\sigma c$
$Dz^* = y^*$

Notes:
[a] *VARIABLES*
'State' variables (3) z, z^*, c
'Costate' variables (4) $p_z, p_{z*}, p_z^*, p_{z*}^*$
'Output' variables (10) $r, r^*, y, y^*, \pi, \pi^*, H_{r*}, H_c, H_r^*, H_c^*$
[b] By substitution: $\quad y = -\kappa\gamma r - \kappa\eta\gamma r^* + \kappa(1-\eta)\delta c,$

$$y^* = -\kappa\eta\gamma r - \kappa\gamma r^* - \kappa(1-\eta)\delta c, \kappa \equiv \frac{1}{(1-\eta)^2}$$

that ignoring the impact of interest rates on the exchange rate leaves the authorities free to neutralise the impact of foreign rates on domestic output. The latter is then steered along the optimal path, whatever the behaviour of foreign rates.

Where the policy makers do take account of the effect of interest rates on the exchange rate, then the outcomes are as shown in the first two columns of Table 5.8, where the time consistent constraint on optimisation $c = \theta_1 z + \theta_2 z^*$, is restricted to match the Riccati coefficients (and the parameter values are as before). In comparison with the coordinated policy outcome shown in column 2 of Table 5.5, the roots have moved closer together and the matrix of the reaction coefficients has a more dominant diagonal. The general nature of the policy response to $z(t_0) = 10\%$, $z^*(t_0) = 0$ is, however, much as before, with real rates being set at 10%

Table 5.8. *Time consistent non-cooperative solutions*[a]

	Symmetric equilibria				Asymmetric equilibria			
	Open-Loop Nash		Closed-Loop Nash		Open-Loop Stackelberg		Feedback Stackelberg	
Roots								
Averages	−0.981		−0.972		−0.9719		−0.9669	
Differences	−0.896		−0.882		−0.8873		−0.8839	
Ricatti Coefficients								
θ_1, θ_2	−0.825	0.825	−0.820	0.820	−0.812	0.826	−0.814	0.820
Reaction Coefficients								
ρ_{11}, ρ_{12}	1.024	0.284	1.012	0.284	0.994	0.282	1.000	0.283
ρ_{21}, ρ_{22}	0.284	1.024	0.284	1.012	0.285	1.024	0.284	1.012
Initial Values								
z, z^*	10	0	10	0	10	0	10	0
c	−8.25		−8.20		−8.14		−8.14	
r, r^*	10.24	2.84	10.12	2.84	9.94	2.85	10.00	2.84
y, y^*	−9.38	−0.42	−9.30	−0.42	−9.21	−0.42	−9.21	−0.42
π, π^*	9.17	0.83	9.18	0.82	9.19	0.81	9.19	0.81
Welfare Costs								
V, V^*	45.79	0.14	45.81	0.14	45.85	0.16	46.06	0.14
Average of V and V^*	22.97		22.98		23.00		23.09	

Notes: [a] Real exchange rate assumed to be a linear function of the stable state variables ($c = \theta_1 z + \theta_2 z^*$).

at home and about 3% overseas, leaving the domestic economy 'uncompetitive' by about 8%.

The welfare costs are correspondingly not very different, but they are in fact marginally *lower* for decentralised policy that was the case for coordinated policy. The reason why the best efforts of the policy coordinator may fail to improve welfare is that the values of θ_1, θ_2 taken as predetermined do in fact vary with the structure of decision making.

In the remainder of Table 5.8 we report the time consistent solutions for asymmetric games with the home country acting as Stackelberg leader. In these cases $\theta_1 \neq \theta_2$, and the reaction coefficients are no longer symmetric.

Given that the overseas reaction function is of the form $r^* = -\eta r + \left(\dfrac{1-\eta^2}{\gamma}\right)(p_{z^*}^* + p_z^*) + \dfrac{(1-\eta)}{\gamma}\delta c$ the necessary conditions for the *Feedback Stackelberg* solution are obtained from those for Closed Loop Nash by adding an extra term $-\eta H_{r^*}$ to the expression for $\partial H/\partial r$ in the top left of the Table 5.7. For *Open Loop Stackelberg* the necessary conditions for Open Loop Nash are modified in the same way and in addition terms equivalent to ρ_{21} and ρ_{22} in Table 5.7 are calculated from the reaction function above and the Riccati coefficients for $p_{z^*}^*$, p_z^* and c. The numerical results for the asymmetric equilibria hardly differ from those for their symmetric counterparts also appearing in Table 5.8. Perhaps the most interesting feature to note is that the costs to the Stackelberg leader *increase* in each case (compare values for V in columns one and three, and in columns two and four). As in the policy co-ordination problem treated earlier, it seems preferable *not* to adopt a leadership role.

(d) Summary and Interpretation of Results

Key features of four of the outcomes can be seen by charting the loss of competitiveness in the home country against z_d the 'difference' between cumulated excess demand at home and overseas. (Only those solutions which share a common unit root for the 'averages' are shown in Figure 5.1, which is not to scale.)

In all four cases there is a significant initial loss of competitiveness. The path starting from A representing the time inconsistent policy is, unlike the others, governed by two stable roots and consequently shows a changing ratio of competitiveness to z_d. This ratio moves towards (minus) 1 as the trajectory approaches asymptotically the $45°$ line (which happens to be the eigenvector associated with the smaller of the two stable roots).

The time inconsistency of this policy is immediately apparent: reoptimisation at t_1, when z_d has reached $z_d(t_1)$, would lead to the selection of a new path, shown as a dotted line, with a starting point on a ray joining

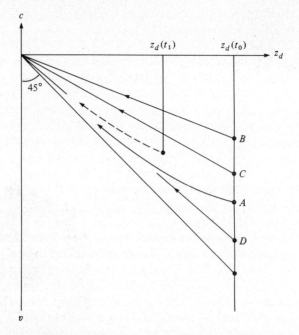

loss of competitiveness

Key:
A: Time Inconsistent Optimal Co-ordinated Policy
B: Time Consistent Co-ordinated Policy ($z_d = \theta_1 c$)
C: Time Consistent Co-ordinated Policy (c given)
D: Time Consistent Open Loop Nash Game ($z_d = \theta_1 c$)

5.1 Policy coordination and the real exchange rate

A to the origin. As this involves some restoration of competitiveness it is evident that, in reoptimising, the policy co-ordinator is tempted to reduce interest differentials below what were promised at time t_0. Consequently optimal policy appears to involve a cut in the initial level of competitiveness and core inflation in the home economy achieved by a path of interest differentials skewed into the future so as to limit the impact on current domestic output.

Imposing the constraint of time consistency on the policy co-ordinator prevents this skewed pattern of interest differentials. As a result, the initial spread of rates is increased to $6\frac{1}{2}\%$ though the initial loss of competitiveness falls to 7.90%, see Table 5.5 and the path starting at B. The use of interest differentials to affect c directly is ruled out by the assumption that $c = \theta_1 z_d$, and the indirect effect of high interest differentials is to reduce the loss of competitiveness by reducing z_d. If the coordinator treats the exchange rate as given, this inhibition is removed and both the initial interest differential and the initial loss of competitiveness increase (see path from point C in the figure).

Since the welfare costs fall when the exchange rate is taken as given in this way, it appears that the perceived ability to exert an influence on the exchange rate is, in the absence of precommitment, counter-productive. This may help to explain why welfare costs also fall in the non-cooperative Open Loop Nash case as lack of co-ordination seems to 'weaken' this time consistency constraint and allows for the choice of policies with higher initial interest differentials, and a greater loss of competitiveness (see path from point D).

It is not, of course, always true that the power to affect the exchange rate proves counter-productive in this way. In an example of fiscal policy co-ordination, Miller and Salmon (1985), we find that it pays the policy co-ordinator to act as a (time-consistent) leader in the foreign exchange markets; and in this case coordinated policy dominates the non-cooperative Nash alternative.

Conclusion

The focus of this paper is on the computation of time consistent equilibria in continuous time 'rational expectations' models where there is more than one decision maker. As an illustration, we have examined the choice of interest rate policies in two countries linked by trade and capital movements with a perfectly flexible exchange rate.

The loss function which policy makers seek to minimise includes only the squared deviation of domestic output from its stable inflation level and the square of core inflation, defined as a moving average of inflation. Such objectives do not, of course, involve any long-run international 'conflict of interest': in each country the equilibrium level of output is determined by the long-run Phillips curve and the floating rate allows for the desired inflation rate to be achieved without coordination.

What gains there may be from coordination must come therefore, in choosing the path towards equilibrium and not in the final equilibrium itself. For the model specified here, however, when the path of the exchange rate is taken to be predetermined in designing policy, there are no such dynamic gains to coordination. And where effects of interest rates on the exchange rate are recognised, coordination so alters the time consistency constraint that average welfare declines marginally, cf. Rogoff (1983) where coordination of monetary policy delivers worse outcomes than decentralised policy.

The failure to reap dynamic benefits from coordination in this case doubtless depends on the particular features of the model, especially the feature that time consistent Stackelberg leadership in setting interest rates appears to be uniformly unattractive in this floating rate environment.

While it is surely useful to focus on these purely dynamic aspects of the problem, it has to be recognised that a more realistic appraisal of the merits of coordination should also make due allowance for international 'conflicts of interest' which persist even in equilibrium, as discussed, for example, by Canzoneri and Gray (1983) and Turner (1983).

Annex. Deriving time consistent equilibria in symmetric and asymmetric dynamic games

In this Annex we derive the four equilibria for full information linear quadratic differential games discussed in the text. In order to focus on the strategic relations between the players, the state vector is taken to be entirely predetermined. The first of the symmetric solutions is for the Open Loop Nash game, where each player takes as given the other's sequence of policy *actions*. This is followed by Closed Loop Nash game where each player takes the other's policy *rule* as given (such rules being restricted to current state feedback only). Where one player is dominant, there are two analogous time consistent solutions, the Open Loop and Feedback Stackelberg equilibria.

The integrals to be minimised are assumed to converge without discounting. By using the 'current value' Hamiltonian and 'current value' shadow prices, these solutions can without difficulty be extended to incorporate discounting if required. Likewise the restriction to only two players is not essential.

1.1 Open loop Nash

Each player is assumed to choose the time path of his or her own control variable(s) so as to minimise the integral of a quadratic cost function defined on the variables of a linear differential equation system, conditional on the assumption that the entire path of the other player's control variable is given.

Since the behaviour of the two players is symmetric, the analysis need only be carried out in detail for the one of them, denoted 1, with a quadratic cost function defined on the set of 'state' variables x, his own controls u, and those of the second player, v. Note that the weights in this function, denoted by the matrix Q_1 below, incorporate any costs attached to other ('output') variables which have been eliminated by substitution in reducing the cost function to one involving only the state variables and the controls.

Thus, for the infinite horizon case, player 1 has to solve the following standard dynamic optimisation problem:

$$\min_{u} \frac{1}{2} \int_{t_0}^{\infty} w^T(s) Q_1 w(s) \, ds, \quad \text{where} \quad w(t) \equiv \begin{bmatrix} x(t) \\ u(t) \\ v(t) \end{bmatrix}, \tag{1}$$

subject to the linear differential 'state' equation

$$\dot{x}(t) = Ax(t) + B_1 u(t) + B_2 v(t), \quad \text{where} \quad \dot{x} \equiv \frac{dx}{dt}, \tag{2}$$

given $x(t_0)$ and $v(t)$, $t \geqslant t_0$. The coefficients of the symmetric matrix Q_1 are assumed to satisfy the usual positive definiteness conditions to ensure that costs are positive and that the values of the control are bounded. (The explicit time-indexing of the elements of w is, for convenience, dropped henceforth).

Using Pontryagin's maximum principle to solve this problem, the appropriate Hamiltonian for player 1 is

$$H^1 = \tfrac{1}{2}(w^T Q_1 w) + p_1^T (Ax + B_1 u + B_2 v) \tag{3}$$

where p_1 is a vector of 'costates', and hence the first order conditions (FOC's) for a minimum may be written

$$\frac{\partial H^1}{\partial x} = Q_{1xx} x + Q_{1xu} u + Q_{1xv} v + A^T p_1 = -\dot{p}_1 \tag{4}$$

$$\frac{\partial H^1}{\partial p_1} = Ax + B_1 u + B_2 v = \dot{x} \tag{5}$$

$$\frac{\partial H^1}{\partial u} = Q_{1xu} x + Q_{1uv} v + Q_{1uu} u + B_1^T p_1 = 0 \tag{6}$$

Since the second player is, in fact, choosing his path for v conditional on u being given, the Nash equilibrium may be obtained as the simultaneous solution of these two optimisation problems. To this end, the state equation and the FOC's of both players (bearing in mind that those of the second player will be symmetric to those of player 1 already described) are first collected together as follows:

$$\begin{bmatrix} \dot{x} \\ -\dot{p}_1 \\ -\dot{p}_2 \\ 0 \\ 0 \end{bmatrix} = \begin{bmatrix} A & 0 & 0 & B_1 & B_2 \\ Q_{1xx} & A^T & 0 & Q_{1xu} & Q_{1xv} \\ Q_{2xx} & 0 & A^T & Q_{2xu} & Q_{2xv} \\ Q_{1ux} & B_1^T & 0 & Q_{1uu} & Q_{1uv} \\ Q_{2vx} & 0 & B_2^T & Q_{2vu} & Q_{2vv} \end{bmatrix} \begin{bmatrix} x \\ p_1 \\ p_2 \\ u \\ v \end{bmatrix} \tag{7}$$

The paths for the states and costates can be more simply described, however, if the control variables are eliminated by substitution. Thus from (7) we obtain

$$
\begin{bmatrix} u \\ v \end{bmatrix} = - \begin{bmatrix} Q_{1uu} & Q_{1uv} \\ Q_{2vu} & Q_{2vv} \end{bmatrix}^{-1} \begin{bmatrix} Q_{1ux} & B_1^T & 0 \\ Q_{2vx} & 0 & B_2^T \end{bmatrix} \begin{bmatrix} x \\ p_1 \\ p_2 \end{bmatrix} \tag{8}
$$

and so

$$
\begin{bmatrix} u \\ v \end{bmatrix} \begin{bmatrix} J_{ux} & J_{up_1} & J_{up_2} \\ J_{vx} & J_{vp_1} & J_{vp_2} \end{bmatrix} \begin{bmatrix} x \\ p_1 \\ p_2 \end{bmatrix} \tag{9}
$$

Hence we can express (7) alternatively as an adjoint system involving only states and costates, which we denote

$$
\begin{bmatrix} \dot{x} \\ \dot{p}_1 \\ \dot{p}_2 \end{bmatrix} = \begin{bmatrix} M_{xx} & M_{xp_1} & M_{xp_2} \\ M_{p_1 x} & M_{p_1 p_1} & M_{p_1 p_2} \\ M_{p_2 x} & M_{p_2 p_1} & M_{p_2 p_2} \end{bmatrix} \begin{bmatrix} x \\ p_1 \\ p_2 \end{bmatrix} \equiv M \begin{bmatrix} x \\ p_1 \\ p_2 \end{bmatrix} \tag{10}
$$

where, for example,

$$
M_{xx} = A + B_1 J_{ux} + B_2 J_{vx}
$$

Since the convergent solution to this infinite time problem involves only the stable roots of this adjoint system, it is straightforward to express the paths for the states and costates in terms of the initial conditions for x and the stable eigenvalues and vectors of the adjoint matrix M in (10).

It is convenient for this purpose first to define a vector of canonical variables, z, each associated with a single root, thus

$$
\begin{bmatrix} x \\ p_1 \\ p_2 \end{bmatrix} = \begin{bmatrix} C_{11} & C_{12} \\ C_{21} & C_{22} \\ C_{31} & C_{32} \end{bmatrix} \begin{bmatrix} z_s \\ z_n \end{bmatrix} = Cz \tag{11}
$$

where

$$
\begin{bmatrix} \dot{z}_s \\ \dot{z}_n \end{bmatrix} = \begin{bmatrix} \Lambda_s & \\ & \Lambda_n \end{bmatrix} \begin{bmatrix} z_s \\ z_n \end{bmatrix} = \Lambda z
$$

letting s, and n denote stable and unstable roots. The matrix C appearing in (11) is simply the matrix of column eigenvectors of M, so $MC = C\Lambda$, where Λ is the diagonal matrix of eigenvalues of M. Partitioning C as shown and setting $z_n = 0$ provides the solution for the states and costates as follows:

$$x(t) = C_{11} z = C_{11} e^{A_s(t-t_0)} C_{11}^{-1} x(t_0),$$

$$p_1(t) = C_{21} C_{11}^{-1} x.$$

$$p_2(t) = C_{31} C_{11}^{-1} x \qquad (12)$$

The time paths for u and v in this open loop Nash equilibrium may now be obtained by substitution of (12) into (9).

1.2 Closed loop or feedback Nash

In contrast to the open loop case, it is now assumed that in minimising the same integral of costs each player observes and reacts to the current state, x. In the Closed Loop Nash game each player takes as given the *feedback rule* of the other, and these closed loop rules, $u = R_1 x$, $v = R_2 x$, alter the players' first-order conditions for cost minimisation. Specifically, when calculating the effect of a change in the state on each player's Hamiltonian, account must be taken of the response of the other player to the change in the state.

Thus for player 1, given (3), and $v = R_2 x$, one calculates

$$\frac{\partial H^1}{\partial x} = Q_{1xx} x + Q_{1xu} u + Q_{1xv} v + A^T p_1 + R_2^T H_v^1 = -\dot{p}_1 \qquad (13)$$

where

$$H_v^1 \equiv Q_{1vx} x + Q_{1vu} u + Q_{1vv} v + B_2^T p_1,$$

which, in comparison with equation (4) above, contains an extra expression representing $\dfrac{\partial H^1}{\partial v} \dfrac{\partial v}{\partial x}$. Player 2 similarly takes into account this closed loop behaviour of player 1, represented by $u = R_1 x$.

As there are no other changes to the FOCs, then collected results for the closed loop Nash equilibrium can be shown by augmenting those for the open loop case as follows

$$
\begin{bmatrix} \dot{x}_1 \\ -\dot{p}_1 \\ -\dot{p}_2 \\ 0 \\ 0 \\ 0 \\ 0 \end{bmatrix}
=
\left[
\begin{array}{ccccc|cc}
 & & & & & 0 & 0 \\
 & & S^{OLN} & & & R_2^T & 0 \\
 & & & & & 0 & R_1^T \\
 & & & & & 0 & 0 \\
\hline
 & & & & & 0 & 0 \\
Q_{1vx} & 0 & 0 & Q_{1vu} & Q_{1vv} & -1 & 0 \\
Q_{2ux} & 0 & 0 & Q_{2uu} & Q_{2uv} & 0 & -1
\end{array}
\right]
\begin{bmatrix} x \\ p_1 \\ p_2 \\ u \\ v \\ H_v^1 \\ H_u^2 \end{bmatrix} \qquad (14)
$$

where S^{OLN} denotes the matrix appearing in equation (7) and H_v^1, H_u^2 are the partial derivatives of the Hamiltonians with respect to the *other* player's controls.

For any given values of R_1, R_2, the system can be reduced by substitution to the adjoint equations in states and costates

$$\begin{bmatrix} \dot{x} \\ \dot{p}_1 \\ \dot{p}_2 \end{bmatrix} = M^{CLN} \begin{bmatrix} x \\ p_1 \\ p_2 \end{bmatrix} \tag{15}$$

and the solution paths may be obtained from the initial condition $x(t_0)$ and the stable eigenvalues and eigenvectors of this adjoint system as described in the last section. It is clear that the eigenvectors so determined will depend on the assumed reaction functions R_1, R_2. Given equation (9) above, it is necessary for the closed loop Nash equilibrium that these reaction functions should simultaneously be related to the eigenvectors as follows:

$$\left. \begin{aligned} R_1 &= J_{ux} + J_{up_1} \Pi_1 + J_{up_2} \Pi_2 \\ R_2 &= J_{vx} + J_{up_2} \Pi_2 + J_{up_2} \Pi_2 \end{aligned} \right\} \tag{16}$$

where Π_1, Π_2 are the Ricatti matrices relating the costates to the states, so

$$\left. \begin{aligned} p_1 &= \Pi_1 x = C_{21} C_{11}^{-1} x \\ p_2 &= \Pi_2 x = C_{31} C_{11}^{-1} x \end{aligned} \right\} \tag{17}$$

The values for R_1, R_2 which characterise the closed loop Nash equilibrium may be determined by applying Jacobi's iterative method to the system after 'modal decomposition', as follows. Given starting values for R_1 and R_2, one may calculate the eigenvectors of M^{CIN}. These can then be used to compute the Ricatti matrices, Π_1 and Π_2, and so a new set of values for R_1 and R_2 (using equations (16) and (17) above). These new values may be substituted back into (14) and the procedure repeated until convergence is obtained. This iterative method was used to compute the closed loop solutions for the example in this paper. Typically R_1 and R_2 were set to zero in the first iteration (which then generates the eigenvectors of the open loop Nash solution in the first round).

An alternative procedure would be to apply numerical methods to the coupled Riccati equations associated with such a closed loop Nash game, namely

$$\left. \begin{aligned} Q_{1xx} + Q_{1xu} R_1 + Q_{1xv} R_2 + A^T \Pi_1 + \Pi_1 A + \Pi_1 B_1 R_1 + \Pi_1 B_3 R_2 = 0 \\ Q_{2xx} + Q_{2xu} R_1 + Q_{2xv} R_2 + A^T \Pi_2 + \Pi_2 A + \Pi_2 B_1 R_1 + \Pi_2 B_2 R_2 = 0 \end{aligned} \right\} \tag{18}$$

where R_1 and R_2 are defined as in (16) above.

Time consistent Stackelberg equilibria

The dynamic games described so far have been symmetric. In many situations, however, one player may be dominant and such a 'leader' can design his policy in part with a view to inducing others ('followers') to act in a manner beneficial to him.

The optimal strategy for the Stackelberg leader in an open loop dynamic game turns out to be time inconsistent, see Simaan and Cruz (1973), and we discussed such time inconsistent strategies in an earlier paper, Miller and Salmon (1983). Here, however, we focus on those time consistent policies which may be obtained using the recursive techniques of dynamic programming.

In what follows, we first describe the time consistent Stackelberg equilibrium derived for an asymmetric *open loop* game along the lines developed by Cohen and Michel (1984); then the *closed loop* equivalent reported earlier by Basar and Haurie (1982).

1.3 Open loop Stackelberg equilibrium

For the linear quadratic problem described in equations (1) and (2) above, Hamiltonians are formed as shown in (3), for the leader, player 1, and likewise for the follower. The first order conditions for optimisation will, of course, be affected by strategic asymmetry.

We begin with the conditions describing how the controls, u and v, are described as functions of the state and costate variables chosen so as to minimise the respective Hamiltonians. While the first order conditions for the follower are unchanged from the symmetric case, the leader, in setting u, will typically take advantage of the follower's reaction to his choice of u.

Thus, for the follower, v will be determined as in equation (7) above, namely

$$\frac{\partial H^2}{\partial v} = Q_{2vx}x + Q_{2vu}u + Q_{2vv}v + B_2^T p_2 = 0 \tag{19}$$

This implies that

$$\left. \begin{aligned} v &= -Q_{2vv}^{-1}(Q_{2vx}x + Q_{2vu}u + B_2^T p_2). \\ &\equiv R_{vx}x + R_{vu}u + R_{vp_2}p_2 \end{aligned} \right\} \tag{20}$$

which will be taken into account by the leader, whose first order condition for setting u therefore becomes

$$\frac{\partial H^1}{\partial u} = Q_{1ux}x + Q_{1uu}u + Q_{1uv}v + B_1^T p_1 + R_{vu}^T H_v^1 = 0 \tag{21}$$

where

$$R_{vu} \equiv \frac{\partial v}{\partial u} = -Q_{2vv}^{-1} Q_{2vu}$$

as shown above, and

$$H_v^1 \equiv \frac{\partial H^1}{\partial v} = Q_{1vx} x + Q_{1vu} u + Q_{1vv} v + B_2^T p_1$$

As this asymmetry exists at a point in time, it does not lead to time inconsistency associated with intertemporal asymmetries.

Turning now to the conditions governing the evolution of the costate variables p_1 and p_2, we note that, as the follower treats the leader's actions as an open loop, the condition for $\dot{p}_2$ will be as in equation (9) above, namely

$$-\dot{p}_2 = \frac{\partial H^2}{\partial x} = Q_{2xx} x + Q_{2xu} u + Q_{2xv} v + A^T p_2 \tag{22}$$

Cohen and Michel have argued that Bellman's Principle of Optimality in the open loop Stackelberg game implies that the leader takes account of the follower's behaviour as summarised here in equation (20), subject *not* to equation (22) but to the 'time consistency' restriction that

$$p_2 = \theta x \tag{23}$$

where θ is taken as given by player 1 but is endogenous to the system. Formally, player 1 chooses u to minimise V_1 subject to (2), (20) and (23).

As a consequence the first order condition describing the evolution of p_1 is

$$\frac{\partial H^1}{\partial K} = Q_{1xx} x + Q_{1xu} u + Q_{1xv} v + A^T p_1 + R^T H_v^1 = -\dot{p}_1 \tag{24}$$

where

$$R \equiv R_{vx} + R_{vp_2} \theta \tag{25}$$

so R is similar to (but not identical with) a closed loop reaction function.

We thus have

$$
\begin{bmatrix} \dot{x}_1 \\ -\dot{p}_1 \\ -\dot{p}_2 \\ 0 \\ 0 \\ 0 \end{bmatrix} =
\begin{bmatrix} & & & & & 0 \\ & & & & & R^T \\ & & S^{OLN} & & & 0 \\ & & & & & R_{vu}^T \\ & & & & & 0 \\ Q_{1vx} & 0 & 0 & Q_{1vu} & Q_{1vv} & -1 \end{bmatrix}
\begin{bmatrix} x \\ p_1 \\ p_2 \\ u \\ v \\ H_v^1 \end{bmatrix} \tag{26}
$$

where S^{OLN} denotes the matrix appearing in (7) above, and R is defined in (25).

Equation (26) can be reduced to an adjoint equation in the state and costate variables of the form

$$
\begin{bmatrix} \dot{x} \\ \dot{p}_1 \\ \dot{p}_2 \end{bmatrix} = M^{OLS} \begin{bmatrix} x \\ p_1 \\ p_2 \end{bmatrix} \tag{27}
$$

using the definition of H_v^1 and the reduced form equations for u and v obtained from (19) and (21) which we denote

$$
\begin{bmatrix} u \\ v \end{bmatrix} = \begin{bmatrix} J_{11} & J_{12} & J_{13} \\ J_{21} & J_{22} & J_{32} \end{bmatrix} \begin{bmatrix} x \\ p_1 \\ p_2 \end{bmatrix} \tag{28}
$$

using a slightly different notation to distinguish this form equation (9).

The equilibrium is defined by the requirement that the matrix θ incorporated in M^{OLS} satisfies the condition that

$$
\theta = C_{31} C_{11}^{-1} \tag{28}
$$

where $\begin{bmatrix} C_{11} \\ C_{21} \\ C_{31} \end{bmatrix}$ denote the stable eigenvectors of (27). This solution may be

obtained either by the Jacobi method used here, or alternatively by solving the non-linear Riccati equations associated with this case.

1.4 Feedback Stackelberg equilibrium

In much the same way, the closed loop asymmetric equilibrium derived using dynamic programming methods by Basar and Haurie can be described as an augmented version of the closed loop Nash game.

The asymmetry will as before mean that v and u are set as in (19) and (21) above. But the closed loop assumption now implies that both players are aware of the other's response to the state, so V_1 is minimised subject to (1) and $v = R_2 x$ and V_2 is minimised subject to (2) and $u = R_1 x$, with each player taking as given the other's reaction function. The resulting first order conditions are almost identical to those for the closed loop Nash game in (4). Specifically

$$
\begin{bmatrix} \dot{x}_1 \\ -\dot{p}_1 \\ -\dot{p}_2 \\ 0 \\ 0 \\ 0 \\ 0 \end{bmatrix} = \begin{bmatrix} A & 0 & 0 & B_1 & B_2 & 0 & 0 \\ Q_{1xx} & A^T & 0 & Q_{1xu} & Q_{1xv} & R_2^T & 0 \\ Q_{2xx} & 0 & A^T & Q_{2xu} & Q_{2xv} & 0 & R_1^T \\ Q_{1ux} & B_1^T & 0 & Q_{1uu} & Q_{1uv} & R_{vu}^T & 0 \\ Q_{2vx} & 0 & B_2^T & Q_{2vu} & Q_{2vv} & 0 & 0 \\ Q_{1vx} & 0 & 0 & Q_{1vu} & Q_{1vv} & -1 & 0 \\ Q_{2ux} & 0 & 0 & Q_{2uu} & Q_{2uv} & 0 & -1 \end{bmatrix} \begin{bmatrix} x_1 \\ p_1 \\ p_2 \\ u \\ v \\ H_v^1 \\ H_u^2 \end{bmatrix} \tag{29}
$$

Of course if the term $R_{vu} = -Q_{2vv}^{-1} Q_{2vu}$ is zero then this solution will coincide with the closed loop Nash. Once again the system may be reduced to the form

$$
\begin{bmatrix} \dot{x} \\ \dot{p}_1 \\ \dot{p}_2 \end{bmatrix} = M^{CLS} \begin{bmatrix} x \\ p_1 \\ p_2 \end{bmatrix} \tag{30}
$$

while the reaction functions both R_1 and R_2 appearing in M^{CLS} must, for the Feedback Stackelberg equilibrium, satisfy the conditions

$$
\left.\begin{aligned}
R_1 &= J_{11} + J_{12} C_{21} C_{11}^{-1} + J_{13} C_{31} C_{11}^{-1} \\
R_2 &= J_{21} + J_{22} C_{21} C_{11}^{-1} + J_{23} C_{31} C_{11}^{-1}
\end{aligned}\right\} \tag{31}
$$

defined with respect to the stable eigenvectors of M^{CLS} in (30).

NOTES

* In revising this paper for publication we have benefitted substantially from comments received at the Conference.
1 The reader is invited to compare the results obtained here for differential games (and the methods used to obtain them) with those presented in the excellent paper by G. Oudiz and J. Sachs included in this volume, which is cast in discrete time and uses explicit dynamic programming methods to obtain time consistent equilibria.
2 Obtained using 'Saddlepoint'; see Austin and Buiter (1982).
3 Cf. Aoki (1981).

REFERENCES

Aoki, M. (1981). *Dynamic Analysis of Open Economies*. New York, Academic Press.
Austin, G. P. and W. H. Buiter (1982). 'Saddlepoint – a programme for solving continuous time linear rational expectation models'. *LSE Econometrics Programme*, D.P. No. 37, November.
Basar, Tamer, and Alain Baurie (1982). 'Feedback Equilibria in Differential Games with Structural and Model Uncertainties'. *Les Cahiers du GERARD*, G-82-09, Montreal, September, forthcoming in J. B. Cruz (ed.) *Advances in Large Scale Systems*, Vol. I, JAI Press.
Basar, Tamer and Geert K. Olsder (1982). *Dynamic Noncooperative Game Theory*. London, Academic Press.
Buiter, Willem (1983). 'Optimal and Time-Consistent Policies in Continuous Time Rational Expectations Models'. *LSE Econometrics Programme* D.P. No. A39, June.
Buiter, W. H. and M. H. Miller (1982). 'Real exchange rate overshooting and the

output cost of bringing down inflation'. *European Economic Review*, 18, May/June, pp. 85–123.

Canzoneri, Matthew and Jo Anna Gray (1983). 'Monetary Policy Games and the Consequences of Non-Cooperative Behavior', NBER Conference on International Co-ordination of Economic Policy (*mimeo*).

Cohen, Daniel and Phillippe Michel (1984). 'Towards a theory of Optimal Precommitment I: An Analysis of the Time Consistent Equilibria'. *CEPREMAP* Discussion Paper No. 8412, May.

Cruz, J. B. Jr. (1975). 'Survey of Nash and Stackelberg Equilibrium Strategies in Dynamic Games', *Annals of Economic and Social Measurement*. **14**, No. 2, pp. 339–44.

Dornbusch, Rudiger (1976). 'Expectations and Exchange Rate Dynamics'. *Journal of Political Economy*, **84**, December, pp. 1161–76.

Driffill, John (1982). 'Optimal Money and Exchange Rate Policies'. *Greek Economic Review*, **4**, December, pp. 261–83.

Hamada, Koichi (1979). 'Macroeconomic Strategy and Coordination under Alternative Exchange Rates' in R. Dornbusch and J. A. Frenkel (eds.) *International Economic Policy*. London: Johns Hopkins Press.

Hamada, Koichi and M. Sakurai (1978). 'International Transmission of Stagflation under Fixed and Flexible Exchange Rates'. *Journal of Political Economy*, **86**, pp. 877–95.

Miller, Marcus and Mark Salmon (1983). 'Dynamic Games and the Time Inconsistency of Optimal Policy in Open Economies'. *Warwick Economic Research Papers* No. 234, July.

Miller, Marcus and Mark Salmon (1985). 'Dynamic Games...' (revised) forthcoming in *Economic Journal*, Supplement.

Oudiz, Gilles and Jeffrey Sachs (1984). 'Macroeconomic Policy Co-ordination among the Industrial Countries'. *Brookings Papers on Economic Activity*, I.

Rogoff, Kenneth (1983). 'Productive and Counterproductive Cooperative Monetary Policies', Board of Governors of the Federal Reserve System, International Financial Division, (*mimeo*), August.

Sachs, Jeffrey (1983). 'International Policy Co-ordination in a Dynamic Macroeconomic Model', *NBER* Working Paper No. 1166, July.

Simaan, M. and J. B. Cruz Jr. (1973). 'Additional Aspects of the Stackelberg Strategy in Non zero-sum Games'. *Journal of Optimization Theory and Application*, 11, No. 6, pp. 613–26.

Turner, Paul (1983). 'A Static Framework for the Analysis of Policy Optimisation with Interdependent Economies'. *Warwick Economic Research Papers* No. 235, Department of Economics, University of Warwick, August.

Turner, Paul (1984). 'Interdependent Monetary Policies in a Two Country Model', Discussion Paper in Economics and Econometrics, No. 8401, University of Southampton.

COMMENT RALPH C. BRYANT

I have mixed reactions about the paper by Miller and Salmon. On the favorable side, the authors make an interesting contribution to a growing technical literature. Researchers working intensively on this topic will benefit from the paper (and the authors' earlier research on which it draws). On the negative side, the authors are not sufficiently clear about *why* the particular aspects of coordination studied here are the issues that most merit analytical attention. Many readers will have difficulty extracting the basic ideas from the technical presentation.

In this written version of my comments I omit specific comments about the authors' model and their empirical results. Instead, I include only some general points that were sparked by my reading of the Miller–Salmon paper and some of the other papers presented at the conference. These points fall under three headings: the characterization of 'solutions' to problems of strategic interactions among national governments; the information and uncertainty aspects of strategic interactions; and some questions about the recent preoccupation with 'time-consistent' policy strategies.

Cooperative and non-cooperative games

The conventional characterization of solutions to problems of strategic interactions distinguishes between 'cooperative' and 'noncooperative' games. I formerly believed that this distinction was clear and that it turned on whether the players in a strategic situation enter into binding agreements with each other. More recently, following conversations with others much more conversant with game theory than I am (for example, Edward Green), I have come to doubt the clarity of this distinction. In particular, the concept of cooperation as customarily used in game theory tends not to highlight the 'enforceability' and 'credibility' aspects of an agreement. And it also fails to pay enough attention to the 'information structure' of the strategic situation.

Every strategic situation can be interpreted as having both 'efficiency' and enforceability aspects. And every game has a particular information structure.[1] The relative importance of the enforceability and the efficiency aspects varies from one game to another, depending on the information structure and the sequencing of decisions. For example, as brought out in the Miller-Salmon paper, a 'Stackelberg' solution can be interpreted as just another Nash solution with a different information structure.

It is interesting to ask whether a steep tradeoff exists between efficiency and enforceability. Does it become more difficult to enforce a solution as the players cooperate to reach an efficient outcome? Alternatively, are the solutions that are most easily enforced and credible likely to be less efficient? For example, we know that a 'noncooperative' Nash solution may be enforceable, yet quite inefficient.

A pessimist about cooperation would probably argue that there is, inevitably, such a tradeoff. I am not clear about this question myself, and my main purpose here is to identify the issue as one deserving careful study. At this rudimentary stage of our knowledge, I tentatively hold an optimistic view. That is, I nourish the hope that negotiators and analysts can be innovative, finding solutions for many types of games that are fairly efficient *and* reasonably enforceable.

International cooperation about national macroeconomic policies is a prime example where I hope an optimistic attitude can be justified. As pointed out in the earlier literature on this subject, the basic inhibitions to and potential gains from collective action apply to this area as well.[2] There is no 'market' in the policy actions of national governments. Governments cannot therefore feasibly 'trade' policy actions with each other. As a result, significant external economies or diseconomies can arise. There thus exists, in principle, a collective ('nonmarket') approach that could bring about more efficient outcomes.

With strong political leadership, a particular efficient solution might be found through bargaining that could make each nation better off. The optimistic view asserts that such a solution not only could be found but could also be enforced. Enforceability requires innovative ideas for containing the 'free-rider' incentives to stay out of the bargaining or to renege on the other players after a putative efficient solution has been bargained and agreed. For any foreseeable future, no international authority will be given strong enough powers to act as a policeman to enforce international agreements. Hence agreements must be 'self-enforcing' – consistent with continued decentralized decisionmaking by national governments.

Information and uncertainty aspects of strategic behavior

Research on international coordination of economic policies could develop in (at least) two ways. Analysts could explore the theoretical aspects of strategic behavior using highly simplified models. This approach – call it type 1 – permits a sharp focus on particular analytical issues, a few at a time. Alternatively, analysts could try to develop the empirical aspects of the issues. As a necessary counterpart to this other approach – type 2 – analysts will have to use empirical structural models of how economies interact; these models must adequately capture the size and nature of transmission of economic forces from one economy to another.

This research by Miller and Salmon, most of the work being discussed at this conference, and indeed the bulk of the interesting recent work by others, has largely been type-1 in nature. This theoretical emphasis has been useful. We certainly have to be clearer about the conceptual and theoretical aspects before we can make significant progress in applying the ideas empirically. At the same time we should not lose sight of the vast need for type-2 work. Theoretical clarity is a necessary, but very far from sufficient, condition for successful empirical application of the ideas.

In real-life discussions among national governments, the most fundamental obstacle to more cooperation is not a lack of awareness of the potential gains from coordination. Nor is it merely a lack of political will. To be sure, both those lacunae are important – especially in the last five years. Yet a still more important obstacle is the tremendous uncertainty about the magnitudes, and even the signs, of cross-border transmissions of economic forces.

In the research discussed at this conference, the players *know* how economic forces are transmitted from one nation to another. So to speak, everyone knows all the details of the relevant matrices in the correct structural model. And each player has the same model in mind. The practical situation confronting policymakers in national governments is of course entirely different.

Even if we cannot yet expect substantial progress in type-2 research, it would be a big advance if we could learn how to put some explicit recognition of uncertainty into our type-1 research. For example, could we incorporate some variances and covariances in our simplified models? Following the lead of the literature started by Brainard (1967), could we try to see how our inferences about strategic behavior and the potential gains from cooperation may be altered if we allow explicitly for uncertainty about what the true model is? A related approach would start by recognizing that two countries (players) disagree about the relevant model characterizing their interdependence. Could we construct and then employ a 'common model' that puts low or zero variance around the parameters not in dispute, but high variances around the parameters where disagreement is strongest?

In a similar vein, I offer a final comment about information and uncertainty. Perhaps we are underplaying the importance of the 'mere' exchange of information among countries? It is true that an exchange of information and forecasts is now virtually all that happens in international discussions about macroeconomic policies. But it does not follow, as is often assumed, that this activity has negligible consequences. When basic uncertainty is so high, 'mere' exchanges of information about recent developments and about national forecasts may be no small thing.

Credibility and time consistency

The credibility and 'time-consistency' aspects of strategic interactions have recently drawn the lion's share of attention in type-1 research. I am doubtful, however, that those aspects most warrant our analytical attention – or at least in the narrow way typical of the recent work.

The questions about time consistency that bother me can be identified with the use of an analogy, the interactions between a parent and young child. One may suppose that the interests of these two players are partly in conflict: what the parent wants for the child at any point in time may differ from what the child wants. Yet there is also a latent commonality of objectives.

In particular, the child dislikes doing homework, likes to watch television, and is often tempted to watch television before the homework is done. The parent lays down behavior rules, including the requirement that all homework has to be done before the TV can be turned on. It is a feature of the situation that the game is 'repeated'; each day is potentially a new test of the homework-before-TV rule.

If the parent were to enforce the rule rigidly, the strategies of both parent and child would be 'time-consistent' (in the sense now popular in the technical literature). Now ask, however, whether it could be sensible for the parent to alter the rule, and if so in what circumstances.

If the child has a tendency to procrastinate, behavior by the parent that 're-optimizes' in a 'time-inconsistent' way can lead to trouble. For example, suppose the parent approves of the child watching certain educational TV programs. If the child procrastinates with his homework and yet at 9:00 p.m. the parent relaxes the rule to permit the child to watch the educational program, the parent's re-optimization can create a credibility problem. On future days the child may again procrastinate, hoping to get the parent to relent again, even for non-educational programs. This result would be an example where re-optimization can induce poor outcomes averaged over longer runs. It is situations of this type into which the recent literature has given us insights.

But now consider a different set of circumstances. Suppose at 3:00 p.m. there is a power failure, which lasts until 8:45 p.m.; suppose the child's homework is to practice typing, and the only typewriter in the house is an electric typewriter. Suppose again at 9:00 p.m. there is an educational TV program that the parent would like the child to watch. Given the unexpected event of the power failure, over which neither player had any control, would a credibility problem be created if the parent permits the child to watch TV? This particular re-optimization could be a constructive breach of the homework rule.

For completeness, imagine a variant of the preceding case. Suppose there is a past history of the child frequently procrastinating. Imagine again the power failure, and again the desirable program on evening TV. How should the parent react to the surprise power failure and its consequent effects on the homework? The parent's decision is more difficult because of the past history. A possible relaxation of policy tonight may induce more procrastination in the future – even though the occasion for contemplating the breach of the rule has nothing to do with the child's behavior today.

My analogy highlights credibility issues. Arguably, child-rearing may be dominantly influenced by such issues.

I now want to ask whether macroeconomic policy is very much, or only partly, like child rearing. One important difference, I would assert, is the greater relative significance in macroeconomic policy of uncertainty about how the rules affect behavior (how policy actions affect performance of the economy). And a second important difference is the much greater prevalence in macroeconomic policy of 'surprises' (like the power failure) that are exogenous from the perspective of individual decisionmaking agents.

Think, for example, of the dilemmas facing policymakers in a significantly open economy. Many types of disturbance originating elsewhere in the world – wars, debt crises, crop failures – will influence the home economy. Many types of nonpolicy shocks may also originate at home.

When uncertainty and unanticipated events are very important, the virtues of unwavering adherence to 'time-consistent' strategies may be much less clear than when the dominant elements of the situation are the interactions between the players themselves. In particular, I conjecture that there are many types of unexpected events for which it is desirable – from the perspective of all players – to re-optimize after the surprise has occurred. More generally, I believe that the recent literature has paid insufficient analytical attention to strategic interactions in the light of uncertainty and surprises.

I do not want to push the argument about exogenous surprises too far, because of the possibility that the subsequent endogenous interactions among the players could be affected adversely by the relaxation of time-consistent policies. Nevertheless, a great deal of macroeconomic policy has to do with responding to contingencies that cannot be anticipated. Policymakers in national governments have opportunities to get to know each others' behavior in international negotiations, and hence to form reasonable judgments about credibility and reputations. With the current state of knowledge of how the world economy functions, on the other hand, they cannot anticipate many contingencies and cannot be confident about how the consequences will be transmitted across national borders. Situations may often arise, therefore, where it could be mutually advantageous for all parties to be time-inconsistent, departing from presumptive rules agreed at an earlier time.

These considerations led me to be a skeptic about whether the recent fad in the profession – preoccupation with credibility problems, and with time-consistent strategies – is leading our research in the most fruitful direction.[3] Perhaps this trend is a bit like other aspects of the so-called rational-expectations revolution? The new emphasis corrects a significant oversight in the previous literature. It forces us to ask important questions. But we need to be careful not to get so swept up in the technically interesting aspects that we forget the old familiar problems that still need attention.

NOTES

1 An outcome or 'solution' is efficient if it is Pareto-optimal. A solution is enforceable if, once reached or agreed, the players have incentives to sustain the behavior generating the solution.
2 See, for example, Niehans (1968); Hamada (1976); Bryant (1980) chapter 25; and Oudiz and Sachs (1984).
3 A possible confusion exists about the use of the term 'time consistency.' In my comments I assert that re-optimization in response to exogenous surprises can – appropriately – lead to 'time-inconsistent' policies. At the conference, a few participants described such policies as 'innovation-contingent feedback rules' and preferred to label the policies as 'time consistent.' Terminology on these matters is still unsettled, and I have no semantic brief for my usage. My essential point is that the credibility aspects of interactions among the agents in a game situation may be receiving excessive attention relative to the aspects generated by uncertainty and exogenous surprises.

REFERENCES

Brainard, Williams G. (1967). 'Uncertainty and the effectiveness of policy'. *American Economic Review*, 57, 411–25.
Bryant, Ralph C. (1980). *Money and Monetary Policy in Interdependent Nations*. Washington DC, Brookings.
Hamada, Koichi (1976). 'A strategic analysis of monetary interdependence'. *Journal of Political Economy*, 84, 677–700.
Niehans, Jurg (1968). 'Monetary and Fiscal Policies in Open Economies under Fixed Exchange Rates: an Optimising Approach'. *Journal of Political Economy*, 76, 893–920.
Oudiz, Gilles and Jeffrey Sachs (1984). 'Macroeconomic policy coordination among the industrial economies'. *Brookings Papers on Economic Activity*, 1–64.

COMMENT STEPHEN J. TURNOVSKY

At the NBER Conference on Policy Coordination held in Cambridge, Massachusetts, in August 1983, Marcus Miller and Mark Salmon presented some results from dynamic (differential) game theory.[1] This paper is an application of some of the results contained in that paper to the problem of monetary policy coordination within the context of a specific two country macroeconomic model. My comments will be in two parts. First, I will make some general remarks on dynamic game theory; secondly, I will make some specific comments on their analysis:

I. Some remarks on dynamic game theory

The analysis of dynamic games has several critical interrelated aspects. These include: (i) the type of strategic behavior being considered; (ii) the information structure available to the policy maker; (iii) the choice of policy instruments. I shall touch briefly on each in turn.

(i) *Types of strategic behavior*

Traditionally, two types of strategic behavior have been analyzed using game theory, namely, *noncooperative* and *cooperative*. In the former, each agent acts independently, under alternative assumptions regarding the interaction of his behavior with that of his competitors. The two most common assumptions are: (i) Nash and (ii) Stackelberg behavior. In the former, each agent takes the actions of his competitors as given and reacts to them. A given set of policies for the agents is in Nash equilibrium when there is no incentive for any one agent to deviate unilaterally from this equilibrium, with the other agents' policies being held fixed as given. In the latter mode of policy making, however, there is a dominance and in a two-player game one of the agents plays the role of a 'leader' and the other a 'follower.' This case applies quite naturally in a situation where the policy coordination involves a large country (leader) and a small country (follower). In determining his equilibrium policy in the Stackelberg sense, the leader anticipates possible rational reactions of the follower to his announced policy and optimizes his objective function accordingly. These two solution concepts are familiar from static game theory. However, they need refinement within a dynamic context, where a proliferation of the equilibrium concepts with dynamic information patterns is possible.

The most important consideration in an intertemporal context is that over time games are played at different stages. Thus for example, the rules of the game can, and probably will, evolve over time. Solution concepts need to be clarified. For example, within the framework of multiact dynamic games, the Stackelberg equilibrium concept is appropriate for the class of decision problems in which the leader has the ability to announce his decisions at all of his possible information sets ahead of time, a solution which forces the leader to commit himself to the actions dictated by these strategies. Thus the Stackelberg solution involves a prior commitment on the part of the leader.[2]

On the other hand, the leader may not have the ability to announce and enforce his strategy at all levels prior to the start of the game. Such a hierarchical equilibrium, which has a Stackelberg property at each level of play, is called a feedback Stackelberg solution. The leader may change over time, depending upon the policies chosen by the agents and the outcome of the dynamic process.

It is also possible that the policy makers in the two countries find it mutually beneficial to coordinate their behavior and to achieve some kind of cooperative equilibrium. This involves the optimization of some joint utility function and is one of the solutions considered by Miller and Salmon.

(ii) *Information structure*

A most important aspect of the solution involves the information structure; see Basar and Olsder (1982). In a dynamic game, a precise delineation of the information pattern, such as which economic agent knows what, how the information pattern available to each agent evolves over time, how much of this is common information shared by all policy makers, and what part of it constitutes private information for each agent, is of paramount importance. An information set is said to be open-loop if only the a priori raw data set is available at all points in time; in this case the policy variables depend only upon time and are called *open-loop* policies. On the other hand if there is some dynamic evolution of the available information and the policy variables are allowed to depend upon this dynamic information, the information pattern is said to be *closed-loop* or *feedback*, with the precise terminology depending upon what is actually available and how it is utilized in the policy making process. Each one of these information structures give rise to a different game and to a different equilibrium structure, some of which are considered in the Miller–Salmon paper.

The definition of the information set is particularly important in the application of strategic behavior to international policy problems. In the first place, certain variables such as exchange rates and interest rates are available with much greater frequency than variables such as output or employment. Secondly, policy makers are likely to have superior information on domestic economic variables than they are likely to have on analogous foreign variables.

(iii) *Choice of policy instruments*

Dynamic games are concerned with determining how policy makers within each economy acting over time choose optimally among some given set of policy instruments. A crucial point, unfamiliar to most economists, is that even within a deterministic context, the choice of policy instruments and the nature of the underlying information pattern is critical to the equilibrium outcome of the differential game. This is in contrast to a single country (agent) dynamic optimization context where, under the assumption of uncertainty, such a choice is unimportant.

Since this distinction between traditional control theory and differential games is so important, it requires further elaboration. Let us abstract from stochastic disturbances and consider for the moment a single agent optimization problem, such as a single government, the objective of which is to tradeoff optimally between the rate of inflation and the rate of unemployment. The optimal solution will be the same whether the policy maker chooses to use say (i) only a fiscal instrument, (ii) only a monetary instrument. (Of course the solution will be different if the policy maker chooses to use both instruments simultaneously.) Furthermore, the end result will be the same regardless of what observables these variables are chosen to depend upon. That is, open-loop and closed-loop policies lead to the same outcome, provided that the same instrument variables are adopted.

By contrast, in the case of a dynamic game version of this problem, involving say two policy makers, even if each policy maker uses only one instrument, the equilibrium outcome will in general depend upon which instrument is being used. Thus, for example, under given behavioral assumptions, the equilibrium outcome will be different, depending upon whether each policy maker is using a fiscal or a monetary (or for that matter some other) policy instrument, and the precise nature of this policy instrument. Consequently, the assumption of the specific policy instrument takes on added importance in a dynamic context. The reason is simply that the policy maker's reaction curve which conditions the optimization of each of the agents depends upon the choice of policy instrument.[3]

Moreover, even if the choice of policy instrument is fixed, the information pattern (whether open-loop or closed-loop feedback information is available to the agents) plays an important role in the characterization and existence of equilibria as Miller and Salmon note, again in contrast to the single-agent case.

II. Specifics of the Miller–Salmon Analysis

I now comment on certain aspects of the Miller–Salmon paper. First, the consistency of the model is critically dependent upon the 'sluggishness' introduced by the core rate of inflation. Using their notation, the critical relationships for say the domestic economy are

$$i = \phi y + \sigma Dc + \pi$$

$$D\pi = \zeta(i - \pi)$$

The first equation is very much like an expectations-augmented Phillips curve, where inflationary expectations (which we may identify with π) are formed adaptively. If one now takes the limiting case where $\zeta \to \infty$, so that the core rate of inflation converges to the current, the model tends to degenerate. With $\zeta \to \infty$, $i = \pi$ and the Phillips curve reduces to

$$\phi y + \sigma Dc = 0 \tag{1}$$

With symmetry, the analogous relationship in the rest of the world is

$$\phi y^* - \sigma Dc = 0 \tag{1'}$$

and combining these two equations yields

$$y + y^* = 0 \tag{2}$$

Further, summing the IS curves for the two countries and noting (2) one finds

$$r + r^* = 0 \tag{3}$$

In the Miller–Salmon model, r and r^* are policy instruments. However, in the limiting case we have considered, the two policy instruments cannot be chosen independently by their respective policy makers. Precisely the same difficulty obtains under the assumption of symmetric economies if one adopts an expectations-augmented Phillips curve, together with the assumption of rational expectations; indeed the two models are observationally equivalent.[4] Thus in either case, the viability of the model depends upon some sluggishness being present. Equation (1) can be viewed as being a manifestation of the ineffectiveness of policy under rational expectations in the aggregate world economy. While due to relative price effects, the output in one country can deviate from its natural level, this is offset by a deviation abroad, so that on balance total output remains unchanged.

In discussing the policy instruments, the authors comment that 'For the design of monetary policy in such a structure it is not necessary to look at the details of the monetary sector, as Driffill (1982) has pointed out.'[5]

This comment is perfectly appropriate in the context of the single agent optimization model analysed by Driffill. But as we have noted above in my general remarks, the specification of policy is important in the context of multiagent optimization problems. Miller and Salmon treat the real interest rate as being the monetary instrument. Since this is not the usual monetary policy instrument, it would be of interest to consider alternatives. Indeed, in the context of multiagent games (either static or dynamic) one can consider a monetary instrument problem analogous to that initially considered by Poole (1970) in a stochastic context. Should the monetary authorities target on the interest rate or some monetary aggregate? Or is some combination of the two preferable? These seem to be interesting questions to consider in the context of this model.

In their earlier paper, Miller and Salmon emphasize the problem of *time consistent* solutions within an intertemporal optimization context. This issue again arises in the present paper. This phenomenon frequently arises in intertemporal optimization models involving forward looking behavior. As a result, certain state variables are not tied to the past, but instead are able to respond freely to unanticipated disturbances. They are often referred to as 'jump' variables and their associated costate variables become zero at the initial point of optimization. The ability to re-optimize at each point of time implies that these costate variables, together with their derivatives, must be zero at all times. Denoting the vector of relevant costate variables by $p(t)$, this leads to an equation

$$\dot{p}(t) = p(t) = 0 \tag{4}$$

In effect, we get an additional dynamic equation and the question of time consistency revolves around whether or not this additional equation conflicts with the other dynamic equations of the system. Note that while conditions such as (4) constrain the dynamics a lot, time inconsistency need not always arise.

Miller and Salmon eliminate the potential problem of time inconsistency by assuming that the time path of the real exchange rate is given, when the policy is designed. That is, they do not allow any jumps in the exchange rate to occur, but instead constrain it to move continuously everywhere. I am somewhat uneasy about this procedure, since much of the current work on exchange rate dynamics emphasizes its role as an information variable and its ability to respond instantaneously to previously unanticipated shocks. I agree with the authors that their paradoxical ranking that increased coordination leads to higher rather than lower joint welfare costs is probably a consequence of their neglect of the jump in the exchange rate.

A simple way of capturing this possibility would be to augment the cost function to

$$\text{Min } C(E(0)-E_0)+\frac{1}{2}\int_0^\infty (\beta\pi^2+y^2)\,dt \tag{5}$$

where E_0 is the inherited exchange rate, $E(0)$ is the endogenously determined exchange rate, following the jump, and $C(\cdot)$ is the cost function attached to the jump. The idea is that when the policy is first introduced, the fact that it is unanticipated will cause the exchange rate to jump. This in turn generates jumps in the relative price and output, which in turn impose real adjustment costs on the economy. These are captured by the cost function C.

For certain classes of cost functions, the problem of time inconsistency may be eliminated. This can be shown to be true, for example, if the cost associated with the initial jump is proportional to its absolute magnitude, although not if it is quadratic.[6] Basically, if such costs are sufficiently high, the costs of recomputing the optimal policy and the associated adjustment costs these impose on the economy, are sufficiently large to eliminate the incentive for the government to revise its previously announced plan and to cheat on the private sector.

The introduction of a cost on unanticipated jumps in the exchange rate could I believe reverse the paradoxical ordering noted earlier, regarding the welfare costs and increased coordination. With more coordination one would expect the jump in the exchange rate to be mitigated, so that this element in the overall cost function would decline with increased cooperation between the policy makers.

Of course, the specification of the cost function $C(\cdot)$ is open to the change that it is arbitrary and that it is not motivated by deep economic considerations. While this may or may not be the case, one can argue that this criterion is just a special case of the more general criterion proposed in the control theory literature, from which the approach adopted in this paper is derived. A general statement of the intertemporal objective function introduces costs on the initial and terminal states of the system, as well as on the states and controls during the transition. In traditional applications of control theory, the initial state is given, so the costs associated with those states are effectively bygones and are given as far as any subsequent optimization is concerned. But when some of the state variables, most notably in the present context the nominal exchange rate, are allowed to undergo initial jumps, a subvector of the initial state vector becomes endogenous and the costs associated with those initial variables become an integral part of the overall optimization.

We may note further that the balancing of costs associated with initial jumps in the system, together with those from having it deviate during the transitional path from some desired target, was the motivation used to justify some of the early distributed lag models; see the survey by Griliches (1967). The modification of the cost function being proposed is along these lines. Furthermore, we may argue that the entire linear-quadratic optimal policy approach, although a convenient representation of the policy maker's problem, is open to the charge of being arbitrary. The specification of an initial cost function C is no less so than the specification of the rest of the cost functional.

We conclude with two further comments. First, the problem of time consistency can be solved by seeking alternative solution concepts. This is the procedure adopted by Oudiz and Sachs (1984) and is superior to either the Miller–Salmon procedure or the modified cost function suggested above. Secondly, instead of working with ad hoc macro models, it may be desirable to work with models based on private sector optimization. In this case, the government's objective is to maximize the utility of the representative individual in the economy. In such models the derivation of equilibrium often eliminates much of the dynamics, thereby possibly eliminating the problem of time inconsistency. To a large degree whether such models are characterized by time inconsistency depends upon how the government policy variables impact on the private sector's optimization.[7]

In summary, the methods of dynamic game theory provide a powerful and fruitful approach to the study of macroeconomic policy making in interdependent economies. The Miller–Salmon paper presents an interesting application of these techniques and serves as a promising start for further research in this area.

NOTES

1 See Miller and Salmon (1983).
2 Further discussion of these issues is given by Basar and Olsder (1982, Chapter 3).
3 A simple static example illustrating this is given by Basar and Olsder (1982, p. 193).
4 The typical specification of the expectations-augmented Phillips curve for an open economy under rational expectations is

$$p = \phi y + i$$

where y, i are as defined in the Miller–Salmon paper, p is the rate of inflation of domestic goods. Defining p^* analogously and letting e denote the rate of exchange depreciation of the domestic currency, we have

$$i = \delta p + (1 - \delta)(p^* + e)$$

where δ is the share of the domestic good in domestic consumption. Writing this equation as

$$i = p + (1 - \delta)(p^* + e - p) = p + (1 - \delta) Dc$$

it is seen that the expectations augmented Phillips curve reduces to

$$\phi y + (1 - \delta) Dc = 0$$

which is equivalent to (1).

5 See p. 10 of the Miller and Salmon text.
6 This result is shown formally by Stemp and Turnovsky (1984).
7 This is one of the conclusions of Turnovsky and Brock (1980).

REFERENCES

Basar, T. and G. J. Olsder (1982). *Dynamic Noncooperative Game Theory*. Academic Press, New York.

Driffill, J. (1982). 'Optimal Money and Exchange Rate Policies'. *Greek Economic Review*.

Griliches, Z. (1967). 'Distributed Lags: A Survey'. *Econometrica*, **35**, 16–49.

Miller, M. and M. Salmon (1983). 'Dynamic Games and the Time Inconsistency of Optimal Policy in Open Economies', paper presented at NBER conference on policy coordination, Cambridge, Mass.

Oudiz, G. and J. Sachs, (1985). 'International Policy Coordination in Dynamic Macroeconomic Models', this volume.

Poole, W. (1970). 'Optimal Choice of Monetary Policy Instruments in a simple Stochastic Macro Model'. *Quarterly Journal of Economics*, **84**, 197–216.

Stemp, P. J. and S. J. Turnovsky (1984). 'Optimal Stabilization Policies under Perfect Foresight', in A. J. Hughes-Hallett (ed.), *Applied Decision Analysis and Economic Behavior*. M. Nijhoff, Amsterdam.

Turnovsky, S. J. and W. A. Brock (1980). 'Time Consistency and Optimal Government Policies in Perfect Foresight Equilibrium'. *Journal of Public Economics*, **13**, 183–212.

6 Macroeconomic policy design in an interdependent world

DAVID CURRIE AND PAUL LEVINE*

I Introduction

Although most of the literature on macroeconomic policy design has focused on policy questions in the single open economy, there is an important strand that is concerned with the issues raised by interdependence between economies. (See, for example, Hamada and Sakurai (1978), Hamada (1979), Canzoneri and Gray (1983), Cooper (1983), Corden (1983), Miller and Salmon (1983, 1984), Sachs (1983), and Turner (1983, 1984).) This literature emphasises the game-theoretic, strategic aspect of policy-making in the international arena, and the prospects that non-cooperative forms of policy, arising from the elements of externality in the effects of policy internationally, may lead to outcomes markedly inferior to those of cooperative policies.

As Corden (1983) notes, analytical tractability has limited this analysis to static models, or to dynamic models with rather rudimentary dynamics, or to neglect of the longer run dynamics by focusing only on short run outcomes. In view of the complexities of the interactions between countries, whether through prices, real demands, asset prices or the flow of funds, this neglect of dynamics is a clear limitation. In this paper, we seek to overcome it by examining policy interactions and interdependence in a stochastic rational expectations model with developed dynamics within a framework that considers both the short and longer run effects of policy.

In the arena of policy debate, there has been evident the objective of formulating policy in terms of simple rules. Thus we may cite the advocacy of monetary or nominal income targeting as a major plank of policy, or the more recent advocacy of particular forms of decoupled control both for the single open economy (see Vines et al. (1983)) and for coping with problems of interdependence (see Meade (1983)). The arguments for simplicity include the perceived advantages in providing an anchor for nominal variables, the gains in understanding derived from stating policy

228

in simple terms, as well as propositions about the relative information advantage in certain variables. (For further discussion, see Currie and Levine (1984).) In the international sphere, such simple rules for the conduct of policy may act to constrain the options for noncooperative behaviour whilst remaining within the agreed rules of the game. Underlying this argument is the notion that it may be easier to secure international agreement on the qualitative aspects of the ground rules for the conduct of policy rather than the quantitative aspects, except within broad ranges. Simple rules, by constraining the range of policy options, may serve to constrain the degree of noncooperative behaviour.

Section II establishes a control theory framework to assist in addressing these questions. Our analysis is conducted throughout in a stochastic context. We also assume rational or consistent expectations, so that the private sector makes no systematic errors in prediction. This provides a useful test-bed for policy regimes, since a policy which performs badly under consistent expectations could perform well only by virtue of systematic forecasting error by the private sector, and this provides an ill-founded and inherently unstable basis for policy. We therefore set out a procedure for deriving optimal linear time-invariant feedback rules in linear stochastic rational expectations models, with the form of the feedback rule constrained as appropriate. This permits, for example, the design of optimal indicator regimes or optimal decoupled systems. We also derive the full optimal rule, noting the rather complex form that this rule takes. To permit analysis of noncooperative game behaviour, we show, for simple rules, how the Nash equilibrium in a two-country game can be derived as the outcome of a Cournot-type adjustment behaviour. However, when extended to the two countries pursuing the full optimal rule this process leads to an ever-expanding state vector, which may provide an additional rationale for simple rules. These procedures are used in Section VI.

In Section III we set up a dynamic stochastic rational expectations model of the open economy with a developed wage/price spiral, a government budget constraint and asset accumulation, and exchange rate dynamics under a floating exchange rate regime. In the context of this model, we review a variety of simple rules for the conduct of monetary and fiscal policy in the single open economy. These include the use of various indicators (the money supply, the exchange rate, nominal income and the price level) for the adjustment of interest rates. They also include a variety of decoupled rules for monetary and fiscal policy, including those advocated by Meade (Meade (1983), Vines et al. (1983)). Of the simple rules considered, the price rule dominates the others. Thus it performs well in the face of a variety of disturbances, and in this sense provides 'a horse for all courses', in contrast to the other simple rules. Moreover, its superior performance continues to hold up in the face of wide parameter variation. Relative to full optimal monetary policy, its performance is good, so that the costs of simplicity for this rule are not high. Its performance relative to full optimal monetary and fiscal policy is not so good, but nonetheless for a simple rule it performs rather well. The form of the full optimal feedback rule suggests that some extra refinements, adding, in particular, an element of integral control, may well improve its performance further.

Thus our methods of policy design for the single open economy suggest that the choice lies between two types of policy: full optimal policy, which is rather complicated to specify and implement, but yields the best performance (by definition); and a form of simple price rule, which is much simpler to specify and implement, but at the cost of some (though not excessive) loss in performance. These results are arrived at by means of methods of policy evaluation that, although non-standard in their use of stochastic control under rational expectations, are typical in their focus on the single economy and their consequent neglect of issues of interdependence. They are therefore of a kind that might be derived from a macroeconometric model of the single open economy which properly models expectations. The focus of the policy analysis is in the remaining section of the paper, where we examine cooperative policy design and compare it with design in the single open economy. In Section VI, we examine policy design in an interdependent world of two identical economies. It is shown that the problem of policy design decomposes into two orthogonal problems, the aggregate problem (which applies equally to a world of many identical economies) and the divergence problem. Optimal cooperative policy is bound to involve rather more fiscal activism and less active use of interest rate policy than for the single open economy policy design. Furthermore, the simple monetary rule for interest rates outperforms the nominal income rule, and this in turn outperforms the price rule, which gives no gain from control. This reverses the ranking of these policies when evaluated for the single open economy.

Of equal interest is the global performance of rules designed for the single open economy. Both the monetary and the nominal income rule perform tolerably when evaluated in this different context. By contrast, the price rule formulated for the single open economy results in total global destabilisation if implemented generally; this appears to be because it relies for its effects on the link between the exchange rate and the domestic price level. Since this cannot operate in the aggregate, it triggers an over-reaction of interest rates to inflationary pressures and consequently leads to instability. In this sense, it is a beggar-my-neighbour policy. The full optimal rule designed for the single open economy also relies significantly on the exchange rate influence on prices, and therefore shares in its beggar-my-neighbour consequences.

These results highlight the externalities inherent in macroeconomic policy design in an interdependent world. They suggest that there may be an incentive for single countries to renege on the optimal cooperative policy and adopt free-riding forms of policy. To shed further light on this issue, we report in Section VI the results of Nash games played between two countries with different constraining ground-rules. These confirm that the incentives to renege on the best cooperative design of monetary or nominal income rules, whilst remaining within the overall constraint of such rules, is not strong. By contrast, there is a strong incentive to renege on the cooperative price rule (which amounts to minimal control), particularly since the country which reneges first retains an advantage even in the long run. Moreover, the threat to retaliate in kind is not credible since it leads to total destabilisation of the system. Clearly the price rule, and other rules (such as the full optimal rule) which rely on the exchange rate influence on domestic prices are inimical to international cooperation.

This analysis highlights the importance of analysing policy in an interdependent, rather than a single country, framework. It also leads to the issue of systems of penalties to sustain cooperative solutions to the policy problem. We offer some thoughts on that question in the conclusions to this paper.

II The solution procedure

We consider the following general linear stochastic rational expectations model:

$$\begin{bmatrix} dz \\ dx^e \end{bmatrix} = A \begin{bmatrix} z \\ x \end{bmatrix} dt + Bwdt + dv \tag{II.1}$$

where $z(t)$ is an $(n-m) \times 1$ vector of variables predetermined at time t, $x(t)$ is an $m \times 1$ vector of non-predetermined or 'free' variables, $dx^e = x^e(t+dt, t) - x(t)$ where $x^e(t, \tau)$ denotes the expectation of $x(t)$ formed at time τ, $w(t)$ is an $r \times 1$ vector of instruments, A and B are $n \times n$ and $n \times r$ matrices respectively with time-invariant coefficients and dv is an $n \times 1$ vector of white noise disturbances independently distributed with $\text{cov}(dv) = \Sigma dt$ where Σ is a positive definite matrix with time-invariant coefficients. Variables z, x and w are all measured as deviations about the long-run equilibrium.

We see a linear time-invariant feedback rule,

$$w = D \begin{bmatrix} z \\ x \end{bmatrix} \tag{II.2}$$

where D is an $r \times n$ matrix with time-invariant coefficients which minimises the asymptotic quadratic loss function, asy $E(W)$, where

$$W = [z^T \ x^T] Q \begin{bmatrix} z \\ x \end{bmatrix} + w^T R w \tag{II.3}$$

and Q and R are $n \times n$ and $r \times r$ time-invariant positive definite matrices respectively. By appropriate restrictions on the coefficients of D, (II.2) can represent a simple feedback rule on only some variables of the system. Such simple rules can include indicator and intermediate target regimes and decoupled rules of the kind advocated by Meade (see Vines, Maciejowski and Meade (1983)).

Our solution procedure may be sketched as follows. We first solve the model for a given feedback rule D, which is assumed to be known by economic agents along with the model and the current state vector. The solution yields the asymptotic variances and covariances of all endogenous variables, and hence permits us to evaluate the loss function. We can then implement an iterative search procedure in which the unconstrained elements of D are varied so as to minimise the loss function.

This procedure yields optimal simple linear time-invariant feedback rules. That policy should be expressible in this form is restrictive for two reasons. First, as we indicate in the following, the full optimal policy cannot be implemented in the form of a linear time-invariant feedback rule of the form of (II.2), so that to insist on policy formulated in this form is restrictive. (This is an important difference between control of models with, and those without, free variables. However, as indicated in Section II.2, the optimal rule can be implemented by means of linear feedback on the z vector, together with integral control terms involving z.) Second, restrictions on the coefficients of the D matrix, such as the zero restrictions that arise naturally from indicator regimes or decoupled control, limit policy design further.

It is helpful to be able to assess the costs of these restrictions on policy design. For if the costs are not high, the benefits of design simplicity discussed in the introduction to this paper may make simple policy desirable. This requires some benchmark against which the performance of simple rules can be judged. The obvious benchmark is that of the performance of the full optimal rule.

The full optimal rule is particularly useful as a benchmark since it has the important property of certainty equivalence. This means that the closed loop feedback solution to the deterministic and stochastic control problems are of the same form, so that the solution to the stochastic problem is independent of the disturbance covariance matrix, Σ. Use of the full optimal rule means that policy makers need not assess the combination of shocks likely to perturb the system. In this sense, the full optimal rule provides 'a horse for all courses'.

By contrast, linear time-invariant feedback rules of the form (II.2) do not satisfy certainty equivalence. This is because the optimal choice of the parameters of D depends on the disturbance covariance matrix, Σ. This is a major disadvantage of simplicity in policy design, for policy makers may have no reasonable estimate of Σ. It is not helpful to policy makers to have a 'horse for each course' if the actual course is not known.

However, the lack of certainty equivalence does not rule out the existence of simple rules that are robust in the sense of performing reasonably well whatever the disturbance covariance matrix, Σ. (We here judge performance relative to that of the full optimal rule.) In our design evaluation of Section IV we pay particular attention to whether robust rules of this kind exist. Of course, robustness with respect to changes in the parameters of the disturbance covariance matrix is merely one aspect of the broader question of robustness with respect to other model parameter and specification changes, which we also consider.

Before turning to the detailed derivation of our control methods, we must briefly consider the issue of time-inconsistency. Both the full optimal rule and the linear time-invariant rules considered here are time-inconsistent, because they offer to policy makers a short term incentive to renege on the rule which the private sector have assumed in formulating their plans. However, reneging imposes longer run costs by undermining faith in the ability of governments to keep to commitments. If such faith is undermined altogether, the result is likely to be a closed-loop Nash equilibrium. This may be arrived at by means of a type of Cournot adjustment process, with each side determining its decision sequentially on the assumption of a given feedback rule on the part of the other.[1] Alternatively, it may come about by the private sector assuming that the government will renege if there is any short run incentive to do so, calculating the government's optimal action accordingly, and then determining its optimal plan in the light of this; the government then determines its optimal plan subject to this procedure for private sector decision making. This equilibrium is time consistent, and is necessarily inferior to the time inconsistent full optimal policy considered in this paper. (See Buiter (1983).)

If the closed-loop Nash equilibrium is markedly inferior to the equilibrium under time-inconsistent optimal policy, whether full or simple, this provides a strong incentive for a far-sighted government not to succumb to the temptation of reneging. Our earlier analysis (Levine and Currie (1983)) suggests this to be the case, at least for certain simple models. It also shows that well-designed simple rules may perform significantly better than the closed-loop Nash equilibrium, so that a similar point applies to this class of rules. This does not, of course, mean that a more myopic government will not renege, but it does suggest that the problems of time-inconsistent policies need not be over-stressed.[2]

We now consider in turn the detailed derivation of optimal simple rules and the full optimal rule, together with the two-player games.

II.1 Optimal simple rule

The first step of the solution procedure is to obtain the rational expectations solution to (II.1) for a given feedback rule (II.2) which is assumed to be known by economic agents along with the model and the current endogenous variables.[3] Substituting (II.2) into (II.3), we obtain

$$\begin{bmatrix} dz \\ dx^e \end{bmatrix} = [A + BD]\begin{bmatrix} z \\ x \end{bmatrix} dt + dv \tag{II.4}$$

We are concerned only with solutions to (II.4) which have the saddle-point property that the number of eigenvalues of $A + BD$ with positive part equals m, the remaining $n - m$ eigenvalues having negative real parts. We shall assume that the pair (A, B) is stabilizable in the sense that there exists at least one D such that $A + BD$ has the saddle-point property. Then stochastic stability follows since we only have additive disturbances (Turnovsky (1977)). We now require the immediate response of the non-predetermined variables x to the feedback rule (II.2). This is found by first forming the matrix of left eigenvectors of $A + BD$, M say, with rows ordered so that the first $n - m$ are the eigenvectors associated with the stable eigenvectors. We then partition so that

$$M = \begin{bmatrix} M_{11} & M_{12} \\ M_{21} & M_{22} \end{bmatrix} \tag{II.5}$$

where M_{11} is an $(n - m) \times (n - m)$ matrix and M_{22} is $m \times m$. Then, provided that $A + BD$ has the saddle-point property, the rational expectations solution places the trajectory on the unique saddle path

$$x = -M_{22}^{-1} M_{21} z = -Nz \tag{II.6}$$

The feedback rule (II.2) now becomes

$$w = (D_1 - D_2 N)z = \tilde{D}z \tag{II.7}$$

where $D = [D_1 D_2]$ with D_1 of dimension $r \times (n - m)$ and D_2 of dimension

$r \times m$. We note that (II.7) is a feedback rule only on the predetermined variables. It follows immediately that D is unique only up to choice of $\tilde{D}$, so that without loss of generality we can confine attention to linear time invariant feedback rules on the predetermined variables, z, alone (i.e. $D_2 = 0$).[4] Let A be partitioned as for M, $B = \begin{bmatrix} B^1 \\ B^2 \end{bmatrix}$ where B^1 is $(n-m) \times r$, B^2 is $m \times r$ and $dv = \begin{bmatrix} dv^1 \\ dv^2 \end{bmatrix}$ where dv^1 is $(n-m) \times 1$ and dv^2 is $m \times 1$. Then substituting (II.6) and (II.7) into (II.1), we have from the first $(n-m)$ rows that

$$dz = [A_{11} - A_{12} N + B^1 \tilde{D}] z \, dt + dv^1. \tag{II.8}$$

The solution to (II.8) is

$$z(t) = \int_0^t e^{C(t-s)} \, dv^1(s) + e^{Ct} z(0) \tag{II.9}$$

where $C = [A_{11} - A_{12} N + B^1 \tilde{D}]$. Equations (II.6) and (II.9) constitute the rational expectations solution to (II.1) for a given feedback rule (II.2).

The second step of the control problem is to optimise with respect to $\tilde{D}$. This requires us to allow for the fact that N depends on $\tilde{D}$. Substituting (II.2) into (II.3), we have

$$\text{asy } E(W) = \text{tr}(\text{asy } E(W)) = \text{tr} \left((Q + D^T R D) Y \right) \tag{II.10}$$

where $Y = \text{asy } \text{cov} \begin{pmatrix} z \\ x \end{pmatrix}$ and we have used the result $\text{tr}(ABC) = \text{tr}(CAB)$. The asymptotic covariance matrix $z = \text{asy } E(z^T z)$ satisfies

$$ZC^{\text{I}} + CZ + \Sigma_{11} = 0 \tag{II.11}$$

where $\Sigma_{11} \, dt = \text{cov}(dv^1)$. Then combining (II.6) and (II.10) we obtain

$$\text{asy } E(W) = \text{tr}(\tilde{Q} Z) \tag{II.12}$$

where

$$\tilde{Q} = Q_{11} + 2N^T Q_{21} + N^T Q_{22} N + \tilde{D}^T R \tilde{D}. \tag{II.13}$$

The welfare loss asy $E(W)$ can now be minimised with respect to $\tilde{D}$ by a standard numerical gradient method, subject to the constraint that the saddle-point property is preserved (i.e. that the number of eigenvalues of $A + B^1 \tilde{D}$ with positive real part is equal to m).

From the form of (II.11) and (II.12), it is clear that, in general, the optimal choice of $\tilde{D}$ is dependent on Σ_{11}, so that certainty equivalence does not hold.

II.2 The full optimal rule

The following is a solution procedure, employing Pontryagin's maximum principle, first proposed by Calvo (1978) and later developed by Driffill (1982) and Miller and Salmon (1983).[5] We consider first the deterministic finite time-horizon problem with objective function

$$W = \int_0^\tau (y^T Q y + w^T R w) \, dt \tag{II.14}$$

and $y = \begin{bmatrix} z \\ x \end{bmatrix}$. Then on introducing the costate row vector $\lambda(t)$, by the maximum principle we minimise

$$J = W + \int_0^\tau \lambda(Ay + Bw - \dot{y}) \, dt \tag{II.15}$$

with respect to w, y and λ. Define the Hamiltonian

$$H = (y^T Q y + w^T R w) + \lambda(Ay + Bw) \tag{II.16}$$

Then

$$J = \int_0^\tau (H - \lambda \dot{y}) \, dt \tag{II.17}$$

Hence, considering arbitrary variations in λ, $\delta J = 0$ if and only if

$$\frac{\partial H}{\partial \lambda} = \dot{y} \tag{II.18}$$

which, from (II.16), is simply the model (II.1) in the deterministic case.

Now consider variations in J due to independent variations in w and y. Integrating (II.17) by parts, we have

$$J = -\lambda(\tau) y(\tau) + \lambda(0) y(0) + \int_0^\tau (H + y\dot{\lambda}) \, dt \tag{II.19}$$

Differentiating (II.19),

$$\delta J = -\lambda(\tau) \delta y(\tau) + \lambda(0) \delta y(0) + \int_0^\tau \left[\left(\frac{\partial H}{\partial y} + \dot{\lambda} \right) \delta y + \frac{\partial H}{\partial w} \delta w \right] dt \tag{II.20}$$

Partition $\lambda(0) = [\lambda_1(0), \lambda_2(0)]$ where λ_1 is $1 \times (n-m)$ and λ_2 is $1 \times m$. Then $\lambda(0) \delta y(0) = \lambda_1(0) \delta z(0) + \lambda_2(0) \delta x(0) = \lambda_2(0) \delta x(0)$ since $z(t)$ is predetermined (i.e. $z(0)$ is given). It follows that $\delta J = 0$ for arbitrary changes $\delta y(\tau)$, $\delta x(0)$, δy and δw if and only if

$$\lambda(\tau) = 0 \tag{II.21}$$

$$\lambda_2(0) = 0 \tag{II.22}$$

$$\frac{\partial H}{\partial w} = 0 \tag{II.23}$$

and

$$\dot{\lambda} = -\frac{\partial H}{\partial y} \tag{II.24}$$

The condition (II.22) can also be obtained (Driffill (1982)) by using the standard result that $\dfrac{\partial W}{\partial y(0)} = \lambda(0)$ at the optimal point. Hence $\dfrac{\partial W}{\partial x(0)} = \lambda_2(0)$. But the welfare loss must be insensitive to changes in the initial values of the non-predetermined variables $x(0)$. Thus $\dfrac{\partial W}{\partial x(0)} = 0$ and the result follows.

From (II.23) and (II.24) with H defined by (II.16), we obtain

$$w = -\tfrac{1}{2}R^{-1}B^T \lambda^T \tag{II.25}$$

and

$$\dot{\lambda} = -(2y^T Q + \lambda A) \tag{II.26}$$

Define $p = \tfrac{1}{2}\lambda^T$. Then the optimal rule for the deterministic control problem is given by

$$w = -R^{-1}B^T p \tag{II.27}$$

where

$$\begin{bmatrix} \dot{y} \\ \dot{p} \end{bmatrix} = \begin{bmatrix} A & -BR^{-1}B^T \\ -Q & -A^T \end{bmatrix} \begin{bmatrix} y \\ p \end{bmatrix} = H \begin{bmatrix} y \\ p \end{bmatrix} \tag{II.28}$$

and z, p satisfy the boundary conditions that $z(0)$ is given, $p_2(0) = 0$ and $p(\tau) = 0$.

It is a standard result in control theory (see, for example, Kwakernaak and Sivan, p. 147) that provided H has $2n$ distinct eigenvalues, n of these associated with predetermined variables $[z^T \, p_2^T]$ will be stable and n associated with non-predetermined variables $[x^T \, p_1^T]$ will be unstable where $p^T = [p_1^T, p_2^T]$. Then re-arranging (II.28) we have

$$\begin{bmatrix} \dot{z} \\ \dot{p}_2 \\ \dot{p}_1 \\ \dot{x} \end{bmatrix} = \begin{bmatrix} A_{11} & -J_{12} & -J_{11} & A_{12} \\ -Q_{21} & -A_{22}^T & -A_{21}^T & -Q_{22} \\ -Q_{11} & -A_{12}^T & -A_{11}^T & -Q_{12} \\ A_{21} & -J_{22} & -J_{21} & A_{22} \end{bmatrix} \begin{bmatrix} z \\ p_2 \\ p_1 \\ x \end{bmatrix} = \tilde{H} \begin{bmatrix} z \\ p_2 \\ p_1 \\ x \end{bmatrix} \tag{II.29}$$

where $J = BR^{-1}B^T$ and matrices A, J and Q are partitioned as before. Equation (II.29) expresses the model in a form analogous to the standard deterministic rational expectations model. The case of the infinite time horizon, $\tau \to \infty$, is analytically tractable. For in this case (using an argument analogous to that leading to (II.6) the rational expectations assumption that $y(t) \to 0$ as $t \to \infty$ (i.e. the model is stable) together with condition (II.21) which implies $p(t) \to 0$ as $t \to \infty$, imposes the relationship

$$\begin{bmatrix} p_1 \\ x \end{bmatrix} = -\tilde{M}_{22}^{-1}\tilde{M}_{21}\begin{bmatrix} z \\ p_2 \end{bmatrix} = -\tilde{N}\begin{bmatrix} z \\ p_2 \end{bmatrix} \tag{II.30}$$

where $\tilde{M}$ is the matrix of left-eigenvectors of H formed and partitioned as for M in (II.6) except that this time we have n stable and n unstable roots.

The feedback rule (II.27) now becomes

$$w = -R^{-1}B^T[-\tilde{N}_{11}z - \tilde{N}_{12}p_2, p_2]^T = D\begin{bmatrix} z \\ p_2 \end{bmatrix} \tag{II.31}$$

where $D = -R^{-1}[-B_1\tilde{N}_{11}, B_2 - B_1\tilde{N}_{12}]$ where $B^T = [B_1, B_2]$ and $\begin{bmatrix} z \\ p_2 \end{bmatrix}$ is given by

$$\begin{bmatrix} \dot{z} \\ \dot{p}_2 \end{bmatrix} = [\tilde{H}_{11} - \tilde{H}_{12}\tilde{N}]\begin{bmatrix} z \\ p_2 \end{bmatrix} = \tilde{C}\begin{bmatrix} z \\ p_2 \end{bmatrix} \tag{II.32}$$

and $\tilde{H}$ is partitioned into four $n \times n$ blocks. The solution to (II.32) is

$$\begin{bmatrix} z \\ p_2 \end{bmatrix} = e^{\tilde{C}t}\begin{bmatrix} z(0) \\ p_2(0) \end{bmatrix} = e^{\tilde{C}t}\begin{bmatrix} z(0) \\ 0 \end{bmatrix} \tag{II.33}$$

which completes the optimal control solution in closed loop and open-loop form.

From the bottom m rows of (II.30) we have that $x = -\tilde{N}_{21}z - \tilde{N}_{22}p_2$ i.e., $p_2 = -\tilde{N}_{22}^{-1}(x + \tilde{N}_{21}z)$. Then substituting into (II.31) we have

$$w = -R^{-1}B^T S\begin{bmatrix} z \\ x \end{bmatrix} \tag{II.34}$$

where
$$S_{11} = -\tilde{N}_{11} + \tilde{N}_{12}\tilde{N}_{22}^{-1}\tilde{N}_{21} \tag{II.35}$$

$$S_{21} = -\tilde{N}_{22}^{-1}\tilde{N}_{21} \tag{II.36}$$

$$S_{12} = \tilde{N}_{12}\tilde{N}_{22}^{-1} \tag{II.37}$$

$$S_{22} = -\tilde{N}_{22}^{-1} \tag{II.38}$$

Matrix S is, of course, the non-negative definite solution to the familiar Riccati equation and (II.35)–(II.38) provide a convenient method of finding such a solution. However the feedback rule (II.34) can only be implemented in conjunction with the nth order system under control, namely (II.28) or (II.29). If the rule were to be announced in the form

(II.34) alone and the private agents' information set consisted of the model (II.1) and current values of z and x, then the argument of Section II.2 shows that it would be equivalent to a feedback rule on z alone, and that the resulting system has order only $(n-m)$. This result contrasts with the standard case where free variables are absent, so that p_2 and x have zero dimension and the optimal rule can be implemented by means of a linear time-invariant feedback rule on the state vector, z. However, the full optimal rule may be implemented by linear feedback on z combined with elements of integral feedback on z; this follows since, from (II.32), p_2 may be expressed as a suitable integral of z.

For the stochastic control problem, we note that it is a standard result of control theory that certainty equivalence applies as between the deterministic and stochastic optimisation problems and this carries over to rational expectations models.[6] This enables us to calculate the loss under the optimal policy for the stochastic case. From (II.30), using $p_2(0) = 0$, we have $p_1(0) = -\tilde{N}_{11} z(0)$. But for the deterministic case, $W = W(z(0))$, with $W(0) = 0$. Also $\dfrac{dW}{dz(0)} = 2p_1(0) = -2\tilde{N}_{11} z(0)$. Hence integrating, we have

$$W = -z^T(0)\, \tilde{N}_{11}\, z(0) \tag{II.39}$$

since $\tilde{N}_{11}$ is symmetric and non-positive definite. The corresponding welfare loss in the stochastic case is the same provided we put $z(0)\, z^T(0) = \Sigma_{11}$ where $\operatorname{cov}(dv^1) = \Sigma_{11}\, dt$. (See Levine and Currie (1984).) Thus since (II.31) and (II.32) define the optimal rule for the deterministic problem, they also define the optimal rule for the stochastic counterpart quite independently of the covariance matrix of the disturbances perturbing the system.

II.3 A two-country closed-loop Nash game

Equation (II.1) is sufficiently general to represent an n-country model of interdependent economies. In particular for the case of two countries denote as unstarred variables those referring to country 1 (the 'home' country) and starred variables for country 2 (the 'overseas' sector). Then we may write a two-country model in the form

$$\begin{bmatrix} dz \\ dz^* \\ dx \\ dx^* \end{bmatrix} = A \begin{bmatrix} z \\ z^* \\ x \\ x^* \end{bmatrix} dt + [B,\ B^*] \begin{bmatrix} w \\ w^* \end{bmatrix} dt + \begin{bmatrix} dv_1 \\ dv_1^* \\ dv_2 \\ dv_2^* \end{bmatrix} \tag{II.40}$$

where the dimensions of z, z^*, x and x^* are $(n-m) \times 1$, $(n^*-m^*) \times 1$, $m \times 1$ and $m^* \times 1$ respectively.

Consider first the case of the two countries pursuing simple rules of the form (II.2). Suppose country 2 adopts a policy given by

$$
w^* = D^* \begin{bmatrix} z \\ z^* \\ x \\ x^* \end{bmatrix}
\tag{II.41}
$$

Then substituting (II.41) into (II.40), country 1 faces the dynamic constraint

$$
\begin{bmatrix} dz \\ dz^* \\ dx \\ dx^* \end{bmatrix} = [A + B^* D^*] \begin{bmatrix} z \\ z^* \\ x \\ x^* \end{bmatrix} + Bwdt + dv
\tag{II.42}
$$

where we denote $dv^T = [dv_1^T \; dv_1^{*T} \; dv_2^T \; dv_2^{*T}]$.

In a Nash game each 'player' chooses its own move taking the current observed 'moves' of other players as given. In a closed-loop Nash game these moves of other players are observed in feedback form on the state vector. For the two-country game presented here this means that country 1 chooses a feedback rule

$$
w = D \begin{bmatrix} z \\ z^* \\ x \\ x^* \end{bmatrix}
\tag{II.43}
$$

taking D^* as *given*. Suppose country 1 has a loss function asy $E(W)$ where

$$
W = [z^T \; z^{*T} \; x^T \; x^{*T}] Q \begin{bmatrix} z \\ z^* \\ x \\ x^* \end{bmatrix} + w^T R w
\tag{II.44}
$$

with a similar loss function asy $E(W^*)$ for country 2, Q and R being replaced with Q^* and R^* respectively. Then the optimisation problem of country 1 – to minimise asy $E(W)$ subject to (II.42) – is in the form of the problem solved in II.1 above and leads to an optimal value for D in the form of a *reaction function* $D = f(D^*)$. Similarly country 2 has a reaction function $D^* = g(D)$ and the Nash equilibrium is at the fixed-point of fg for D and gf for D^*.

A plausible adjustment process by which countries move towards a closed-loop Nash equilibrium is the following Cournot-type sequence of moves. Given an initial feedback rule for country 2 with D^* denoted by $D^*(0)$, country 1 chooses $D = D(1) = f(D^*(0))$. Then country 2 revises its choice of D^* to $D^*(1) = g(D(1))$. Country 1 then re-optimises and so on.

This process may or may not converge to an equilibrium depending on the initial value of D^*. Indeed a Nash equilibrium may not exist and if it does it may not be unique. Given the complexity of models with rational expectations, it seems a formidable task to obtain analytical conditions for the existence, uniqueness and convergence of a Nash equilibrium and we do not attempt to do so here.

Consider next the full optimal policy for the two-country model. Suppose country 2 adopts an optimal rule which from section II.2 can be implemented in the form

$$w^* = D^* \begin{bmatrix} z \\ z^* \\ p_2^* \end{bmatrix} \tag{II.45}$$

where

$$dp_2^* = P^* \begin{bmatrix} z \\ z^* \\ p_2^* \end{bmatrix} \tag{II.46}$$

p_2^* has dimensions $(m+m^*) \times 1$ and P^* depends on A, B, B^* and country 2's loss function. (Country 2 could arrive at (II.45) by assuming country 1 was pursuing a simple rule of the type considered above.) In a closed-loop Nash game country 1 takes (II.45) as given and optimises subject to the dynamic constraint

$$\begin{bmatrix} dz \\ dz^* \\ dp_2^* \\ dx \\ dx^* \end{bmatrix} = \tilde{A} \begin{bmatrix} z \\ z^* \\ p_2^* \\ x \\ x^* \end{bmatrix} dt + \begin{bmatrix} B^1 \\ 0 \\ B^2 \end{bmatrix} wdt + \begin{bmatrix} dv_1 \\ dv_1^* \\ 0 \\ dv_2 \\ dv_2^* \end{bmatrix} \tag{II.47}$$

where

$$\tilde{A} = \begin{bmatrix} A_{11}+B^{*1}D_1^* & B^{*1}D_2^* \\ P_1^* & P_2^* \\ A_{21}+B^{*2}D_1^* & B^{*2}D_2^* \end{bmatrix} \begin{bmatrix} A_{12} \\ 0 \\ A_{22} \end{bmatrix} \tag{II.48}$$

and we have partitioned A so that A_{11} is $(n+n^*-m-m^*) \times (n+n^*-mn^*)$, B so that B^1 is $(n+n^*-m-m^*) \times r$, $D^* = [D_1^*, D_2^*]$ with $D_1^* r \times (n+n^*-m-m^*)$ and P^* similarly. The optimal feedback rule of country 1 is then of the form

$$w = D \begin{bmatrix} z \\ z^* \\ p_2^* \\ p_2 \end{bmatrix} \tag{II.49}$$

where

$$dp_2^* = P \begin{bmatrix} z \\ z^* \\ p_2^* \\ p_2 \end{bmatrix} \tag{II.50}$$

and p_2 has dimensions $(m+m^*) \times 1$. Comparing (II.45) and (II.49) we see that matrices D and D^* defining the feedback rules are not comparable as they have different dimensions.

The reaction function analysis adopted from simple rules is now not applicable. If we envisaged a Cournot-type adjustment process, then with each iteration the model defining the dynamic constraint for the optimising country increases its dimension by the number of non-predetermined variables $m+m^*$. The game may well converge in the sense that the coefficients of D and D^* relating to the additional p_2 and p_2^* terms tend to zero and the welfare loss tends to a finite quantity. However, the possibility of countries actually engaging in games of such complexity seems remote and it would appear that the full optimal closed-loop Nash game is not a plausible form of non-cooperative behaviour. The problem with the full optimal closed-loop Nash game arises because for a single country the full optimal (time inconsistent) rule cannot be implemented as a linear feedback on the state vector alone (Levine and Currie (1984)). If we confine ourselves to simple (and, in general, time-inconsistent) rules of the form (II.41) and (II.43) the problem does not arise. Nor does it arise if one focuses on time-consistent (but sub-optimal) policies for government or on Nash *open-loop* games between countries (see Miller and Salmon (1984)). All these options form interesting directions for research; but in this paper we shall analyse non-cooperative behaviour only in terms of the first, namely simple policy rules.

III The model

Throughout the rest of this paper we use variants of the following eleven equation continuous time stochastic model:

$$dy = \psi_1[\alpha_1 q - \alpha_2(r - \dot{p}^e) + \alpha_3 v - \alpha_4 s + \alpha_5 y^* - y]\,dt + du_1 \tag{III.1}$$

$$dm = \psi_2[\gamma_1 y - \gamma_2 r + p + \gamma_3 v - m]\,dt + du_2 \tag{III.2}$$

$$dv = [-\phi_0 s - \phi_1 y + \phi_2 q + \phi_3 y^*]\,dt - dp \tag{III.3}$$

$$dw = \psi_3\left[\beta_1 \int_{-\infty}^{t} y(\tau)\,d\tau + p^e - w\right]dt + du_3 \tag{III.4}$$

$$\bar{p}^d = c_1 w + (1 - c_1)(w^* + e) \tag{III.5}$$

$$\bar{p} = \theta\bar{p}^d + (1 - \theta)(w^* + e) \tag{III.6}$$

$$dp = \psi_4(\bar{p} - p)\,dt \tag{III.7}$$

$$de^e = (r - r^*)\,dt \tag{III.8}$$

$$q = w^* + e - w \tag{III.9}$$

$$dw^* = -\mu_1 w^* dt + du_4 \tag{III.10}$$

$$dr^* = -\mu_2 r^* dt + du_5 \tag{III.11}$$

where the following notation is used:

  e nominal exchange rate (defined as the price of foreign exchange)
  y real output
  q competitiveness
  r domestic nominal rate of interest
  s autonomous taxation
  v real net financial wealth of the private sector
  m nominal money supply
  p general price index
  p^d price index of domestic output
  w nominal wages
  w^* nominal wages overseas
  r^* foreign nominal rate of interest
  du_i white noise disturbance

Because we are concerned in this paper only with stabilization of the system around an exogenously given long run equilibrium (which may incorporate trends), all variables are measured in terms of deviations of their logarithm from equilibrium, except for interest rates which are measured as deviations of proportions. All parameters are defined to be positive. An 'e' superscript denotes an expectation formed at time t on the basis of information available up to time t; while a '*' superscript denotes the foreign counterpart to the variable in question. A bar denotes a partial equilibrium value. Equation (III.1) represents the IS curve with output adjusting sluggishly with a mean lag of ψ_1^{-1} to competitiveness, the real interest rate, real financial wealth, autonomous taxes and foreign demand. Equation (III.2) represent the LM curve. The money supply is assumed to be demand determined for any given level of interest rates, and money demand adjusts sluggishly to output, interest rates and real financial wealth with a mean lag of ψ_2^{-1}. Equation (III.3) determines the change in real wealth from the determinants of the sum of the government budget deficit and the current account of the balance of payments. Neglecting interesting payments and approximating this relationship log-linearly, this makes the change in real wealth depend positively on competitiveness and foreign output, and negatively on domestic output, autonomous taxes and inflation. Equation (III.4) determines the level of nominal wages. Taking the derivative of its deterministic part, we have that long-run wage inflation is determined by an expectations-augmented Phillips curve, but with actual wage inflation adjusting sluggishly towards this long-run relationship. The sluggishness of wave adjustment generates fluctuations in real output in the face of demand disturbances, even under rational expectations. (See, for example, Buiter (1980)). Equation (III.5) is a partial equilibrium relationship giving the price index of domestic output in equilibrium as a weighted average of domestic and foreign wages (the influence of the latter variable working partly through a mark-up on costs and partly through competitive pricing effects). The corresponding general price index in partial equilibrium is given from (III.6) as a weighted average of domestic prices and foreign wages. Actual prices adjust quickly but not instantly according to (III.7) where ψ_4 is large.[7] Equation (III.8) models the exchange rate as asset market determined under conditions of perfect capital mobility.[8] The expected rate of depreciation of the exchange rate in an interval dt (denoted by d$e^e = e^e(t+dt, t) - e(t)$ where $e^e(\tau, t)$ is the expected exchange rate at time τ, formed at time t) exactly offsets the interest rate differential in favour of the home currency. (Note that $r = 0$ in equilibrium corresponds to the domestic and foreign interest rates being equal.) Unlike other variables, which adjust slowly and are predetermined variables, the exchange rate is non-predetermined and can make discrete jumps in response to changes in exogenous variables or policy rules. Equation (III.9) defines competitiveness in terms of relative costs. Equations (III.10) and (III.11) specify exogenous first order autoregressive processes for foreign wages and foreign interest rates respectively. Some persistence in these disturbances is required if they are to have any impact on domestic variables, and this process involves the minimum additional complication.

Equations (III.1) and (III.11) specify our model of the small open economy. For the two-country analysis of interdependent economies, we assume an identical structure for the overseas economy. Our model of the overseas sector is therefore given by equations (III.1)–(III.9), with unstarred variables being replaced by starred variables and *vice versa*.[9] In the Appendix we set out the single country model and the two country model in the form of equation (II.1).

For our subsequent policy design analysis, we need to define a suitable loss function. Our loss function for the single country is assumed to take the form

$$W = ay^2 + bp^2 + cr^2 + s^2 \qquad (III.12)$$

while for the two country case we assume an aggregate loss function of the form

$$W^a = a(y^a)^2 + b(p^a)^2 + c(r^a)^2 + (s^a)^2 \qquad (III.13)$$

where the 'a' superscript denotes the sum of the relevant variables over the two countries (e.g. $y^a = y + y^*$). We may also consider a divergence loss function given by:

$$W^d = a(y^d)^2 + b(p^d)^2 + c(r^d)^2 + (s^d)^2 \tag{III.14}$$

where the 'd' superscript denotes the divergence of the relevant variable between the two countries (e.g. $y^d = y - y^*$). As shown in the Appendix, the assumption of two identical countries permits us to decompose the two country model into two orthogonal parts, the aggregate model (given by (A.4)) and the divergence model (given by (A.5)). As explained in Section VI, we may therefore choose aggregate rules to minimise the aggregate loss function, given the aggregate model; and, quite separately, choose divergence rules to minimise the divergence loss function, given the divergence model. Since

$$W^a + W^d = 2(W + W^*)$$

where W^* is the value of (III.12) evaluated over foreign variables, this amounts to minimising a loss function consisting of the sum of the individual countries' loss functions.

Our assumed parameter values are set out in Table 6.1, together with variants of a number of parameter values to test for robustness of policies with respect to parameter change. The parameter α_5 is set equal to the degree of openness, $1 - \theta_1 c_1$. For the parameter of the objective function, we assume $c = 1$, penalising equally variations in r and s. We penalise price fluctuations twice as much ($b = 2$) relative to the instruments, and for our central assumptions penalise output and price fluctuations equally ($a = 2$). We also consider a Keynesian variant in which output fluctuations are penalised much more heavily ($a = 5$). Only results for central parameter values are reported in Tables 6.2–14.

IV The design of rules for monetary and fiscal policy in a small open economy

In this section we review results considered in more detail in Currie and Levine (1985) for the small open economy. We first consider monetary policy alone, thus holding the fiscal instrument, autonomous taxes, constant. Since tax receipts fluctuate with the level of economic activity, this amounts to allowing automatic fiscal stabilisers to operate unimpeded.

Our simple rules for monetary policy alone take the form

$$r = \begin{cases} \beta m & \text{monetary rule} \\ \beta e & \text{exchange rate rule} \\ \beta(y+p) & \text{nominal income rule} \\ \beta p & \text{price level rule} \end{cases} \tag{IV.1}$$

where β is chosen optimally by the procedure outlined in Section II.1. Each of the rules provides a long run anchor for expected nominal variables provided that disturbances to the system follow stationary processes.[10] In the case of the exchange rate target, this anchor depends on foreign prices following a stationary process, but trends in foreign prices may be offset by a suitable trend in the exchange rate along the long run equilibrium path.

We next consider the use of fiscal policy (represented in the model by autonomous tax changes) in conjunction with monetary policy. We consider three forms of decoupled control rules given by

$$\text{DCR I} \quad \begin{cases} r = \beta_1(e+w^*-w) \\ s = \beta_2(y+p) \end{cases}$$

$$\text{DCR II} \quad \begin{cases} r = \beta_1 e \\ s = \beta_2(y+p) \end{cases} \tag{IV.2}$$

$$\text{DCR III} \begin{cases} r = \beta_1 p \\ s = \beta_2 y \end{cases}$$

The first, DCR I, represents a Meade-type assignment of using fiscal policy to keep nominal income on track and monetary policy to stabilise the real exchange rate. DCR II is similar, except monetary policy now tracks the nominal, rather than the real, exchange rate. DCR III represents an extension of the price rule in (IV.1) whereby monetary policy is assigned to the price level while fiscal policy reacts to real output fluctuations. This rule implies that a rise in output, for example, generates a contraction of fiscal policy, with a subsequent tightening of monetary policy as and when there is an effect of higher output on inflation. All these rules are of a simple proportioned form: as noted below, elements of integral control may also be desirable.

The solution procedure described in Section II.1 can now be used to find values of β for rule (IV.1), and of β_1 and β_2 for (IV.2), that minimise asy (W) with W given by (III.12).[11] As noted in that section certainty equivalence does not apply for simple rules so that the design of each category of rules depends on the covariance matrix of the disturbances. Our approach to this problem is to consider one disturbance at a time and choose the optimal value of the parameter (or parameters) for each rule. We then evaluate the welfare loss for the chosen optimal rule when each of the other shocks in turn hits the system.

For each form of simple rule then there exist up to five optimal rules corresponding to anticipated disturbances u_i, $i = 1, 5$. In Table 6.2 we report only those with superior performance for central parameter values

Table 6.1. *Parameter values*

parameter	low	central	high
ψ_1		0.5	
ψ_2		0.5	
ψ_3		0.5	
ψ_4		10.0	
α_1		0.3	
α_2		0.1	0.5
α_3	0.1	1.0	2.0
α_4		0.4	
γ_1		1.0	
γ_2		1.0	
γ_3	0.1	1.0	
β_1		0.3	2.0
ϕ_0		1.0	
ϕ_1		1.3	
ϕ_2		0.1	
ϕ_3		0.5	
c_1	0.5	0.7	
θ	0.5	0.7	
μ_1		0.5	
μ_2		0.5	
a		2.0	5.0
b		2.0	
c		1.0	

Table 6.2. *Best policy rules and welfare losses for the single open economy*

Policy rule	Disturbances				
	du_1	du_2	du_3	du_4	du_5
Minimal control	2.44	0.00	1.22	0.96	3.83
Optimal monetary	2.28	0.00	0.39	0.09	0.39
Optimal monetary + fiscal	1.50	0.00	0.22	0.09	0.31
$r = 0.56\,(y+p)$	3.08	0.00	0.82	0.16	1.04
$r = 0.77\,m$	3.82	0.48	0.68	0.27	1.09
$r = 4.02\,p$	2.31	0.00	0.47	0.16	0.46
$r = 10\,p$ $s = 0.46\,y$	2.04	0.00	0.38	0.19	0.75
$r = 2.87\,p$ $s = 1.24\,y$	2.49	0.00	0.33	0.15	0.60

and loss function asy $E(2y^2+2p^2+r^2+s^2)$. For monetary policy alone the exchange rate rule, because of the segmentation of the model under this regime, gives no improvement on minimal control for all disturbances except u_5 and even for that disturbance it performs relatively badly.[12] There is little to choose between the best nominal income and monetary rules reported; the former performs better for u_1 and u_2 shocks and the latter for a u_3 shock. but the rule that completely dominates in category (IV.1) is the price rule, i.e. irrespective of the nature of the disturbance the best price rule is superior to the best monetary rule, nominal income or exchange rate rules. In addition, comparison with the performance of the full optimal rule shows that its performance compares quite well with this benchmark, particularly for domestic shocks. Thus the costs of simplicity do not appear to be enormous for this rule. The other simple rules, by contrast, perform rather badly overall.

It is a familiar result from the government budget constraint literature (see, for example, Blinder and Solow (1973), Christ (1979)) that monetary targeting may be unstable if the wealth effects on money demand are large relative to those on expenditure. To check whether this was at the root of the poor performance of the monetary targets, we examined the consequences of increasing β so that the money supply is kept strictly on a fixed track. The results reported in Table 6.3 indicate that there is no tendency for instability of the model under strict monetary targeting, suggesting that monetary targets perform badly because of their failure to dampen volatility rather than because of inherent instability.

For the central parameter set we also find the price rule is rather robust in its performance. A choice of β somewhere in the range between 2 and 10 yields a similar performance that is insensitive to disturbance uncertainty. To examine the consequences of parameter variation, we subjected the model to a variety of parameter changes (see Table 6.1). These include a more Keynesian objective function, an increased degree of openness, a large impact of demand on inflation, an increased effect of wealth on money demand, an increased direct influence of monetary policy on demand, and reduced wealth effects on aggregate demand and money demand. While the details of these results vary, the superiority and robustness of the price level rule remains intact; while the performance of the other simple rules remains poor. The only significant difference is if the influence of demand on inflation is stepped up, when the performance of the price level rule relative to the full optimal rule falls significantly in dealing with domestic shocks.

Turning to rule (IV.2) we find that DCR I and DCR II perform badly and are ruled out as plausible policy rules. DCR III in the form of two variants performs well but in neither case is there a clear-cut improvement

Table 6.3. *The consequences of monetary targeting. Policy rules* $r = \beta m$, *with increasing values of* β

β		asy var (m)	asy var (r)	asy var (p)	asy var (y)	Welfare loss
du_1	5	0.07	1.72	1.07	1.20	6.25
	10	0.02	2.07	1.17	1.16	6.73
	15	0.01	2.20	1.20	1.15	6.90
	20	0.01	2.27	1.22	1.14	6.99
	Optimal = minimal	1.00	0.00	0.03	1.19	2.44
	Minimal control	1.00	0.00	0.03	1.19	2.44
du_2	5	0.16	4.11	0.09	0.00	4.29
	10	0.09	9.01	0.06	0.01	9.13
	15	0.06	9.01	0.06	0.01	14.06
	20	0.05	18.95	0.03	0.01	19.03
	Optimal = minimal	1.00	0.00	0.00	0.00	0.00
	Minimal control	1.00	0.00	0.00	0.00	0.00
du_3	5	0.01	0.22	0.13	0.15	0.77
	10	0.00	0.25	0.13	0.14	0.79
	15	0.00	0.26	0.13	0.14	0.79
	20	0.00	0.27	0.13	0.14	0.68
	Optimal ($\beta = 0.77$)	0.12	0.07	0.12	0.19	0.68
	Minimal control	0.62	0.00	0.37	0.24	1.22
du_4	5	0.00	0.03	0.07	0.01	0.18
	10	0.00	0.03	0.07	0.01	0.17
	15	0.00	0.03	0.06	0.01	0.17
	20	0.00	0.03	0.06	0.01	0.16
	Optimal ($\beta > 40$)	0.00	0.003	0.06	0.01	0.16
	Minimal control	0.29	0.00	0.46	0.02	0.96
du_5	5	0.01	0.12	0.28	0.02	0.72
	10	0.00	0.13	0.26	0.02	0.68
	15	0.00	0.13	0.25	0.02	0.66
	20	0.00	0.13	0.24	0.02	0.65
	Optimal ($\beta > 40$)	0.00	0.13	0.24	0.02	0.64
	Minimal control	1.14	0.00	1.82	0.10	3.83

on the best price rule using monetary policy alone. The first variant of DCR III improves the performance in the face of u_1 and u_3 shocks at the expense of a deterioration in the face of u_4 and u_5. The second variant provides still more improvement in the face of u_3 shocks at the expense of a deterioration for u_1 and u_5 shocks.

The top of Table 6.2 presents comparisons with full optimal policies, both for monetary policy alone and for fiscal and monetary policy together. The additional use of fiscal policy gives a significant gain in handling domestic disturbances. In consequence, optimal policy significantly outperforms our best simple rules with respect to all disturbances. Moreover, additional simulations showed that the performance of the optimal rule is robust with respect to parameter changes. When fiscal policy is considered, therefore, the costs of simplicity are high. However, the price level rule continues to perform well relative to other forms of simple rule. The poorer performance of the price rule relative to optimal policy when fiscal policy is considered may reflect the absence of any elements of integral control in the design of our simple rules. It remains to be investigated whether better rules can be devised that incorporate integral as well as proportional feedback, whilst remaining simple in design.

V The cooperative two country control problem

Hitherto in this paper, we have considered policy design in the small open economy, treating the rest of the world as exogenous. In this section, we examine the consequences of assuming two interdependent economies, each identical to the model described in Section III and assumed throughout our previous analysis.

Our assumed loss function for the aggregate problem is described by (III.13), and penalises deviations in aggregate variables summed over the two countries. An orthogonal divergence problem is that defined by minimising a loss function (III.14) defined over deviations of the differences in variables between the two countries (see Appendix). The joint solution to the aggregate and divergence problem is equivalent to minimising a loss function which is the sum of the individual country loss functions defined by (III.12).

We focus first on the aggregate problem, and consider the performance of simple rules in this context. Since the exchange rate does not enter the aggregate problem, we ignore the exchange rate rule given in IV.1, as well as DCR I and DCR II. We also consider three new variants of rule defined by:

$$\text{NIR} \quad \begin{cases} r = \beta_1(y+p) \\ s = \beta_2(y+p) \end{cases}$$

$$\text{DCR IV} \quad \begin{cases} r = \beta_1 m \\ s = \beta_2(y+p) \end{cases} \tag{V.1}$$

$$\text{NIFR} \quad s = \beta_2(y+p)$$

NIR represents a nominal income rule where both monetary and fiscal policy are used jointly to track nominal income. DCR IV represents a form of decoupled control, where interest rates are used to track the money supply and fiscal policy tracks nominal income. NIFR represents a nominal income target pursued by fiscal policy alone.

Table 6.4. *The aggregate two country problem: monetary policy alone*

Expected disturbance (unit variance)	Policy rule		Actual disturbance (unit variance)	
			du_1^a	du_3^a
all	Minimal Control	$(r = 0.00\ p)$	19.30	17.05
	Optimal		14.79	14.50
du_1^a	Nominal Income	$(r = 1.01\ (y+p))$	15.45	17.84
	Monetary	$(r = 0.66\ m)$	16.18	15.71
	Price	$(r = 0.006\ p)$	19.26	17.05
du_3^a	Nominal Income	$(r = 0.38\ (y+p))$	16.70	16.40
	Monetary	$(r = 0.50\ m)$	16.27	15.61
	Price	$(r = 0.02\ p)$	19.35	17.05
	Open Economy Best Rules:			
	$r = 0.56\ (y+p)$		16.03	16.53
	$r = 0.77\ m$		16.23	15.86
	$r = 4.02\ p$		unstable	
	Optimal		16.90	23.02

Table 6.4 presents results for the aggregate problem for the rules using monetary policy alone (to be compared with the results of Section IV. Because the scope for monetary policy is much less for the aggregate problem, with the channel of influence via the exchange rate ruled out, the gain from control is not large. This may be seen by comparing the results reported for minimal and optimal control respectively. Of the simple rules, the price rule gives no gain whatever relative to minimal control. Both nominal income and monetary rules give some gain, the nominal income rule coping better with demand (u_1) shocks and the monetary rule performing better for supply shocks (u_3).

The bottom part of Table 6.4 reports the performance of the best simple rules designed for the single economy reported in Section IV when applied in both countries simultaneously. The nominal income and monetary rules are not dissimilar to those devised for the aggregate country. The price rule, by contrast represents a rather active feedback on prices, and for the aggregate economy it is totally destabilising. Thus the best rule designed for the single open economy is disastrous in its performance when applied generally. Similar problems apply to the full optimal rule designed for the single economy, when applied generally. Although it is stable, Table 6.4 shows its performance to be very poor. This highlights the dangers of the usual approach to policy design which focuses on the single open economy.

Table 6.5. *The aggregate two country problem: fiscal and monetary policy*

Expected disturbance (unit variance)	Policy rule		Actual disturbance (unit variance)	
			du_1^a	du_3^1
all	optimal		3.30	8.31
d_1^a	DCR III	$r = 0.0001\,p$ $s = 1.16\,y$	4.48	13.66
	NIR	$r = 0.25\,(y+p)$ $s = 1.29\,(y+p)$	5.28	38.84
	DCR IV	$r = 0.09\,m$ $s = 1.29\,(y+p)$	5.32	37.33
	NI FR	$s = 1.30\,(y+p)$	5.34	37.36
du_3^a	DCR III	$r = 0.0005\,p$ $s = 0.34\,y$	6.54	10.52
	NIR	$r = 0.21\,(y+p)$ $s = 0.14\,(y+p)$	11.59	14.86
	DCR IV	$r = 0.29\,m$ $s = 0.12\,(y+p)$	12.02	14.83
	NI FR	$s = 0.15\,(y+p)$	11.98	15.00
	Open Economy Best Rules			
		$r = 10\,p$ $s = 0.46\,y$	7.36	18.12
		$r = 2.87\,p$ $s = 1.24\,y$	5.35	35.70
		optimal	unstable	

The results in Table 6.5 for the two country problem with joint fiscal and monetary policy indicate the important role for fiscal policy in the aggregate problem. The optimal policy gives very considerable gain when fiscal policy is used. Of the simple rules examined in Table 6.5, DCR III gives the best performance. However, the parameter in the interest rate part of this rule indicates that monetary policy is playing a minimal part in this rule, and the full burden of control falls on fiscal policy. This rule reduces to simple Keynesian policy of controlling output by fiscal feedback on output. The performance of the other rules is broadly similar, because of the limited influence of monetary policy, and amounts to fiscal feedback on nominal income. This performs poorly relative to optimal policy or DCR III.

The performance of the best rules for monetary and fiscal policy reported in Section IV for the single open economy are reported at the

Table 6.6. *The divergence component of the two-country problem*

Monetary policy alone ($s = 0$)			Actual disturbance	
Expected disturbance	Policy rule		$d\tilde{u}_1$	$d\tilde{u}_3$
all	optimal		1.39	0.10
	minimal control	($r = 0.0001\ m$)	1.40	0.10
du_1	exchange rate		1.40	0.10
	nominal income	($r = 0.0001\ (y+p)$)	1.40	0.10
	monetary	($r = 0.0001\ m$)	1.40	0.10
	price	($r = 0.008\ p$)	1.40	0.10
du_3	exchange rate		1.40	0.10
	nominal income	($r = 0.0001\ (y+p)$)	1.40	0.10
	monetary	($r = 0.0001\ m$)	1.40	0.10
	price	($r = 0.005\ p$)	1.40	0.10

Monetary plus fiscal policy			Actual disturbance	
Expected disturbance	Policy rule		$d\tilde{u}_1$	$d\tilde{u}_3$
all	optimal		1.15	0.07
du_1	DCR III	$r = 0.01\ p$ $s = 0.29\ y$	1.34	0.09
du_3	DCR III	$r = 0.0001\ p$ $s = 0.70\ y$	1.47	0.08

bottom of Table 6.5. In contrast to the use of monetary policy alone, the simple rules do not totally destabilise the system. However, their performance is poor, whilst the full optimal rule designed for the single open economy is totally destabilising when applied in the aggregate.

We have not carried out any thorough testing of the robustness of the results of this section. However, we have examined the effects of giving monetary policy a greater channel of influence in the aggregate problem by choosing the higher variant for α_2 in Table 6.1. Although this gave monetary policy a greater role it did not alter the broad results. In particular, the result that policies devised for the single open economy perform badly in the aggregate continues strikingly to stand out.

We have derived these results for the two-country case, but they have a more general interpretation. This is because the aggregate problem can be derived from the aggregation of the n-country generalisation of the two country analysis presented in the Appendix. The larger the number of countries, the greater will be the difficulty in sustaining the optimal rules for the aggregate stabilisation problem presented in Tables 6.4 and 6.5, and in preventing single countries adopting the optimal rules reported in Section IV. Our results focus attention directly on the incentive to renege on cooperative forms of international behaviour, despite the rather serious consequences for performance if all countries do, indeed, renege.

The results for the cooperative solution to the divergence problem are reported in Table 6.6. For monetary policy alone (reported in the upper part of the table), there is no gain whatever to control, whether simple or full optimal. This contrasts markedly with the solution to the single country problem. The lower part of the Table shows that there is some scope for fiscal action of a mild kind. However, these benefits of control show up only for the optimal rule, and the simple fiscal rules show little or no benefit relative to minimal control.

These results one more highlight the marked differences between the cooperative two country solution to the control problem and that thrown up by single country optimisation. They suggest that there is a serious free-rider problem in the design of international policy. To examine this further, in the next section we consider policy design in an explicit game theoretic framework.

VI Two-country non-cooperative games

In this section we consider non-cooperative behaviour for two identical countries in the form of a Cournot-type adjustment process leading to a closed-loop Nash equilibrium. We assume that each country pursues the same form of simple rule and we consider monetary policy only. To simplify matters still further we consider shocks (u_1, u_1^*), and (u_3, u_3^*) in pairs so that each country is experiencing either an aggregate demand shock or a supply shock in common. We put $\text{var}(du_i) = \text{var}(du_i^*) = 0.5 \, dt$ for $i = 1$ and 3 and assume that disturbances in different countries are independent.[13] Then $\text{var}(du_i^q) = \text{var}(du_i^q) = dt$ and the welfare loss may be compared with that for cooperative policies already considered.

Suppose a cooperative policy is agreed in the form of the simple rules examined in Table 6.4. We can investigate the incentive to renege (i.e., the short-term gain) and the long-term consequence by following a Cournot-type sequence of decisions. The results are displayed in Tables 6.7–14 below for central parameter values with loss functions asy $E(2y^2 + 2p^2 + r^2)$ and asy $E(2y^{*2} + 2p^{*2} + r^{*2})$, for a monetary rule ($r = \beta m$ and $r^* = \beta m^*$), a nominal income rule ($r = \beta(y+p)$ and $r^* = \beta(y^*+p^*)$) and a price level rule ($r = \beta p$ and $r^* = \beta p^*$). An exchange rate rule ($r = \beta e$ and $r^* = -\beta e$)

Table 6.7. *The Cournot adjustment process for policy rule* $r = \beta m$

Iteration number	Expected disturbance du_1^a $\text{var}(du_1) = \text{var}(du_1^*) = 0.5\, dt$ $\text{cov}(du_1, du_1^*) = 0$				Expected disturbance du_3^a $\text{var}(du_3) = \text{var}(du_3^*) = 0.5\, dt$ $\text{cov}(du_3, du_3^*) = 0$			
	Country 1		Country 2		Country 1		Country 2	
	β	Welfare loss	β	Welfare loss	β	Welfare loss	β	Welfare loss
0	0.66	4.73	0.66	4.73	0.50	3.95	0.50	3.95
1	0.88	4.70	0.66	4.92	3.13	3.16	0.50	6.17
2	0.88	4.92	0.95	4.88	3.13	5.10	3.34	5.03
3	0.98	4.92	0.95	4.97	3.31	5.10	3.34	5.09
4	0.98	4.94	0.98	4.94	3.31	5.10	3.34	5.09
5	0.98	4.94	0.98	4.94	3.32	5.10	3.34	5.10

Parameters: central loss function: asy $E\,(2y^2 + 2p^2 + r^2)$

Table 6.8. *Welfare loss for Nash equilibrium for policy rule:* $r = \beta m$

Expected disturbance (unit variance)	Policy rule	Actual disturbance (unit variance)	
		du_1^a	du_3^a
du_1^a	$r = 0.98\ m$	4.94	4.10
du_3^a	$r = 3.33\ m$	6.44	5.10

is not considered because in this case an optimal β is indeterminate ruling out the existence of unique reaction functions.

Consider first the monetary rule. For a demand disturbance in view of the slight benefits of divergence control the aggregate policy $r^d = 0.71\ m^d$ of Table 6.4 implies that $r = 0.71\ m$ and $r^* = 0.71\ m^*$ for the two countries. From Table 6.7 it can be seen from iteration 1 that the benefits to country 1 from reneging and pursuing an optimal policy given country 2's policy $r^* = 0.71\ m^*$ are very small and the eventual Nash equilibrium results in a rather greater (but still small) welfare loss. By contrast, for a supply disturbance, both the short-term gains and the long-term losses are quite considerable and at the Nash equilibrium the monetary rule is far stronger ($r = 3.32\ m$) than at the cooperative policy ($r = 0.53\ m$). These results suggest that if a joint policy is agreed between two countries in the form of a monetary rule, a supply shock is far more likely to undermine that agreement than a demand shock if the countries indulge in short-sighted behaviour.

For a nominal income rule from Table 6.9 both types of disturbances result in similar incentives to renege with only a slight long-term loss for a demand shock as against a significant long-term loss for a supply shock. This suggests that even a far-sighted country would be tempted to renege when faced with a demand disturbance. An interesting point to note about both monetary and nominal income rules is that if countries are engaged in a Nash closed-loop game it may actually pay if they are wrong about the nature of the shock hitting the two countries. Thus from Table 6.8 a monetary rule designed with u_1^a in mind results in a better outcome than a rule designed form u_3^a even when u_3^a actually occurs. It follows that countries pursuing a monetary rule benefit if they wrongly rule out the possibility of a u_3^a shock. For a nominal income rule Table 6.10 indicates that countries will benefit if they are wrong on all occasions. If a u_1^a shock occurs it is better if countries expect a u_3^a shock and if a u_3^a shock occurs it is better if they expect a u_1^a shock!

Table 6.9. *The Cournot adjustment process for policy rule:* $r = \beta(y+p)$

Iteration number	Expected disturbance du_1^a var(du_1) = var(du_1^*) = 0.5 dt cov(du_1, du_1^*) = 0				Expected disturbance du_3^a var(du_3) = var(du_3^*) = 0.5 dt cov(du_3, du_3^*) = 0			
	Country 1		Country 2		Country 1		Country 2	
	β	Welfare loss	β	Welfare loss	β	Welfare loss	β	Welfare loss
0	1.01	4.47	1.01	4.47	0.38	4.13	0.38	4.13
1	0.49	4.20	1.10	4.89	0.98	3.64	0.38	5.10
2	0.49	4.56	0.43	4.51	0.98	4.62	1.10	4.47
3	0.42	4.55	0.43	4.56	1.07	4.61	1.10	4.59
4	0.42	4.56	0.42	4.56	1.07	4.59	1.08	4.59
5	0.42	4.56	0.42	4.56	1.08	4.59	1.08	4.59

Table 6.10. *Welfare loss for Nash equilibrium for policy rule:* $r = \beta(y+p)$

Expected disturbance (unit variance)	Policy rule	Actual disturbance (unit variance)	
		du_1^a	du_3^a
du_1^a	$r = 0.42\ (y+p)$	4.56	4.14
du_3^a	$r = 1.08\ (y+p)$	4.49	4.59

For both monetary and nominal income rules that closed-loop Nash equilibrium is symmetrical. For our final regime, a price level rule, this is no longer the case. Starting at the best cooperative policy which in this case is minimal control, the Cournot process converges to an asymmetrical outcome with the country that moves first benefiting considerably at the expense of the other, in both the short-term and long-term. (Note that we have imposed an upper limit of $\beta = 10$ for all the rules.) For both demand and supply shocks the country that reneges moves immediately to the strongest possible feedback rule $r = 10\,p$ leaving the second country's best rule as minimal control (see Tables 6.11 and 6.12). Tables 6.13 and 6.13 report results starting at $r = p$ rather than minimal control. For disturbance du_1^a the country that moves *first* loses out and the second country benefits whereas for a u_3^a disturbance, the final outcome is a symmetrical Nash equilibrium at $r = 0.76\,p$. As yet we have not been able to find a starting point which yields a symmetrical equilibrium for a u_1^a shock.

These results suggest that the incentive to renege on the cooperative monetary or nominal income rule, while adhering to the overall constraint of such a simple rule, is not large. By contrast, the price rule offers a very considerable incentive to renege, particularly since the country that reneges first secures long run, not just short run, benefit. It seems that the price rule, and policies like it, are inimical to international cooperation.

VII Conclusions

In this paper, we have been concerned with the design of macroeconomic policy in a stochastic interdependent world. This analysis was conducted in terms of a model that is rather more complex in its interactions and dynamics than is usual in the analytical literature on policy interdependence, allowing for wage/price dynamics, asset accumulation and exchange rate dynamics.

Section II set out techniques for deriving optimal control rules in

Table 6.11. *The Cournot adjustment process for policy rule:* $r = \beta p$

Iteration number	Expected disturbance du_1^a var(du_1) = var(du_1^*) = 0.5 dt cov(du_1, du_1^*) = 0				Expected disturbance du_3^a var(du_3) = var(du_3^*) = 0.5 dt cov(du_3, du_3^*) = 0			
	Country 1		Country 2		Country 1		Country 2	
	β	Welfare loss	β	Welfare loss	β	Welfare loss	β	Welfare loss
0	0.006	5.18	0.006	5.18	0.02	4.23	0.02	4.32
1	10.00	4.74	0.006	8.53	10.00	2.63	0.02	10.68
2	10.00	4.74	0.0002	8.53	10.00	2.55	0.0002	10.64
3	10.00	4.73	0.0002	8.53	10.00	2.55	0.0002	10.64
4	10.00	4.73	0.0002	8.53	10.00	2.55	0.0002	10.64
5	10.00	4.73	0.0002	8.53	10.00	2.55	0.0002	10.64

Table 6.12. *Welfare loss for Nash equilibrium for policy rule: $r = \beta p$*

Expected disturbance (unit variance)	Policy rule	Actual disturbance (unit variance)	
		du_1^a	du_3^a
du_1^a	$r = 10\, p$ $(r = 0.0002\, p)^*$	4.73 (8.53)	2.55 (10.64)
du_3^a	$r = 10\, p$ $(r = 0.0002\, p)^*$	4.73 (8.53)	2.55 (10.64)

* Country 2 in brackets (where different).

stochastic rational expectations models with complex dynamics, and also showed how restricted or simple optimal rules may be derived. This latter aspect of policy design assumes significance in view of the importance attached to restrictions on policy design (e.g. monetary or nominal income targeting) in current policy debates. But simple or restricted design carries with it the cost that certainty equivalence no longer holds, so that the design of policy is no longer independent of the nature of the shocks perturbing the system. Methods of handling these complications are set out in Sections II and IV. In addition, Section II sets out the method for deriving the Nash solution to a two country policy game as the outcome of a Nash game between the countries pursuing simple rules. The Nash game between the countries pursuing the optimal rule is shown to lead to an ever-expanding state vector.

In our subsequent analysis, we applied these methods to an examination of the effectiveness of the full optimal policy and a variety of simple rules in stabilisation. What our results bring out clearly is the divergence between policy design in the single open economy and in the global economy. This divergence arises from externalities in policy design in an interdependent world. It leads to the possibility of free-riding behaviour, as countries renege on cooperative policy design.

This raises the question as to how best to contain such free-riding behaviour within a system of international policy coordination. Advances in the theory of noncooperative game theory suggest that this may not be as intractable a problem as is usually assumed.[14] This is because forms of tit-for-tat strategy can be shown to be rather robust strategies in dealing with repeated games of the prisoner's dilemma type so frequently encountered in problems of international policy coordination. However, our results also show that not all aspects of the international policy game are of the prisoner's dilemma type. This is illustrated by the Nash game under

Table 6.13. *The Cournot adjustment process for policy rule: $r = \beta p$*

Iteration number	Expected disturbance du_1^a $\mathrm{var}(du_1) = \mathrm{var}(du_1^*) = 0.5\,dt$ $\mathrm{cov}(du_1, du_1^*) = 0$				Expected disturbance du_1^a $\mathrm{var}(du_3) = \mathrm{var}(du_3^*) = 0.5\,dt$ $\mathrm{cov}(du_3, du_3^*) = 0$			
	Country 1		Country 2		Country 1		Country 2	
	β	Welfare loss	β	Welfare loss	β	Welfare loss	β	Welfare loss
0	1.00	7.69	1.00	7.69	1.00	7.23	1.00	7.23
1	0.17	6.99	1.00	5.62	0.61	7.03	1.00	5.56
2	0.17	9.30	10.00	5.30	0.61	6.67	0.89	5.55
3	0.0002	8.53	10.00	4.73	0.67	6.66	0.89	5.80
4	0.0002	8.53	10.00	4.73	0.66	6.46	0.84	6.65
5	0.0002	8.53	10.00	4.73	0.70	6.46	0.84	6.65
20	0.0002	8.53	10.00	4.73	0.76	6.16	0.76	6.16

Table 6.14. *Welfare loss for Nash equilibrium for policy rule:* $r = \beta p$

Expected disturbance (unit variance)	Policy rule	Actual disturbance (unit variance)	
		du_1^a	du_3^a
du_1^a	$r = 10\,p$	4.73	2.55
	$(r = 0.0002\,p)^*$	(8.53)	(10.64)
du_3^a	$r = 0.76\,p$	6.82	6.16

* Country 2 in brackets (where different).

the price rule, where one country can secure a lasting gain at the expense of the other. This arises because, in this game, tit-for-tat amounts to the threat to destabilise the system totally, and may therefore not be credible. Similar results may well apply more generally to strategies that rely on manipulating the exchange rate under a regime of floating rates to secure domestic objectives at the expense of global aims.

It may be that other forms of macropolicy threats may be credible in containing this form of behaviour, and this is an issue that needs more detailed consideration. Alternatively, it may be that a wider class of threats, involving factors outside the field of international policy, is required to sustain international cooperation. If this is so, our analysis offers a possible additional argument for simple rules, particularly concerning the targeting of the money supply or nominal income: that by formulating policy in these terms, one may rule out the noncooperative forms of behaviour implied by the price level rule and by full optimal behaviour.

Appendix

In this appendix, we set out the models analysed in the main paper in the form of equation (II.1); that is,

$$\begin{bmatrix} dz \\ dx^e \end{bmatrix} = A \begin{bmatrix} z \\ x \end{bmatrix} dt + Bw\,dt + dv \tag{A.1}$$

(i) The single country model

We let $n = \int_{-\infty}^{t} y\,ds$, so that $dn = y\,dt$. We also treat y^* as given exogenously, and therefore incorporated into the disturbance terms in

(III.1) and (III.3). Then we may write (III.1)–(III.9) in the form of (A.2), where $x = e$ and:

$$A = \begin{bmatrix}
-\psi_1 & 0 & \psi_1\alpha_3 & \psi_1(\psi_4\alpha_2\delta_1-\alpha_1) & -\psi_1\psi_4\alpha_2 & 0 & \psi_1(\alpha_1+\psi_4\alpha_2\delta_2) & 0 & \psi_1(\alpha_1+\psi_4\alpha_2\delta_2) \\
\psi_2\gamma_1 & -\psi_2 & \psi_2\gamma_3 & 0 & \psi_2 & 0 & 0 & 0 & 0 \\
-\phi_1 & 0 & 0 & -(\psi_4\delta_1+\phi_2) & \psi_4 & 0 & \phi_2-\psi_4\delta_2 & 0 & \phi_2-\psi_4\delta_2 \\
0 & 0 & 0 & -\psi_3 & \psi_3 & \psi_3\beta_1 & 0 & 0 & 0 \\
0 & 0 & 0 & \psi_4\delta_1 & -\psi_4 & 0 & \psi_4\delta_2 & 0 & \psi_4\delta_2 \\
1 & 0 & 0 & 0 & 0 & 0 & 0 & 0 & 0 \\
0 & 0 & 0 & 0 & 0 & 0 & -\mu_1 & 0 & 0 \\
0 & 0 & 0 & 0 & 0 & 0 & 0 & -\mu_2 & 0 \\
0 & 0 & 0 & 0 & 0 & 0 & 0 & -1 & 0
\end{bmatrix}$$

$$z = \begin{bmatrix} y \\ m \\ v \\ w \\ p \\ n \\ w^* \\ r^* \end{bmatrix}, \quad
B = \begin{bmatrix}
-\psi_1\alpha_2 & -\psi_1\alpha_4 \\
-\psi_2\gamma_2 & 0 \\
0 & -\phi_0 \\
0 & 0 \\
0 & 0 \\
0 & 0 \\
0 & 0 \\
1 & 0
\end{bmatrix}, \quad
dv = \begin{bmatrix}
1 & 0 & 0 & 0 & 0 \\
0 & 1 & 0 & 0 & 0 \\
0 & 0 & 0 & 0 & 0 \\
0 & 0 & 1 & 0 & 0 \\
0 & 0 & 0 & 0 & 0 \\
0 & 0 & 0 & 0 & 0 \\
0 & 0 & 0 & 0 & 0 \\
0 & 0 & 0 & 0 & 1
\end{bmatrix}
\begin{bmatrix} du_1 \\ du_2 \\ du_3 \\ du_4 \\ du_5 \end{bmatrix}$$

$$w = \begin{bmatrix} r \\ s \end{bmatrix} \tag{A.2}$$

and where $\delta_1 = \theta c_1$, $\delta_2 = (1-\theta c_1)$.

(ii) The two country model

For this case, from equations (III.1)–(III.7) we may write the system in the form of (A.1) where A is given in Table A.1, where $x = e$, and where:

$$z = \begin{bmatrix} y \\ m \\ v \\ w \\ p \\ n \\ y^* \\ m^* \\ v^* \\ w^* \\ p^* \\ n^* \end{bmatrix}, \quad
B = \begin{bmatrix}
-\psi_1\alpha_2 & -\psi_1\alpha_4 & 0 & 0 \\
-\psi_2\gamma_2 & 0 & 0 & 0 \\
0 & -\phi_0 & 0 & 0 \\
0 & 0 & 0 & 0 \\
0 & 0 & 0 & 0 \\
0 & 0 & 0 & 0 \\
0 & 0 & -\psi_1\alpha_2 & -\psi_1\alpha_4 \\
0 & 0 & -\psi_2\gamma_2 & 0 \\
0 & 0 & 0 & -\phi_0 \\
0 & 0 & 0 & 0 \\
0 & 1 & 0 & 0 \\
1 & 0 & -1 & 0
\end{bmatrix}, \quad
dv = \begin{bmatrix}
1 & 0 & 0 & 0 & 0 & 0 \\
0 & 1 & 0 & 0 & 0 & 0 \\
0 & 0 & 0 & 0 & 0 & 0 \\
0 & 0 & 1 & 0 & 0 & 0 \\
0 & 0 & 0 & 0 & 0 & 0 \\
0 & 0 & 0 & 0 & 0 & 0 \\
0 & 0 & 0 & 1 & 0 & 0 \\
0 & 0 & 0 & 0 & 1 & 0 \\
0 & 0 & 0 & 0 & 0 & 0 \\
0 & 0 & 0 & 0 & 0 & 1 \\
0 & 0 & 0 & 0 & 0 & 0 \\
0 & 0 & 0 & 0 & 0 & 0
\end{bmatrix}
\begin{bmatrix} du_1 \\ du_2 \\ du_3 \\ du_1^* \\ du_2^* \\ du_3^* \end{bmatrix}$$

$$w = \begin{bmatrix} r \\ s \\ r^* \\ s^* \end{bmatrix} \tag{A.3}$$

Exploiting the symmetry of this model, we may follow Aoki (1981) by decomposing this model into two orthogonal components, the aggregate model and the divergence model. Thus let $z^a = z+z^*$, $u_i^a = u_i+u_i^*$,

Table 6A.1. *A matrix for the two-country model*

$$
\begin{bmatrix}
-\psi_1 & 0 & \psi_1\alpha_3 & \psi_1(\psi_4\alpha_2\delta_1-\alpha_1) & -\psi_1\psi_4\alpha_2 & 0 & \psi_1\alpha_5 & 0 & 0 & \psi_1(\alpha_1+\psi_4\alpha_2\delta_2) & 0 & \psi_1(\alpha_1+\psi_4\alpha_2\delta_2) \\
\psi_2\gamma_1 & -\psi_2 & \psi_2\gamma_3 & 0 & \psi_2 & 0 & 0 & 0 & 0 & 0 & 0 & 0 \\
-\phi_1 & 0 & 0 & -(\psi_4\delta_1+\phi_2) & \psi_4 & \psi_3\beta_1 & \phi_3 & 0 & 0 & \phi_2-\psi_4\delta_2 & 0 & \phi_2-\psi_4\delta_2 \\
0 & 0 & 0 & -\psi_3 & \psi_3 & 0 & 0 & 0 & 0 & 0 & 0 & 0 \\
1 & 0 & 0 & \psi_4\delta_1 & -\psi_4 & 0 & 0 & 0 & \psi_4\delta_2 & \psi_4\delta_2 & 0 & \psi_4\delta_2 \\
\psi_1\alpha_5 & 0 & \psi_1(\alpha_1+\psi_4\alpha_2\delta_2) & 0 & 0 & 0 & -\psi_1 & 0 & \psi_1(\psi_4\alpha_2\delta_1-\alpha_1) & \psi_1(\alpha_1+\psi_4\alpha_2\delta_2) & -\psi_1\psi_4\alpha_2 & -\psi_1(\alpha_1+\psi_4\alpha_2\delta_2) \\
\phi_3 & 0 & \phi_2-\psi_4\delta_2 & -\psi_3 & 0 & 0 & \psi_2\gamma_1 & 0 & 0 & 0 & \psi_2 & 0 \\
0 & 0 & \psi_4\delta_2 & -\psi_4 & 0 & 0 & -\phi_1 & 0 & -(\psi_4\delta_1+\phi_2) & -\psi_3 & \psi_4 & -(\phi_2-\psi_4\delta_2) \\
0 & 0 & 0 & 0 & 0 & 0 & 0 & 0 & -\psi_3 & -\psi_3 & \psi_3 & -\psi_4\delta_2 \\
0 & 0 & 0 & 0 & 0 & 0 & 1 & 0 & \psi_4\delta_1 & \psi_4\delta_1 & -\psi_4 & 0 \\
0 & 0 & 0 & 0 & 0 & 0 & 0 & 0 & 0 & 0 & \psi_3\beta_1 & 0 \\
0 & 0 & 0 & 0 & 0 & 0 & 0 & 0 & 0 & 0 & 0 & 0
\end{bmatrix}
$$

$r^a = r + r^*$, $s^a = s + s^*$. Then the aggregate model (denoted by an 'a' superscript) is given by (A.1) with

$$A^a = \begin{bmatrix} -\psi_1(1-\alpha_5) & 0 & \psi_1\alpha_3 & \psi_1\psi_4\alpha_2 & -\psi_1\psi_4\alpha_2 & 0 \\ \psi_2\gamma_1 & -\psi_2 & \psi_2\gamma_2 & 0 & \psi_2 & 0 \\ -(\phi_1-\phi_3) & 0 & 0 & -\psi_4 & \psi_4 & 0 \\ 0 & 0 & 0 & -\psi_3 & \psi_3 & \psi_3\beta_1 \\ 0 & 0 & 0 & \psi_4 & -\psi_4 & 0 \\ 1 & 0 & 0 & 0 & 0 & 0 \end{bmatrix}, \quad z^a = \begin{bmatrix} y^a \\ m^a \\ v^a \\ w^a \\ p^a \\ n^a \end{bmatrix}$$

$$B^a = \begin{bmatrix} -\psi_1\alpha_2 & \psi_1\alpha_4 \\ -\psi_2\alpha_2 & 0 \\ 0 & -\phi_0 \\ 0 & 0 \\ 0 & 0 \\ 0 & 0 \end{bmatrix}, \quad w^a = \begin{bmatrix} r^a \\ s^a \end{bmatrix}, \quad dv^a = \begin{bmatrix} 1 & 0 & 0 \\ 0 & 1 & 0 \\ 0 & 0 & 0 \\ 0 & 0 & 1 \\ 0 & 0 & 0 \\ 0 & 0 & 0 \end{bmatrix} \begin{bmatrix} du_1^a \\ du_2^a \\ du_3^a \end{bmatrix} \qquad (A.4)$$

and where the x vector has zero dimension. It will be noted that the aggregate model contains no free variables.

Using a 'd' superscript to denote the divergence model, and letting $z^d = z - z^*$, $u_i^d = u_i - u_i^*$, $r^d = r - r^*$, $s^d = s - s^*$, then the divergence model is given by (A.1) with:

$$A^d = \begin{bmatrix} -\psi_1(1+\alpha_5) & 0 & \psi_1\alpha_3 & \psi_1(\psi_4\alpha_2(\delta_1-\delta_2)-2\alpha_1) & -\psi_1\psi_4\alpha_2 & 0 & 2\psi_1(\alpha_1+\psi_4\alpha_2\delta_2) \\ \psi_2\gamma_1 & -\psi_2 & \psi_2\gamma_3 & 0 & \psi_2 & 0 & 0 \\ -(\phi_1+\phi_3) & 0 & 0 & -(\psi_4(\delta_1-\delta_2)+2\phi_2) & \psi_4 & 0 & 2(\phi_2-\psi_4\delta_2) \\ 0 & 0 & 0 & -\psi_3 & \psi_3 & \psi_3\beta_1 & 0 \\ 0 & 0 & 0 & \psi_4(\delta_1-\delta_2) & -\psi_4 & 0 & 2\psi_4\delta_2 \\ 0 & 0 & 0 & 0 & 0 & 0 & 0 \\ 0 & 0 & 0 & 0 & 0 & 0 & 0 \end{bmatrix}$$

$$z^d = \begin{bmatrix} y^d \\ m^d \\ v^d \\ w^d \\ p^d \\ n^d \end{bmatrix}, \quad B^d = \begin{bmatrix} -\psi_1\alpha_2 & -\psi_1\alpha_4 \\ -\psi_2\gamma_2 & 0 \\ 0 & -\phi_0 \\ 0 & 0 \\ 0 & 0 \\ 0 & 0 \\ 1 & 0 \end{bmatrix}, \quad dv^d = \begin{bmatrix} 1 & 0 & 0 \\ 0 & 1 & 0 \\ 0 & 0 & 0 \\ 0 & 0 & 0 \\ 0 & 0 & 0 \\ 0 & 0 & 0 \\ 0 & 0 & 0 \end{bmatrix} \begin{bmatrix} du_1^d \\ du_2^d \\ du_3^d \end{bmatrix}, \quad w^d = \begin{bmatrix} r^d \\ s^d \end{bmatrix} \qquad (A.5)$$

and where $x = e$.

NOTES

* David Currie acknowledges the financial support of the ESRC and H.M. Treasury; Paul Levine acknowledges the financial support of the Nuffield Foundation and the ESRC.
1 The rational expectations equilibria considered in this paper may be thought of as Stackelberg equilibria, with the government as leader and the private

sector as follower. By reneging consistently, the government relinquishes its leadership role.

2 We can formally evaluate the incentive to renege faced by a myopic government by assuming a given discount rate. This requires us to consider the derivation of optimal rules with time-discounting, as in Levine and Currie (1984).

3 This solution is based on Blanchard and Kahn (1980) and Dixit (1980). For further details, see Currie and Levine (1982).

4 This result does not carry over to the discrete time cases. See Levine and Currie (1984).

5 For further discussion, see Levine and Currie (1984).

6 For further analysis, see Levine and Currie (1984).

7 This partial adjustment process is incorporated for technical reasons. If ψ_4 is large, as it is in the subsequent analysis, it is as though (III.5) and (III.6) hold instantaneously.

8 We are concerned with deviations of the system from long run equilibrium. Assuming that the current account is in equilibrium in this long run equilibrium, it is plausible to assume that transitory current account imbalances cause no divergence between *ex ante* domestic and foreign interest rates expressed in the same currency.

9 Since foreign wages and interest rates are now separately determined (with persistence), equations (3.10) and (3.11) are dropped. Note that $e^* = -e$.

10 Non-stationary disturbance require the addition of integral control to tie down nominal variables, though at the cost of making instruments non-stationary. We exclude this case here.

11 FORTRAN programs have been written to implement the solution procedures of section II.

12 Strictly speaking, setting $\beta = 0$ for the other rules leads to indeterminacy of nominal variables. However, this problem can be avoided and the loss made as close to zero as desired by choosing β to be positive but small. We refer to this case as 'minimal control' in what follows.

13 We have also considered the opposite extreme, u_i and u_i^* perfectly correlated. The same qualitative conclusions reached for uncorrelated disturbances still hold.

14 See Axelrod (1983) and Basar and Olsder (1982). For further discussion, see Currie (1985).

REFERENCES

Aoki, M. (1981). *Dynamic Analysis of Open Economies*. Academic Press.

Axelrod, R. (1983). *The Evolution of Cooperation*. Basic Books.

Basar, T. and Olsder, G. K. (1982). *Dynamic Noncooperative Game Theory*. Academic Press, London.

Blanchard, O. J. and Kahn, C. M. (1980). 'The Solution of Linear Difference Models under Rational Expectations'; *Econometrica*, **48**, pp. 1305–9.

Blinder, A. S. and Solow, R. M. (1973). 'Does Fiscal Policy Matter?; *Journal of Public Economics*, Vol. 2, pp. 314–37.

Buiter, W. H. (1980). 'The Macroeconomics of Dr. Pangloss'; *Economic Journal*, **90**, pp. 34–50.

(1980). 'The Superiority of Contingent Rules over Fixed Rules in Models with Rational Expectations'; *Economic Journal*, **91**, pp.647–70.

Calvo, G. A. (1978). 'On the Time-Consistency of Optimal Policy in a Monetary Economy'; *Econometrica*, **46**, pp. 1411–28.

Canzoneri, M. B. and Gray, J. A. (1983). 'Two Essays on Monetary Policy in an Interdependent World'; Federal Reserve Board, International Finance Discussion Paper No. 219, Washington.

Christ, C. F. (1979). 'On Fiscal and Monetary Policies and the Government Budget Restraint', *American Economic Review*, **69**, pp. 526–38.

Cooper, R. N. (1983). 'Economic Interdependence and Coordination of Economic Policies'; in R. Jones and P. B. Kenen (eds.), *Handbook in International Economics*, Vol. II, Amsterdam, North-Holland.

Corden, W. M. (1983). 'Macroeconomic Policy Interaction under Flexible Exchange Rates: A two-Country Model'; Institute for International Economic Studies, Seminar Paper No. 264.

Currie, D. A. (1985). 'Macroeconomic Policy Design and Control Theory: A Failed Partnership?' *Economic Journal*, **95**, June.

and Levine, P. L. (1982). 'A Solution Technique for Discrete and Continuous Time Stochastic Dynamic Models under Rational Expectations with Full and Partial Information Sets'; *PRISM* Paper No. 1.

(1985). 'Simple Macropolicy Rules for the Open Economy'. *Economic Journal*, **95**, Supplement.

Dixit, A. (1980). 'A Solution Technique for Rational Expectations Models with Applications to Exchange Rate and Interest Rate Determination'; *mimeo*, University of Warwick.

Driffill, E. J. (1982). 'Optimal Money and Exchange Rate Policies'; *Greek Economic Review*, December.

Hamada, K. (1979). 'Macroeconomic Strategy and Coordination under Alternative Exchange Rates'; in R. Dornbusch and J. A. Frenkel (eds.), *International Economic Policy*. The Johns Hopkins Press, Baltimore.

and Sakurai, M. (1978). 'International Transmission of Stagflation under Fixed and Flexible Exchange Rates'; *Journal of Political Economy*, **86**, pp. 877–95.

Kwakernaak, H. and Sivan, R. (1972). *Linear Optimal Control Systems*. Wiley-Interscience.

Levine, P. L. and Currie, D. A. (1983). 'Optimal Feedback Rules in an Open Economy Macromodel with Rational Expectations'; *PRISM* Paper No. 5, presented to the 1983 European Meeting of the Econometric Society.

(1984). 'The Design of Feedback Rules in Stochastic Rational Expectations models'. *PRISM* Paper No. 20.

Meade, J. (1983): 'International Cooperation in Macroeconomic Policies'. *mimeo*.

Miller, M. and Salmon, M. (1983). Dynamic Games and Time Inconsistency of Optimal Policy in Open Economies'; *mimeo*. University of Warwick.

(1984): 'Policy Coordination and Dynamic Games'; this volume.

Sachs, J. (1983). 'International Economic Policy Coordination in a Dynamic Macroeconomic Game'. National Bureau of Economic Research, Working Paper No. 1166.

Turner, P. (1983). 'A Static Framework for the Analysis of Policy Optimisation with Interdependent Economies'. University of Warwick, Department of Economics Research Paper No. 235.

(1984). 'Interdependent Monetary Policies in a Two Country Model'. University of Southampton, Department of Economics Discussion Paper No. 8401.

Turnovsky, S. J. (1977). *Macroeconomic Analysis and Stabilisation Policies.* Cambridge University Press.

Vines, D., Maciejowski, J. and Meade, J. (1983). *Demand Management.* Allen and Unwin.

COMMENT DAVID K. H. BEGG

David Currie and Paul Levine have given us an interesting paper. They emphasise the need for *simple* rules, yet, aside from some general remarks about the ease of securing international cooperation, they offer little formal justification for the advantages of simple rules. I begin by arguing that the issues of time consistency and credibility can be used to suggest why we might be interested in formulating rules in a simple way.

Given a deterministic model with full information, there is no distinction between open-loop and closed-loop rules, and I suggest optimal policy design is as follows. If future actions can truly be precommitted, the possibility of time inconsistency simply does not arise. If precommitment is not possible, a time consistent plan can be formulated by adopting the backward recursion of dynamic programming, which recognises that bygones are bygone as real time elapses and as decisions can be reconsidered. In a deterministic perfect foresight model, time inconsistent policies are simply *incredible*.

Now consider a stochastic model. Partition all possible rules into those components based exclusively on today's information set and those innovation-contingent rules which specify how new information is reflected in policy. Notice two things: first, it will generally pay to use new information as it arrives. Innovation-contingent components are valuable to policy makers. Second, the preceding perfect foresight discussion of time consistency and credibility formally carries over to the stochastic model, provided it is applied to the part of the rules which conditions on today's information set.

Suppose, however, that it is not costless for agents to monitor the actions of the policy maker or to diagnose and process new information. There will then arise an ambiguity. Suppose policy this period is different from agents' expectation of policy this period, conditional on information in some previous period. Should agents believe a policy maker who says that this merely represents the implementation of a previously announced innovation-contingent feedback rule? Or does it represent an attempt to renege on that part of the policy rule based purely on previous information? In such circumstances, there may be much to be said for the pursuit of simple rules if they are easier for agents to understand and to monitor. In so doing, they may remove most of the problems which arise in a world in which reneging is easy, whilst simultaneously preferring the policy maker's ability to implement an innovation-contingent feedback rule which blunts the effects of genuine surprises as they hit the system.

Ideally, of course, reneging should be endogenous to the model, and the asymmetric information on which its possibility depends should be made explicit. In such a framework, one could then determine credibility endogenously and thus conduct an examination of the incentives to cheat today at the cost of losing reputation for the future.

Before leaving the overall framework of the paper, I note that the authors adopt an asymptotic approximation to the policy maker's objective function. Thus the paper really complicates the dynamics of the structural constraints for the sake of simplifying the dynamics of the intertemporal objective function. For some purposes this may be an advance; in other cases it may not. For example, many people would argue that a vital component of the Thatcher revolution in policy attitudes in Britain is the changed priority of the future against the present.

I now consider the main sections of the paper. Section II presents a standard linear-quadratic forward looking stochastic model in which the second best time-invariant rule is compared with the 'fully optimal' rule. The latter is time inconsistent, and I have already made clear my objection to this terminology. To be credible, such a rule must rely either on the ability to make binding precommitments of policy or on its voluntary precommitment through an analysis of the cost of losing reputation when this is recognised as endogenous. Section II then specifies a two-country closed-loop Nash game. Although preferable to an open-loop Nash game, this specification still seems to me to have its drawbacks. Individual players are modelled as assessing their own strategies subject to the belief that the other player's reaction function is invariant, yet it is knowable that different strategies by one player will cause the other player to revise that reaction function. The Lucas critique applies in game theory too.

Section III specialises the structural model to a familiar open economy model with sluggish domestic price adjustment and perfect international capital mobility. These seem reasonable. However, the loss function contains a term in the square of the *level* of prices. This is certainly not the same as the notion that inflation is undesirable, nor is it a trivial discrepancy: it is a major conclusion of the paper that simple rules formulated as *price* rules behave rather differently from other types of simple rule. Before attributing too much importance to this result, I should like to know the extent to which it reflects the particular specification of the loss function. Some sensitivity analysis would be valuable here.

Section IV begins with the third best problem of simple monetary rules, for example having nominal interest rates proportional to the price level or to nominal income. At some stage, the authors refer to this as 'targeting'. This seems to me rather misleading. Even if one wishes to target an intermediate variable, it is generally optimal to use all available policy instruments to achieve this end. Next, the robustness of various rules to specific shocks is examined. As I read it, the authors perturb each disturbance separately. Yet in Section II they show that their simple rules do not obey certainty equivalence, and that the parameters of these rules are functions of the variance-covariance matrix of disturbances. That being so, it would be nice if sensitivity analysis utilised shocks with a variance-covariance matrix similar to that implicitly embodied in the parameters of the simple rules whose robustness is being investigated. This leads on to a related point. The authors' search for robust simple rules is very much a hit-and-miss affair. Particular specifications are contemplated, as if out of a hat, and their properties assessed. Why not start from the other end? In Section II we are shown how to calculate the optimal rule. Alternatively, we could calculate the optimal linear time-invariant rule. From one of these more general specifications, could we not examine the coefficient parameters and hence make a more informed judgement about which exclusion restrictions to impose in order to acquire a simple rule?

Having examined at length the question of a monetary rule alone, Currie and Levine then consider the simultaneous choice of simple monetary and fiscal rules. Here simplicity means decoupling: each policy variable has a rule with a single argument. Basically, the authors conclude that fiscal policy matters in their model, but that it should be accompanied by a monetary rule which takes the form of a price rule. Again, my earlier remark applies. Without an examination of alternative loss functions, we cannot be sure at this stage that the preference for a price rule does not reflect the particular way prices enter the loss function.

Section V extends the analysis to two countries, using the Aoki trick of dividing the problem into two orthogonal ones, the first dealing with aggregate variables across countries and the second dealing with divergences between countries. Here I find the conclusions sensible and appealing. There is less scope for monetary policy than fiscal policy to affect aggregate variables. And it is shown that the interaction of unharmonised national policies can easily lead to undesirable outcomes.

Section VI deals briefly with 2-country non-cooperative games, and begins to examine the incentive to renege. Short term gains are compared with long term losses from a reduction in credibility. Given my earlier remarks, I applaud the effort in this section. As yet, as the authors recognise, this work is rather preliminary. For example, time discounting is likely to be important in evaluating how to trade off present and future. Here the simplified intertemporal objective function is concealing more than it reveals. Similarly, conjectures which are based on the Cournot-adjustment of the other player's reaction function are clearly systematically and knowably in error.

COMMENT KOICHI HAMADA

I feel very privileged to have this opportunity to discuss the paper by Professor Currie and Dr Levine, because it is rich in content and neatly written.

In the first part of this paper, the authors sort out various ramifications of optimal control. Being a 'back of the envelope' theorist myself, I learned a lot from their clear exposition of modern control technology combined with the assumption of rational expectations. There are so many layers of categories: constrained variables vs. free variables in initial conditions, full optimisation vs. time-invariant rules, general vs. simple rules, joint utility maximisation vs. Cournot-Nash games, closed loop vs. open loop, time consistent vs. unconstrained rules, and so forth. This paper sorts out these complex layers. The description is compact but gives us a full understanding of the basic structure of the issues.

The second part of this paper develops an expectations augmented Phillips curve model consisting of two countries. Since a time-invariant feedback rule is dependent on the covariance matrix, they examine simple rules corresponding to each type of shock on LM, IS and supply curves, look for the best rule for each particular kind of shock, and examine vulnerability of the system under the simple rule against types of shock other than the system is designed for. The most reliable feedback rule is the price rule for the domestic economy, but this rule collapses when two countries play a game with these simple rules.

When I was reading this paper, I was reminded of a conversation I had with Dr. Hirotsugu Akaike, the founder of AIC of the time series model. He was quite successful in reducing the variance in quality of concrete production by applying some feedbacks to the system according to his methods. He also succeeded in smoothing temperature fluctuations in electricity generation. Incidentally his institute is now studying adminis-trative reform (fiscal consolidation) in Japan. He has to defend the raison d'être of his institute by pointing out that the feedback system saved trillions of Yen. Dr Akaike is interested in the possibility of applying feedback systems to our economy as well. This paper gives us hope that some day, unfortunately seemingly not in the immediate future, we may be able to control the economy like a concrete production process.

One of the most surprising results of this paper is that the simple price rule, which is stabilising in a closed economy, can cause total global destablisation in a two country context. This is somewhat counter-intuitive, because a combination of two stable systems of differential equations will normally result in a stable system unless off-diagonal blocks expressing the interdependence are extremely important. My first question is how, in an analytic as well as an economic sense, the authors interpret this phenomenon.

My next question concerns the statement of the authors on the last page, saying 'in this game, tit-for-tat amounts to the threat of destabilising the system totally, and may therefore not be credible'. This is an interesting remark, but I do not consider that this statement is the result of deduction from the analytical part of the paper. I would like to hear more clarification.

My comments are on the economics of these interesting experiments. My first comment concerns the validity of the asymptotic system. We are all constrained by history, that is by initial conditions at any time. It may take a very long time to achieve the asymptotic state of stochastic equilibrium. I wonder how fast is the convergence speed of the deterministic part of the system to a stationary equilibrium. It would be possible to tell the speed of convergence by examining the magnitude of the stable roots of the system. If it takes a rather short time to reach equilibrium, these experiments are useful although we have to add some learning period for agents to understand the working of the system. If it takes a rather long time, then historical programming taking account of the initial conditions is more relevant than the analysis of stochastic equilibria.

Incidentally, I was talking about this paper with Dr Georges de Ménil on the plane, and his related point, which I should like to quote if he does not mind, was that if we are examining the properties of long run equilibrium, why do we need inertia like the short run Phillips curve? If the asymptotic state is in question, does it not suffice to examine only a new-classical model with a vertical long run Phillips curve?

My second comment concerns the use of simple rules. As a pedagogical device it is fine, but I have an ambivalent feeling about the adoption of very simple rules. In this world of rational expectations, agents know the structure correctly and they know exactly what the government is doing. The simpler the rule, the easier it is for private agents to learn about it.

This is an attractive side of the analysis. On the other hand, I cannot help feeling some uneasiness about the asymmetry in the degree of sophistication assumed between private agents and governments. Private agents know economic structures and government policies completely, and pick the right saddle point paths in spite of various disturbances. Governments, on the other hand, can only choose the value of β. According to Professor Morishima, in the UK the best students go after graduation to the academic world as university or high school teachers, the next best go to public service, and the least good to the private business sector. In Japan, on the other hand, I feel that the best and brightest go to the public service, next to private business, and perhaps the least bright to the academic world. Thus while this model may reflect some aspects of British society, the strong asymmetry in the model does not seem to fit my conception of the real world.

Third, on the simple rules. First of all, though simple minded the government has perfect control of the nominal interest rate. Thus monetary shocks u_2 are completely offset. Imagine a world where a case of missing money appears; can the government still just smooth the shock as assumed here? A more basic question is why one has to choose the *nominal* interest rate. The well known criticism of Keynesian economics developed by the monetarist school was that if one only aims at the nominal interest rate, one cannot distinguish whether a high level of the nominal rate reflects a high real rate of interest that has a depressionary effect, or a high rate of inflationary expectations reflecting a boom. If you stick to the rule of trying to keep nominal interest rates constant in an inflationary situation, you may end up with severe inflation because the attempt may reduce the real rate. Thus it is no wonder that the price rule will do a better job. Here again, even though control of the real rate of interest is hard, the government could be a little smarter.

Finally, there is an interesting structure connecting the choice among simple rules and the possible outcomes under any given rule. Here again temptation arises for the government to renege on the committed rule that private agents are counting on.

7 International policy coordination in dynamic macroeconomic models

GILLES OUDIZ AND JEFFREY SACHS*

I Introduction

In an earlier essay (Oudiz and Sachs, 1984) we investigated the quantitative gains to international policy coordination in a static environment. In this paper, we begin to extend the analysis to a dynamic setting. However, because of several new methodological issues, this first step is more theoretical than empirical. The extension to dynamics introduces three important points of realism to the static game. First, the payoffs to beggar-thy-neighbor policies may look very different in one-period and multiperiod games, so that the need for policy coordination may be different in the two games. Second, it is often claimed that governments are shortsighted in macroeconomic planning, and support for this view has come from the literature on political business cycles.[1] We should therefore investigate whether international policy coordination is likely to exacerbate or meliorate this shortsighted behavior. Third, governments act under a fundamental constraint that they cannot bind the actions of later governments (or even of themselves at a future date). In principle, therefore, optimizing governments must take into account how future governments will behave in view of the economic environment that they inherit. We study the implications for policy coordination of this inability to bind future governments.

Let us consider these three points in turn. In the static game, uncoordinated macroeconomic policy-making is typically inefficient because of a prisoner's dilemma in policy choices. Consider, for example, two countries that are attempting to move optimally along short-run Phillips curves. It may be that each country will choose contractionary policies no matter what the other country selects, though the policy pair (expand, expand) is better for both countries than the non-cooperative equilibrium (contract, contract). As we showed in our earlier study, this situation arises naturally under flexible exchange rates, since by contracting while the other country

274

is expanding a country can appreciate its currency and export some of its inflation abroad. It is this beggar-thy-neighbor action that gives rise to the prisoner's dilemma. Cooperation, say in the form of a binding international commitment to expand, may be useful in moving the countries to the efficient equilibrium.

The question arises whether the payoff structure in a multiperiod, or infinite-horizon, game will look the same. The reason for doubt is simple. In almost all macroeconomic models, policies which lead to a short-run real appreciation also lead to long-run real depreciation, or at least a return to the initial real exchange rate. In this circumstance, farsighted players would understand that a short-run beggar-thy-neighbor appreciation is less attractive than it looks, since it will be reversed in the long run, at which point the country reimports the inflation that it earlier sent abroad. To this extent, the beggar-thy-neighbor policy loses its appeal, and the need for coordination is reduced.

The second theme introduced in a multiperiod setting is the myopic behavior of governments. In considering public welfare in a multiperiod game, it is natural to consider a payoff of the form:

$$U_0^i = \sum_{t=0}^{T} \beta^t u(T_t^i) \tag{1}$$

Here, U_0^i is the intertemporal utility of country i as of time zero. $u(T_t^i)$ is the instantaneous utility of the country at time t, as a function of a vector of macroeconomic targets T_t^i. β is a pure rate of time preference, with $\beta < 1$, so that the future is discounted relative to the present. The planning interval is for t between 0 and T.

In view of the evidence on political business cycles, in which governments attempt to manipulate T_t^i in conjunction with upcoming elections, it seems natural to suggest that if (1) is the 'true' social welfare function, the government's social welfare function take the form:

$$U_0^{Gi} = \sum_{t=0}^{T^G} \beta^{Gt} u(T_t^i) \tag{2}$$

where $T^G \leqslant T$ and $\beta^G < \beta$. That is, its planning horizon is shorter than the economy's, or its discounting of the future is higher.

In this view, the public is partly a hostage of a self-serving government. The policy choices reflect the incumbent government's goals, and not the public's. If this is so, we can ask whether international policy coordination is likely to improve or worsen this sub-optimal situation. At an abstract level, the arguments seem to fall on both sides. Some critics, for example, have characterized policy coordination as a cartel of the incumbents, in which each policymaker helps the others to manipulate the political business cycle. As an example of this, policymakers may have a short-run expansionary bias if expansion shows up as output today and as inflation only many years in the future. To some extent, the fear of currency depreciation following a unilateral expansion keeps this bias in check. That is, the flexible exchange rate provides discipline on the shortsighted government. With policy coordination, the fear of currency depreciation can be removed by a commitment of *all* countries to expand. In this way, policy coordination may give incumbent governments a free hand to undertake overly inflationary policies.

On the other hand, we can think of circumstances in which policy coordination ties the hand of incumbents, and thus prevents such self-serving policies. An international gold standard, for example, might impose discipline on governments that would not exist in each country alone. To analyse this possibility fully we would have to examine each government's incentive to stick with a particular rule, and the extent to which internationally certified rules are more or less durable than rules undertaken unilaterally. For example, each country on its own could adopt a gold standard. What, if anything, is added by a multicountry commitment?

The third theme introduced in a multiperiod setting is that of 'time-consistency' of optimal plans. Even in circumstances in which the current government (or current administration) has the public's interest at heart, its ability to maximize social welfare may be limited by its inability to pre-commit the actions of (well-meaning) future governments. In these circumstances, the current government must choose its optimal policy *taking as given* the policy rules that will be pursued in the future. That is, it must optimize today, assuming that future governments will optimize under the assumption that yet future governments will optimize, and so on. In general this constrained optimization yields a lower level of social welfare than does the case in which the government can choose not only its own policies but those of future governments as well.

Many authors, including Barro and Gordon (1983) and Rogoff (1983), have given examples in which the inability to bind future policies imparts an inflationary bias to the economy. In these examples, wage setters set wages before macroeconomic policy is set. Once the wages are set, policymakers have an incentive to expand the economy to reduce real wages, and raise output. Wage setters anticipate these policies, and choose inflationary wage settlements in anticipation. If the government can pre-commit to avoid inflationary policies, the economy can get the same *ex post* output levels at a lower rate of inflation. Unfortunately, such a pre-commitment is not credible since the government has an incentive to renege on it after the wages are set.

As Rogoff stresses, this time consistency problem may have important consequences for international policy coordination. If the inability to bind future policies leads to an inflationary bias, international policy coordination may further exacerbate this bias by eliminating each country's concern about currency depreciation. Thus, even when a sequence of governments within each country is trying to maximize that country's true social welfare function, policy coordination may make the situation worse rather than better.

We consider later on several factors that tend to weaken this pessimistic conclusion. First, in infinite-horizon games, governments may be able to invest in a 'reputation' in order to overcome the time-inconsistency problem (as illustrated in Barro and Gordon (1983)). In other words, a government's credibility may be judged by its willingness to honor a program laid down by an earlier government, so much that it continues the policy rather than reoptimizing during its incumbency. We will provide an example of this solution to the time inconsistency problem. Second, to the extent that the time inconsistency problem revolves around the exchange rate, policy coordination may actually eliminate the problem. In examples later in the paper, optimal coordinated policies in our two-country model turn out to be time-consistent.

The plan of the paper is as follows. In the next section we set out a simple dynamic macroeconomic model characterized by flexible exchange rates and perfect foresight on the part of the private and public sectors. In Section III, we describe various equilibria in a one-country version of the model, to highlight the implications of time inconsistency. Next, in Section IV, we describe the various equilibria in the two-country version of the game, including the welfare gains or losses from policy coordination. Extensions and conclusions are discussed in a final section.

II A simple dynamic macroeconomic model

We consider a simple model of the sort explored by Dornbusch (1976). The home country produces output Q, at price P, and trades with a foreign country, which produces Q^* at price P^*. The domestic exchange rate E measures units of home currency per unit of foreign currency, so that the relative price of the home good is $P/(EP^*)$. Demand for the home good is a decreasing function of $P/(EP^*)$ and of the real interest rate, and an increasing function of Q^*. Letting lower case variables p, q, and e represent the logarithms of their upper-case counterparts, we write demand for home goods as:

$$q_t = -\delta(p_t - e_t - p_t^*) - \sigma[i_t - (p_{t+1}^e - p_t)] + \gamma q_t^* \tag{3}$$

Here, i is the nominal interest rate, and $i_t - (p_{t+1}^e - p_t)$ the home real interest rate at time t (p_{t+1}^e is the expectation of p_{t+1} at time t). Under the perfect foresight assumption, which we hereafter maintain, $p^e_{t+1} = p_{t+1}$ for all $t \geqslant 0$.

The money demand equations take the standard transactions form:

$$m_t - p_t = \zeta q_t - \epsilon i_t \tag{4}$$

For convenience, we will invert this equation and write

$$i_t = \mu q_t - \rho(m_t - p_t) \tag{5}$$

with $\mu = \zeta/\epsilon$ and $\rho = 1/\epsilon$. Following Dornbusch, we assume perfect capital mobility, so that uncovered interest arbitrage holds:

$$e^e_{t+1} - e_t = i_t - i^*_t \tag{6}$$

Again, assuming perfect foresight, we solve for equilibria with $e^e_{t+1} = e_{t+1}$ for all t.

It remains to specify wage and price dynamics. First, the (log) consumer price index (p^c) is written as a weighted average of home (p) and foreign ($p^* + e$) prices:

$$p^c_t = \lambda p_t + (1 - \lambda)(p^*_t + e_t) \tag{7}$$

Home prices are written as a fixed markup over wages:

$$p_t = w_t \tag{8}$$

Finally, nominal wage change, $w_{t+1} - w_t$, is made a function of lagged consumer price change, $p^c_t - p^c_{t-1}$, output, and output change:

$$(w_{t+1} - w_t) = (p^c_t - p^c_{t-1}) + \psi q_t + \theta(q_t - q_{t-1}) \tag{9}$$

Note that since $w_{t+1} - w_t$ is a function of *lagged* rather than contemporaneous price change, the system will display typical Keynesian features, particularly the non-neutrality of q_t with respect to contemporaneous and future anticipated changes in m_t. This is the standard presumption in the Dornbusch model that the labor market clears more slowly than the asset markets.

In the next section, we will introduce corresponding equations for the second country, in order to construct a two-country model. Here, we focus on the one-country case by making the small-country assumption for the home economy that p^*, i^*, and q^* are given for all $t \geqslant 0$. By doing so, we can write the one-country model as a four-dimensional difference equation system as in (10):[2]

$$\begin{bmatrix} p_{t+1} \\ p^c_t \\ q_t \\ e_{t+1} \end{bmatrix} = A \begin{bmatrix} p_t \\ p^c_{t-1} \\ q_{t-1} \\ e_t \end{bmatrix} + Bm_t + C \begin{bmatrix} p^*_t \\ i^*_t \\ q^*_t \end{bmatrix} \tag{10}$$

In any given period, p_t, p_{t-1}^c, and q_{t-1} are given by the past history of the economy. These are the 'pre-determined' variables of the economy. m_t, and indeed the entire sequence of m, is chosen as a policy variable. p_t^*, i_t^*, and q_t^* are exogenous forcing variables of the system from the point of view of the home economy.

As is typical of perfect foresight models, an asset price such as e_t is determined not by past history but by forward-looking behavior of asset holders. In particular, for given values of p_t, p_{t-1}^c, q_{t-1}, and given sequences of p^*, i^*, and q^* from t to infinity, there is typically a unique value of e_t such that the exchange rate does not grow or collapse explosively (technically, this unique value of e_t puts the economy on its stable manifold). Such a unique value of e_t exists as long as the eigenvalue associated with e_t in the A matrix is outside the unit circle, and the remaining eigenvalues are on or within the unit circle. In the simulations reported below, this condition is always satisfied.

The goal of economic policy in our model will be to maximize a social welfare function as in (1) or (2), subject to the constraint in (10). The assumption that e_t is always such as to keep the economy on the saddlepoint path (or stable manifold) requires that economic agents have complete knowledge as to the path of future policies. In this sense, the government is like a Stackelberg leader with respect to the private sector, choosing monetary policy with a view to affecting e_t and thereby more basic economic targets, while e_t is chosen taking as given the future sequence of m. This is not to say, however, that governments can necessarily choose any sequence of m that they desire. A large part of the discussion that follows describes the 'admissible' sequences of policies.

As a concrete example of this model, we will suppose that instantaneous utility $u(T_t^i)$ is a quadratic function of inflation, $\pi_t = p_t^c - p_{t-1}^c$, and the deviation of output from full employment q_t. That is, $u_t = -(\frac{1}{2})(q_t^2 + \phi \pi_t^2)$. Thus, intertemporal utility is

$$U_0 = -(\tfrac{1}{2}) \sum_{t=0}^{\infty} \beta^t (q_t^2 + \phi \pi_t^2) \tag{11}$$

Note that ϕ is a parameter reflecting the weight attached to π_t relative to q_t. β is the discount factor. We have written the utility function with an infinite horizon, and we will point out shortly some special features of the problem that arise with such a formulation.

We now turn to the optimal policy for m. It may seem straightforward to maximize (11) subject to (10), but as Phelps and Pollak (1968) first explained, and Kydland and Prescott (1977) further elucidated, the maximization is quite problematic. Here we sketch the problem, and treat it in greater detail below.

Suppose that we apply optimal control techniques to the problem of maximizing U_0 subject to (10), taking as given p_0, p_{-1}^c, q_{-1}. For simplicity, we set $p_t^* = i_t^* = q_t^* = 0$ for all $t \geq 0$. The result of this straightforward control problem will be an infinite sequence m_0, m_1, ..., denoted hereafter $\{m\}_0^\infty$, that maximizes U_0. Let us write this optimal choice of monetary policy as $\{\hat{m}\}_0^\infty$. We have already noted that e_0 will in general be a function of p_0, p_{-1}^c, q_{-1} and the *entire* sequence $\{\hat{m}\}_0^\infty$. The first step of this sequence is $\hat{m}_0$.

Given $\hat{m}_0$, e_0, p_0, p_{-1}^c, and q_{-1}, we can use (10) to find p_1^c, p_0, q_0. Suppose now that at time 1 the policymakers reoptimize, in order to maximize U_1 subject to (10). Once again, a simple control problem will yield a sequence m_1, m_2, ..., now denoted as $\{\tilde{m}\}_1^\infty$. In general, $\hat{m}_t$ will not equal $\tilde{m}_t$ for $t \geq 1$, so that the government at time 1 will not want to carry on with the optimal plan as of time zero. If the government at time 1 is not bound (e.g. by a constitution) to carry out $\{\hat{m}\}_1^\infty$, the earlier plan will be scrapped.

As Kydland and Prescott stressed, we cannot simply assume away this problem by letting the initial government choose $\hat{m}_0$, the next choose $\tilde{m}_1$, etc.; i.e. by letting each succeeding government optimize anew, using the optimal control solution (this is close to what Buiter (1983) and Miller and Salmon (1983) propose, incorrectly we believe, as discussed below). The problem is much deeper, for the following reason. The choice $\hat{m}_0$ is optimal only under the assumption that it is followed by $\hat{m}_1$, $\hat{m}_2$, ... It has no particular attractiveness given that it will be followed by $\tilde{m}_1$ and other $m_t \neq \hat{m}_t$ for $t \geq 2$. Moreover, the exchange rate e_0 will be a function not of $\{\hat{m}_0\}$, as the original government's solution assumed, but rather of the actual m_t that will be selected.

Phelps and Pollak, and Kydland and Prescott, provided the answer to this difficulty. Unless the original government can act to bind all future governments, it must optimize with the full knowledge that all future governments will be free to optimize. A *time consistent* equilibrium is one in which each government optimizes its policy choice taking as given the policy rules (or specific policy actions) that *future* governments will use. With a finite time horizon, such an optimization is easy to carry out. Let x_T represent the inherited state of the economy in the final period T. In our example x_T would be the vector $\langle p_T, p_{T-1}^c, q_{T-1} \rangle$. Given x_T, it is easy to find the best policy $m_T = f_T(x_T)$ that maximizes $\Sigma_{t=T}^T \beta^t U_t$. At time $T-1$, the penultimate government knows that its successor will follow $m_T = f_T(x_T)$. It is then an easy task to maximize $\Sigma_{t=T-1}^T \beta^t U_t$ subject to (10) *and* the constraint $m_T = f_T(x_T)$. This second optimization will yield the rule $m_{T-1} = f_{T-1}(x_{t-1})$. By backward recursion, every government could thereby find a policy rule $f_i(x_i)$ that is optimal given the rule that *succeeding* administrations will follow. Such rules will be credible to the private sector (e.g. the asset holders in the foreign exchange market) because each government is doing the best that it can given the freedom of action of future governments.

In an infinite-horizon setting, the solution of the time-consistency issue is a bit more complex, as we shall soon see. The problem is that there is likely to be a *multiplicity*, perhaps an infinity, of policy rules that have the property that they are optimal given that future governments will also choose the rule. There is an embarrassing abundance of time-consistent policies. Not only is it hard to find all of these solutions, but it is not necessarily straightforward to choose among them.

In summary, there are typically two types of equilibria in multiperiod planning problems. The first type assumes that the initial government can pre-commit to an entire sequence of moves, or to a policy rule. For this type of problem, optimal control suffices. The second types of problem more realistically assumes that each government can make its 'move,' but cannot bind the hand of future governments. It must therefore optimize, taking as given the freedom of choice of future governments. Before proceeding to the multicountry setting, it is useful to study some more technical aspects of these two approaches.

Pre-commitment equilibria

There are two types of pre-commitment equilibria. In the first, the government selects an entire sequence $\{\hat{m}\}_0^\infty$ that by assumption will be carried out at all future dates. In the second, the initial government selects a *rule* $m_t = f(x_t, x_{t-1}, \ldots)$ that is also assumed to bind all future governments. The first equilibrium is termed an open-loop solution, and the second, a closed-loop solution. Both solutions will tend to be time-inconsistent, except in special cases, in the sense that future governments will want to deviate from the original sequence (in the open-loop case), or the original rule (in the closed-loop case), even if they believe that other governments will abide by the original plans.

We now calculate the optimal open-loop equilibrium in order to pinpoint the source of the time inconsistency. Starting with (10), we write the elements of the A matrix as a_{ij}, the B matrix as b_{ij}, and the C matrix as c_{ij} (the specific values of a_{ij}, b_{ij}, and c_{ij} are given in the footnote preceding equation (10)). In fact C can be ignored under our simplifying assumption that $p_t^* = q_t^* = i_t^* = 0$ for $t \geqslant 0$. Thus $p_{t+1} = a_{11}p_t + a_{12}p_{t-1}^c + a_{13}q_{t-1} + a_{14}e_t + b_{11}m_t$, while similar expressions hold for p_t^c, q_t, and e_{t+1}. The goal is to choose the sequence $\{m\}_0^\infty$ that maximizes U_0 in (11) subject to (10). To solve this problem, we write down the Lagrangian $\mathscr{L}$ as follows:

$$\max_{\{m\}_0^\infty} \mathcal{L} = -(\tfrac{1}{2}) \sum_{t=0}^{\infty} \beta^t \{[q_t^2 + \phi \pi_t^2]$$

$$+ \mu_{1,t+1}[a_{11} p_t + a_{12} p_{t-1}^c + a_{13} q_{t-1} + a_{14} e_t + b_{11} m_t - p_{t+1}]$$

$$+ \mu_{2,t+1}[a_{21} p_t + a_{22} p_{t-1}^c + a_{23} q_{t-1} + a_{24} e_t + b_{21} m_t - p_t^c]$$

$$+ \mu_{3,t+1}[a_{31} p_t + a_{32} p_{t-1}^c + a_{33} q_{t-1} + a_{34} e_t + b_{31} m_t - q_t]$$

$$+ \mu_{4,t+1}[a_{41} p_t + a_{42} p_{t-1}^c + a_{43} q_{t-1} + a_{44} e_t + b_{41} m_t - e_{t+1}]\}$$

$$(12)$$

As is well known, $\mu_{1,0}$, $\mu_{2,0}$, and $\mu_{3,0}$ are shadow values which describe how U_0 is affected by different inherited values of p_0, p_{-1}^c, and q_{-1}. In particular, $\mu_{1,0} = \partial U_0/\partial p_0$; $\mu_{2,0} = \partial U_0/\partial p_{-1}^c$; and $\mu_{3,0} = \partial U_0/\partial q_{-1}$.

By analogy, $\mu_{4,0}$ equals $\partial U_0/\partial e_0$; that is $\mu_{4,0}$ measures the change in intertemporal utility for a small change in e_0. Unlike p_0, p_{-1}^c, and q_{-1}, however, the policymaker does not inherit e_0, but rather determines e_0 as a function of the policies that are selected. Because e_0 is a policy *choice*, a necessary condition of the optimization must therefore be that $\partial U_0/\partial e_0 = \mu_{4,0} = 0$. At the optimum, μ_{4t} will equal zero at $t = 0$.

The time consistency problem arises because along the optimum sequence $\{m\}_0^\infty$, μ_{4t} will (in general) not always equal zero. (μ_{4t} will follow a difference equation of the form described in the Appendix). Since μ_{4t} will tend to move away from zero, reoptimization at any t when $\mu_{4t} \neq 0$ would lead to a new sequence of m such that μ_{4t} would again start at zero (a necessary condition of the optimization). From a technical point of view, the open-loop sequence is time consistent if and only if the equation for μ_{4t} can be satisfied with $\mu_{4,t} \equiv 0$ for all $t \geq 0$. If this condition is met, then future governments will choose $\{\hat{m}\}_0^\infty$ at all dates t even if they are not bound by the original government. If the condition is not satisfied, the open-loop solution makes sense only if future governments are not allowed to reoptimize.

Consider a simple illustration using our model. We select simulation values for the key parameters of the model, as shown in Table 7.1. The economy inherits a *ten-percent* domestic inflation rate, and lagged full employment (i.e. $p_0 = 0.10$; $p_{-1} = 0.0$; $p_{-1}^c = 0.0$; $q_{-1} = 0.0$). With a constant exchange rate ($e_0 = 0$), CPI inflation will equal ten percent in period zero (i.e. $\pi_0 = 0.10$), while a currency appreciation can reduce the initial CPI inflation rate. Given our parameter values, the optimal sequence $\{\hat{m}\}_0^\infty$ is sharply contractionary at $t = 0$, so that output is pushed below zero, with the goal of reducing inflation. The real exchange rate $p_0^* + e_0 - p_0$ appreciates at $t = 0$, 4.7 percent above its long run value, with the currency appreciation helping to export inflation abroad. Figure 7.1 shows the optimal paths of inflation, output, and the real exchange rate. (1984 is taken as $t = 0$).

Table 7.1. *Parameter values*

$\xi = 1.00$	$\epsilon = 0.50$	$\psi = 0.10$
$\beta = 0.75$	$\theta = 0.30$	$\phi = 2.00$
$\gamma = 0.00$	$\lambda = 0.75$	
$\delta = 1.50$	$\sigma = 1.50$	

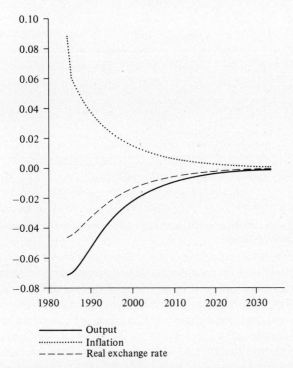

———— Output
············ Inflation
– – – – Real exchange rate

7.1 Open-loop control in the one-country model

Consider the behavior of $\mu_{4,t}$, as shown in Figure 7.2. After $t = 0$, μ_4 turns positive, meaning that an increase in e would raise welfare. From the point of view of the government at time $t = 3$ (1987), for example, the original plan is too contractionary, since a currency depreciation would raise welfare. A new optimization at $t = 3$ would lead to a new sequence $\{\overline{m}\}_0^\infty$, with $\overline{m}_3 > \hat{m}_3$. This is shown in Figure 7.3, where we superimpose $\{\hat{m}\}_0^\infty$ and $\{\overline{m}\}_3^\infty$. Loosely speaking, the initial government, at $t = 0$, has an incentive to announce a stern set of future monetary policies in order to induce a currency appreciation at $t = 0$, and thereby to reduce π_0 (which is otherwise very high). Of course, e_0 can be reduced by extremely low m_0

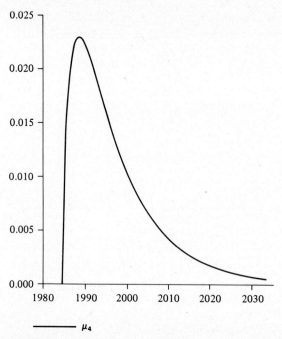

7.2 Shadow price on the exchange rate (μ_{4t}) in open-loop control (one-country model)

and higher m_t for $t \geqslant 1$, or by more moderate m_0 and somewhat lower m_t for $t \geqslant 1$. The *optimal* policy is to opt for moderate m_0 and low future m, rather than extremely restrictive m_0, since the approach with restrictive future m achieves the same currency appreciation with a somewhat lower loss of initial output, q_0.

Thus, from the perspective at $t = 0$, it is worthwhile to commit future m to low values for the sake of e_0. However, from the perspective of future governments, e_0 is a bygone, and m should reflect tradeoffs in the present and future, not the past. Thus, by the time a future government assumes office, part of the original incentive to keep m low has disappeared, and the new optimization in period t consequently yields a higher value of m_t.

It is interesting to note that there is a single special case in which the open-loop policy is also time consistent, and that is when $\sigma = 0$ in the original model (i.e. output is not affected by the real interest rate). In that case, $\mu_{4t} \equiv 0$ satisfies the equation for μ_{4t} derived in the Appendix.[3] From an economic point of view, when $\sigma = 0$, only the exchange rate e_0, but *not* the sequence of future m, affects q_0 and π_0, so that there is no reason to prefer one path of m over another as long as they both lead to the same

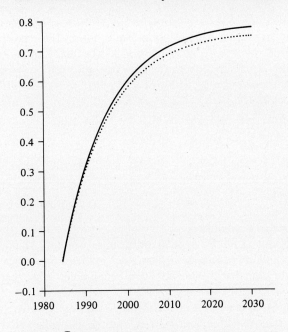

——— $\bar{M}$: Open-loop policy with reoptimization in 1987
·············· $\hat{M}$: Open-loop policy

7.3 Reoptimization of open-loop control in 1987 (comparison with original solution; one-country model)

e_0. The same is true about all future e_t. This property allows the original government to specify a path $\{\hat{m}\}_0^\infty$ that all future governments will be content to honor.

The open-loop equilibrium is the best pre-commitment equilibrium available. It is sometimes argued, however, that while governments cannot credibly pre-commit future governments to a sequence of policy moves, they may be able to pre-commit governments to a specific policy *rule* for m_t. Such a closed-loop rule might not be as good as the open-loop result, but it might be better than no rule at all. There is some merit to this argument, as we shall soon see. The rule can of course be of varying complexity. We illustrate this case by choosing a simple rule, which links m_t to the *current* state of the economy, as described by the vector x_t $\langle p_t, p_{t-1}^c, q_{t-1} \rangle$. Such a rule is termed memoryless, in that the past history of the economy, in arriving at $\langle p_t, p_{t-1}^c, q_{t-1} \rangle$, is not permitted to affect m_t. We simplify further by specifying m_t as a *linear* function of p_t, p_{t-1}^c, and q_{t-1}:

$$m_t = \beta_0 + \beta_1 p_t + \beta_2 p_{t-1}^c + \beta_3 q_{t-1} \tag{13}$$

Our method of solution is straightforward. A solution of the form (13) is guessed. Using (10) and the assumption that e_0 places the economy on the stable manifold, we find U_0 as a function of the rule. Implicitly then $U_0 = U_0(\beta_0, \beta_1, \beta_2, \beta_3)$. Using a standard numerical optimization technique, we then proceed to maximize U_0 with respect to $\beta_0, \beta_1, \beta_2, \beta_3$, to arrive at the optimal rule $m_t = \hat{\beta}_0 + \hat{\beta}_1 p_t + \hat{\beta}_2 p_{t-1}^c + \hat{\beta}_3 q_{t-1}$. Given our assumed parameter values for the structural model, we find:

$$m_t = -0.038\, p_t + 1.027\, p_{t-1}^c + 0.322\, q_{t-1} \tag{14}$$

Note that this is the optimal linear rule for a given $x_0 = \langle p_0, p_1^c, q_{-1} \rangle = \langle 0.1, 0.0, 0.0 \rangle$. For a different starting point, we would find a different rule.

Time-consistent equilibria

The previous equilibria depend on the unsatisfactory assumption that future governments can be bound by rules made at an earlier date. Some writers have suggested that macroeconomic policies must therefore be formulated as constitutional rules, in order to bind successfully at a later date. For many reasons, including conflicting views about the correct rules, unwillingness to tamper with a constitution, and the realization that even constitutions can be amended at a later date, there is little likelihood that the macroeconomic policy will soon be etched in constitutional stone. In practice, therefore, governments must operate with the knowledge that future governments have freedom to change course and will have incentives to do so, relative to the open-loop or closed-loop optimum, even when the future governments share the goals of the earlier governments.

In this circumstance, we can reformulate the policy problem as a game among an infinite number of players (i.e. governments), who are identified by the time period in which they act. The initial move is made by the government at $t = 0$ (hereafter G_0), then by G_1, and so on. The payoff functions for G_t is $\Sigma_{i=t}^{\infty} \beta^t U_t(T_t^i)$, and the move is m_t.

Now, we can think of various types of *Nash equilibria* among these governments. In analogy to the pre-commitment case, we can think of Nash equilibria in which each government takes as given the *moves* of other governments, or Nash equilibria in which each government takes as given *policy rules* of other governments. A Nash equilibrium in moves will be called 'open-loop,' and a Nash equilibrium in strategies or policy rules will be called 'closed-loop.'

Consider first the case of open-loop Nash equilibrium. Let $\{m\}_{-t}$ denote the sequence of *moves* before and after, but not including, period t: $m_0, m_1, \ldots, m_{t-1}, m_{t+1}, m_{t+2}, \ldots$. An open-loop Nash equilibrium is a sequence $\{m^N\}_0^\infty$, with the property that for all governments m^N is optimal taking as given $\{m^N\}_{-t}$:

> $\{m_0^N\}^\infty$ is an open-loop Nash equilibrium if and only if for
>
> all t, m_t^N maximizes $\sum\limits_{i=t}^{\infty} \beta^i U_i$ subject to (10) and given $\{m^N\}_{-t}$. (15)

In performing the optimization at period t, the government assumes that e_t adjusts to keep the economy on the stable manifold, given the past history of m, the current policy choice m_t, and the assumed future path $m_{t+1}^N, m_{t+2}^N, \ldots$.

With this definition, the problem with the precommitment equilibrium is that the resulting path is not a Nash equilibrium among the infinite sequence of governments (this was verified in Figure 7.3). Taking as given that other governments will play $\hat{m}_t$ (the open-loop sequence), only the initial government will want its part of the sequence (i.e. $\hat{m}_0$). For all other governments (in general), there will exist a superior choice of policy.

Now, consider the 'closed-loop' version of Nash equilibrium, in which we assume that G_t plays a *rule* (or strategy) f_t, which maps $(x_t, x_{t-1}, \ldots)$ to m_t, rather than just a move m_t. As before, define the sequence $\{f\}_{-t}$ as $(f_0, f_1, \ldots f_{t-1}, f_{t+1}, \ldots)$. Now, we define a Nash equilibrium in this strategy space as follows:

> $\{f^N\}_0^\infty$ is a closed-loop Nash equilibrium if and only if for all
>
> t, $m_t = f_t^N(x_t, x_{t-1}, \ldots)$ maximizes $\sum\limits_{i=t}^{\infty} \beta^i U_i$ subject to (10),
>
> and given $\{f^N\}_{-t}$. (16)

In general, there will be many such Nash equilibria, some of which (as we shall see) are not very desirable.

As is typical in such circumstances, we further refine the nature of the equilibrium to include only Nash *perfect* equilibria. A strategy sequence $\{f\}_0^\infty$ is said to be a perfect equilibrium if for any history of the economy from time 0 to t (even histories not resulting from a Nash equilibrium during periods 0 to t), strategies $\{f\}_0^\infty$ constitute a Nash equilibrium in the sub-game from t to ∞. We now define *time consistency*:

> $\{f\}_0^\infty$ time consistent if and only if $\{f\}_0^\infty$ is a Nash
> perfect equilibrium. (17)

In general, open-loop Nash equilibria, as in (15), will not be perfect equilibria. Suppose, for example, that the sequence $\tilde{m}_1, \tilde{m}_2, \ldots$ has the Nash property. In most models, including those in our paper, the sequence

$\tilde{m}_2, \tilde{m}_3, \ldots$ will not be subgame Nash (starting at period 2), if m_1 is set differently from $\tilde{m}_1$. Thus, from this point on, we restrict our search for time-consistent equilibria to closed-loop Nash equilibria, in which governments take as given the policy rules of other governments.

Unfortunately, even the perfectness concept does not eliminate the problem of a multiplicity of equilibria. There will in general be many truly time-consistent equilibria. To narrow the search, we begin with the simplest case, in which m_t is a function of the current state x_t ($= \langle p^c_{t-1}, p_t, q_{t-1} \rangle$) alone (see Maskin and Tirole (1983) for some justification for restricting our search to such 'memoryless' strategies). Thus, we are searching for a function $m_t = f(x_t)$ such that:

$$m_t = f(x_t) \text{ maximizes } \sum_{i=t}^{\infty} \beta^i u_i \text{ subject to (10) and to the}$$

restriction that $m_i = f(x_i)$ for all $i \neq t$. \hfill (18)

(Note that in this case the government at time t does not actually care about the rules up to time t, since the past is fully summarized in x_t). Implicit throughout is the assumption that e_t is always such as to keep the economy on the stable manifold. In practice, this means that along with f there is another function h linking e_t and x_t: $e_t = h(x_t)$.

Our strategy is to search for f among the class of linear functions. Although we cannot prove that the resulting function is the unique memoryless, time-consistent equilibrium, we suspect that it is in fact unique, in view of the linear-quadratic structure of the underlying problem. Consider the necessary conditions for a time-consistent optimum. Let $m_t = \gamma_0 + \gamma_1 p_t + \gamma_2 p^c_{t-1} + \gamma_3 q_{t-1}$ be a candidate solution (call it the γ-rule). Plugging this rule into (10), we can also determine a unique linear rule $e_t = h_0 + h_1 p_t + h_2 p^c_{t-1} + h_3 q_{t-1}$ that keeps the economy on the stable manifold. Now, suppose that these rules hold for all $t \geqslant 1$. It is possible to calculate $\Sigma_{t=1}^{\infty} \beta^t U_t$ as a function of the rule and the state of the economy at $t = 1$, i.e. x_1. Let us call the value of the utility function $V_1^{\gamma}(x_1)$, where V^{γ} denotes the dependence of utility on the rule γ.

At time zero, the 0th government wants to maximize $\Sigma_{t=0}^{\infty} \beta^t U_t$, which equals $U_0 + \beta V_1^{\gamma}(x_1)$ under the assumption that future governments will use the γ-rule. Note that $x_1 = \langle p_1, p_0^c, q_0 \rangle$. Specifically, the initial government solves the following:

$$\max_{m_0} U_0 + \beta V_1^{\gamma}(p_1, p_0^c, q_0)$$

Subject to:

(a) $e_1 = h_0 + h_1 p_1 + h_2 p_0^c + h_3 q_0$

(b) $p_1 = a_{11} p_0 + a_{12} p^c_{-1} + a_{13} q_{-1} + a_{14} e_0 + b_{11} m_0$

(c) $p_0^c = a_{21} p_0 + a_{22} p_{-1}^c + a_{23} q_{-1} + a_{24} e_0 + b_{21} m_0$

(d) $q_0 = a_{31} p_0 + a_{32} p_{-1}^c + a_{33} q_{-1} + a_{34} e_0 + b_{31} m_0$

(e) $e_1 = a_{41} p_0 + a_{42} p_{-1}^c + a_{43} q_{-1} + a_{44} e_0 + b_{41} m_0$

(f) $U_0 = -(q_0^2 + \phi \pi_0^2)$

(g) p_0, p_{-1}^c, q_{-1} and V_1^γ given $\qquad$ (19)

In this optimization problem, (a) is determined by the candidate γ-rule. (b)–(e) are the structural dynamic equations summarized in (10). (f) is the instantaneous utility function (note that $\pi_0 = p_0^c - p_{-1}^c$). Finally, (g) defines the state of the economy for the initial government.

The optimization is straightforward. Using (a) and (e) we can write $e_0 = (1/a_{44})[h_0 + h_1 p_1 + h_2 p_0^c + h_3 q_0 - a_{41} p_0 - a_{42} p_{-1}^c - a_{43} q_{-1} - b_{41} m_0]$. Now using (b), (c) and (d) together with the new equation for e_0, we have four equations that make e_0, p_0^c, q_0, and p_1 linear functions of m_0 and the pre-determined variables p_0, p_{-1}^c, q_{-1}. Let us write this system as:

$$\left.\begin{array}{l} e_0 = d_{11} p_0 + d_{12} p_{-1}^c + d_{13} q_{-1} + d_{14} m_0 \\ p_0^c = d_{21} p_0 + d_{22} p_{-1}^c + d_{23} q_{-1} + d_{24} m_0 \\[6pt] q_0 = d_{31} p_0 + d_{32} p_{-1}^c + d_{33} q_{-1} + d_{34} m_0 \\ p_1 = d_{41} p_0 + d_{42} p_{-1}^c + d_{43} q_{-1} + d_{44} m_0 \end{array}\right\} \qquad (20)$$

Now simply impose the first-order condition that $d[-(q_0^2 + \phi \pi_0^2) + \beta V_1^\gamma(p_1, p_0^c, q_0)]/dm_0$ equals zero. By direct substitution we have:

$$\begin{aligned} 0 = &-2 d_{34}(d_{31} p_0 + d_{32} p_{-1}^c + d_{33} q_{-1} + d_{34} m_0) \\ &- 2\phi d_{24}(d_{21} p_0 + d_{22} p_{-1}^c + d_{23} q_{-1} + d_{24} m_0 - p_{-1}^c) \\ &+ \beta(\partial V_1^\gamma/\partial p_1) d_{44} \\ &+ \beta(\partial V_1^\gamma/\partial p_0^c) d_{24} \\ &+ \beta(\partial V_1^\gamma/\partial q_0) d_{34} \end{aligned} \qquad (21)$$

This gives us a linear rule for m_0 as a function of p_0, p_{-1}^c, q_{-1} and implicitly (through V_1^γ) the γ rule:

$$\begin{aligned} m_0 = &[1/(d_{34} + \phi d_{24}^2)] [(d_{34} d_{31} + \phi d_{24} d_{21}) p_0 \\ &+ (d_{34} d_{32} + \phi d_{24} d_{22}) p_{-1}^c + (d_{33}^2 + \phi d_{23}^2) q_{-1} \\ &+ (\tfrac{1}{2}\beta)(\partial V_1^\gamma/\partial p_1) d_{44} + (\tfrac{1}{2}\beta)(\partial V_1^\gamma/\partial p_0^c) d_{24} \\ &+ (\tfrac{1}{2}\beta)(\partial V_1^\gamma/\partial q_0) d_{34}] \end{aligned} \qquad (22)$$

Under our assumptions, the partial derivatives of V_1^γ are linear functions of p_0, p_{-1}^c, and q_{-1} (though not easy to write down analytically!). Thus, m_0 is a linear rule in p_0, p_{-1}^c, and q_{-1}:

$$m_0 = \delta_0 + \delta_1 p_0 + \delta_2 p_{-1}^c + \delta_3 q_{-1} \qquad (23)$$

As long as (23) is the same as the γ rule, we have found a stationary, time-consistent rule. That is, for $\delta_0 = \gamma_0$, $\delta_1 = \gamma_1$, $\delta_2 = \gamma_2$, $\delta_3 = \gamma_3$, the γ rule is validated as a time-consistent policy. Starting at *any* period t and any state t, the tth government will choose the γ rule given that all future governments will make that choice.

In general, the time-consistent rule must be found numerically (see Cohen and Michel (1984) for an elegant treatment of the one-dimensional case for the state vector x, for which an analytical solution is found). To do so, we start with a finite-period problem, in which $U_0^i = \Sigma_{t=0}^T \beta^t u_t$. It is then easy to find the optimal final period rule $m_T = f_T(x_T)$. Given f_T, f_{T-1} is readily found by the type of backward recursion just described. For each T, we can readily compute $f_0(x_0)$. Denote this rule as $f_0^T(x_0)$ to denote the dependence of the rule on the periods remaining. Then it is a simple matter to find the limiting value of $f_0^T(x_0)$ as $T \to \infty$. The rule $f(x_0) = \lim_{T \to \infty} f_0^T(x_0)$ can then be verified directly to have the time-consistency, Nash equilibrium property for the infinite-horizon game. We provide details of this method in the Appendix.

Using the parameter values described earlier, the time-consistent rule is calculated to be:

$$m_t = -0.032\, p_t + 1.032\, p_{t-1}^c + 0.275\, q_{t-1} \tag{24}$$

As is shown in the Appendix, the open-loop optimal policy can be written as a linear function of the state variables *and* μ_{4t}:

$$m_t = -0.019\, p_t + 1.019\, p_{t-1}^c + 0.272\, q_{t-1} + 0.389\, \mu_{4t} \tag{25}$$

Starting, as before, with 10 percent inflation, we can compute the path of output and inflation for the time-consistent policy, for comparison with the open-loop pre-commitment equilibrium. In Figure 7.4a, we compare the inflation performance in the two cases; in Figure 7.4b, we compare the exchange rates; and in Figure 7.4c, we compare the output paths. We have already seen that the open-loop control holds future governments to an *over-contractionary* policy relative to the one that they would select upon reoptimization. Since the time-consistent policy explicitly allows for (expansionary) reoptimization in the future, it is not surprising that the real exchange rate is less appreciated in the time-consistent (TC) case than in the open-loop (OL) case. Simply, agents recognize that future governments will select more expansionary m, and e_t is an increasing function of the entire sequence of m. Thus, $\pi_0^{OL} < \pi_0^{TC}$, via the exchange rate effect. In general, $q_t^{OL} < q_t^{TC}$ in the early periods, as governments in the OL case pursue a steady, contractionary policy. After a certain period (shown as $\bar{t}$ in Figure 7.4c), the inequality is reversed. Both policies reduce the inherited inflation to zero in the long run.

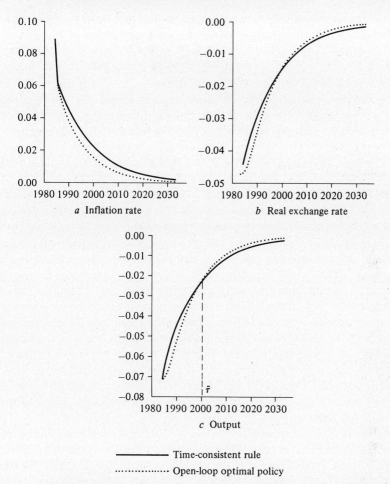

a Inflation rate

b Real exchange rate

c Output

——— Time-consistent rule

.... Open-loop optimal policy

7.4 A comparison of open-loop and time-consistent policies (one-country model)

Before turning to a welfare ranking of the various policies, we must note a key feature of the disinflation process (pointed out earlier in Buiter and Miller (1982) and elsewhere). The price equation is:

$$(p_{t+1}-p_t) = (p_t^c-p_{t-1}^c)+\psi q_t+\theta(q_t-q_{t-1}).$$

Also $p_t^c = p_t+(1-\lambda)(p_t^*+e_t-p_t) = p_t+(1-\lambda)r_t$, where $r_t (= p_t^*+e_t-p_t)$ is the real exchange rate. Thus,

$$(p_{t+1}-p_t) = (p_t-p_{t-1})+(1-\lambda)(r_t-r_{t-1})+\psi q_t+\theta(q_t-q_{t-1}) \quad (26)$$

Suppose an economy inherits an inflation rate of $\Delta_0 = p_0-p_{-1}$, with

$r_{-1} = q_{-1} = 0$. By simple forward integration of (26) from $t = 0$, we have

$$(p_{t+1} - p_t) = \Delta_0 + (1 - \lambda) r_t + \psi \sum_{i=0}^{t} q_i + \theta q_t \qquad (27)$$

Now, for all of the equilibria so far considered, $p_{t+1} - p_t$ equals zero in the long run (i.e. inflation is eliminated), r_t returns to zero (i.e. no long-run change in competitiveness), and q_t returns to zero (i.e. long-run full employment). Thus, taking limits of (27), we find $0 = \Delta_0 + \psi \Sigma_{i=0}^{\infty} q_i$, or

$$\sum_{i=0}^{\infty} q_i = -\Delta_0 / \psi \qquad (28)$$

All policies have the same cumulative output loss, no matter what is the time path of exchange rates, money, etc.! Thus, the welfare issue is always one of *timing*, rather than the overall magnitude of lost output.

On purely logical grounds, we can rank the welfare achieved by the three policies so far studied: open-loop control, closed-loop control (with pre-commitment), and time-consistent control. The open-loop control is clearly first best, since both of the other solutions reflect the same optimization, but under additional constraints. The closed-loop, linear feedback rule also must produce higher utility than the time-consistent rule. Both the linear rule and time-consistent solution choose m_t as a linear function of x_t; the linear rule is chosen as the *best* among this class of functions, so in particular it is better than the time-consistent rule. Thus we know that $U_0^{\text{OL}} \geqslant U_0^{\text{CL}} \geqslant U_0^{\text{TC}}$. In general, the inequalities will be strict, though we have already noted special cases (e.g. $\sigma = 0$) in which all of the policies are identical.

Buiter (1983) has recently proposed an alternative strategy for finding a time-consistent linear rule, which has also been treated at length by Miller and Salmon (1983); (we describe Buiter's approach at length in the appendix). His reasoning is as follows. Consider the open-loop control solution, with shadow prices μ_1, μ_2, and μ_3 on the state variables, and μ_4 on the exchange rate. At $t = 0$, the initial government chooses policies so that $\mu_{4,0} = 0$. For $t > 0$, we know that $\mu_{4,t}$ will tend to deviate from zero. Each government in period t would like to reset $\mu_{4,t}' = 0$. Buiter proposes, therefore, that a time-consistent solution is found by *assuming* that $\mu_{4,t} \equiv 0$ for all t, and *dropping* the open-loop dynamic equation for $\mu_{4,t}$. When this procedure is followed, we obtain the following linear rule:

$$m_t = 0.237 \, p_t + 0.763 \, p_{t-1}^e + 0.229 \, q_{t-1} \qquad (29)$$

There are two counts against this proposed solution. Most important, it is simply not time consistent. If all governments for $t \geqslant 1$ adopt the Buiter rule, the government at $t = 0$ would *not* choose this rule. By following the procedures described earlier (for calculating the best rule at $t = 0$ for a given rule at $t \geqslant 1$) we find that the initial government would choose:

$$m_t = -0.147\, p_0 + 1.147\, p^c_{-1} + 0.309\, q_{-1} \tag{30}$$

The logic underlying the Buiter solution seems problematic as well. The merit for a government to choose $\mu_{4,t} = 0$ comes if the sequence of m corresponding to $\mu_{4,t} = 0$ will in fact be carried out by future governments. But, by construction, each succeeding government alters the chosen sequence of m. There is simply no attraction to choosing $\mu_{4,t} = 0$ if the government knows that its plans will not be carried forward. The private sector understands this point perfectly, by setting e_t to correspond to the actual sequence of m rather than to the sequence planned by each government. In a nutshell, Buiter's government is naive in assuming that future governments will carry out its open-loop optimum, at the same time that the private sector is completely on top of the policy-making process, and knows that future governments will reoptimize.

Reputation and time-consistency

In the previous section we simplified our search for a time-consistent policy to 'memoryless' rules. Such rules make m_t a function of the contemporaneous state vector x_t, but not of the past history of x and m. Many policies in the real world depend on the history of a game as much as the current state. In competitive environments, for example, aggressive behavior by one player at time $t-1$ might bring forward retaliation by others at period t, as in 'tit-for-tat' strategies. Game theorists have long understood that such history-dependent strategies can help competing players to achieve more efficient outcomes than those obtainable from memoryless strategies alone.

It turns out that similar complex strategies can help a sequence of governments to achieve a better equilibrium than the one obtained by the memoryless rule $m_t = f(x_t)$. Consider a compound rule of the sort:

(a) Government t chooses its policy according to $m_t = g(x_t)$, as long as all governments $j < t$ have also selected policy this way;
(b) If any government $j < t$ selects $m_j \neq g(x_j)$, then government t selects $m_t = f(x_t)$, where f is the memoryless, time-consistent rule. (31)

Suppose now that the rule $g(x_t)$ is better than $f(x_t)$ in the sense that if all governments $t \geqslant 0$ choose $g(x_t)$ they achieve utility $U^g_t > U^f_t$. Also, suppose that $g(x_t)$ itself is *not* time consistent in the sense of (19): If all governments $t \geqslant 1$ are known to choose $g(x_t)$, it is not optimal for the government at $t = 0$ to select $g(x_0)$.

The surprising result is that while $g(x_t)$ is not time consistent, a compound strategy like (31)(a)–(b) can be time consistent with the result that all governments end up playing $g(x_t)$, leading to higher social welfare. In the memoryless time-consistency problem, each government takes as given the choice of policy *rule* followed by future governments. If future governments are going to choose $m_t = g(x_t)$, the current government may have no particular incentive to choose g. With a compound rule as in (31), the government at time t knows that it affects the policy rule selected by future governments. It takes as given the *two-part decision mechanism* (a)–(b), but it recognizes that if it is the first government to deviate from $g(x_t)$, it will cause all future governments to choose $f(x_t)$ instead of $g(x_t)$. Since $U^g > U^f$ by assumption, this deviation from $g(x_t)$ imposes a cost, which deters the government from deviating from $g(x_t)$.

Thus, each government operates under a 'threat' that future governments will revert to $f(x_t)$ if the current government fails to play $m_t = g(x_t)$. Game theorists have long recognized that such a threat mechanism is viable only if the reversion to $f(x_t)$ is credible. For example, suppose that the rule is 'let money growth obey the open-loop strategy or else each future government lets money grow by one million percent.' If every government takes it *as given* that future governments hold this rule, then money growth will indeed obey the open-loop strategy (governments would seek to avoid the hyperinflation that they fear would otherwise ensue). A true intertemporal Nash equilibrium is obtained, in which the open-loop sequence is carried out by every government. The problem here, of course, is that the threat of hyperinflation is not rational. Surely, if any government does violate the open-loop rule, the next government will not exercise the threat. Knowing this, no government really has an incentive to persist in the open-loop path.

Game theorists therefore restrict the threats to actions that would indeed be carried out if deviations from $g(x_t)$ occur (even if, as in the example, the threats need never actually be carried out). It is here that the assumption of *perfection* of equilibrium becomes important. In the hyperinflation example just cited, not all subgames are Nash, and thus the proposed equilibrium is not perfect. To see this, suppose that G_0 deviates. Even if G_1 assumes that all future governments will play the hyperinflation threat, it is not optimal for government 1 to play the threat. Thus the subgame in which government 0 deviates, and all G_t ($t \geq 1$) let m grow by 1 million percent per period, is not a Nash equilibrium. G_1 can do better unilaterally, taking as given the actions of other G_t.

As long as the reversion is to $f(x_t)$, i.e. the threat is to return to the time-consistent rule, the threat is credible. After all, if a government believes that all future governments will play $f(x_t)$, it is optimal for the government itself to play $f(x_t)$. Every subgame consisting of the infinite sequence of governments playing $f(x_t)$ is therefore a Nash equilibrium.

Now we argue that by this mechanism the sequence of governments can sustain any linear rule $m_t = l(x_t)$, as long as the utility from this rule is higher than the utility from the memoryless time-consistent rule for any x_t. We want to show, therefore, that the following strategy for each government constitutes a perfect Nash equilibrium, in which $m_t = l(x_t)$ is always played.

(a) Each government chooses $m_t = l(x_t)$ as long as all governments $j < t$ have also selected this rule;

(b) If any government $j < t$ selects a different m_t, then all governments t select $m_t = f(x_t)$. (32)

Now let us examine the incentive of any government to deviate from $m_t = l(x_t)$. It knows that all future governments will then play $f(x_t)$. But knowing that all future governments will play $f(x_t)$, it is optimal for the government in question to choose $m_t = f(x_t)$ as well, by the definition of f. In other words, if a government is going to deviate, the best deviation is simply to revert to $f(x_t)$ immediately. Thus, the cost of defecting from the $m_t = l(x_t)$ rule is to revert immediately and permanently to the $m_t = f(x_t)$ rule. Since utility is higher under l than f, there is never an incentive to deviate from l. The equilibrium is perfect, since in any subgame in which a defection from $m_t = l(x_t)$ has occurred, it will be a Nash equilibrium for all governments to revert to $f(x_t)$.

For the case $\theta = 0.0$, we have found a rule $m_t = l(x_t)$ that has the property that $U_t^l(x_t) \geqslant U_t^f(x_t)$, and thus have verified that such reputational equilibria exist in our model. With $\theta = 0$, and all other parameter values as in Table 7.1, the time consistent rule is:

$$m_t = f(x_t) = -0.165 \, p_t + 1.165 \, p_{t-1}^c$$

The following rule has higher utility for all x_t:

$$m_t = l(x_t) = -0.185 \, p_t + 1.185 \, p_{t-1}^c$$

The loss functions corresponding to these rules are:

$$U^f(x_t) = -(\tfrac{1}{2}) \, x_t' \begin{bmatrix} 1.726 & -1.726 \\ -1.726 & 1.726 \end{bmatrix} x_t = -x_t' S^f x_t$$

$$U^l(x_t) = -(\tfrac{1}{2}) \, x_t' \begin{bmatrix} 1.725 & -1.725 \\ -1.725 & 1.725 \end{bmatrix} x_t = -x_t' S^l x_t$$

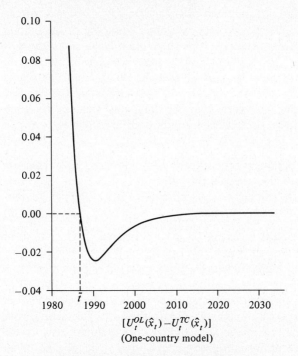

$$[U_t^{OL}(\hat{x}_t) - U_t^{TC}(\hat{x}_t)]$$
(One-country model)

[a] Note that the y-axis has been adjusted by a
multiplicative factor for graphical convenience.

7.5 The cost of reversion to time-consistent control

Since $S^f - S^l$ is positive definite, we have for all x_t that

$$U^l - U^f = x_t'(S^f - S^l)x_t > 0.$$

We have not found such an example for $\theta > 0.0$.

In an important sense, then, the time inconsistency problem is exagger-ated, in that many 'pre-commitment' equilibria can probably be sustained even in situations where actions of future governments cannot be bound. The memoryless time-consistent equilibrium is the *lower limit* of what can be obtained by a sequence of governments, not the only outcome. We should stress, however, that time consistency does impose costs, since the first-best, open-loop strategy almost surely cannot be sustained as a perfect equilibrium. The reason is as follows. Suppose that the sequence of governments pursues the open-loop solution under the threat of reversion to $m_t = f(x_t)$ if it ever violates the open loop rule. We know that it will follow the sequence $\{\hat{m}\}_0^\infty$, to which corresponds a sequence of states, denoted $\{\hat{x}\}_0^\infty$. At each t, we may calculate the utility of continuing with

Table 7.2. *Two-country model*

Aggregate demand
$$q_t = -\delta(p_t - e_t - p_t^*) + \gamma q_t^* - \sigma[i_t - (p_{t+1} - p_t)]$$
$$q_t^* = -\delta(p_t^* + e_t - p_t) + \gamma q_t - \sigma[i_t^* - (p_{t+1}^* - p_t^*)]$$

Money demand
$$m_t - p_t = \xi q_t - \epsilon i$$
$$m_t^* - p_t^* = \xi q_t^* - \epsilon i^*$$

Consumer price index
$$p_t^c = \lambda p_t + (1-\lambda)(p_t^* + e_t)$$
$$p_t^{c*} = \lambda p_t^* + (1-\lambda)(p_t - e_t)$$

Domestic price level
$$p_t = w_t$$
$$p_t^* = w_t^*$$

Nominal wage change
$$(w_{t+1} - w_t) = \pi_t + \psi q_t + \theta(q_t - q_{t-1})$$
$$(w_{t+1}^* - w_t^*) = \pi_t^* + \psi q_t^* + \theta(q_t^* - q_{t-1}^*)$$

Inflation
$$\pi_t = p_t^c - p_{t-1}^c$$
$$\pi_t^* = p_t^{c*} - p_{t-1}^{c*}$$

Exchange rate
$$e_{t+1} = e_t + i_t - i_t^*$$

---

the open-loop sequence, $U_t^{\mathrm{OL}}(\hat{x}_t)$, with the utility of reverting to the time-consistent equilibrium, $U_t^{\mathrm{TC}}(\hat{x}_t)$. The threat of reverting to f will continue to work only when $U_t^{\mathrm{OL}}(\hat{x}_t) \geqslant U_t^{\mathrm{TC}}(\hat{x}_t)$. However, at some point this equality is reversed, and the government at that date actually prefers to revert to the time-consistent equilibrium. Knowing that such a date will be reached, earlier governments will also know that the open-loop path cannot be sustained. This phenomenon is shown in Figure 7.5, where at each t, we graph $U_t^{\mathrm{OL}}(\hat{x}_t) - U^{\mathrm{TC}}(\hat{x}_t)$, with the $\hat{x}_t$ calculated along the open-loop path. As long as $U_t^{\mathrm{OL}}(\hat{x}_t) - U_t^{\mathrm{TC}}(\hat{x}_t)$ is positive, the government at t does not have an incentive to deviate. At time $\tilde{t}$ (here 1987), the government prefers to revert to the time-consistent solution.

III Policy coordination in the two-country model

The first part of the paper has dealt with economic policy in a single economy. We now extend the same set of techniques to a two-country setting. The goal is to compare 'non-cooperative' equilibria (NC), in which each country optimizes while taking as given the policies abroad, with 'cooperative' equilibria (C), in which binding commitments can be made between the two countries. Formally, we treat the cooperative case as one in which a single controller chooses the policies of the two countries. As in the early section, we must treat two separate types of equilibria: (1) the *pre-commitment* case, in which the two countries (in NC) or the single controller (in C), can credibly pre-commit to a rule or to an infinite sequence of actions; and (2) the *time-consistent* case, in which no pre-commitment in future periods is possible. We turn first to the pre-commitment case.

Open-loop control and policy coordination

The open-loop case is most easily dealt with (policy coordination in the open-loop case is also discussed in Buiter and Miller (1983) and Sachs (1983)). We first append a symmetric foreign-country model to the home-country model just discussed. The model is shown in Table 7.2. In the NC solution, each government at $t = 0$ solves for an optimal sequence of monetary policies taking as given the sequence selected from abroad. In the C solution, a single controller chooses $\{m\}_0^\infty$ and $\{m^*\}_0^\infty$ to maximize a weighted average of intertemporal utilities at home and abroad. In view of the symmetry assumed between the countries, $\{m\}_0^\infty$ will equal $\{m^*\}_0^\infty$ as a feature of both solutions, with the adjustment paths at home and abroad identical. The key result is that non-cooperative control leads to over-contractionary anti-inflation policies relative to the social optimum. Both countries are made better off by a coordinated policy of less rapid disinflation.

In general, the dimensionality of the control problem is too high to analyze the NC case analytically. An important special case, however, allows us to establish analytically the key features of the NC versus C solutions. Since the findings are insightful, we begin with that special case. In particular, we first assume that aggregate demand and money demand are not interest sensitive ($\sigma = \epsilon = 0$ in the original model). This simplification allows us to determine e_t as a function of the current state vector together with m_t and m_t^*, rather than as a forward-looking variable dependent on the entire future sequence of policies. Also, to reduce further the dimensionality, we set $\theta = 0$, so that wage change depends on the level of output but not its lagged rate of change.

Denoting the real exchange rate as $r_t = p_t^* + e_t - p_t$, we can write $p_t^c = p_t + (1-\lambda) r_t$, and $\pi_t = p_t^c - p_{t-1}^c = (p_t - p_{t-1}) + (1-\lambda)(r_t - r_{t-1})$. Therefore, from the wage equation, and the fact that $p_t = w_t$, we have $\pi_{t+1} = \pi_t + (1-\lambda)(r_{t+1} - r_t) + \psi q_t$. Note from this expression that inflation accelerated when $r_{t+1} > r_t$ or $q_t > 0$. In other words, a real depreciation between periods t and $t+1$ causes inflation to accelerate, basically because real import prices rise. Carrying out the same manipulation for the foreign country yields $\pi_{t+1}^* = \pi_t^* - (1-\lambda)(r_{t+1}-r_t) + \psi q_t^*$. Note that a real depreciation at home causes inflation to *fall* abroad, while an appreciation at home causes foreign inflation to rise. Here is the nub of the coordination problem: each country may have an incentive to contract the economy in order to appreciate the currency and thereby export inflation abroad at the expense of the other country. Since the exchange rate effects are bound to cancel out if each country chooses contractionary policies to appreciate its currency, a coordinated policy can avoid the contractionary policies, to the mutual benefit of both countries.

It only remains to determine r_t before solving for the two equilibria. Subtracting the foreign aggregate demand schedule from the home schedule we find:

$$r_t = \alpha(q_t - q_t^*) \quad \alpha = (1+\gamma)/2\delta > 0 \tag{33}$$

From (33), we see that the key to a real appreciation is to be more contractionary than one's neighbor. The effort towards contraction leads to the inefficiency of the non-cooperative outcome.

In any period, p_t and p_t^* are predetermined variables, so that the choice of m_t and m_t^* fix q_t and q_t^* respectively, in view of the money demand schedules. Thus, we may think of the policy authorities as controlling q_t and q_t^* directly, and then use the sequences $\{q_t\}_0^\infty$ and $\{q_t^*\}_0^\infty$ to find the paths of prices and the policies m_t and m_t^* as $p_t + \alpha q_t$ and $p_t^* + \alpha q_t^*$.

We now write the home country's optimization problem in canonical form. At any moment, there are two state variables, p_t and p_{t-1}^c, and we write the dynamic system in terms of these states:

$$\begin{bmatrix} p_{t+1} \\ p_t^c \end{bmatrix} = \begin{bmatrix} 2 & -1 \\ 1 & 0 \end{bmatrix} \begin{bmatrix} p_t \\ p_{t-1}^c \end{bmatrix} + \begin{bmatrix} \alpha(1-\gamma)+\psi \\ \alpha(1-\gamma) \end{bmatrix} q_t - \begin{bmatrix} \alpha(1-\gamma) \\ \alpha(1-\gamma) \end{bmatrix} q_t^* \tag{34}$$

Note that q_t is the control variable, and q_t^* is an exogenous forcing variable from the point of view of the home country. The objective function is again a discounted sum of quadratic loss functions in q_t and π_t:

$$U_0 = -(\tfrac{1}{2}) \sum_{t=0}^{\infty} \beta^t (q_t^2 + \phi \pi_t^2) \tag{35}$$

Note that $\pi_t = p_t^c - p_{t-1}^c = (p_t - p_{t-1}^c) + \alpha(1-\gamma)(q_t - q_t^*)$.

We set up a Lagrangian $\mathscr{L}$ and take first-order conditions in the standard way (note that μ_{1t} is the co-state variable for p_t, and μ_{2t} for p_{t-1}^c).

$$\begin{aligned}
\mathscr{L} = -\tfrac{1}{2} \sum_{t=0}^{\infty} \beta^t \{ & q_t^2 + \phi[(p_t - p_{t-1}^c) + \alpha(1-\gamma)(q_t - q_t^*)]^2 \\
& + \mu_{1t}[2p_t - p_{t-1}^c + \psi q_t + \alpha(1-\gamma)(q_t - q_t^*) - p_{t+1}] \\
& + \mu_{2t}[p_t + \alpha(1-\gamma)(q_t - q_t^*) - p_t^c]
\end{aligned} \tag{36}$$

First order conditions are:

$$\partial \mathscr{L} / \partial q_t = 0 = \Rightarrow q_t + \phi \alpha (1 - \gamma) [(p_t - p_{t-1}^c) + \alpha (1 - \gamma)(q_t - q_t^*)]$$
$$+ \mu_{1t} \psi + \mu_{1t} \alpha (1 - \gamma) + \mu_{2t} \alpha (1 - \gamma) = 0$$
$$\partial \mathscr{L} / \partial p_t = 0 = \Rightarrow \phi [(p_t - p_{t-1}^c) + \alpha (1 - \gamma)(q_t - q_t^*)]$$
$$+ 2 \mu_{1t} - \mu_{1t-1} / \beta + \mu_{2t} = 0$$
$$\partial \mathscr{L} / \partial \mu_{1t} = 0 = \Rightarrow p_{t+1} = 2 p_t - p_{t-1}^c + \psi q_t + \alpha (1 - \gamma)(q_t - q_t^*)$$
$$\partial \mathscr{L} / \partial \mu_{2t} = 0 = \Rightarrow p_t^c = p_t + \alpha (1 - \gamma)(q_t - q_t^*)$$
$$\partial \mathscr{L} / \partial p_{t-1}^c = 0 = \Rightarrow - \phi [(p_t - p_{t-1}^c) + \alpha (1 - \gamma)(q_t - q_t^*)]$$
$$- \mu_{1t} - \mu_{2t-1} / \beta = 0$$

We now invoke a sleight of hand. The foreign country is carrying out an identical optimization, which by symmetry must yield $q_t = q_t^*$. Without specifying the foreign country's problem, we simply invoke this symmetry condition as a property of the equilibrium, in order to simplify the first-order conditions. Note that when $q_t = q_t^*$, p_t^c equals p_t, so that $\pi_t = p_t^c - p_{t-1}^c = p_t - p_{t-1}^c$. Using these facts, we rewrite the first-order conditions as:

(a) $\mu_{1t} [\psi + \alpha (1 - \gamma)] + \mu_{2t} \alpha (1 - \gamma) + \phi \alpha (1 - \gamma) \pi_t + q_t = 0$

(b) $2 \mu_{1t} - \mu_{1t-1} / \beta + \mu_{2t} + \phi \pi_t = 0$

(c) $\mu_{1t} + \mu_{2t-1} / \beta + \phi \pi_t = 0$

(d) $\pi_{t+1} - \pi_t - \psi q_t = 0$

$$\left. \right\} \quad (37)$$

By direct inspection of (37)(b) and (c), we can see that the system will satisfy $\mu_{2t} = - \mu_{1t}$.[4] We now make that substitution and also substitute for q_t, to write a 2×2 system in μ_{1t} and π_t:

$$\begin{bmatrix} \mu_{1t+1} \\ \pi_{t+1} \end{bmatrix} = \begin{bmatrix} 1/\beta + \phi \psi^2 & \phi^2 \psi \alpha (1 - \gamma) - \phi \\ -\psi^2 & 1 - \psi \alpha (1 - \gamma) \phi \end{bmatrix} \begin{bmatrix} \mu_{1t} \\ \pi_t \end{bmatrix} \qquad (38)$$

As long as $\beta < [1 - \psi \alpha (1 - \gamma) \phi]$, this system has a single root within the unit circle and a single root outside the unit circle (the condition is sufficient, though not necessary).[5] Denote the stable root as λ_1^N (the superscript N denotes non-cooperative case). Thus, the dynamics of inflation are:

$$\pi_{t+1} = \lambda_1^N \pi_t \qquad (39)$$

Starting from an inherited inflation rate π_0, the two economies converge to zero inflation, with a mean lag of $\lambda_1^N / (1 - \lambda_1^N)$ years.

Now let us consider the cooperative case. Here, a single controller chooses q_t and q_t^* to maximize an average of utilities in the two countries. Since the countries are identical, we may assume simply that the controller maximizes domestic utility subject to the constraint that $q_t = q_t^*$ for

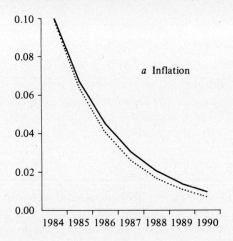

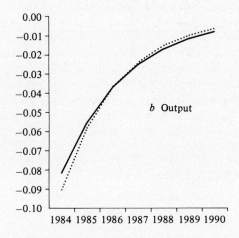

Cooperation

Non-cooperation

7.6 A comparison of non-cooperative and cooperative control (simplified two-country model)

all t. With this constraint, the inflation equation is $\pi_{t+1} = \pi_t + \psi q_t$. The Lagrangian for the single controller problem is therefore:

$$\max_{\{q\}_{t=0}^{\infty}} \mathcal{L} = -\tfrac{1}{2} \sum_{t=0}^{\infty} \beta^t \{q_t^2 + \phi \pi_t^2 + \mu_{1t}[\pi_t + \psi q_t - \pi_{t+1}]\} \tag{40}$$

The dynamic equation for the first-order conditions of (40) are:

$$\begin{bmatrix} \mu_{1t+1} \\ \pi_{t+1} \end{bmatrix} = \begin{bmatrix} 1/\beta + \phi\psi^2 & -\phi \\ -\psi^2 & 1 \end{bmatrix} \begin{bmatrix} \mu_{1t} \\ \pi_t \end{bmatrix} \tag{41}$$

Note the relationship between (38) and (41). The cooperative dynamics are found by setting $\alpha = 0$ in (38). α is the parameter which measures how large a real appreciation is achieved for a given contraction of q relative to q^*. It thus indicates the importance of the 'beggar-thy-neighbor' phenomenon, which each country (vainly) attempts to keep output lower at home than abroad in order to export inflation. Since the single controller recognizes the futility of each country, in a closed system, trying to export inflation, the controller simply sets $\alpha = 0$. That is the root of the gain to cooperation.

The matrix in (41) again has a single stable root, this time denoted λ_1^C.[6] The dynamics of inflation are now

$$\pi_{t+1} = \lambda_1^C \pi_t \tag{42}$$

It is a simple matter to prove that $\lambda_1^C > \lambda_1^N$ for $\alpha > 0$, so that cooperative control results in *slower disinflation* than non-cooperative control.[7] Figure 7.6 illustrates the inflation and output paths of the home economy under cooperation and non-cooperation. The faster disinflation under NC is clearly brought about by increased unemployment (i.e. reduced output) in the early years of the disinflation process. Remember from our earlier discussion that the *cumulative* output loss is the same for all paths that asymptotically reduce inflation to zero.

Welfare aspects of cooperation

Assuming that governments are pursuing appropriate objectives (e.g. that they use the 'right' discount rate), it is easy to show that the cooperative path, with less extreme disinflation, dominates the non-cooperative path. A simple argument is as follows (direct computation would also make the same point). Define the set of pareto efficient (E) pairs of sequences $[\{q\}_0^\infty, \{q^*\}_0^\infty]^E$ that have the property that U_0 is maximized given U_0^*, and U_0^* is maximized given U_0. It is well known that the set of pareto efficient pairs may be found by maximizing $wU_0 + (1-w)U_0^*$ with respect to $\{q\}_0^\infty$ and $\{q^*\}_0^\infty$ for all weights $w \in [0, 1]$. Every pareto efficient sequence pair maximizes some weighted average of U_0 and U_0^*, and every sequence pair that maximizes $wU_0 + (1-w)U_0^*$ is pareto efficient.

The cooperative solution, by construction, gives the sequence pair corresponding to $w = 0.5$ (i.e. equal weighting of the countries). It is the unique solution to the problem. Since the non-cooperative solution also yields a symmetric equilibrium, with $U_0 = U_0^*$, it must be that $U_0^{NC} < U_0^C$,

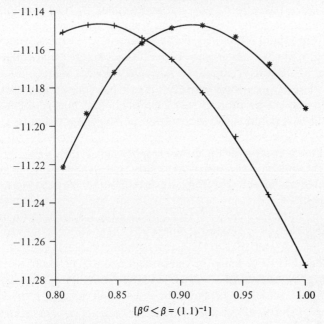

* Cooperation
+ Non-cooperation

[a] Note that the welfare scale on the y-axis has been adjusted by a multiplicative factor for graphical convenience.

7.7 The gains from cooperation with myopic governments

since otherwise the non-cooperative solution would pareto dominate a known pareto efficient solution.

We mentioned in the introduction that some critics of cooperation are dubious of the assumption that governments maximize the proper social welfare function. In particular, plausible arguments have been made that the government's discount rate β^G is less than the 'true' β. If so, cooperation might exacerbate rather than meliorate social welfare. The point is that cooperation allows governments to pursue a more 'leisurely' disinflation. However, short-sighted governments might already be postponing the necessary disinflation, in return for short-run gains to output. In an already distorted policy environment, cooperation might further retard the necessary adjustment.

To examine this view, we computed the open-loop cooperative and non-cooperative intertemporal utilities for a range of β^G, holding fixed the 'true' β at $(1.1)^{-1}$ (we use the simplified version of the two-country model for these calculations). For each β^G, we calculate the two equilibria and then evaluate the social welfare of the resulting paths using $\beta = (1.1)^{-1}$. As seen from Figure 7.7 non-cooperation dominates cooperation when β^G is sufficiently smaller than β, and cooperation dominates non-cooperation as long as β^G is 'close enough' or somewhat greater than β. Of course, for any $\beta^G = \beta$, open-loop cooperation will necessarily be superior to open-loop non-cooperation. It is not the level of β^G but the difference of β^G and β which might cause cooperation to be welfare reducing.

Policy coordination and time consistency

We now leave the case of open-loop control and return to the more realistic assumption that governments cannot bind their successors. In the non-cooperative setting we are looking for an equilibrium characterized by rules $m_t = f(x_t)$ and $m_t^* = f^*(x_t)$ that have the following property: for the home country, f is optimal at time t *given* that all future governments at home play f and that abroad the contemporaneous and all future governments play f^*; while for the foreign country f^* is optimal under the analogous conditions. Note that x_t is the state vector including predetermined variables of both the home and foreign economy. In particular, $x_t = \langle p_t, p_t^*, p_{t-1}^c, p_{t-1}^{c*}, q_{t-1}, q_{t-1}^* \rangle$.

There are two key differences with the open-loop model previously described. First, of course, is the inability of G_0 and G_0^* to bind the entire sequence of future moves. Second is the assumption that each government takes as given the foreign *rule* rather than the foreign actions, so that optimal moves today take into account the effects of today's actions on tomorrow's state vector, and thus on the foreign governments' moves. It would be possible instead to calculate a time-consistent multicountry equilibrium in which each government takes as given the sequence of future moves (i.e. open-loop time consistency), but we have not pursued that choice here.

As in the one-country case, the time-consistent equilibrium is solved as the limit of a backward recursion. (For the calculations that follow, we revert to the complete two-country model, with non-zero values of σ, ϵ, and θ.) Using the parameter values of the one-country model, we arrive at the following rules:

$$m_t = -0.19\, p_t + 1.19\, p_{t-1}^c - 0.181\, p_t^* + 0.181\, p_{t-1}^{c*}$$
$$+ 0.328\, q_t + 0.05\, q_t^* \tag{43}$$

Figure 7.8 compares the paths of the home economy output for the non-cooperative open-loop and non-cooperative time-consistent equilibria. As in the one-country model, output losses are smaller in the early periods for TC than OL. The inability to bind one's successors causes a bias

Output

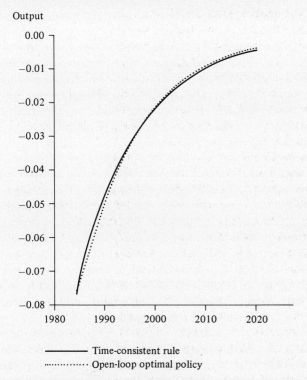

7.8 A comparison of non-cooperative control: open-loop versus time-consistent solutions (two-country model)

towards more expansionary policies and thus more rapid inflation, relative to the open-loop solution.

Significantly, it is no longer possible to rank social welfare under open-loop versus time-consistent policies (for non-cooperative equilibria), as it was in the one-country model. Remember the argument in the one-country context. Open-loop control, by definition, picks the optimal sequence; time-consistent policy, on the other hand, reflects an optimization under additional constraints and therefore is inferior to the open-loop control. In the two-country setting, the same logic does not apply. The open-loop sequence is no longer the optimal sequence. Indeed we have seen that open-loop, non-cooperative control is typically Pareto inefficient. There is no presumption that adding constraints to the optimization will now lower welfare, particularly since constraints are being added abroad as well as at home. It is true that the home country can no longer pre-commit to a sequence of moves, but now neither can the foreign country. It is true that the home country prefers an open-loop to time consistent policy assuming that the other country is *fixed* at one or the other. With the other country's policy fixed, an open-loop policy at home can exactly replicate the time-consistent sequence, and presumably it can do better.

There are good economic reasons to believe that the time-consistent policy may actually dominate the open-loop solution in the non-cooperative game. The open-loop policy, we know, is over-contractionary relative to the efficient equilibrium. Moving from open-loop control to time consistency causes policy to become less contractionary and therefore pushes the economy towards the efficient equilibrium.

Now, let us consider the time-consistent *cooperative* equilibrium. Here we imagine that a single controller each period sets m and m^*, but now subject to the time-consistency constraint. The single cooperative controller must optimize while taking as given the actions of single cooperative controllers in later periods. We should like to determine whether time-consistent cooperation is superior to time-consistent non-cooperation. As we have noted in several places Rogoff (1983) has devised an ingenious example where cooperation reduces welfare. Simply, time-consistency leads governments to be over-inflationary relative to the open-loop pre-commitment equilibrium. Cooperation further exacerbates this over-inflationary bias by removing each government's fear of currency depreciation.

Interestingly, our results run counter to Rogoff's: cooperation is superior in welfare terms to non-cooperation. While the cooperative solution is more inflationary (see Figure 7.9), as we might expect, it is not overly inflationary in a welfare sense. The less rapid disinflation merely corrects the contractionary bias of the non-cooperative case. The key point here is as follows. In the symmetric country model, the single controller always adopts symmetric rules so that $e_t = 0$ for all t. Since the exchange rate is the sole potential source of time inconsistency in this model, and since it is always equal to zero, the cooperative time-consistent solution is also the open-loop cooperative solution. For a cooperative controller, there is no time-consistency problem in our model (since the countries are symmetric). The single controller can reach the first-best optimum solution for open-loop cooperative control.

In sum, we have shown examples where cooperative control is *more* inflationary than open-loop non-cooperative control and time-consistent non-cooperative control. In both cases, the cooperative solution is welfare improving relative to the non-cooperative equilibrium. In view of Rogoff's example, it will be difficult indeed to set out general principles on the gains from cooperation under the constraint of time consistency. Comparing our example with his, the key difference seems to rest on the source of the time-consistency problem. In Rogoff's case, the problem arises from

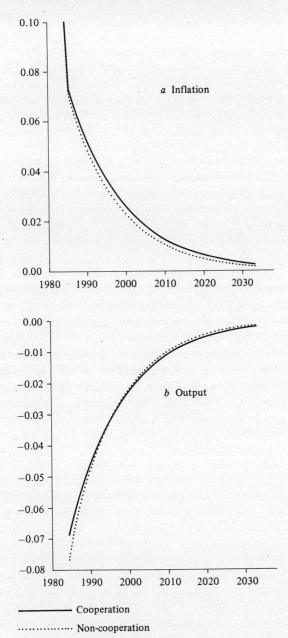

7.9 A comparison of non-cooperative and cooperative control: the case of time-consistency (two-country model)

forward-looking *wage* setters and cooperation exacerbates the problem. In our model, the problem arises from forward-looking exchange market participants, and cooperation eliminates the problem.

Conclusions

This study represents work in progress on the gains to coordination in dynamic macroeconomic models. Our focus has been purely methodological, and preparatory to attempts at a quantitative assessment of international policy coordination. The methodological issues arise from the wide variety of possible equilibrium concepts in multicountry dynamic games. The games can be solved under the assumption of pre-commitment versus time-consistency; open-loop versus closed-loop behavior; and non-cooperative versus cooperative decision-making. These three dimensions are all independent, so any choice along each dimension is possible.

Moreover, in some cases there may be multiple equilibria. For example, there are probably many time-consistent, non-cooperative equilibria that depend on the 'threat-reputation' mechanism outlined in the paper. As yet, we have made no systematic attempt to search for such equilibria.

This work should now be used to gain empirical insight into the cooperation issue. For all of the discussion surrounding time consistency, for example, there is not a single empirical investigation of its importance in the macroeconomics literature. Similarly, there are no reliable measures of the gains to cooperation the simpler, pre-commitment equilibria. Such quantitative work deserves a high priority.

Appendix

We shall present in this appendix the derivation of the four policy rules discussed in this paper. All of these rules are obtained as the stationary limit of backward recursions using a methodology similar to Basar and Olsder (1982) or Kydland (1975). The only significant difference with these authors is the fact the followers' actions are represented here by a forwardlooking variable, the exchange rate.

Let us consider a two-country world. The world economy is characterized by an n-dimensional vector of state variables, x_t and the domestic currency price of the foreign currency is e_t. In each country the authorities seek to maximize a welfare function W_i, $i = 1$, 2, and can use a set of policy instruments denoted U_{it}, where U_{it} is an m_i-dimensional vector. The dynamics of the world economy can be represented by a system of difference equations.

$$\left.\begin{array}{l} x_{t+1} = Ax_t + Be_t + CU_t \\ e_{t+1} = Dx_t + Fe_t + GU_t \end{array}\right\} \tag{A1}$$

where U_t denotes the stacked vector of instruments for the world economy and A, B, C, D, F and G are matrixes of parameters. Note that matrixes A, B, C are defined differently than matrixes A, B, C in the rest of the chapter.

Let us denote by τ_{it} the vectors of targets for each country. τ_{1t} and τ_{2t} are linear functions of the state variables, the exchange rate and the values of the policy instruments:

$$\tau_{it} = M_i x_t + L_i e_t + N_i U_t \quad i = 1, 2 \tag{A2}$$

where M_i, L_i and N_i are matrixes of parameters.

The optimization problem for the authorities of country i is then:

$$\underset{U_{it}}{\text{Max}} - (\tfrac{1}{2}) \sum_{t=0}^{\infty} \beta_i^t \tau_{it} \Omega_i \tau_{it}$$
$$\text{s.t. (A1), (A2)}$$

where Ω_i is a matrix of parameters and β_i is a discount factor.

The time-consistent solution

The time-consistent, non-cooperative equilibrium is found as a limit to a finite-time (T period) problem, for T large. The solution is derived in two steps. The finite-horizon problem is solved for the last period, T, and then it is solved for period t given the solution for period $t+1$. We find the limit of the rule for period 0, as $T \to \infty$.

In period $T+1$ we assume that the exchange rate has stabilized, and that the value functions $V_{1T+1}(x_{T+1})$ and $V_{2T+1}(x_{T+1})$ are equal to zero:

$$e_{T+1} = e_T \tag{A3}$$

$$V_{iT+1}(x_{T+1}) = 0 \quad i = 1, 2 \tag{A4}$$

(A1) and (A3) imply that:

$$e_T = (1 - F)^{-1}(Dx_T + GU_T) = J_T x_T + K_T U_T \tag{A5}$$

Given x_T, the authorities of country 1 choose U_{1T} such as to maximize welfare in the last period:

$$\underset{U_{1T}}{\text{Max}} - (\tfrac{1}{2})\beta^T \tau'_{1T} \Omega_1 \tau_{1T}, \text{ given } x_T$$

Substituting (A5) into (A2) leads to the following first order condition:

$$[N_{1i} + L_1(1-F)^{-1}G_1]' \Omega_1[N_1 + L_1(1-F)^{-1}G] U_T$$
$$= [N_{1i} + L_1(1-F)^{-1}G_1]\Omega_1[M_1 + L_1(1-F)^{-1}D] x_T \tag{A6}$$

Where N_{1i} and G_i are the submatrixes of N_1 and G which correspond to U_{it}.

A similar condition can be derived for country 2 which yields:

$$MM_T U_T = -NN_T x_T$$

where MM_T is an $(m_1 + m_2) \times (m_1 + m_2)$ dimensional matrix. We shall give below the explicit forms of MM_T and NN_T as functions of J_T and K_T. Thus under the assumption that MM_T is invertible we get a linear policy rule:

$$U_T = \Gamma_T x_T \tag{A7}$$

Substituting (A7) into (A5) yields:

$$e_T = (1-F)^{-1}(D + G\Gamma_T) x_T = H_T x_T \tag{A8}$$

Finally we can derive the value functions $V_{iT}(x_T)$ for period T:

$$V_{iT}(x_T) = -(\tfrac{1}{2}) x'_T S_{iT} x_T; \quad i = 1, 2$$

where

$$S_{iT} = [M_i + L_i H_T + N_i \Gamma_T]' \Omega_i [M_i + L_i H_T + N_i \Gamma_T]; \quad i = 1, 2 \tag{A9}$$

Let us now consider period t assuming that S_{it+1}, Γ_{t+1}, and H_{t+1} are given, i.e.

$$V_{it+1} = -(\tfrac{1}{2}) x'_{t+1} S_{it+1} x_{t+1} \tag{A10}$$

$$U_{t+1} = \Gamma_{t+1} x_{t+1} \tag{A11}$$

$$e_{t+1} = H_{t+1} x_{t+1} \tag{A12}$$

Substituting (A12) into (A1) yields:

$$e_t = J_t x_t + K_t U_t \tag{A13}$$

where

$$\left. \begin{array}{l} J_t = (F - H_{t+1} B)^{-1} (H_{t+1} A - D) \\ K_t = (F - H_{t+1} B)^{-1} (H_{t+1} C - G) \end{array} \right\} \tag{A14}$$

The value function of country 1 for period t is defined by:

$$V_{1t}(x_t) = \underset{U_{1t}}{\mathrm{Max}} -(\tfrac{1}{2}) \tau'_{1t} \Omega_1 \tau_{1t} + \beta_1 V_{1t+1}(x_{t+1}), \quad \text{given } x_t \tag{A15}$$

Substituting (A13) into (A1) and (A2) leads to the following first order conditions:

$$[(N_{11} + L_1 K_{1t})' \Omega_1 (N_1 + L_1 K_t) + \beta_1 (C_1 + BK_{1t})' S_{1t+1} (C + BK_t)] U_t$$
$$= -[(N_{11} + L_1 K_{1t})' \Omega_1 (M_1 + L_1 J_t)$$
$$+ \beta_1 (C_1 + BK_{1t})' S_{1t+1} (A + BJ_t)] x_t \tag{A16}$$

where K_{1t} and C_1 are the submatrixes of K_t and C corresponding to U_{1t}.

A similar set of conditions holds for country 2. We thus obtain:

$$MM_t U_t = -NN_t x_t \tag{A17}$$

where MM_t is an $(m_1 + m_2) \times (m_1 + m_2)$ dimensional matrix and NN_t is an $(m_1 + m_2) \times n$ dimensional matrix.

Let us divide MM_t and NN_t in submatrixes corresponding to U_{1t} and U_{2t}:

$$MM_t = \begin{bmatrix} MM_{11t} & MM_{12t} \\ MM_{21t} & MM_{21t} \end{bmatrix}; \quad NN_t = \begin{bmatrix} NN_{1t} \\ NN_{2t} \end{bmatrix} \tag{A18}$$

Then we have:

$$MM_{ijt} = (N_{ii} + L_i K_{it})' \, \Omega_i (N_{ij} + L_i K_{jt}) + \beta_i (C_{it} + BK_{it})' \, S_{it+1}(C_j + BK_{jt}) \tag{A19}$$

$$NN_{it} = (N_{ii} + L_i K_{it})' \, \Omega_i (M_i + L_i J_t) + \beta_i (C_i + BK_{it})' \, S_{it+1}(A + BJ_t) \tag{A20}$$

These formulae hold for period T with J_T and K_T defined as above and $S_{iT+1} = 0$. Finally we can derive Γ_t, H_t and S_{it}:

$$\Gamma_\tau = -MM_t^{-1} NN_t \tag{A21}$$

$$H_t = J_t + K_t \Gamma_t \tag{A22}$$

$$S_{it} = (M_i + L_i H_t + N_i \Gamma_t)' \, \Omega_i (M_i + L_i H_t + N_i \Gamma_t) \\ + \beta_i (A + BH_t + C\Gamma_t)' \, S_{it+1}(A + BH_t + C\Gamma_t); \quad i = 1, 2 \tag{A23}$$

We have thus obtained both recursion rules and starting values for the set of matrixes Γ_t, H_t, S_{1t} and S_{2t}. We define as the time consistent solution the stationary solution to which this system converges for $t = 0$ as T goes to infinity. We do not know of any general result concerning the convergence of this process. However in our empirical applications we have not run into major problems. Cohen and Michel (1984) show that in a one dimensional case this kind of a recursion does have a fix-point.

The open-loop solution

The open-loop solution corresponds to a one-shot game where the authorities announce at time zero the whole path of their policies. It thus does not by definition require the use of a backward recursion procedure. The set of dynamic equations formed by the state variable difference equations and the first-order conditions corresponding to the optimal control problem of the authorities could for example be solved explicitly by using the method proposed in Blanchard and Kahn (1980) or numerically with a multiple shooting algorithm (see Lipton, Poterba, Sachs and Summers (1982)). However, we shall present here a backward recursion procedure which leads to a simple algorithm.

The optimal control problem faced by the authorities of country i leads to the definition of the Hamiltonian H_{it}:

$$H_{it} = (\tfrac{1}{2})\tau'_{it}\,\beta^t_i\,\Omega_i\,\tau_{it} + \beta^{t+1}_i\,p'_{it+1}(Ax_t + Be_t + CU_t - x_{t+1})$$
$$+ \beta^{t+1}_i\,\mu_{it+1}(Dx_t + Fe_t + GU_t - e_{t+1}) \tag{A24}$$

where p_{it+1} is the vector of co-state variables or shadow costs which the authorities of country i associate with each of the state variables and, similarly μ_{it+1} is the co-state variable corresponding to the exchange rate.[8]

The set of first-order conditions is then:

$$\partial H_{it}/\partial U_{it} = N'_{ii}\,\Omega_i\,\tau_{it} + \beta_i\,C'_i\,p_{it+1} + \beta_i\,G'_i\,\mu_{it+1} = 0 \tag{A25}$$

$$\partial H_{it}/\partial x_t = M'_i\,\Omega_i\,\tau_{it} + \beta_i\,A'\,p_{it+1} + \beta_i\,D'\mu_{it+1} = p_{it} \tag{A26}$$

$$\partial H_{it}/\partial e_t = L'_t\,\Omega_i\,\tau_{it} + \beta_i\,B'\,p_{it+1} + \beta_i\,F'\mu_{it+1} = q_{it} \tag{A27}$$

Let us first of all derive the recursion equations at period t. One major difference with the time consistent case is the existence of μ_t, the co-state variable corresponding to the exchange rate at time t. Since e_0 is not pre-determined, it can be set freely by the authorities in the initial period by announcing a proper path of future policies. Its shadow cost in the first period, μ_1, is zero. μ_t is thus a predetermined variable equal to zero in the first period and has to be added to the vector of state variables, x_t, when the recursion relations are defined.

More precisely we shall assume that the problem is solved for $t+1$ and that the following relations hold:

$$e_{t+1} = H_{t+1}x_{t+1} + h_{t+1}\mu_{t+1} \tag{A28}$$

$$p_{t+1} = \Delta_{t+1}x_{t+1} + \delta_{t+1}\mu_{t+1} \tag{A29}$$

$$U_{t+1} = \Gamma_{t+1}x_{t+1} + \gamma_{t+1}\mu_{t+1} \tag{A30}$$

Let us now define the following matrixes:

$$A^i_{11} = N'_{ii}\,\Omega_i; \quad A^i_{21} = M'_i\,\Omega_i; \quad A^i_{31} = L'_i\,\Omega_i$$
$$A^i_{12} = \beta_i\,C'_i; \quad A^i_{22} = \beta_i\,A'; \quad A^i_{32} = \beta_i\,B'; \quad i = 1,2 \left.\right\} \tag{A31}$$
$$A^i_{13} = \beta_i\,G'_i; \quad A^i_{23} = \beta_i\,D'; \quad A^i_{33} = \beta_i\,F$$

$$A_{kl} = \begin{bmatrix} A^1_{kl} & 0 \\ 0 & A^2_{kl} \end{bmatrix} \tag{A32}$$

$$A_1 = \begin{bmatrix} A_{11} & A_{12} & A_{13} \\ A_{21} & A_{22} & A_{23} \\ A_{31} & A_{32} & A_{33} \end{bmatrix} \tag{A33}$$

Equations (A25) to (A27) can be rewritten in matrix form:

$$A_1 \begin{bmatrix} \tau_t \\ p_{t+1} \\ \mu_{t+1} \end{bmatrix} = \begin{bmatrix} 0 & 0 & 0 \\ 0 & 0 & I_{2n} \\ 0 & 0 & 0 \end{bmatrix} \begin{bmatrix} U_t \\ \mu_{t+1} \\ p_t \end{bmatrix} + \begin{bmatrix} 0 & 0 \\ 0 & 0 \\ 0 & I_2 \end{bmatrix} \begin{bmatrix} x_t \\ \mu_t \end{bmatrix} \tag{A34}$$

where I_{2n} and I_2 denote identity matrixes of dimensions $2n$ and 2 respectively. Then using equations (A28) to (A30) we get:

$$e_t = J_t x_t + k_t U_t + R_t \mu_{t+1} \tag{A35}$$

$$\tau_t = B_{1t} x_t + B_{2t} U_t + B_{3t} \mu_{t+1} \tag{A36}$$

$$\begin{bmatrix} \tau_t \\ p_{t+1} \\ \mu_{t+1} \end{bmatrix} = A_{2t} \begin{bmatrix} U_t \\ \mu_{t+1} \\ p_t \end{bmatrix} + A_{3t} \begin{bmatrix} x_t \\ \mu_t \end{bmatrix} \tag{A37}$$

where τ_t and p_{t+1} are the stacked vectors of targets and co-state variables and

$$A_{2t} = \begin{bmatrix} B_{2t} & 0 & 0 \\ \Delta_{t+1}(C+BK_t) & \Delta_{t+1}BR_t+\delta_{t+1} & 0 \\ 0 & T_2 & 0 \end{bmatrix}$$

$$A_{3t} = \begin{bmatrix} B_{1t} & B_{3t} \\ \Delta_{t+1}(A+BJ_t) & 0 \\ 0 & 0 \end{bmatrix}$$

$$B_{1t} = \begin{bmatrix} M_1+L_1J_t \\ M_2+L_2J_t \end{bmatrix} ; \quad B_{2t} = \begin{bmatrix} N_1+L_1K_1 \\ N_2+L_2K_2 \end{bmatrix} ; \quad B_{3t} = \begin{bmatrix} L_1R_t \\ L_2R_t \end{bmatrix}$$

$$J_t = (F-H_{t+1}B)^{-1}(H_{t+1}A-D)$$

$$K_t = (F-H_{t+1}B)^{-1}(H_{t+1}C-G)$$

$$R_t = (F-H_{t+1}B)^{-1}h_{t+1}$$

$$\begin{bmatrix} U_t \\ \mu_{t+1} \\ p_t \end{bmatrix} = -MM_t^{-1}NN_t \begin{bmatrix} x_t \\ \mu_t \end{bmatrix} \tag{A38}$$

where:

$$MM_t = A_1 A_{2t} - \begin{bmatrix} 0 & 0 & 0 \\ 0 & 0 & I_{2n} \\ 0 & 0 & 0 \end{bmatrix} ; \quad NN_t = A_1 A_{3t} - \begin{bmatrix} 0 & 0 \\ 0 & 0 \\ 0 & I_2 \end{bmatrix}$$

From (A38) we can derive Γ_t, γ_t, Δ_t, δ_t, Λ_t and λ_t where the two last variables are defined by:

$$\mu_{t+1} = \Lambda_t x_t + \lambda_t \mu_t$$

Lastly we get:

$$H_t = J_t + K_t \Gamma_t + R_t \Lambda_t$$
$$h_t = K_t \gamma_t + R_t \lambda_t$$

We now need to obtain starting values for the recursions thus defined. If we assume as above that the exchange rate stabilizes at time T and that $p_{T+1} = 0$, we get:

$$J_T = 0 ; (1-F)^{-1} D; \quad K_T = (1-F)^{-1} G; \quad R_T = 0; \quad \Delta_{t+1} = 0;$$
$$\delta_{T+1} = 0$$

The open-loop solution is the stationary limit to which this recursion converges. It should be noted that here the policy rule is not only a function of the state variables, x_t, but also of the costate variables μ_t.

Let us give a simple example in the case where each country has a single policy instrument. The policy rule is $U_t = \Gamma x_t + \gamma \mu_t$, where γ is a (2×2) matrix. We also have:

$$\mu_t = \Lambda x_{t-1} + \lambda \mu_{t-1}$$

which, given the policy rule, yields:

$$\mu_t = \Lambda x_{t-1} + \lambda(\gamma^{-1} U_{t-1} - \gamma^{-1} \Gamma x_{t-1})$$

Thus we finally obtain

$$U_t = \gamma \lambda \gamma^{-1} U_{t-1} + \gamma(\Lambda - \lambda \gamma^{-1}) x_{t-1} + \Gamma x_t$$

The policy rule appears to be of a more complicated form than the time consistent rule. It is a function not only of the current state variables but of the lagged values of these state variables and of the lagged moves.

The Buiter solution

Buiter (1983) proposes a solution to the time inconsistency problem which we discuss in the paper. Formally his strategy amounts to setting μ_t equal to zero and suppressing equations (A37).

Using the same notation the set of first order conditions becomes:

$$A_1 \begin{bmatrix} \tau_t \\ p_{t+1} \end{bmatrix} = \begin{bmatrix} 0 \\ p_t \end{bmatrix}$$

where

$$A_1 = \begin{bmatrix} A_{11} & A_{12} \\ A_{21} & A_{22} \end{bmatrix}$$

Equations (A28) to (A30) become:

$$e_{t+1} = H_{t+1} x_{t+1} \tag{A28'}$$

$$p_{t+1} = \Delta_{t+1} x_{t+1} \tag{A29'}$$

$$U_{t+1} = \Gamma_{t+1} x_{t+1} \tag{30'}$$

Then we get:

$$e_t = J_t x_t + K_t U_t = H_t x_t \tag{A35'}$$

$$\tau_t = B_{1t} x_t + B_{2t} U_t \tag{A36'}$$

$$\begin{bmatrix} \tau_t \\ p_{t+1} \end{bmatrix} = A_{2t} \begin{bmatrix} U_t \\ p_t \end{bmatrix} + A_{3t} x_t \tag{A37'}$$

where

$$A_{2t} \begin{bmatrix} B_{2t} & 0 \\ \Delta_{t+1}(C + Bk_t) & 0 \end{bmatrix}; \quad A_{3t} = \begin{bmatrix} B_{1t} \\ \Delta_{t+1}(A + BJ_t) \end{bmatrix}$$

and finally:

$$\begin{bmatrix} U_t \\ p_t \end{bmatrix} = -MM_t^{-1} NN_t x_t \tag{A38}$$

where

$$MM_t = A_1 A_{2t} - \begin{bmatrix} 0 & 0 \\ 0 & I_{2n} \end{bmatrix}$$

$$NN_t = A_1 A_{3t}$$

From (A38) we derive Γ_t and Δ_t which give H_t:

$$H_t = J_t + K_t \Gamma_t$$

The system of recursive equations thus obtained is solved backward from T with the same starting values as above:

$$J_T = (1 - F)^{-1} D; \quad K_T (1 - F)^{-1} G; \quad \Delta_{T+1} = 0$$

The optimal linear rule

The problem here is to derive the optimal linear rule, i.e. the constant feedback rule which yields the highest welfare for the authorities of each country. It can be divided into two steps. The first step consists in obtaining for a given rule

$$\Gamma = \begin{bmatrix} \Gamma_1 \\ \Gamma_2 \end{bmatrix} \text{ such that}$$

$U_t = \Gamma x_t$, the value of the welfare for each country, $W_1(\Gamma)$ and $W_2(\Gamma)$. Then, in a second step, the optimal values of Γ_1 and Γ_2 are calculated using a numerical gradient method. We shall not discuss here the second step. The first step is again solved by backward recursion which proved more tractable for the repeated calculations imposed by the gradient method.

Substituting $U_t = \Gamma x_t$ into (A1) yields:

$$\begin{bmatrix} x_{t+1} \\ e_{t+1} \end{bmatrix} = \begin{bmatrix} A+C\Gamma & B \\ D+G\Gamma & F \end{bmatrix} \begin{bmatrix} x_t \\ e_t \end{bmatrix} \tag{A39}$$

For period T assuming $e_{T+1} = e_T$ yields

$$e_T = (1-F)^{-1}(D+G\Gamma)x_T = H_T x_T \tag{A40}$$

Then if we assume: $e_{t+1} = H_{t+1} x_{t+1}$,

$$e_t = (F-H_{t+1}B)^{-1}[H_{t+1}(A+C\Gamma)-(D+G\Gamma)]x_t \tag{A41}$$

the recursion is thus simply

$$H_t = (F-H_{t+1}B)^{-1}[H_{t+1}(A+C\Gamma)-(D+G\Gamma)] \tag{A42}$$

which, starting with H_T, has a stationary solution for values of the parameters such that the transition matrix in (A39) has only one eigenvalue greater than unity. More precisely:

$$\lim_{T\to\infty} H_0 = -C_{22}^{-1} C_{21}$$

where C_{22} and C_{21} are submatrixes of C, the matrix of row eigenvectors of the transition matrix defined by

$$C = \begin{bmatrix} C_{11} & C_{12} \\ n \times n & n \times 1 \\ C_{21} & C_{22} \\ 1 \times n & 1 \times 1 \end{bmatrix}$$

NOTES

* We thank Warwick McKibbin for very able research assistance. We also wish to thank Dilip Abreu, Antoine d'Autume, Daniel Cohen, Jerry Green, and Barry Nalebuff for helpful comments. We also thank DRI for generously

allowing us the use of computer facilities. This work was begun while Sachs was a visiting professor at the École des Hautes Études en Sciences Sociales in 1983, and was completed while Oudiz was a visiting scholar at MIT and the NBER during 1984. Oudiz gratefully acknowledges the financial support of NATO and the Fulbright Fellowship Program.

1 See, for example, Nordhaus (1975).

2

$$A = \begin{bmatrix} 1+\lambda-(\psi+\theta)\Delta(\delta+\sigma\rho-\sigma\lambda) & -1-(\psi+\theta)\sigma\Delta & -\theta(1+(\psi+\theta)\sigma\Delta) \\ \lambda & 0 & 0 \\ -(\delta+\sigma\rho-\sigma\lambda)\Delta & -\sigma\Delta & -\sigma\theta\Delta \\ \rho-\mu\Delta(\delta+\sigma\rho-\sigma\lambda) & -\sigma\mu\Delta & -\mu\theta\sigma\Delta \end{bmatrix}$$

$$\begin{bmatrix} 1-\lambda+(\psi+\theta)\Delta[\delta+\sigma(1-\lambda)] \\ 1-\lambda \\ [\delta+\sigma(1-\lambda)]\Delta \\ 1+\mu\Delta[\delta+\sigma(1-\lambda)] \end{bmatrix}$$

$$B = \begin{bmatrix} \sigma\rho(\psi+\theta)\Delta \\ 0 \\ \sigma\rho\Delta \\ -\rho+\mu\Delta\sigma\rho \end{bmatrix}$$

$$C = \begin{bmatrix} 1-\lambda+(\psi+\theta)\Delta[\delta+\sigma(1-\lambda)] & 0 & \gamma(\psi+\theta)\Delta \\ 1-\lambda & 0 & 0 \\ [\delta+\sigma(1-\lambda)]\Delta & 0 & \gamma\Delta \\ [\delta+\sigma(1-\lambda)]\mu\Delta & -1 & \gamma\mu\Delta \end{bmatrix}$$

where $\Delta = [1+\sigma(\mu-\psi-\theta)]^{-1}$

3 Using the notation of the appendix, it is readily checked that if $\sigma = 0$, C and N_1 in (A1) are null matrixes, and G in (A1) is equal to $-\rho$. This implies that the money stock has no direct effect on either the state variables or on the government's targets: output and inflation. Thus the first-order condition (A25) reduces to $-\beta\rho\mu_{t+1} = 0$.

4 This point is easily proved by considering the following change of variables:

$$(\pi_t, \mu_{1t}, \mu_{2t}) = \Rightarrow (\pi_t, \mu_{1t}, \zeta_t)$$

where $\zeta_t = \mu_{1t} + \mu_{1t}$

The differential system (38) becomes:

$$\begin{bmatrix} \mu_{1t+1} \\ \pi_{t+1} \\ \zeta_{t+1} \end{bmatrix} = \begin{bmatrix} 1/\beta+\phi\psi^2 & \phi^2\psi\alpha(1-\gamma)-\phi & -1/\beta \\ -\psi^2 & 1-\psi\alpha(1-\gamma)\phi & -\psi\alpha(1-\gamma) \\ 0 & 0 & 1/\beta \end{bmatrix} \begin{bmatrix} \mu_{1t} \\ \pi_t \\ \zeta_t \end{bmatrix}$$

This system is saddle point stable under the conditions discussed in the text and has one stable root λ_1^N and two unstable roots λ_2^N and $1/\beta$. One variable π_r is backward looking while μ_{1t} and ζ_t are forward looking. Given that $1/\beta > 1$, it is clear from the third equation that along the stable path ζ_t must always be equal to zero, so that $\mu_{1t} = -\mu_{2t}$ for all t.

5 The roots of the system can be found by solving the characteristic equation:

$$\lambda^2-(\omega+1/\beta+\phi\psi^2)\lambda+(1/\beta)\omega = 0, \text{ where } \omega = [1-\psi\alpha(1-\gamma)\phi]$$

We assume $\omega > 0$. To show that there is exactly one stable root $0 < \lambda_1^N < 1$ and one unstable root $1 < \lambda_2^N$, observe the values of the characteristic equation $C(\lambda)$ at $\lambda = 0$ and $\lambda = 1$. $C(0) = (1/\beta)\omega > 0$ and $C(1) = -\phi\psi^2 - [1/\beta - 1]\psi\alpha(1-\gamma)\phi < 0$. Also, for $\lambda \gg 1, C(\lambda) > 0$. Thus, there is exactly one root between 0 and 1, and one root exceeding 1.

The stable root is

$$\lambda_1^N = (\omega + 1/\beta + \phi\psi^2)/2 - (\tfrac{1}{2})[(\omega + 1/\beta + \phi\psi^2)^2 - 4\omega/\beta]^{\frac{1}{2}}.$$

The unstable root is:

$$\lambda_2^N = (\omega + 1/\beta + \phi\psi^2)/2 + (\tfrac{1}{2})[(\omega + 1/\beta + \phi\psi^2)^2 - 4\omega/\beta]^{\frac{1}{2}}.$$

6 The roots for the cooperative case can be found by setting $\alpha = 0$ (i.e. $\omega = 1$) in the equations for the roots derived in note 5.

The stable root is

$$\lambda_1^C = (\tfrac{1}{2})(1 + 1/\beta + \phi\psi^2) - (\tfrac{1}{2})[(1 + 1/\beta + \phi\psi^2)^2 - 4/\beta]^{\frac{1}{2}}.$$

The unstable root is

$$\lambda_2^C = (\tfrac{1}{2})(1 + 1/\beta + \phi\psi^2) + (\tfrac{1}{2})[(1 + 1\beta + \phi\psi^2)^2 - 4/\beta]^{\frac{1}{2}}.$$

7 It was shown in note 6 that $\lambda_1^C = \lambda_1^N$ when $\alpha = 0$. To prove that $\lambda_1^N > \lambda_1^C$ for $\alpha > 0$, we need only show that $\partial(\lambda_1^C - \lambda_1^N)/\partial\alpha > 0$ for all α. We know that $\partial(\lambda_1^C)/\partial\alpha = 0$. Consider $\partial(\lambda_1^N)/\partial\alpha$

$$\partial(\lambda_1^N)/\partial\alpha = (\tfrac{1}{2})\psi(1-\gamma)\phi[-1 + (\omega - 1/\beta + \phi\psi^2)\{(\omega + 1/\beta + \phi\psi^2)^2 - 4\omega/\beta\}^{-\frac{1}{2}}]$$

We want to prove that the last expression is negative. We know $-4\phi\psi^2/\beta < 0$. Therefore,

$$-4/\beta(\phi\psi^2 + \omega + 1/\beta) + 4/\beta^2 + (\omega + 1/\beta + \phi\psi^2)^2 < (\omega + 1/\beta + \phi\psi^2)^2 - 4\omega/\beta,$$

or

$$(\omega - 1/\beta + \phi\psi^2)^2 < (\omega + 1/\beta + \phi\psi^2)^2 - 4\omega/\beta.$$

Taking the square root of both sides and dividing gives

$$(\omega - 1/\beta + \phi\psi^2)\{(\omega - 1/\beta + \phi\psi^2)^2 - 4\omega/\beta\}^{\frac{1}{2}} < 1$$

Substituting into the expression for $\partial(\lambda_1^N)/\partial\alpha$, we see

$$\partial(\lambda_1^N)/\partial\alpha < 0 \text{ for all } \alpha.$$

Thus $\partial(\lambda_1^C - \lambda_1^N)/\partial\alpha > 0$ for all α.

8 Note that in the paper the notation is slightly different, with μ_{4t} being the co-state variable corresponding to the exchange rate in the one-country case.

REFERENCES

d'Autume, A. (1984). 'Closed-Loop Dynamic Games and the Time-inconsistency Problem.' Brown University, processed, June.

Barro, R. J. and D. B. Gordon (1983). 'Rules, Discretion and Reputation in a Model of Monetary Policy.' *Journal of Monetary Economics* **12**, pp. 101–21.

Basar, T. and G. J. Olsder (1982). *Dynamic Noncooperative Game Theory*. Academic Press.

Blanchard, O. J. and C. Kahn (1980). 'The Solution of Linear Difference Models Under Rational Expectations.' *Econometrica* **48**.

Buiter, W. H. (1983). 'Optimal and Time-Consistent Policies in Continuous Time Rational Expectations Models.' NBER Technical Working Paper.

 and M. H. Miller (1982). 'Real Exchange Rate Overshooting and the Output Cost of Bringing Down Inflation.' *European Economic Review* **18**, May/June, pp. 85–123.

Calvo, G. A. (1978). 'On the Time Consistency of Optimal Policy in a Monetary Economy.' *Econometrica* **46**, no. 6.

Cohen, D. and P. Michel (1984). 'Toward a Theory of Optimal Precommitment. I. An Analysis of the Time-Consistent Solutions in a Discrete Time Economy.' CEPREMAP.

Dornbusch, R. (1976). 'Expectations and Exchange Rate Dynamics.' *Journal of Political Economy* **84**, pp. 1161–76.

Kydland, F. (1975). 'Noncooperative and Dominant Player Solutions in Discrete Dynamic Games.' *International Economic Review* **16**, no. 2.

 (1977). 'Equilibrium Solutions in Dynamic Dominant-Player Models.' *Journal of Economic Theory* **15**, pp. 307–324.

 and E. C. Prescott (1977). 'Rules Rather than Discretion: The Inconsistency of Optimal Plans.' *Journal of Political Economy* **85**, no. 3.

Lipton, D., J. M. Poterba, J. Sachs and L. H. Summers (1982). 'Multiple Shooting in Rational Expectations Models.' *Econometrica* **50**, September, 1329–1333.

Maskin, E. and J. Tirole (1982). 'A Theory of Dynamic Oligopoly, Part I.' M.I.T. Department of Economics Working Paper No. 320, November.

Nordhaus, W. (1975). 'The Political Business Cycle.' *Review of Economic Studies* **42**, pp. 169–190.

Miller, M. and M. Salmon (1983). 'Dynamic Games and the Time Inconsistency of Optimal Policies in Open Economies,' mimeo, University of Warwick.

Oudiz, G. and J. Sachs (1984). 'Macroeconomic Policy Coordination Among the Industrial Economies.' *Brookings Papers on Economic Activity*.

Phelps, E. S. and R. A. Pollak (1982). 'On Second-best National Savings and Game Equilibrium Growth.' *Review of Economic Studies* **49**, pp. 185–199.

Rogoff, K. (1983). 'Productive and Counter-productive Monetary Policies.' International Finance Discussion Paper 223 (Board of Governors of the Federal Reserve System), December.

Sachs, J. (1983). 'International Policy Coordination in a Dynamic Macroeconomic Model.' NBER Discussion Paper No. 1166, July.

COMMENT JORGE BRAGA DE MACEDO

Between the Fall of 1982 and the early Summer of 1984, Sachs has written three (or four depending on the count) papers on international policy coordination. In the Spring of 1983, with the collaboration of Oudiz, line output accelerated tremendously. It also became more quantitative: only a few months ago, Gilles and Jeff found the gains from international policy coordination to be empirically modest.

Unlike the remarkable *Brookings* paper, however, this one has no punch line. Called 'research in progress' in the conclusion, it sets out to investigate three points: whether dynamics make a difference; how international policy coordination interacts with the political business cycle; and the implications of the inability of governments to bind their successors. The last point, by investigating time-consistent solutions, is an elaboration of the first. The second point is discussed graphically toward the end of the paper. It is ignored in the discussion to follow. The same for the empirical significance of time-consistency, which deserves 'high priority' in the authors' concluding judgement. Whilst in agreement, I deleted remarks on empirical models of policy coordination to share the 'pure methodological focus' of the paper.[1] The model used to illustrate the method will be discussed first. It is presented in Table 7.2 while parameter values used in the numerical simulations are in Table 7.1.

The first pair of equations defines the IS curves at home and abroad:

$$q = \delta r + \gamma q^* - \sigma(i - \dot{p}) \tag{1}$$

Since the parameter γ is set to zero in Table 7.1, trade between the two countries is unresponsive to output (marginal propensities to import are zero). As a consequence, the coefficient on the real exchange rate (r) is to be interpreted as the average propensity to import times the sum of the trade elasticities less one times the inverse of the (common) marginal propensity to save. Unitary elasticities, and an average propensity to import of 0.25 (the same as $1 - \lambda$, the share of foreign goods in the consumer price index) would give $\delta = 1.5$ – as in Table 7.1 – if the savings propensity is 0.17. But the experiments where δ is infinite require infinite elasticities which are implausible in a two-country world. The parameter σ represents the real interest semi-elasticity of investment. Given the value of the savings propensity and a share of investment like the share of imports, the value $\sigma = 1.5$ implies an elasticity higher than the steady-state real interest rate. If there is no steady-state inflation, a nominal interest rate of 10% would given an elasticity of 0.125. Since the nominal interest rate is deflated by the proportional change in domestic prices rather than in the consumer price index, the change in the real exchange rate does not affect investment.[2]

The second pair of equations defines the LM curve at home and abroad.

$$m - p = \alpha q - \epsilon i \tag{2}$$

Money balances are also deflated by domestic prices, so that there is no direct effect of the real exchange rate on money demand.[3] The parameter α is set to one in Table 7.1. The value of $\epsilon = 0.5$ implies that the interest elasticity of money demand is one half of the steady-state level of the interest rate or 0.05. This makes it 2.5 times smaller than the real interest elasticity of investment.

Equations (1) and (2) can be combined into an aggregate demand curve which involves the real exchange rate, the domestic real money stock (denoted by a bar) and the rate of domestic price inflation (denoted by y):

$$\left(1+\frac{\sigma}{\epsilon}\right)q = \delta r + \frac{\sigma}{\epsilon}\bar{m} + \sigma y \tag{3}$$

Unlike the *Brookings* paper, which introduced an elegant portfolio balance model, this one makes the usual assumption that domestic and foreign money are perfect substitutes ($\dot{e} = i - i^*$). The rate of change in the real exchange rate can therefore be expressed as:

$$\dot{r} = \frac{1}{\epsilon}(q - q^* - \bar{m} - \bar{m}^*) - y + y^* \tag{4}$$

Substituting for q and q^* from (3), there obtains a steady-state proportional relationship between the real exchange rate and relative real money balances, with coefficient $\frac{1}{2}\gamma$. Using this in (1), we get output as:

$$q = \frac{2\sigma+\epsilon}{2(\sigma+\epsilon)}\bar{m} - \frac{\epsilon}{2(\sigma+\epsilon)}\bar{m}^* \tag{5}$$

Suppose the two countries set m and m^* so as to minimize a quadratic function of the deviation of domestic output and the consumer price index from steady-state:[4]

$$U = -\tfrac{1}{2}\{q^2 + \phi[p + (1-\lambda)r]^2\} \tag{6}$$

Then a price rigidity $p = p^* = \bar{p}$ will imply a loss of $\phi\bar{p}^2$ if both countries set $\bar{m} = \bar{m}^* = 0$ since it is evident from (5) that, in that case, $q = q^* = 0$.

If, instead, each country attempts to appreciate the exchange rate, taking the other country's money stock as given, they will both end up with a lower money stock. Loss in this Cournot-Nash non-cooperative solution is magnified by $\phi[(1-\lambda)(\sigma+\epsilon)/\gamma(2\sigma+\epsilon)]^2$. Other non-cooperative solutions, allowing for a non-zero conjectural variation, imply a lower loss than the Nash.[5] Still, with the parameter values of Table 7.1, the squared term is less than 1%, so that loss varies from $2\bar{p}^2$ in the cooperative solution to $2.02\,\bar{p}^2$ in the Nash non-cooperative solution. This summarizes the results of a static policy game.

Coming back to the dynamics, they are certainly not confined to (4) above. There is also an equation for the change in nominal wages which is a function of the change in consumer prices (with a one-period lag), the change in output and its level in the previous period. The model does not distinguish between wages and the price of domestic output, so that this is also the equation for domestic price inflation (y). Usually, domestic inflation is made proportional to the difference between demand and supply for domestic output. Aggregate supply is in turn derived from a Cobb-Douglas production function with capital fixed, labor demand responding to the product wage and labor supply responding to the wage deflated by the consumer price index:[6]

$$\dot{p} = \theta\left[q + \frac{(1-c')}{1+nc'}n(1-\lambda)r\right] \tag{7}$$

where c' is the share of capital in output and n is the labor supply elasticity

The author's formulation is, instead:

$$\dot{y} = (1-\lambda)\dot{r} + \theta\dot{q} + \psi q \tag{8}$$

Equation (8) assumes that $\theta(1-c')n = 1$ (or, with $c' = 0.5$, a labor supply elasticity of 6.7) since the real exchange rate elasticity is larger by $1/(1+nc')$ when the product wage is fixed. More importantly, it incorporates the effect of cumulative output on inflation. If there is some inherited domestic price inflation, say y_0, then it allows full employment, no inflation and no change in the real exchange rate in steady-state:

$$y = y_0 + (1-\lambda)r + \theta q + \psi_0 \int^t q_\tau \, d\tau \tag{8'}$$

The welfare effect of different policies refers only to the timing of output losses, given by $-y_0/\psi$. Alternatively, even with $\psi = 0$, as in Buiter and Miller (1982), the measure of output losses could be $-(1-\lambda)(r_\infty - r_0)/\theta$, or the change in the real exchange rate.

Using m as a policy variable, and ignoring the foreign variables, the system of (3), (4) and (8) has a block-triangular state-space representation in terms of p, r, y and q:

$$
\begin{bmatrix} 1 & 0 & 0 & 0 \\ 0 & 1 & 0 & 0 \\ 0 & -1+\lambda & 1 & -\theta \\ 0 & -\delta & -\sigma & 1+\dfrac{\sigma}{\epsilon} \end{bmatrix}
\begin{bmatrix} \dot{p} \\ \dot{r} \\ \dot{y} \\ \dot{q} \end{bmatrix}
=
\begin{bmatrix} 0 & 0 & 1 & 0 \\ \dfrac{1}{\epsilon} & 0 & -1 & \dfrac{1}{\epsilon} \\ 0 & 0 & 0 & \psi \\ 0 & 0 & -\dfrac{\sigma}{\epsilon} & 0 \end{bmatrix}
\begin{bmatrix} p \\ r \\ y \\ q \end{bmatrix}
+
\begin{bmatrix} 0 \\ -\dfrac{1}{\epsilon} \\ 0 \\ 0 \end{bmatrix} m
$$

The system in (9) has one positive root, associated with the jump variable r, and three negative roots, as required for saddle-point stability. The objective function of the domestic authorities is expressed in terms of the output gap and the rate of consumer price inflation:

$$U_0 = -\frac{1}{2} \int_0^\infty e^{-\beta t}(q^2 + \phi\pi^2)\, dt \tag{10}$$

where $\pi = y + (1-\lambda)\dot{r}$

Several numerical solutions of the maximization of (10) subject to (9) are presented in Section II of the paper, about two-thirds of the text.

A natural welfare ranking, based on the constraints to optimization, is given for the one-country model: open-loop control first, closed-loop control second and time-consistent control third. Time-consistent control, though, does not rely on precommitments, so that the first best policy may not be feasible. If the search is not confined to linear memoryless rules, so that the threat of reversion to the undesirable line consistent rule is credible (because $U^{OL} > U^{TC}$), then the first best open-loop strategy can be sustained.[7] At the end of Section II, of the model with $\theta = 0$ in (8) is used to suggest that the utility difference between the first best rule and the time consistent rule is given by $(y - 0.25\, r)^2/1000$. For the 10% inherited inflation rate mentioned in the paper and $r = 0$, this would be 10^{-6}.

The numerical rules presented before this example reflect the version of the model where $\theta \neq 0$. They seem to suggest that m^{OL} is superior to m^{CL} which in turn is superior to m^{TC}. This involves comparing the following expressions (we keep here the discrete time notation of the authors and their equation numbers preceded by a):

$$\bar{m}_t^{OL} = -1.038\,\pi_t + 0.257\,r_{t-1} + 0.322\,q_{t-1} - 0.011\,p_{t-1} \tag{a14}$$

$$\bar{m}_t^{CL} = -1.019\,\pi_t + 0.255\,r_{t-1} + 0.272\,q_{t-1} + 0.389\,\mu_{4t} \tag{a25}$$

$$\bar{m}_t^{TC} = -1.032\,\pi_t + 0.258\,r_{t-1} + 0.275\,q_{t-1} \tag{a24}$$

It is noted that $\pi_0^{OL} < \pi_0^{TC}$ and that $q_t^{OL} < q_t^{TC}$ in the early periods.

The open-loop policy is overcontractionary (given the total output loss) as far as future governments are concerned. While no ranking is given, the Buiter (1983) notion of time consistency (which does not allow the government to optimize on the exchange rate and thus sets $\mu_{4t} = 0$) involves:

$$\bar{m}_t^{Bu} = -0.763\,\pi_t + 0.191\,r_{t-1} + 0.229\,q_{t-1} \tag{a29}$$

The time inconsistency of the rule is demonstrated by computing the first period money stock under the Buiter criterion:

$$\bar{m}_0^{Bu} = 1.147\,\mu_0 + 0.287\,r_{-1} + 0.309\,q_{-1} \tag{a30}$$

There is no guidance in the paper as to the interpretation of these results, in contrast with the experiments the authors run in the Brookings paper. The research design seems to change in Section II, where the two-country model is solved analytically in a special case and the cooperative and non-cooperative solutions are rooted in the size of the parameter δ. When $\sigma = \epsilon = 0$, then $q = \delta r$ and $\bar{m} = q$ in (2). This allows output to be controlled directly, as in Sachs (1983). It is also assumed that $\theta = 0$ in (8). Since $\bar{m} = -y$, the system in this case reduces to one state-variable:

$$\dot{y} = -\Lambda(y-y^*)+\psi q \tag{11}$$

where $\Lambda = (1-\lambda)/2\delta$

The Hamiltonian for the Nash non-cooperative solution is:

$$H = e^{-\beta t}\{-\tfrac{1}{2}(q^2+\phi\pi^2)+\mu[-\Lambda(y-y^*)+\psi q]\} \tag{12}$$

where $\pi = (1-\Lambda)y+\Lambda y^*$ and μ is the shadow price of domestic inflation.

From the canonical equation for the costate variable and the first order condition for a maximum, we obtain a differential equation for the control variable:

$$\dot{q} = (\Lambda+\beta)q+\phi\psi(1-\Lambda)^2 y+\phi\psi\Lambda(1-\Lambda)y^* \tag{13}$$

Ignoring foreign inflation, (11) and (12) give a system with two roots (R) of opposite sign (and equal magnitude when $\beta = 0$):

$$2R = \beta\pm[(\beta+2\Lambda)^2+4(1-\Lambda)^2\,\phi\psi^2]^{\tfrac{1}{2}} \tag{14}$$

The cooperative solution is obtained by setting $r = 0$ so that $\pi = y = y^*$. This is equivalent to making $\Lambda = 0$ in (11) and (13).[8] The stable root is larger in this case so that, as we found in the steady-state example, there is less of a contractionary bias under cooperation. The more efficient timing of inflation implies also a lower loss in this case. However, in the two-country world, it is not possible to rank policies because the open-loop is no longer first best. Indeed, even among time consistent policies, there is no presumption in favor of cooperation which may be as overinflationary as the open-loop non-cooperative is overdeflationary. This is, of course, one of the basic insights drawn from early (but as yet largely unpublished) contributions by Canzoneri and Gray (1983), Eichengreen (1984), Cooper (1984), Rogoff (1983), Laskar (1984) and others.[9]

One is left hoping that a forthcoming Oudiz–Sachs paper will consolidate the gains in insight by providing empirical evidence on the gains from (time consistent?) policy coordination in a multicountry model.

NOTES

1 There are many references in this literature, which in a sense goes back to project LINK. Aside from the *Brookings* paper, the asymmetry between the

U.S. and other industrial countries or groups thereof is analyzed in Brandsma and Hallett (1983) and Hallett (1984). There is also the exciting work of Taylor, say his (1984). Another deleted strand of literature assesses attitudes toward cooperation. See Axelrod (1984) and the survey of policy makers reported in Deane and Pringle (1984).

2 Solving the two-country IS model, we would obtain:

$$q = \delta r - \sigma(i - \pi) - \sigma^*(i^* - \pi^*)$$
$$q^* = -\delta r^* - \sigma(i^* - \pi^*) - \sigma(i - \pi)$$

Note that the consumer price indices are used to deflate interest rates, so that

$$q - q^* = 2\delta r + (\sigma - \sigma^*)(1 - \lambda - \lambda^*)\dot{r}$$

It can be shown that $\sigma > \sigma^*$. If $1 - \lambda = \lambda^*$ the effect disappears. The expected negative effect stems from the transfer condition: $\lambda + \lambda^* > 1$ if the exchange rate does not enter, the coefficient becomes $-(\sigma - \sigma^*)$. See Macedo (1983a).

3 The LM curve would become

$$m - p^c = \alpha(q + p - p^c) - \epsilon i$$

Using the definition of the consumer price index, we get the right hand side of (2) as a α-weighted average of q and $(1 - \lambda)r$. The real exchange rate effect drops when $\alpha = 1$. See, for example, Macedo (1984).

4 This example, as discussed in Cooper (1982), may be counted as the first paper of Sachs on the subject. It represents a tutorial exposition of the beggar-thy-neighbor world of Canzoneri and Gray (1981). Along the same lines, Sachs (1983) includes a traded intermediate input with weight a and a real price (s) fixed in terms of a basket with weight $\frac{1}{2}$ so that, if p^v is the price of domestic value added, the consumer price index is given by:

$$p^c = \lambda a p^v + \lambda(1 - a)s + 0.5\lambda(1 - a)p + 0.5(1 - \lambda)(1 - a)(p^* + e)$$

5 This is shown in Macedo (1984).
6 This is elaborated in Macedo (1983a and b). See also Rogoff (1983).
7 On reputation equilibria, see Backus and Drifill (1984a and b). A good survey of differential games is in Tirole (1982).
8 This requires either that foreign prices do not enter the consumer price index ($\lambda = 1$) or that δ be infinite. As mentioned, the implied trade elasticities would be implausible in a two-country model. In the first case, there would be no relevant link between the two economies.
9 The classic contributions are Johnson on tariffs and retaliation, Niehans and Hamada, who dealt lastly with fiscal interdependence in a Diamond debt setup; see his (1984). In a sense, it all began with Hamada's application of game-theory to the choice of the savings ratio in a two-country model of capital movements; see his (1965, 98–113). Cooper (one of his thesis advisers) and his classmate Bryant were encouraging. The field remained dormant for many years, until well after Bryant (1980). Thanks largely to the Sachs machine, it began to arouse attention in 1983.

REFERENCES

Note: References in the paper, e.g. Buiter (1984), Buiter and Miller (1982), Oudiz and Sachs (1984), Rogoff (1983) and Sachs (1983) are not repeated here.

Axelrod, R. (1984). *The Evolution of Cooperation*. Basic Books.

Backus, D. and J. Driffill (1984a). 'Inflation and Reputation'. Institute for Economic Research, Queen's University, Discussion Paper No. 560, Feburary.

   (1984b). 'Rational Expectations and Policy Credibility Following a Change in Regime'. Institute for Economic Research, Queen's University, Discussion Paper no. 564, June.

Brandsma, A. and A. Hallett (1984). 'Optimal Policies for Interdependent Economies: Risk Aversion and the Problem of Information', in T. Basar and L. Pau, eds., *Dynamic Modelling and Control of National Economies*, Pergamon Press.

Bryant, R. (1980), *Money and Monetary Policy in Interdependent Economies*. Brookings Institution.

Canzoneri, M. and J. Gray (1981). 'Monetary Policy Games Following an Oil Price Shock', draft. Federal Reserve Board, December (revised as 'Monetary Policy Games and the Consequences of Non Cooperative Behavior', 1983).

Cooper, R. (1984). 'Economic Interdependence and Coordination of Economic Policies', in R. Jones and P. Kenen, eds., *Handbook of International Economics*. North Holland (first draft November 1982).

Deane, M. and R. Pringle (1984). *Economic Cooperation from the Inside*. New York, Group of Thirty.

Eichengreen, B. (1984). 'Central Bank Cooperation under the Interwar Gold Standard'. *Explorations in Economic History*. January (first draft January 1983).

Hallett, A. (1984). 'Policy Design in Interdependent Economies: The Case for Coordinating US and EEC Policies', draft. Erasmus University, June.

Hamada, K. (1965). 'Economic Growth and long-term International Capital Movement', Ph.D. dissertation, Yale University

   (1984). 'Strategic Aspects of International Fiscal Interdependence', draft. University of Tokyo, June.

Laskar, D. (1984). 'Foreign Exchange Intervention Policies in a Two-Country World: Optimum and Non-Cooperative Equilibrium', draft. CEPREMAP, April.

Macedo, J. (1983a). 'Policy Interdependence under Flexible Exchange Rates'. Woodrow Wilson School, Princeton University, Discussion Paper in Economics No. 62, May.

   (1983b). 'Small Countries in Monetary Unions: The Case of Senegal', draft. Princeton University, September.

   (1984). 'Trade and Financial Interdependence under Flexible Exchange Rates: The Pacific Area', draft. Princeton University, August.

Taylor, J. (1984). 'International Coordination in the Design of Macroeconomic Policy Rules', draft. Princeton University, June.

Tirole, J. (1982). 'Jeux Dynamiques: Un guide de l'utilisation'. CERAS Document du Travail no. 7, June.

COMMENT KENNETH ROGOFF*

In this remarkably clear-headed paper, Gilles Oudiz and Jeff Sachs have succeeded in both consolidating and extending the more technical game-theoretic literature on international monetary policy cooperation. One important contribution of their paper is to provide relatively simple examples of some difficult dynamic game theory concepts in the context of a well-known international macro model. My specific comments on the paper will deal with the question, raised here and in my 1983 paper, as to whether cooperation between central banks exacerbates or ameliorates the credibility problem of the central banks vis-à-vis the private sector. But I will also make some general remarks about applications of game theory to international macroeconomics.

Until recently, the literature on international monetary cooperation focused almost exclusively on the strategic interactions of sovereign central banks, each concerned solely with its own country's welfare. Because little attention was paid to the problem of maintaining low time-consistent rates of inflation, the strong presumption was that cooperation beween central banks in stabilization policy is unambiguously beneficial. In Rogoff (1983b), I formally demonstrated that this presumption was incorrect. In the absence of institutional constraints on systematic inflation, a cooperative regime may quite possibly be characterized by higher mean inflation rates than a noncooperative regime. Suppose, for example, that private agents are concerned that the central bank will try to exploit the existence of nominal wage contracts to raise employment. Wage setters can frustrate the central bank by setting wage inflation high enough so that in the absence of disturbances, the central bank will choose to ratify wage setters' target real wage. At a high enough rate of inflation, the central bank finds that the marginal gain from trying to lower employment below wage setters' target level is offset by the marginal loss from still higher inflation. Consider how this inflationary bias may be exacerbated in a cooperative regime. When central banks inflate jointly, none of them need worry about having their real exchange rate depreciate. On the other hand, in a noncooperative regime, real depreciation provides an important check on each central bank's incentive to unanticipatedly expand its money supply, since depreciation lowers the employment gains and raises the inflation costs. Because cooperation removes this check on the central banks' incentives to inflate, it raises the time-consistent level of nominal wage inflation. This basic result can be extended to alternative non-neutralities and alternative sources of time-consistency problems. Depending on the central banks' objective functions, it is also possible that the cooperative regime will be characterized by lower inflation. (The cooperative regime may have lower time-consistent inflation rates if (a) the central banks' objective functions depend on employment and money supply growth (as in Canzoneri–Gray (1984)) rather than employment and inflation, and (b) the coefficients of the macro model are such that an unanticipated foreign monetary expansion lowers employment at home.) Note also that in all cases, cooperation produces superior responses to disturbances.

Oudiz and Sachs have produced an example in which cooperation actually removes the source of the time-consistency problem, and is unambiguously welfare-improving. Their analysis seems particularly relevant to the disinflation problems faced by many countries over the past ten years. In the Oudiz–Sachs model, time-consistency problems arise because if a government unilaterally announces future right monetary policies, it causes its exchange rate to appreciate today thereby improving its current-period Phillips curve trade-off. Since future governments will not be concerned with how expectations of their policies affect today's exchange rate, the optimal unilateral policy will not be time-consistent. Cooperation ensures that central banks will not try to manipulate the exchange rate to their advantage and therefore removes this source of time inconsistency. Note that there is no long-run systematic inflationary bias in Oudiz and Sachs' model. En passant, it is worth mentioning that time-consistency problems can arise through a similar channel as in the Oudiz–Sachs paper in a closed-economy model in which both the price level and the real interest rate enter the central bank's objective function.

I want to conclude with a few general remarks on the game theory approach to international macroeconomics embodied in many of the papers in this conference. One issue is whether or not it is realistic to model the game between countries in monetary policy separately from the games involved in setting trade policy, defense policy, etc. There are certainly cases where countries tie commercial relations to defense relations. And it is also not unusual for countries to simultaneously negotiate over trade and monetary issues. The problem becomes especially acute when we consider some of the dynamic concepts introduced by Oudiz and Sachs. Consider reputational equilibria, for example. If a country has recently misbehaved in trade policy, might that not affect its credibility in monetary policy? Secondly, I commend Oudiz and Sachs for reminding us in their interesting theoretical paper, that an important goal of this research should be its ultimate application. In fact, Oudiz and Sachs' (1984a) Brookings paper is one of the very few empirical papers in this literature. Matthew Canzoneri has stressed in his comments here that empirical implementation appears difficult even for the Canzoneri–Gray (1984) model. In that relatively simple model, one can deduce quite a lot simply by knowing whether an unanticipated foreign money increase raises or lowers domestic employment. Unfortunately, Canzoneri points out, the empirical evidence on the sign of this effect is not decisive. In models with multiple instruments, and in which foreign policy affects multiple domestic objectives, the problem is even harder. For then, as in Oudiz and Sachs' Brookings paper, we need to know the magnitudes of all the multipliers, and not just their signs. It is also clear from analyses such as the present Oudiz–Sachs paper, that empirical implementation requires knowing quite a bit about the strategic behavior of the central banks. What type of game they are playing and with whom: the other country's central bank, their own private sector and/or their own fiscal authorities? Clearly, it will be a challenge to embody the new game-theoretic approach in future empirical work.

Finally, we should recognize that game theory leads to thinking about how to modify institutions rather than policies. Hamada (1976) stressed that the problem of international monetary cooperation is best viewed as one in which countries cooperate to set up the system which works best on a day-to-day basis without cooperation. The new focus on institutions rather than just policies is a logical extension of the early work on rational expectations, which emphasized the importance of analyzing systematic policies rather than individual actions. (See Rogoff (1983a).)

NOTE

* The views expressed here are those of the author and should not be interpreted as reflecting the views of the Board of Governors of the Federal Reserve System.

REFERENCES

Canzoneri, Matthew B. and Jo Anna Gray (1984). 'Monetary policy games and the consequences of non-cooperative behavior'. *International Economic Review*, forthcoming.

Hamada, Koichi (1976). 'A strategic analysis of monetary interdependence'. *Journal of Political Economy* **84**, Aug., 667–700.

Oudiz, Gilles and Jeffrey Sachs (1984a). 'Macroeconomic policy coordination among the industrial economies'. *Brooking papers on economic activity* **1**, 1–64.

Oudiz, Gilles and Jeffrey Sachs (1984b). 'International policy coordination in dynamic macroeconomic models', this volume.

Rogoff, Kenneth (1983a). 'The optimal degree of commitment to an intermediate monetary target: Inflation gains versus stabilization costs'. *International Finance Discussion Paper* No. 230, Sept. (Board of Governors of the Federal Reserve System, Washington, D.C.).

Rogoff, Kenneth (1983b). 'Productive and counterproductive cooperative monetary policies.' *International Finance Discussion Paper* No. 233, December (Board of Governors of the Federal Reserve System, Washington, D.C.).

8　Policy cooperation and the EMS experience

TOMMASO PADOA SCHIOPPA*

I Introduction

To many academic observers the European Monetary System is a somewhat mysterious animal. It cannot be classified as a fixed rate regime since it has allowed much more flexibility than the Bretton Woods system. It is even less a floating rate regime since it is based on the commitment of member countries to defend agreed parities. The effects and consequences of the EMS are also difficult to define precisely. If skepticism was the prevailing attitude five years ago, surprise at what is often recognized as the 'success' of the System is the attitude today.

The purpose of this paper is to assess the significance and performance of the EMS by drawing on the author's involvement with economic policy-making rather than economic analysis. While the two professions of economic policy making and economic analysis have much in common, since they deal essentially with the same problems, important differences in perspectives, objectives and tools make the dialogue between them difficult at times. Factors which are central to policy making seem difficult to incorporate into rigorous analysis, to the point that academic economists sometimes prefer to ignore them altogether. Policy makers, on the other hand, are hard pressed to catch the relevant messages generated by increasingly sophisticated techniques of formal analysis.

Most of the academic literature on exchange rate relationships in the last ten years or so has, perhaps not surprisingly, usually concluded that better results can be obtained if the exchange rate is allowed to move, or at least if a fixed rate constraint can be switched on and off at will. The policy maker, however, emerges with the disturbing feeling that this fails to capture the essence of a system like the EMS. To him the basic reason for adopting such a system is the structural change it brings in the interplay between the exchange rate and other areas of policy. After the adoption of a system like the EMS, the policy-making structure of a group of inter-

331

dependent countries is not simply the previous one *plus* an exchange rate constraint – it is a new structure, in which policy behaviour, the ranking of objectives, and the procedures for coordination between sovereign countries are profoundly affected by the new regime, although they have not been formally reformed.

The policy maker is well aware of the limits of his analysis and will want to check his conclusions with those obtained by professional economists. However, he is only likely to accept the results of this check if it incorporates the elements he deems essential or if it convincingly argues that they are of negligible importance.

This paper presents three aspects of the European Monetary System. It first discusses (Section II) systemic issues which in the view of the author are at the heart of the policy process of multicountry economies, that is economies that embrace several sovereign countries. It is argued that the crucial question in the process of policy cooperation is to combine the necessary degree of discretion with the need to take action at the multicountry rather than at the individual country level. The members of a multicountry economy are unlikely to opt for a cooperative game unless an appropriate institutional framework is established. The collapse of the Bretton Woods fixed exchange rate system can be explained in the light of the double alternative 'rules versus discretion' and 'ad hoc versus institutionalized cooperation'. The European Monetary System can be seen as an example of a more successful solution of this double alternative. Section III presents quantitative evidence concerning the ability of the System to achieve some of the objectives that were set for it at the beginning. This evidence covers four topics; variability of nominal exchange rates; dollar policy; coordination of monetary policy; and 'real' convergence. Statistical evidence, however, is only one of the tools that need to be used for a thorough assessment of the EMS. Section IV presents some of the 'non-quantitative' elements that throw light of the working of the System. This shows how the System has combined the necessary degree of discretion with the implementation of institutionalized cooperation.

II Systemic issues

Rules versus discretion

In the last fifteen years the conduct of macroeconomic policy has moved in opposite directions in the international and domestic spheres. Domestically, there has been a movement towards greater reliance on rules, as can be seen in the adoption of quantitative targeting and the abandonment of fine tuning in monetary policy, and in the proposals in several countries for constitutional amendments requiring a balanced budget.

By contrast, there has been a major shift from rules to discretion in the international sphere, and in the conduct of exchange rate policy in particular. In the early seventies the increasing rigidity of the Bretton Woods system combined with the influence of academic thinking induced policy makers to adopt floating exchange rates in an attempt to free domestic policy from the external constraint. Major countries failed to agree on an alternative set of rules or guidelines for the management of international monetary relationships. In particular, no rules were established for intervening in the foreign exchange markets and the only check to purely discretionary action by individual governments was the judgemental surveillance of the IMF.

There are several factors at work in these contrasting developments. At the national level stronger rules have been seen as a way of shielding policy authorities from the pressures of political constituencies. In addition, in the early 1970s the domestic sphere was marked by greater discretion than the international one. Finally, the complexity of economic interactions combined with the degree of integration that had developed among countries, contributed to the abandonment of the fixed exchange rate rule.

In general, discretion should be exerted whenever there are conflicting objectives, while fixed rules are preferable when conflicts between objectives are only apparent, or when the costs – in terms of uncertainty – associated with greater discretion exceed the benefits deriving from improved achievement of final objectives. This general principle underlies the various reasons for the movement towards greater discretion in the management of the world economy.

The nature of the present exchange rate system is the first of these reasons. A return to a fixed parity system is at present inconceivable, but the rule of pure floating has also been severely criticized. What lies between these extremes, however, is the discretionary management of a floating system by policy-oriented institutions that interact with private profit-oriented agents.

A second reason is the increased complexity of coordinating the macroeconomic policies of a group of sovereign countries. This, in turn, is due to the emergence of several centers of economic power, all of which are on a par and tied together by highly integrated financial markets under a system of floating exchange rates that appears to reinforce rather than attenuate the transmission of disturbances. In these circumstances, cooperation requires coordinated action involving a wide range of instruments and policies, something that can only be achieved through judgemental decisions.

A third reason is the increasing frequency of exogenous shocks and disturbances, such as oil embargos, economic sanctions and sudden financial crises, that require many countries to respond consistently and effectively.

Finally, discretion may be necessary to avoid the 'moral hazard' created by knowledge of government behavioural rules. A case in point is the function of lender of last resort, which should operate without a predetermined set of rules in order to discourage excessive risk-taking by private agents; another, with an adjustable peg system, is the need to avoid setting rules for currency realignment in order to avoid speculation.

In conclusion, an increasingly complex and integrated world requires that discretionary decisions should play a greater role in the solution of multicountry cooperation problems. This does not imply a loosening of the government function at either the global or the national level. Firstly, in some cases discretion should actually replace rules, but more generally it should be complementary to existing rules. Moreover, discretion should be implemented in order to increase the area of government's responsibilities and increase its effectiveness and adaptability in the face of unexpected events.

Institutions and cooperation

Discretion needs to be increased, but it should be exercised *jointly* by the agents operating in the international sphere so that action is taken at the system level. This raises the question of the role institutions should play in the management of multicountry economies.

A crucial distinction must be drawn between 'institutionalized' and 'ad-hoc' cooperation.

Ad hoc cooperation is based on discussions among the interested parties, but joint action is taken only if agreement is reached. In the last ten years this type of cooperation has prevailed and in many cases – probably the majority – no common action was taken as a result of failure to reach agreement. There was therefore a usually uncoordinated response at the level of individual countries.

Institutionalized cooperation, by contrast, ensures that decisions and actions are taken at the multicountry level even when the parties fail to agree; therefore institutional responsiveness is more permanent and more certain in character. Within an institution the need for action to achieve public goals is established 'a priori', whereas with the cooperative approach this need has to be established each time. For institutionalized cooperation to work effectively, some national powers must be transferred to the supra-national sphere. However, this does not necessarily imply a reduction in national governments' control nor an increase in overall public intervention in the economic sphere; on the contrary, it makes it possible to regain control over phenomena that would otherwise escape any form of management and possibly to avoid the distortive actions often taken at the national level in an attempt to reconcile conflicting domestic objectives.

The difference in the nature of the two approaches indicates several reasons why improving multicountry coordination requires a strengthening of institutions.

First of all, even when cooperative methods work at their best, they are generally too slow, a feature that conflicts with the increasing need for discretionary decisions in the management of a multicountry economy. Failure to produce timely responses may even exacerbate existing problems by inducing action at the lower, national, level and thus causing welfare losses and unnecessary friction.

A second reason is that cooperative methods rarely work at their best since they are subject to greater constraints associated with the pressure exerted by local constituencies and public opinion on the officials and politicians who run the cooperative process. Especially in periods of recession it is not unusual for the electorate to be more prone to selfish and inward looking measures than either Ministers or officials. Thus ad hoc cooperation is less ready to compromise or to give general goals priority over particular interests.

A third reason is that political instability in the 1970s considerably increased the turnover of governments and officials in many countries. Consequently negotiators did not have time to complete the learning process or develop the personal relationships and good-will that are indispensable to the success of ad hoc cooperation.

Fourth, the growth in the number of negotiating parties makes the cooperative process exceedingly difficult. Consensus becomes harder to obtain, and even if decisions were taken by a select group, it might be difficult to implement them or have them accepted by those excluded from the negotiations.

Fifth, the growing complexity of the information base leads to a dilemma that is well known to those who have been involved in international cooperation. Officials with a broader perspective and the authority to make decisions often fail to master the many intricacies of the problems: they 'see the forest but fail to see the trees'. By contrast, those who master the details, often do not appropriately perceive the relevant priorities or the correct perspective of the issues and tend to consider relatively small points of controversy as sufficient reason for delaying or even preventing agreements.

Finally, an increasing number of problems are at the intersections of different domains: exchange rates and trade, trade and financial markets, exchange rates and EC common agricultural policy etc. The interdisciplinary approach required to tackle such problems effectively is at odds with the highly specialized nature of the existing fora. This information base dilemma makes 'package deals' very difficult to achieve.

The basic proposition

To improve the management of multicountry economies will require coordinated steps to increase the role of discretionary decisions and strengthen the institutional framework. The basic proposition then reads: the scope for discretionary decisions in the government of multicountry economies will have to be greater than in the 1950s and 1960s but international institutions will have to be strengthened if such decisions are to be taken at the appropriate level.

The experience of the last 15 years in the field of international monetary relationships, among large currencies and at the European level respectively, clarify the importance of this basic proposition. A brief reference is made in this section to the international monetary system while the two that follow focus on the EMS.

In the pre-1971 monetary world the emphasis was on rules: exchange rates were fixed and parity change, a discretionary decision almost by definition, was considered an exception to be avoided whenever possible. Moreover, discretion tended to be exercised at the national rather than at the international level, since parity changes were essentially unilateral decisions. It can be argued that the Bretton Woods system would have functioned more efficiently, and perhaps lasted longer, if the right to make parity changes had been exercised in a more timely and multilateral fashion. The combination of a weak institutional framework for the discretionary part of the system, and the bias in favour of exchange rate rigidity contributed to the final collapse.

Under the floating exchange rate regime introduced in 1973 monetary and trade relationships have again suffered from persistent misalignments of real exchange rates, thus reproducing the negative features of the previous regime. The rule of fixed parities has been replaced by the rule of exchange rate variability, but the object of discretion, the 'disciplinary element', has again been confined to unilateral decisions. Viewed in the light of the two issues of 'rules versus discretion' and 'institutional versus ad hoc cooperation' the two systems are very much alike: 'in both cases what was missing was the exercise of the required discretion, and this was due, in both cases, to a fundamental weakness of the institution which should have practiced this discretionality' (Padoa Schioppa 1983).

We turn now to the case of monetary cooperation in Europe.

III The EMS: quantitative evidence

Compared to the developments at the international level, the EMS can be regarded, five years after its creation, as a successful example of institutionalized cooperation. The objectives of the System – as defined in the Bremen Annex to the conclusions of the European Council of July 1978 and in the Brussels Resolution of the European Council of December 1978 – can be summed up in two points. First, to create a 'zone of monetary stability in Europe', to be understood as 'internal and external stability'. This meant a reduction in the overall inflation level and in the differentials between member countries, coupled with more stable and less volatile exchange rates. Second, 'to coordinate members' policies vis-à-vis third countries', i.e. to increase the cohesiveness of European currencies in the face of dollar instability and to offer a 'European' instrument to the growing reserve currency status of the mark.

The best way to assess the EMS performance would be to compare it with the estimated development of monetary conditions in member countries in its absence. Such an analysis, however, is impossible. Not only do we lack a sufficiently complete model to simulate a non-EMS path of the European economies in the 1979–84 period; but our knowledge of the behaviour of policy makers is too anecdotal to construct a realistic hypothesis of the interactions between economic events and policy decisions in a non-EMS environment over the last five years. Thus we have chosen to identify four key elements on the basis of the above objectives and to compare their behaviour *before and after* the inception of the EMS in *participating and non-participating* countries in an attempt to identify the effects of the System. The four elements are: (i) nominal exchange rates; (ii) dollar policy; (iii) monetary policy; (iv) 'real' convergence. It is clear, however, that the methodology we propose would be equivalent to the appropriate method, only if the EMS was the unique innovation between the two periods; although this assumption is unwarranted in principle, in practice the EMS was such a major change that our exercise is a good approximation of the one comparing an EMS versus a non-EMS world.

Nominal exchange rates

We shall start by evaluating the impact of the System in terms of exchange rate stability.

Empirical studies on the effect of the EMS on exchange rates have been carried out at the Commission of the EC and the IMF. The analysis of the Commission[1] utilizes general standard indicators of variability. This contribution is useful for the large number of currencies considered and for the emphasis given to the variability of the mark with respect to EMS and non-EMS currencies. The overall conclusion is that 'the System has made a positive contribution to exchange rate stability'.

The IMF official position can be found in the 1983 Annual Report which states that '...the EMS has not yet achieved its intended goal of fostering the emergence of a zone of greater monetary stability in Europe. In fact, the cumulative changes in nominal exchange rates that have taken place over the past four years have been larger than those during the previous four years'. However an IMF analysis of the EMS performance[2] concludes with regard to variability that '...it appears that the exchange rate variability of the EMS currencies has diminished since the introduction of the System...'

Compared with these studies, the original contribution of this section lies in the express consideration given to separate measures of total variability and variability around trend, and in the use of daily observations for the entire period of floating and for all the effective exchange rates considered. As will be shown, this provides *strong evidence that in the first five EMS years member currencies behaved in a way that was substantially different both from that of the same currencies in previous years, and from that of non-EMS currencies throughout the 1973–84 period.*

Recent academic literature on exchange rate variability has not analysed the EMS, but rather the dollar and other reserve currencies. To do this, it has used several measures, such as averages of absolute changes, standard deviations and deviations from long-term trends.[3] As Kenen (1979) has demonstrated, most measures show the same basic patterns over time and across countries. Three such standard indicators have been used here: MAP, which measures total movements of the exchange rate along trend as well as around trend;[4] VEER, which measures movements around trend;[5] EV, defined as the weighted average of standard deviations of bilateral exchange rate percentage changes.[6]

Considering *nominal exchange rate behaviour* these three measures have been applied to monthly and daily data of two sets of three respectively non-EMS and EMS currencies. The non-EMS currencies considered were the dollar, the yen and the pound sterling, which does not participate in the European exchange rate agreement; the EMS ones were the Deutsche mark, the French franc and the lira. These are the three 'major' EMS currencies and those which had been unable to stay together for long in the previous 'snake' arrangements. The DM represents the lower inflation currencies in the System as well as the group of 'minor' currencies that belonged to the 'snake'; the lira and the French franc, the higher inflation ones.

Comparison of the chosen indicators *before* and *after* the inception of the System (Table 8.1) shows that total (MAP) and around trend (EV,

Table 8.1. *Nominal exchange rate variability*

	Mean absolute percentage change (MAP)				Effective exchange rates (VEER)[1]				Effective variation (EV)[2]			
	before EMS[3]		after EMS[4]		before EMS[3]		after EMS[4]		before EMS[3]		after EMS[4]	
	daily	monthly	daily	monthly	daily	monthly	daily	monthly	daily	monthly	daily	monthly
Non-EMS currencies												
Against major currencies[5]												
US Dollar	0.21	1.01	0.36	1.51	0.32	1.33	0.51	1.86	0.47	1.99	0.64	2.30
Yen	0.29	1.52	0.41	1.88	0.47	1.97	0.58	2.52	0.53	2.43	0.69	2.90
Pound sterling	0.27	1.56	0.35	1.53	0.43	1.68	0.52	2.04	0.55	2.17	0.63	2.46
EMS currencies												
Against major currencies[5]												
D. Mark	0.19	1.00	0.14	0.80	0.29	1.41	0.22	0.88	0.45	1.87	0.38	1.41
Lira	0.23	1.38	0.10	0.58	0.46	2.00	0.20	0.65	0.56	2.37	0.36	1.32
F. Franc	0.21	1.00	0.14	0.70	0.34	1.40	0.28	0.98	0.47	1.97	0.40	1.44
Against EMS currencies												
D. Mark	0.20	1.04	0.11	0.57	0.30	1.42	0.22	0.75	0.41	1.76	0.31	1.09
Lira	0.26	1.52	0.11	0.55	0.48	2.13	0.21	0.69	0.55	2.36	0.31	1.08
F. Franc	0.21	1.03	0.12	0.57	0.34	1.44	0.26	0.89	0.44	1.88	0.34	1.16

[1] Standard deviation of percentage changes of the trade weighted effective exchange rate.
[2] Measured by weighted average of standard deviations of percentage changes of bilateral exchange rates, with wieghts equal to foreign trade shares.
[3] March '73–March '79.
[4] March '79–March '84.
[5] Major 14 currencies.

VEER) variability of the three EMS currencies fell substantially both on a monthly and on a daily basis. The variability of the DM, the lira and the French franc against the aggregate of the EMS currencies also decreased. By contrast, the variability of the non-EMS currencies increased in every case except for a (negligible) fall in the monthly MAP measure for the pound sterling.

When the currencies *inside* and *outside* the System are compared, all three measures of daily and monthly variability indicate that the three currencies belonging to the European exchange agreement were more stable than the freely floating currencies during the EMS period. Moreover, some of these currencies had shown greater variability than the dollar and the pound sterling in the pre-EMS period of floating, thus confirming that participation increased their exchange rate stability.

In summary, the variability of the EMS currencies in the EMS years was significantly less than in previous years and approximately half that recorded by non-EMS currencies.

Dollar policy

The need for, and lack of, a 'common dollar policy' has been and still is one of the main sources of controversy and complaint about the EMS. Undeniably, the aim of the System 'to coordinate members' policies vis-à-vis third countries' is difficult to formulate both conceptually and operationally.

It might be argued that a bloc of currencies tied together by fixed parities and floating vis-à-vis the outside should not require any such coordination. In the EMS, however, one of these currencies has a special position in two respects: first, it is the only one that plays the role of an international reserve currency and, second, having a superior price performance, it normally tends to appreciate within the System. The impact on the DM of dollar movements is thus generally greater than the DM's share of the ECU, so that the German currency tends to rise or fall vis-à-vis EMS currencies when it rises or falls vis-à-vis the dollar.

In this situation, and given that the floating of the EMS bloc vis-à-vis the outside is managed, coordination may range from an attempt to avoid inconsistent actions and objectives to a search for an 'optimum' ECU/dollar exchange rate. This would presumably correspond to an agreed-upon combination of the objective of minimizing intra-EMS tensions with other objectives, such as price stability and employment.

In reality what has emerged as a 'common dollar policy', is more a coordination of other member countries' monetary policy with that of Germany, which, in turn, has increasingly become the monetary 'center of gravity' of the EMS (Micossi and Padoa Schioppa (1984)). Hence, the

Table 8.2. *Correlation coefficient of D.mark exchange rate changes*[1]

	Before EMS[2]	After EMS[3]
$/DM, EMS/DM[4]	0.61 (0.57)	0.36 (0.47)
„ HFL/DM	0.32 (0.32)	0.26 (0.13)
„ LIT/DM	0.59 (0.50)	0.50 (0.57)
„ FF/DM	0.44 (0.42)	0.16 (0.42)
„ BF/DM	0.36 (0.41)	0.20 (0.13)
„ DK/DM	0.43 (0.46)	0.31 (0.26)
„ IRP/DM	0.68 (0.63)	0.22 (0.44)

[1] Based on weekly average observations. Numbers in parenthesis are correlation coefficients of exchange rate changes during periods of dollar depreciation.
[2] March '73–March '79.
[3] March '79–March '84.
[4] Effective exchange rate of the DM vis-à-vis the EMS currencies excluding pound sterling.

fact that the exchange rate, especially vis-à-vis the DM, has become a key indicator of national monetary conditions and of their consistency within the System, in conjunction with the increased attractiveness of the DM in international portfolios as a substitute for the dollar, implies that Germany's monetary policy has also come to play a significant role in determining the external value of the EMS currencies.

In conclusion, to the extent that the EMS has added to the attractiveness of the DM by making it the reference standard of a large and increasingly 'harmonized' area and that the exchange rate agreement has forced countries to adopt domestic policies consistent with Germany's monetary developments it can be argued that the System has been able to implement a common policy vis-à-vis third currencies.

In practice, movements in the dollar/mark exchange rate have still been matched by movements in the DM against the EMS currencies, but at least the frequency of such simultaneous movements has been reduced. In Table 8.2 we report the correlation coefficients of the dollar/mark exchange rate against the mark's exchange rate in terms of all the EMS currencies. *In the EMS period the correlation with the dollar has decreased, which constitutes indirect evidence of the ability of the System to shield the DM rates of other EMS currencies from dollar movements.* The same correlation coefficients calculated for the periods in which the dollar was depreciating and in which strains within the EMS tended to be greater, have also been lower since March 1979 (figures in parenthesis in Table 8.2).

Table 8.3. *Money growth rates in the EMS countries**

(Quarterly data, annual change in per cent)

	nominal		real[3]	
	before EMS[1]	after EMS[2]	before EMS[1]	after EMS[2]
	M1		M1	
Average	12.4	9.0	1.4	−1.5
Standard Deviation	6.6	6.2	7.0	5.8
	M2		M2	
Average	15.2	12.6	5.8	1.7
Standard Deviation	8.9	6.8	8.7	5.8

[1] From 73.II to 79.I.
[2] From 79.II to 83.III.
[3] Deflated by consumer price changes.
Source: IMF, *International Financial Statistics*
* Aggregates refer to the 9 EMS countries.

Monetary policy

At the inception of the System it was feared that the constraint imposed by a fixed rate regime would undermine countries' ability to pursue domestic monetary targets in their anti-inflationary strategies. The evidence, however, suggests that the EMS has not prevented a general slowdown in the growth of monetary aggregates. Today nobody, in any EMS country, seriously claims that the System has encouraged inflationary policies.

Analysis of member countries' monetary aggregates before and after the creation of the EMS shows a significant drop in growth rates compared with the years of floating rates. The growth rates of M1 and M2 have fallen from 12.4 and 15.2 per cent to 9.0 and 12.6 per cent respectively, with an even greater slowdown in 'real' M1 and M2 growth. Furthermore, dispersion around average, as measured by standard deviation, has also been reduced (Table 8.3).

Indirect evidence on the degree of monetary policy *coordination* is provided by the correlation coefficients of monetary indicators (Table 8.4).

Table 8.4. *Correlation between monetary aggregates in the EMS countries*

	Nominal growth rate						Real growth rate[1]					
	FRG		IT		UK		FRG		IT		UK	
Countries	before EMS²	after EMS³	before EMS²	after EMS³	before EMS²	after EMS³	before EMS²	after EMS³	before EMS²	after EMS³	before EMS²	after EMS³
M1												
FR	0.24	−0.70	0.17	−0.40	0.07	0.36	0.19	0.45	0.57	0.32	0.34	0.79
FRG	—	—	−0.36	0.46	0.69	0.58	—	—	−0.06	0.60	0.47	0.69
IT	—	—	—	—	0.08	0.24	—	—	—	—	0.68	0.25
M2												
FR	0.27	−0.05	−0.25	−0.30	0.12	−0.17	0.05	0.12	0.18	0.09	0.50	−0.84
FRG	—	—	−0.44	0.06	0.11	−0.20	—	—	−0.30	0.66	0.10	−0.21
IT	—	—	—	—	0.05	−0.79	—	—	—	—	−0.37	−0.30

[1] Real growth rates are calculated on the basis of consumer price changes.
[2] Correlation before the EMS: 1973 II–1979 I.
[3] Correlation after the EMS: 1979 II–1983 III.

Table 8.5. *Correlation between interest rates in the EMS countries*

	Nominal interest rate						Real interest rate[1]					
	FRG		IT		UK		FRG		IT		UK	
Countries	before EMS[2]	after EMS[3]	before EMS[2]	after EMS[3]	before EMS[2]	after EMS[3]	before EMS[2]	after EMS[3]	before EMS[2]	after EMS[3]	before EMS[2]	after EMS[3]
			short term						short term			
FR	0.56	0.62	0.37	0.79	0.29	0.11	0.69	0.08	0.19	0.65	0.54	0.67
FRG	—	—	−0.33	0.38	0.24	0.57	—	—	−0.11	−0.03	0.65	−0.27
IT	—	—	—	—	0.23	−0.15	—	—	—	—	0.42	0.75
			long term						long term			
FR	0.32	0.73	0.14	0.94	0.59	0.31	−0.33	0.55	0.60	0.66	0.30	0.82
FRG	—	—	−0.79	0.68	0.28	0.69	—	—	−0.05	0.58	0.37	0.70
IT	—	—	—	—	0.25	0.24	—	—	—	—	0.31	0.80

[1] Nominal interest rates deflated by changes in the consumer price index.
[2] Correlation before the EMS: March 1973–March 1979.
[3] Correlation after the EMS: April 1979–February 1984.

Nominal as well as real *interest rates* have shown a marked increase in correlation among the EMS countries (Table 8.5). In part this can be attributed to the response to interest rate developments in the United States (IMF (1983)) but it also reflects the need to equalize interest rate developments among member countries in order to maintain exchange rate stability. It should be noted that correlation has increased more among long-term than short-term rates, especially for real rates. This development reflects the need, with a system of limited floating exchange rates, to manage short-term interest rates with the aim of influencing capital flows and correcting for fundamental disequilibria in exchange rates. This applies particularly to Italy's and France's real short-term rate movements vis-à-vis Germany's and is consistent with the changes in their relative prices and exchange rates. Indirect evidence of the leading role played by Germany's monetary policy can be deteced in the fact that the correlation of its interest rates with all the countries considered has increased during the EMS period in almost all cases.

Nominal money growth rates provide only scanty evidence of increased correlation after March 1979. But if one looks at real money aggregates often considered a more reliable indicator of the 'tightness' of monetary policy, a stronger correlation can be detected, especially for M1.

Finally, it can be noted that since the start of the EMS the number of cases in which the correlation has increased for UK monetary aggregates is smaller than for other countries; the fact that sterling does not participate in the exchange rate agreement may partly explain such difference.

'Real convergence'

The most radical criticisms heard in 1978 and 1979 against the EMS can be summarized as follows: 'The System cannot by itself enforce convergence of costs and prices. The artificial exchange rate stabilization of widely diverging currencies will generate increasing misalignments of real exchange rates, trade distortions and protectionist pressures. Worse, it may force stable members to inflate. If, on the other hand, high inflation countries were to adopt a more stability oriented policy, the fruits of it could be reaped even without the EMS'.

Preliminary quantitative evidence on some of the relevant variables suggests that the System has indeed been less than successful in taming inflation, but that the too pessimistic expectations have not been borne out.

As regards *real exchange rates* (Table 8.6a), monthly observations show all the EMS currencies, as well as the pound sterling, as having reduced their total (MAP) variability since March 1979, while the dollar and the yen recorded increases. This development seems to indicate that, in spite of

Table 8.6a. *Real exchange rate variability*[1]

| | Monthly observations | | | |
| | MAP[2] | | VEER[3] | |
	Before EMS[4]	After EMS[5]	Before EMS[4]	After EMS[5]
Non-EMS currencies				
Against major currencies[6]				
US Dollar	1.00	1.60	1.32	1.98
Yen	1.58	2.01	2.07	2.67
Pound sterling	1.78	1.61	1.69	2.12
EMS currencies				
Against major currencies[6]				
D. Mark	1.01	0.69	1.45	0.86
Lira	1.23	0.62	1.90	0.83
F. Franc	0.97	0.83	1.30	1.09
Against EMS currencies				
D. Mark	1.02	0.54	1.42	0.75
Lira	1.38	0.60	2.04	0.82
F. Franc	1.04	0.80	1.38	1.08

[1] Real exchange rates are calculated on the basis of wholesale prices.
[2] Mean of absolute percentage changes.
[3] Standard deviations of percentage changes.
[4] March 73–March 79.
[5] March 79–December 83.
[6] Major 14 currencies.

fixed parities and inflation differentials, exchange rates have been allowed to move enough to avoid excessive changes in relative competitiveness. Moreover, the changes have tended to foster internal adjustment, in the sense that weak currencies have shown an appreciating real exchange rate and thus a loss of competitiveness. Variability around trend (VEER) has been reduced during the EMS period for the mark, the lira and the French franc.

In terms of *price stability* the EMS can only claim some modest results. This is presumably due to the fact that the inception of the System was followed by the second oil shock and the rapid rise of the dollar, two external factors which caused inflation rates to accelerate and diverge in Europe.

Consumer price inflation during the five EMS years did not come down in some member countries compared with the pre-EMS period, although

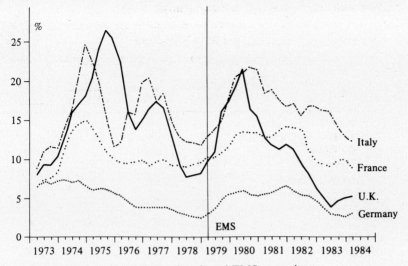

8.1 Consumer price inflation in selected EMS countries

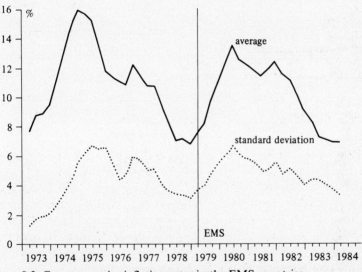

8.2 Consumer price inflation rates in the EMS countries

the average inflation rate of the member countries was reduced (Figure 8.1 and Table 8.6b). In the first two years of the EMS inflation rates rose and the differentials between member countries widened. This was partly due to the above mentioned external factors but also to the fact that France, Ireland and Italy had joined the System with depreciated real exchange

Table 8.6b. *Consumer price changes in the EMS*

(Quarterly data, annual changes in per cent)

	Before EMS[1]	After EMS[2]	
		[3]	[4]
FRG	4.9	5.0	4.8
U.K.	15.1	16.6	8.1
FR	10.3	12.4	11.4
IT	15.7	18.7	16.0
Average EMS[5]	11.0	11.5	9.8
Standard Deviation	5.1	5.6	4.8

[1] From 73.II to 79.I.
[2] From 79.II to 84.I.
[3] From 79.II to 80.IV.
[4] From 81.I to 84.I.
[5] All EMS countries.

Table 8.6c. *Correlation between inflation rates and between industrial activity in the EMS countries*

	FRG		IT		UK	
Countries	before EMS[1]	after EMS[2]	before EMS[1]	after EMS[2]	before EMS[1]	after EMS[2]
			inflation rates[3]			
FR	0.35	0.85	0.73	0.71	0.47	0.71
FRG	—	—	0.15	0.65	0.34	0.61
IT	—	—	—	—	0.46	0.73
			industrial activity[4]			
FR	0.91	0.85	0.94	0.61	0.64	0.60
FRG	—	—	0.82	0.66	0.71	0.52
IT	—	—	—	—	0.54	0.05

[1] Correlation before the EMS: March 1973–March 1979.
[2] Correlation after the EMS: April 1979–March 1984 (inflation rates), Dec. 1983 (industrial activity).
[3] Consumer price inflation rates.
[4] Growth rates of industrial production.

rates that allowed inflation rates to diverge before the exchange rate constraint made itself felt.

Starting in 1980 the disciplinary effects began to exert pressure, the average inflation rate fell and the divergence of inflation rates was slowly reduced. Although the two oil shocks had a very similar effect on industrial countries, it seems that the inflationary impact was parried better by the EMS countries in the second case. After the first oil price increase, inflation rose on average from 9 per cent in the third quarter of 1973 to a maximum of almost 16 per cent at the end of 1974, while in 1980 it peaked at about 13.5 per cent. On the contrary, in most of the remaining industrial countries including Canada and the US, inflation after the second oil shock peaked at a higher level than after the first. Finally, an improvement can be claimed by the System in terms of a uniform pattern of inflation rates as revealed by bilateral correlation coefficients (Table 8.6c). These increased significantly in every case, except one.

As for the EMS effects on economic activity, results are mixed. The aggregate growth rate of industrial production in the EMS fell considerably in the EMS period; the cross-border standard deviation of these growth rates also decreased pointing to greater convergence of economic activity. By contrast, coordination seems to have decreased as indicated by the fall in the bilateral correlation coefficients among the major EMS countries (Table 8.6c).

IV The system at work

Early criticisms

In early 1978 the decision to set up the EMS was viewed with skepticism by many market operators, economists and experts, and even by some officials.

It was considered another invention of politicians, rather than a serious remedy for the shortcomings of the existing situation. At best the potential benefits were minimized and seen as limited to fostering intra-EEC trade, while intervention in the foreign exchange market was considered useless or even harmful.

Several arguments were used to support this attitude of skepticism. It was said that a fixed exchange rate regime would undermine national monetary targets; defense of the parity would cause strong currency countries' domestic targets to be overshot and produce an unacceptable inflationary bias. It was argued that real exchange rate movements would be amplified by nominal exchange rate rigidity and stubborn defense of agreed parities, thus increasing protectionist pressures. It was claimed that the asymmetry of the burden of adjustment would soon force weak currencies to abandon the exchange rate arrangements. It was also thought that the enlarged credit facilities – a key element of the System – would create a 'moral hazard' and allow diverging countries to postpone adjustment. Finally, it was suggested that the need to sustain exchange rate parities in the face of massive speculation would prove a serious threat to the stock of official reserves.

Even after five years of experience with the System the validity of these criticisms cannot be definitely upheld or refuted by quantitative analysis alone. An element of judgement, based on a priori arguments and a subjective reading of events, is still necessary. As we said earlier, we believe that the System has had a significant influence on the formulation of policy objectives, particularly in certain countries and at certain critical junctures, and that it has modified the nature of the 'cooperative game' between member countries in areas that go well beyond exchange rates.

To support this view, a careful examination of the actual working of the System at both the Community and the national levels would be necessary. Policy decisions, their choronology and their determinants would have to be assessed to detect the role played by the EMS. Since such an analysis would go beyond the scope of this paper, we shall only present some anectodal evidence of the way the System has actually worked, drawn largely from direct personal experience.

Institutional aspects

To understand the way the System has actually functioned, it is not enough to read the written provisions. It is also necessary to consider the practices and interpretations that have gradually been established in five years of sometimes turbulent operation. This has generated new, unwritten rules, that are now just as important as the original written ones. Some of them regard the fundamental, constitutional aspects of the System; others its management. Taken together they have made the European Monetary System differ from the Bretton Woods regime much more than most observers, and perhaps also the founders, originally expected.

In the first place, central rates have been realigned in a much more timely and pragmatic way than ever occurred under the Bretton Woods arrangements. The contradiction inherent in the expression 'adjustable peg' has been resolved in a fairly balanced way. Over-protracted defense of parities has not been a feature of the System. On some occasions realignments were delayed, thus giving ground to speculation, but the delay was never too long, and generally allowed conditions favourable to the adoption of adjustment measures to mature. The experience of the 'snake' has been very important in this respect, since it showed that an adjustable peg system could be managed with a fair amount of flexibility and still retain credibility.

The second and, we believe, the most important aspect of constitutional practice, is that the setting of new central rates in the EMS has become a truly collective decision. The importance of this cannot be stressed too much. A basic aim of a system like the EMS is precisely to eliminate the scope for obtaining trade advantages by unilateral exchange rate management. The past offers significant previous experiences of this process of collective decisions. Under the Bretton Woods System the rare changes in central rates were basically decided by the interested country, while the role of the other countries and the IMF was virtually limited to formal ratification. In the 'snake', the leadership of Germany was so strong that there was little room left for bargaining.

Realignments in the EMS have only gradually become collective decisions. The first, in September 1979, largely repeated the 'snake' pattern: one country, Germany, took the initiative of calling a ministerial meeting, at which it presented a complete set of new rates. It was then realized that this method could not work a second time, as the number of parties around the table and their relative importance were very different from those of the 'snake'. The following two realignments (Denmark, November 1979, and Italy, March 1981) were essentially unilateral, and limited to exchange rates: no meeting was called, only one currency was involved and no policy measures were presented and discussed, the Community procedures were limited to giving a sort of 'multilateral approval' to the decision taken by one member. After these three realignments the procedure has become one of collective decision, much closer to those of he other Community areas, such as trade and agriculture, than to those of monetary cooperation. The actual outcome of realignment sessions rarely met the requests of member countries in full; countries often emerged from negotiations with a somewhat different grid of parities from the one they were seeking at the start.

The third institutional aspect of the System that has been shaped by practice is that changes in parities have coincided with the adoption of substantial policy measures. This, of course, had always been part of the spirit of an adjustable peg system, and had been stressed many times by theorists. However, experience justified a certain degree of skepticism about the ability of member countries to follow this line. And indeed, as we have recalled, the first realignments were not satisfactory in this respect. Increasingly, however, changes in parities have been part of major policy changes, which has also meant that policies of domestic adjustment have been increasingly discussed in Community fora as a result of the working of the EMS.

Functional aspects

These three features are 'constitutional' aspects of the System, and they distinguish it sharply from the Bretton Woods approach to multicountry cooperation. Their nature is best clarified in terms of the systemic issues analyzed in Section II above. The System has succeeded in coupling the appropriate degree of discretion with the appropriate level of decision making. It has achieved a form of institutionalized cooperation unknown with earlier regimes.

Other aspects of the experience of the last five years, do not belong to the 'unwritten constitution', but rather to the operation of the System. Nevertheless they help explain how this has actually worked and what its achievements have been.

Many observers have noted that, contrary to world exchange rates (the dollar, the yen, the Deutsche mark), EMS exchange rates have always moved 'in the right direction', which is in itself a positive result, from the point of view of what could be termed the 'trade objective' of the System: i.e. to keep trade open and avoid distortions due to protracted misalignments of real exchange rates.

Less attention has been given to the fact that the timing and the size of realignments have not fully accommodated divergencies in price and cost behaviour in member countries. From the point of view of the 'stability objective' of the System this is very important because it means the greater flexibility with which the System has been managed compared with the Bretton Woods regime has not been pushed to the point of losing the benefits of a disciplinary exchange rate effect. Pressure to restore cost and price competitiveness through internal adjustment has been maintained.

The third important aspect of the way the System has been managed is that compared with the asymmetrical changes of the Bretton Woods system parity changes have been spread more evenly between weak and strong currencies. The philosophy expressed by the European Commission concerning such decisions has been that 'strong currencies should revalue while weak currencies should adjust'. In the eight realignments that have occurred so far, the mark and the guilder have been revalued against all other currencies respectively four and three times.

Finally, in addition to the 'constitutional' and management aspects of the System, mention must be made of a third. This is the fact that the very existence of the EMS has significantly deepened the cooperative character of the policy coordination game among member countries. Procedures for such coordination that had been legislated by the Community well before 1979, were given a new life by the fact that a new commitment had been made in the field of exchange rates. The level of representation in the relevant policy committees, the qulity and openness of the debates held in such fora, the readiness of the Commission to 'speak out' and of member countries to listen improved after 1979.

V Conclusions

The increasing complexity of the management of multicountry economies requires a greater role for discretionary decisions and a strengthening of multilateral institutions. The EMS has been fairly successful so far in striking a good balance between 'rules' and 'discretion', absorbing major external shocks without incurring a disruption in its structure or a weakening of its commitments. On decisive occasions the System has played a crucial role in catalyzing the necessary political will to take the difficult and often unpopular decisions that were required to achieve better monetary stability.

However, this relatively successful experience should not cause us to overlook the inherent vulnerability of the System in its present setting. That is the conflict between unrestrained national sovereignty in fiscal and monetary policies, on the one side, and capital mobility and supranationalism in trade and exchange rates, on the other. Political and economic pressures could cause member countries to choose a non-cooperative course of action in any moment of the future. Seen in this light, the System has not yet achieved the degree of institutional strength that is necessary to bring European monetary cooperation beyond the 'point of no return'.

NOTES

* The author is indebted to S. Rebecchini for valuable help in the preparation of this paper. He retains full responsibility for both the errors and the opinions contained in these pages.
1 See: Commisson of the European Communities (1982) and (1984).
2 The European Monetary System: The Experience, 1979–1982; IMF Occasional Paper no. 19, May 1983.
3 For examples and comparisons between different measures see: Hooper and Kohlhagen (1978), Kenen (1979), Frenkel and Mussa (1980), Levich (1981), Lanyi and Suss (1982), Bergstrand (1983).
4 This indicator is defined as the mean absolute percentage change of the effective exchange rate. It would be equal to zero if the exchange rate was constant over time, greater than zero otherwise.
5 This indicator is defined as the standard deviation of the percentage changes in the effective exchange rate. The reason for considering only the variability around trend is that costs for traders and investors derive not so much from

exchange rate variations or their size as from the *uncertainty* and *unpredictability* of such changes (see: Bergstrand (1983), Lanyi and Suss (1982)). VEER would be equal to zero if the exchange rate was a constant or, unlike MAP, if it was changing at a constant rate; it would be greater than zero if the exchange rate oscillated around a constant or a trend. This indicator focuses on variability as it influences the competitiveness of domestic firms and the levels of domestic prices, wages and activity.

6 The reason for using EV is that it captures a variability that is likely to entail costs to economic agents but that is not reflected in VEER, which is defined as the standard deviation of a linear combination of random variables (the bilateral exchange rates composing the effective exchange rate) that are likely to be negatively correlated. For example, importers or exporters of a country whose currency is simultaneously appreciating against one currency and depreciating against another are facing a costly variability which causes changes in foreign expenditures and receipts, yet the VEER index remains stable. Being a measure of variability around trend, EV has the same properties as VEER.

In calculating VEER and EV we have utilized percentage changes in exchange rates rather than deviations from a moving average or a trend, because the latter induce an element of arbitrariness and distortions in the measures. The reasons are indicated by Lanyi and Suss (1982): calculating a moving average implies an arbitrary decision on the number of elements to be utilized; in addition a moving average may understate actual exchange rate changes by smoothing movements too much. Therefore the first order percentage change has been utilized to remove the trend in the exchange rate series.

REFERENCES

Bergstrand J. (1983). 'Is exchange rate variability "excessive"'?. *New England Economic Review*.

Commission of the European Communities (1982). 'Exchange rate variability and interventions within the European Monetary System', mimeo.

(1984). 'Five years of monetary cooperation in Europe (March 1979–March 1984)', II/74/84-E.

Frenkel J. (1981). 'Flexible exchange rates, prices and the role of news'. *Journal of Political Economy*.

and Mussa M. (1980). 'The efficiency of foreign exchange markets and measures of turbulence'. *American Economic Review*.

Hooper P. and Kohlhagen S. (1978). 'The effect of exchange rate uncertainty on the prices and volume of international trade'. *Journal of International Economics*.

IMF (1983). *The European Monetary System*. IMF occasional paper no. 19.

Kenen P. (1979). *Exchange rate instability: measurement and implications*. International Finance Section, Research memorandum, Princeton University.

(1983). 'A note on the volatility of floating exchange rates, mimeo, Princeton University.

Lanyi A. and Suss E. (1982). 'Exchange rate variability: alternative measures and interpretation. *IMF Staff Papers*.

Levich R. (1981). *Overshooting in the Foreign Exchange Market.* Group of Thirty occasional paper no. 5.

Micossi S. and Padoa Schioppa T. (1984). *Short term interest rates linkages between the United States and Europe.* Banca d'Italia, Temi di Discussione no. 33.

Padoa Schioppa T. (1983). 'Rules and institutions in the government of multi-country economies'. Banca d'Italia, mimeo; forthcoming in L. Tsoukalis (ed.), *The political economy of international money.* Royal Institute of International Affairs.

COMMENT MICHAEL J. ARTIS

Padoa Schioppa's paper falls into two parts, one devoted to some quantitative assessment of the EMS, and the other devoted to more general issues of policy co-ordination with special reference to the way these arise, and are resolved within the EMS. I shall deal with the quantitative assessment first.

Quantitative evidence

The kinds of measures which Dr Padoa Schioppa presents us with here are familiar for this type of problem. In his paper they are brought up to date, and implemented on daily as well as on monthly data. The basic procedure is to compare a measure of exchange rate, inflation or monetary stability across member-EMS countries for the period since the inception of the system with the value of that measure for the same countries prior to the inception of the EMS, and with the behaviour of similar measures constructed for a control group of non-EMS countries over the same two pre- and post-EMS periods. Padoa Schioppa's results confirm those obtained by other authors: for the EMS countries, the EMS period gives greater stability, and the trend is more favourable than that to be found among the control group (where, by and large, volatility has increased). The same basic result, moreover, tends to come through whichever one of a wide variety of statistical definitions of stability, the exchange rate or the money supply is used (though, perhaps not surprisingly, the coefficient of variation and the standard deviation give different verdicts on the convergence of monetary growth rates over a period of general decline).

These exercises, and others like it must be supplied with caveats, of course. A major one is that, rather obviously, the method is only a crude and indirect means of measuring the preferred counterfactual 'what would have happened if the EMS had not been created?'. Necessarily, the results of applying the method can only be a part of an attempt to answer that question.

2   Second, the stability measures need to be handled with some care. We would not think it a good idea to have perfect stability of nominal exchange rates with fluctuating relative inflation and hence, gyrating real exchange rates. Nor would stability of real exchange rates, if accompanied by extreme but offsetting fluctuations in nominal exchange rates and relative inflation rates, be particularly desirable. The measures have to be taken together, for these reasons.

3   Third, it is important to be clear why we attach any value at all to measures of stability *per se*. Arguably, the preferred measure is one of predictability. Interpreted in this light, the author's measures assume, variously, that the market could be held to have been capable of predicting, *ex ante* the trends revealed *ex post*, or that the exchange rate is a random walk. Whilst neither hypothesis is completely unreasonable, such hypotheses are not the outcome of standard exchange rate modelling. An alternative suggestion would be to ask whether forward rates are better forecasters of actual rates in the EMS (post-inception) period for member countries than before it and relative to the forecasting performance of forward rates in the control group. It would be interesting to see this checked out on a similar data base to the one used for the principal calculations reported. Batchelor, who performed calculations of this type for his evidence to the *House of Lords Committee on the EMS* (1983), found that forward rate evidence favoured the same conclusion as that arrived at by the means used in the present paper.

4   Fourth, just to complicate matters, it needs to be said that in any event predictability is not all. In the short run forward markets provide facilities for cover, but these markets are very thin for longer horizons and far-seeing capital markets seem equally rare. In this case, being able to predict future exchange rates is not enough. The episode of the overappreciation of sterling seems to show that many traders understood that the exchange rate would decline in the future but, due to the high fixed cost of re-entry into export markets, found it appropriate to stay in these markets at a marginal loss in the short term. This perception, it would seem, was not shared by the capital market, with the result that firms in this position were forced to self-finance their far-sightedness by liquidating stocks of goods and men on a large scale, or to go out of business. A major benefit of the EMS is to have reduced for its members the prospect of an overshooting exchange rate and experiences of this sort. What is not clear is that the methods used in the paper wholly capture this benefit, for they are primarily addressed to the shorter run.

Other evidence

Since a full verdict on the EMS requires the quantitative assessment to be supplemented by other kinds of evidence, the author proceeds to supply some. There is a possibility that, in doing so, he has 'over-rationalized' the success of the EMS in an understandable desire to see its survival as the embodiment of the development of a multi-country government institution pointing the way to a regeneration of international monetary co-operation and stability of a very desirable kind. That the author's account may involve such an 'error of sentiment' could be sustained by noting the following points:

(1) The major institutional innovation of the EMS (at least as it seemed upon its inception) was the 'divergence indicator'. But this has proven deeply flawed. Technical flaws in its construction have been amply revealed by Spaventa (1982) whilst in practice it is clear (a) that the position of sterling and the lira in relation to the ECU induced a sluggishness in the indicator and (b) (I would hazard) that had the indicator been triggered in the 'strong' direction by Germany, it would have had few, if any, of the consequences supposed of it. Germany would not have accepted them.

(2) The reason for thinking this is related to the second point. Despite the second oil price shock and other 'noises' the EMS has had an easy time in its first 5 years for a number of highly specific reasons. (i) France began with and persisted in an attitude – then somewhat new for her – of sensitivity to inflation which aligned her more closely with Germany. To a degree it was true more generally that there was a predisposition to a greater degree than before to emphasize the control of inflation. (ii) In any case, those countries who wished it, obtained comparatively considerable freedom to change parity (Denmark is the obvious example). (iii) For reasons unconnected with the EMS, the DM was weak against the dollar most of the time and this dispelled the vision of a 'hard' DM which had governed the animosity of many critics of the EMS.

(3) It is too easy to forget that only a little over a year ago there were grave doubts about the ability of France to stay within the EMS.

(4) The durability of the system has, to a degree, been purchased at the price of a flexibility which some consider *too* accommodating. It has been described as a 'mere crawling peg', by those who consider this a term of abuse to suggest that in the compromise of flexibility and rigidity the EMS has fatally erred on the side of the former.

All these considerations should be borne in mind. It is easy to over-rationalize the success of EMS. A final point would be the following: on a broader political front the foundation of the EMS met the need for some new creation to fill the gap in the progress of Europe. Another gap has opened up now. Some people (Roy Jenkins, (1984) for one; but see also Layard et al. (1984)) have advocated that a second phase of the EMS – a recovery plan, in effect – should fill that gap. This poses altogether more difficult issues than the EMS has so far had to face. But if there is no concentration of measures to promote recovery it seems a good bet that the stresses must show themselves. There is in progress some switch of emphasis from control of inflation to reduction of unemployment. This seems bound to occur, if left to itself, non-uniformly across countries, producing a scenario for policy divergence.

On would like, of course, to believe that the EMS could rise to this challenge. It seems one of the few hopes we have.

General issues

The author's development of his general themes regarding the actual historical and future desirable development of multi-country institutions and decision-making is very appealing. The distinction between rules and institutions is obviously useful. The limits of *ad hoc* cooperation are usefully and sensibly stressed. This form of decision-making is woefully expensive in set-up and bargaining costs. The paper also draws out the difference in developments at the national and international level – at the former, away from discretion towards rules, at the latter away from rules. Few comments seem called for. Below, there follow just two.

(1) Although it is *mentioned*, the author arguably *does not make enough of* the desire of governments to escape the pressure of domestic interest groups, especially trades unions, in this process. This desire favours the establishment of rules, such as monetary growth rules, which have the dual purpose of making a commitment to foreign agents and of exposing unions to political odium if their actions seem to lead either to a breach of the commitment or alternatively to unemployment. As a result of the inflationary experiences of the 60s and 70s, this desire to create more room for governments and less for trades unions became (and remains to some extent) a significant theme of national policy development. Of course, generalisation is risky here. The search for rules which serve to isolate trade union pressure groups and make for confrontation in place of 'consensus' is a somewhat Anglo-Saxon phenomenon. Monetary rules in some other countries have, by contrast, emerged as a *result* of consensus.

(2) Second, for the same reason, governments have been rather disposed *against* protectionism. One thing that can certainly be said of free trade is that it provides protection against sectional producer interests. It is arguable that too much attention, this last decade and a half, may have been diverted to the need to avoid protectionism. The analogy with the

30s was false: then, floating rates led to the abuse of undervaluation initiatives and attempts to export unemployment. In the 70s and 80s, the problem has been rather than countries have accepted or pursued *over*valued exchange rates for the sake of the purchase over inflation thus obtained. Relative to the level of unemployment, and its industrial and geographical concentration, protectionism has not been a great danger. This situation could of course now change as the inflation danger is seen to recede, and that of unemployment to loom larger.

REFERENCES

Batchelor R. A. (1983). 'The Functioning of the European Monetary System', evidence to the House of Lords Select Committee on the European Community, *Report on the European Monetary System*. HMSO.

Jenkins R. (1984). 'European Monetary System and Sterling', Midland Bank Lecture at Brunel University repr. *Midland Bank Review*. Summer.

Layard R., G. Basevi, O. Blanchard, W. Buiter and R. Dornbusch (1984). Europe: the case for unsustainable growth'. *CEPS Papers* 8/9.

Spaventa L. (1982). 'Algebraic properties and economic improprieties of "the indicator of divergence" in the European Monetary System'. *Discussion Papers on International Economics and Finance*, 1. Banca d'Italia, Research Department.

COMMENT   JEFFREY R. SHAFER*

Tommaso Padoa Schioppa has provided a broad-brush review of experience with the European Monetary System, now more than five years old. He writes as a close friend of the system, emphasizing positive aspects of the experience. In doing so, he covers a lot of ground – from broad theoretical issues of a political nature to some quantitative indications of how exchange rates and other key economic variables have performed before and after the establishment of the EMS. I will focus my comments on two issues discussed by Padoa Schioppa. One is a rather narrow one – what is the case for discretionary policies? The other involves a range of questions about exchange rate volatility.

Rules versus discretion

One context in which Padoa Schioppa places the development of the EMS is that of the search for a workable balance between rules and discretion in international economic policies. The case for discretion does not, in my view, arise from conflicting objectives as he claims. The essence of economics is dealing with conflicting objectives – how to make a decision when one wants more of everything. The economist's approach to such a problem is to specify an objective function that weights the conflicting objectives and solve for its maximum, subject to constraints. The set of solutions corresponding to different inputs imbedded in the constraints is a rule. It may be simple or conditional in very complex ways depending on how many factors are taken into account. There is not, except in some gaming situations, any economic logic to introducing indeterminacy. If the objectives and constraints can be clearly specified, not following a rule only adds noise and inefficiency to the economic environment.

What, then, is the case for discretion? It is that all of the contingencies for a feedback policy may not be anticipated in advance. Discretion becomes the way in which policies are adjusted in light of contingencies that often cannot, as a practical matter, be exhaustively spelled out – many contingencies may be too complex to set out clearly or even to recognize in advance. The case against discretion has two elements: first, it is too tolerant of unstructured decisionmaking. And second, it carries an inherent temptation to pursue time-inconsistent policies, which over the long-haul erode the credibility and predictability that enhance the economic efficiency and effectiveness of a policy strategy.

These considerations pro and con are at odds with one another. Hence policymakers must seek a balance between discretion and formal, not too complicated rules which balance them. But discretionary acts need to be explicable in terms of a broad policy philosophy. I see few situations in which there is an economic, let alone a political, case for capricious policies.

The EMS seems to represent an attempt to balance these considerations. There are a lot of rules – about central rates, margins, credits and other matters. But they are not intended to be a strait-jacket. Intervention policies within margins are vague, and central rates can be changed judgmentally as the outcome of deliberation. Whether the rules are ideal or the balance of rules and discretion is just right is hard to say. But a rigid and immutable set of rules of any conceivable degree of complexity would not avert situations where one would want to set them aside – not primarily for reasons of time inconsistency but because the rules had not covered some contingency that arose. On the other hand, I cannot see that a policy of intervening in exchange markets in amounts and at rates that were determined day-by-day according to the animal spirits of authorities would do anything but add noise to international macroeconomic relationships.

The ideal for policy should be rules, but as a practical matter, prudent populations will settle for something less from their policymakers.

Exchange rate volatility

As an outside observer of the EMS, I have reacted much as aeronautical engineers once reacted after studying the bumblebee – I have to admit that it flies, but I don't understand how. Padoa Schioppa gives us some evidence that the EMS flies – that is, that it has reduced exchange rate volatility by a number of measures. He gives some hints as to what might be going on behind the scenes. But they are not sufficient to answer two questions about the EMS experiment that seem particularly compelling:

– What does the experiment tell us about our theories of exchange rate determination?
– If, in fact, exchange rate variability, however measured, has been reduced within the EMS, has that resulted in an improvement in economic welfare? The answer depends on the nature of the exchange rate fluctuations that were suppressed and on the other consequences of the means by which this was accomplished.

Before turning to some thoughts on what answering these questions entails, I have a few comments on the evidence presented in the paper that exchange-rates within the EMS member countries have been more stable as a result of its establishment. This evidence consists of comparisons of the volatility of short-run (that is, daily and monthly) exchange rate *changes* among the EMS currencies before and after its establishment and comparisons of EMS and non-EMS currency volatility before and after its establishment. The results constitute powerful evidence that the EMS has made a difference in reducing the nominal short-run volatility of exchange rates among participating currencies. A number of technical issues could be raised about how to interpret the statistics (indeed, the author discusses some of them). But the results seem fairly robust as judged both from the various measures presented in the paper and from similar studies done by others. I don't believe it is worth quibbling over just how short-run variability should be measured, given the robust findings.

But I do have some reservations as to whether reducing *short-run* nominal or real exchange variability is a very important achievement, in and of itself. Exchange rate fluctuations are unlikely to have large welfare costs if they average out over relatively short time periods. Well developed forward markets and other hedging opportunities would seem to reduce to a low level the potential inhibiting and distorting effects on trade and business planning of purely short-run exchange rate uncertainties. Evidence reviewed recently by the IMF tends to confirm this view of the micro effects of short-run exchange rate fluctuation. I suspect that the architects of the EMS were after bigger game in seeking to establish a zone of monetary stability in Europe.

One thing I think they were looking for was more stable exchange rate relationships in the medium-term. Large uncertainties over a period ranging from six months to several years are difficult, if not impossible, to hedge not only because forward markets are thin or nonexistent but also because they involve decisions on investment and business development more than specific transactions of known size and timing. It is not clear whether this objective of more stable exchange rates was seen primarily in real or in nominal terms, and each has some appeal as a proximate objective. I would judge the EMS by both standards, and if it did better on either one and no worse on the other I would be prepared to say that the EMS had achieved what it was intended to do – setting aside the question of at what cost or to what ultimate benefits beyond that of creating a more stable price environment for integrated European commerce. Hence I would find measures of deviations from some baseline – be it an average level, a PPP rate, a trend, or a model prediction – more informative than the volatility of short-run exchange rate changes. I took a quick look at some charts, and the question is too close to call with confidence by eyeball. But I would not be surprised if the EMS passed a before-and-after test using this sort of criteria, and I would be extremely surprised if it did not pass a before-and-after test relative to non-EMS currencies.

But what of the costs, and what of the benefits? The author finds greater convergence of inflation rates and real monetary growth rates among EMS countries averaged after 1979. The mixed comparisons with other countries do not make a completely convincing case that the EMS inflation convergence is markedly different from other groups of countries. Moreover, real money supplies are notoriously dangerous indicators of the stance of monetary policy: because velocity tends to be positively correlated with expected inflation, it is not unusual to find the *real* money supply decelerating when monetary policy is fueling an acceleration of inflation. The question of the contribution of the EMS to convergence must be considered as still open.

The paper offers some tantalizing hints on how exchange rates have been kept in line to the extent that they have been. But we need to know more to evaluate the benefits of the System. Has the existence of central rates and sterilized intervention activities reduced noise in exchange markets – noise which otherwise might have been associated with unstable expectations? And has this been achieved without any change in fundamental macroeconomic policies? That is to say, has the EMS been a cheap lunch in that there has been little need to subordinate domestic policy instruments to its operation? If so, has this stabilization of expectations reduced only short-run volatility or has the reduction of noise had a stabilizing effect over the medium-term? My own reading of the evidence on exchange market efficiency and on the small percentage of exchange rate changes over the medium-term that seem systematically explainable on the basis of fundamentals (even ex-post), leave me disposed to believe that there is a potential for sterilized intervention that is coordinated and undertaken according to a well-understood set of principles to reduce exchange rate volatility. Excess noise in the system might well be reduced without sacrificing domestic policy objectives. The benefits would be better micro-decisionmaking and less aggravation of vicious and virtuous cycles. But we have, as yet, no evidence that the EMS has achieved this.

Padoa Schioppa suggests that the EMS has been held together by more coordination of monetary policy than meets the eye – the 'unwritten rules'. I take this to mean, in analytical terms, that intervention has not been fully sterilized, whether this was the direct result of the way intervention was technically executed or the result of keying of domestic monetary policy operations to EMS exchange rate obligations. For starters, it would be nice to know the facts. What does the record have to say about correlations between EMS intervention and changes in central bank assets net of non-monetary liabilities? If there is a correlation, is it only apparent in the short-run or over longer periods as well? How symmetrical is the behaviour between large and small countries? Between weak currencies and strong currencies?

If the evidence suggested that central banks' balance sheets expanded and contracted in response to pressures on their currencies within the EMS, different interpretations could still be offered. For a broad spectrum of open-economy macro-economists who are skeptical of the power of sterilized exchange market intervention, such evidence would make sense of a finding of reduced exchange rate volatility within the EMS: it could be attributed to monetary policy reactions. But would such a reduction represent an improvement in welfare? The answer would depend on where the disturbances that led to larger exchange rate fluctuations were coming from before the EMS was established and on this there would be many priors within the spectrum. A fundamentalist monetarist economist – one who believed in the absolute stability of velocity – would expect to see greater stability of exchange rates only as a result of more stable *relative* money growth rates. Perhaps this would be a good thing, but not necessarily if it came at a cost of more unstable money growth for EMS countries taken together. In the middle ground, fallen away monetarists and lapsed Keynesians, who saw money demand as the central determinant of nominal income but also as subject to unpredictable shocks, would expect to see more volatility of money growth as exchange rate pressures signalled central banks to adjust money supplies in response to money demand disturbances. This volatility might well be associated both with greater exchange rate stability and with more stable economic conditions domestically. Once again, however, macroeconomic stability within the EMS bloc would depend on success in offsetting, rather than exacerbating, aggregate money demand disturbances in the bloc. Reducing *relative* disturbances between participants would not be sufficient.

A third group in the spectrum, comprised of those who see floating exchange rates as a source of additional noise in macroeconomic relationships – and I suspect this was a prevailing view among the architects of the EMS – ought to view greater money supply volatility in response to exchange market pressures with some misgiving. Greater exchange rate stability would then have been purchased at a cost of more unstable domestic monetary conditions. It would no longer be clear that it was worth it in strictly economic terms.

This leads me to the more fundamental agenda behind the EMS. It was established, in part, as a gesture to restore momentum towards greater political and economic unification in the community. If it were successful in this respect, it would be hard to fault the EMS, whether or not it made a large direct contribution to macroeconomic stability. But in this respect, the EMS has not provided as visible an impetus as one might have hoped. The commitment made at the time of its establishment, to take further steps towards monetary integration in Europe, has apparently been set aside. From the outside, it seems that as time has passed it has become more difficult – both politically and economically – to change central rates. Padoa Schioppa argues that this is because those decisions are becoming more collaborative, but this is a charitable view. Moreover, the system is held together, in part, with capital controls and even intra-EEC trade restrictions. Finally, one large member of the Community remains outside the exchange rate arrangements. These tensions may be as much a threat to European integration as more volatile exchange rates would be.

The book on the EMS is not finished yet. I have indicated some economic questions that seem answerable now. And it is important to answer them – not just from the standpoint of evaluating the EMS but for understanding better how alternatives to the present exchange rate arrangements among major currencies and blocs of currencies might function. However, the answer to the most important question, whether external monetary arrangements can contribute to closer economic and political integration in Europe, will remain open for some time. I, for one, hope the answer will be yes.

NOTE

* The views expressed herein are those of the author and not necessarily those of OECD Member governments or its Secretariat.

9 Panel discussion: the prospects for international economic policy coordination

WILLIAM H. BRANSON – *Chairman*

To conclude the conference we have chosen four distinguished panellists, who will place the proceedings in perspective, or as Dick Cooper said 'make statespersonlike pronouncements on the proceedings'. The panel consists of Richard Cooper from Harvard, Michael Emerson from the European Commission, Louka Katseli from the Centre of Planning and Economic Research in Athens, on leave from Yale, and Stephen Marris from the Institute for International Economics in Washington. I'd like to introduce the discussion with a quote which Jeff Sachs somehow missed. It is from the 19th Century American expert on time consistency, Ralph Waldo Emerson, who said 'A foolish consistency is the hobgoblin of little minds, adored by little statesmen and philosophers and divines' (my thanks to Joan Pearce for identifying the source). I'll leave it to the conference to decide into which category the disputants from this morning's discussion should be put.

RICHARD N. COOPER

Today we have a new perspective compared with policy discussions ten or twenty years ago. It is that governments can be viewed as economic agents that respond, like firms and households, to the economic environment in which they operate. A government is not a deus ex machina which can just do anything that is technically possible. Viewing governments this way raises a host of questions that economists have asked about firms and households, concerning the existence and nature of what might be called a 'policy equilibrium'. That is to say, does the collection of actions of interdependent nations settle down to an equilibrium as soon as the environment settles down? My own answer to that question is negative because the preferences of governments are ever-shifting. That is a point to which I want to return, but let us waive it for the moment.

If policy does settle down to an equilibrium, then we can ask questions about its efficiency. Is it Pareto-optimal or not? If it is Pareto-optimal then the question of cooperation, the topic of this conference, is moot. It is worth noting that only economists would even think of looking at things this way. The layman would take for granted that cooperation between governments would surely make things better than they otherwise would be. That does not mean that cooperation is easy or that it will necessarily take place, but surely it would make things better. But the economist's stock-in-trade is to point out that there are circumstances under which a system of highly decentralized decision-making is socially optimal – that was Adam Smith's great insight. It is at least a logical possibility that a series of decentralized independent decisions by governments – taking into account the environment in which they operate – will settle down into a position that is socially optimal. Max Corden has written that the policy equilibrium might have this property, and in a different context I made a similar observation in my Wicksell Lectures ten years ago.

We therefore have to ask: what is the case in principle for policy coordination? To continue the analogy with firms and households, we have the same kind of case that we do for private markets. I would identify four reasons for coordination.

The first is the existence of public goods – that is to say, an expenditure or activity which would benefit all but which without conscious coordination will not be supplied at all, or will be under-supplied, because of the free-rider problem, the possibility of benefiting without paying the costs that is the nature of a public good.

The second, closely related, reason is the presence of externalities of some kind that are not transmitted entirely through the 'market' as it bears on the decision-makers. Much of what we have seen talking about here falls into this category – externalities, spillovers from the action of one government to the environment of another, operating in most cases through the international terms of trade, but one can imagine other kinds of transmission as well.

Third, the world of governments hardly fits the model of atomistic competition that we typically use for households and firms. There are only about 160 governments in the world, of very unequal size and influence on their environment. The assumption of 'other things being equal' that is usually plausible for households and sometimes for firms is not at all plausible for the ten to twenty governments in which we are most interested. They usually dispose of some monopoly power over at least some of their international transactions, and attempts – even frustrated attempts – to exercise this power will in general assure that the policy equilibrium is not socially optimal.

Those are the three standard cases of 'market failure' to come out of microeconomic analysis. I would add a fourth one in the case of policy coordination. Even in the absence of public goods, externalities, and monopoly power there might be a case for policy coordination because of time lags in the system and the fact that as a practical matter decision-making cannot be taken continuously, particularly as regards fiscal policy. As a consequence, a sequence that we are confident ultimately will settle down to an equilibrium that would be Pareto-optimal may nonetheless take a long time to reach if there is no coordination. There are therefore avoidable costs to not coordinating. If the system as a whole is impacted by disturbances all of the time, on average it will always be farther away from policy equilibrium than necessary. Because of the lags and the iterative nature of the policy process, avoidable losses can be reduced through coordination. So I would add that as a fourth circumstance under which we might want policy coordination.

Now let me shift course and say something about the kinds of coordination that we have actually observed, successful examples of international cooperation in historical experience. A leading example is the adoption of the metric system – an international decision, stimulated, it is true, by the imperial ambitions of France in the early 19th century, but it stuck. Britain did not join until over a century later, and the United States is still only inching toward it. A second example, of which 1984 is the centenary, is the adoption of Greenwich Mean Time, the world's time system, and the closely related geographic grid system. Both of these have the attributes of public goods. It needed conscious effort and coordination to adopt them, and to get the full benefits from them.

An example which is more interesting from our point of view, and which I want to come back to, is international public health. Around the turn of the century, there was a major breakthrough, after over a half-century of attempts, in establishing an international regime for the containment of contagious diseases. We can draw some illuminating lessons from that.

There are more specialized examples: the International Telegraphic Union took responsibility for the allocation of the electro-magnetic radio frequencies spectrum; ICAO, the International Civil Aviation Organization, which is concerned not only with civil aviation safety standards but also with air traffic control. Once again, standardization, an international public good, is crucial.

We can turn to the domains which are closer analytically to the topic of this conference. There was the Bretton Woods Agreement, which was a framework agreement for monetary cooperation; the GATT; and I put in this category also the Non-Proliferation Treaty. All of these have the feature that the Nash non-cooperative equilibrium appeared to the participants to be far inferior to a cooperative solution. The non-cooperative approach resulted, the Bretton Woods architects thought, in mutually disadvantageous competitive currency devaluation. In the case of trade, the world was riddled with trade restrictions which analysts realized was a sub-optimal equilibrium. GATT was really a tariff disarmament regime. The Non-Proliferation Treaty, although non-economic in content, displays a similar analytic structure; it is a GATT before the event, so to speak, designed to prevent a world in which the Nash uncooperative equilibrium involves the proliferation of nuclear weapons.

We also have the various international fisheries agreements, which involve stock depletion externalities which can be beneficially limited by some cooperative regime. More recently we have the International Energy Agency, which has been at least partially successful as an exercise in international cooperation. In the macroeconomic area we have the efforts at coordination by the OECD and, in the last ten years, by the economic summits; in my judgement they have been less successful.

What generalizations can one make from looking at this list? – and this list could be greatly augmented. The first is that international coordination of national policy is in fact possible. We have been talking here about macroeconomic policy, but if we look over the whole domain of inter-national cooperative activities there are a number which have been highly successful. I would conjecture that when they are successful it is because the benefit-cost ratio is high and – this is very important – is manifest. It must be high and manifest – clear, not just to technicians, but to a wider public as well. That condition is necessary to overcome the temptation to become a free-rider, or the irritation at those who remain free-riders.

Another lesson we can learn from this historical list is that there are many forms of coordination. We should not speak of coordination as though it is a well-defined thing. It can mean literal harmonization of policies – the extreme case would be adoption of common standards, the metric system or the Greenwich Mean Time System. It can mean joint expenditures – for example, to maintain the international air-traffic control system. It can involve, thirdly, a rule-based framework, where nations remain free to make their decisions autonomously but within an environment which involves agreed rules. Fourth, it can involve a virtually continuous exchange of information, which would not take place without an institu-tional mechanism. That was especially important in the public health case, and it is in my view especially important in macroeconomic matters.

Finally, what we most often have in mind when we speak of policy coordination, it can involve continuous joint decision-making. But it is worth emphasizing that that is only one form of coordination, and probably the most difficult form of cooperation for nations to undertake.

We have experienced difficulties in macroeconomic policy coordination, and the reasons for those difficulties are worth enumerating. I will return to public health to provide contrast. The first is that there is typically – not always, but typically – a disagreement on the economic outlook, the prognosis for the future. Those disagreements often reflect deeper biases in the observers. Without agreement on the economic outlook, it is difficult to coordinate policy actions.

Secondly, there is often no agreement on objectives. That is worth developing a bit because literal agreement on objectives is not necessary to enjoy gains from cooperation. But where there are deep philosophical differences on such matters as the role of government, or on the degree of interference that is acceptable in private markets, then cooperation becomes especially difficult among governments. More serious even than disagreement on objectives is that governments do not actually know what their objectives are until they have to make decisions involving choice among difficult alternatives.

Robert Putnam, a Harvard political scientist who has done a careful study of the economic summits, makes the interesting observation that the most successful summits, including the Bonn summit and the moderately successful Venice summit, were the summits when there were substantial disagreements within governments – not between governments, but within governments – that went to the summit. That made it possible to form coalitions across governmental lines, among various parties within each government, in order to push a particular line. In contrast, on those occasions when governments held well-defined views about what they wanted, it was very much more difficult to get agreement among governments. That is an interesting and astute observation. A more general observation is that governments do not know what their objectives are until they are forced by circumstances to make decisions.

Third, what is a special challenge to the economics profession, there is no agreement on what I would call means-ends relationships, or the 'technology' of policy, the mechanism by which pulling a particular policy lever influences a particular ultimate objective. We are more at sea now than we were ten years ago in macroeconomics. We heard yesterday Pat Minford's view of how economies work, which is radically different from other views on how economies work. Economists these days sometimes cannot agree even on the sign of the effect of a particular policy instrument on target variables, much less the magnitude. These sharp disagreements on means-ends relationships make macroeconomic policy cooperation impossible.

I draw your attention to an interesting recent exhibit of our uncertainties here: a description by Henry Wallich, a full-fledged member of our profession, a professor of economics for many years, now a decision-maker who sits on the US Federal Open Market Committee. He recently described how monetary policy works in the United States today. Wallich ought to be as informed as anyone is; he has considerable talent and professional expertise at his disposal, including some of those here. And yet his statement is suffused with uncertainty and agnosticism. The slippage between what the trading desk can do and the effect on our ultimate economic objectives, the uncertainty about means-ends relationships with which we are operating, is just enormous. That leaves enormous scope for disagreement even between people who share prognosis and who share objectives.

Finally, there is always disagreement on the distribution of gains from cooperation. Every negotiation is, at its core, a zero-sum game, even when there are substantial mutual gains to be had from it. If the mutual gains are obvious, the negotiators quickly take those for granted, and the bargaining immediately focuses on the distribution of gains. While analysts, standing away from the problem, can draw a sharp distinction between zero-sum and non-zero-sum games, every negotiation is actually a zero-sum game, because the gains – assuming they are quickly recognized, which is not always the case – become taken for granted and the negotiation becomes one over the distribution of gains. The free-rider problem is of course a special example of that, where every country wants the world to go ahead with a recognized public good, and they want the United States to bear the cost. We see that phenomenon again and again, whether one is talking about NATO or reduction of world inflation.

For all of these reasons, since the topic of this afternoon's discussion is the prospects for economic cooperation, I think the prospects in the macroeconomic area are rather dim. I said I would come back to the question of international public health because that experience is extremely illuminating. Today we take for granted the desirability of some kind of international regime to prevent the spread around the world of contagious diseases, which is especially important with as much travelling as occurs these days. We do not want cholera showing up in Philadelphia or London. We have a regime to make sure that does not take place. The interesting historical point is that it took over fifty – 50 – years from the first identification of contagious disease as an international problem, with a cholera epidemic in London in the 1840s which it was assumed was imported from the Far East, to the time at which the beginnings of a satisfactory regime for quarantining and for the containment of the spread of contagious diseases was established. I would hypothesize that the principal reason that it took half a century was the enormous ignorance that prevailed throughout most of that period on the nature of contagious diseases – how people were infected, how diseases were transmitted, how long their incubation period was, and so forth. Those disagreements left every party free to choose the scientific hypothesis that imposed least costs on him, even with a widely shared objective that disease should be controlled. It was not until the 1890s and the emergence of solid scientific knowledge on the transmission of contagious diseases that the whole field of hypotheses for each disease collapsed to a single one, at which point it became possible for each disease to say 'the incubation period is x days, the quarantine period need not be longer than x days, you do not have to burn all the merchandise on the ship, etc.' Only then did we get agreement on an international regime. Technical information then became meaningful, it was quickly transmitted, and countries acted on it.

Unfortunately, in the macroeconomic area, we are still back in the 1840s; maybe the 1850s. I will resist the temptation to offer my view on the contemporary macroeconomic counterpart of the phlogiston theory.

MICHAEL EMERSON

This is the moment when we have to draw conclusions on whether the international coordination of economic policy can really be a beneficial activity, or one so riddled with difficulties to be just an illusion. The latter view is being heard these days from many voices on the other side of the Atlantic, and even from some on this side. My remarks basically support the former view, that coordination can be really beneficial. It is a sign of the times that this view has to be defended.

The minimal efficient agenda for coordination

Recently some senior representatives of the US administration have been arguing that the realistic agenda for international economic coordination has four main points (i) trade rules for the world community, (ii) a sub-set of rules circumscribing trade in strategic goods with Communist countries, (iii) international debt management problems and (iv) rules for the international respect of private property rights. Macroeconomic policy – monetary, exchange rates, budgetary – is off the agenda.

I would put the point of view that this list is inadequate. For who, one may then ask? For Europeans in their more interdependent regional affairs, yes, almost all would agree. For the international community of industrialised countries also, I would argue that this agenda is insufficient to be efficient. It is doubtful whether this limited agenda can stand the test of time. The trade and debt repayment systems are already cracking, to say the least. I would speculate that the US and Japan at some stage will find it be in their interests in due course to participate more actively in macroeconomic and monetary cooperation in order to support other parts of the international system, and for this I will describe one possible scenario in a moment.

Having made one point addressed to other countries, I would readily balance it with another addressed to the Europeans, a point which came out clearly in this conference. If the US is to be interested in coordination it has to have someone to coordinate with, and a large collection of medium-sized or small countries arguing different positions is a sure formula for getting nowhere. Thus Europe needs to get its act together. This is gradually taking place, but at times it appears to be progressing at the speed of an Alpine glacier. But we have at least moved beyond the stage of debating whether better EC coordination is in competition with the pursuit of better international coordination. There is, I think, now widespread recognition that an EC organisation of coordination, mixed with elements of integration, is a natural feature of a multi-tiered world system. The special case of the EC warrants may be spelt out more explicitly.

Some particular features of coordination in the EC

The special features of the EC case are that:

- first, relatively explicit objectives are recognized for both 'nominal' and 'real' convergence of economic performance of Member States, and
- secondly, coordination is one technique of collective action that fits in with a fairly extensive array of legal and financial instruments of common policy. Macroeconomic policy is a subject of coordination, with the European Monetary System standing as its centre piece. Microeconomics and supply side policies are the subject of many legal and financial instruments of common action.

I will illustrate this outline a little.

Monetary convergence and coordination

The European Monetary System is addressed to the objective of nominal convergence and stabilisation. The system appears to have become accepted – by private economic agents as well as governments – as a permanent institution. Credibility and stability appear to be reinforcing each other increasingly. During the first three years of the system's life one might well have been disappointed at the rather sparse evidence of improved convergence in supporting budgetary policies and in the evolution of wage incomes. In the last two years, though, this convergence has become clearer, in particular with widespread budget policy initiatives in the direction of what in Germany is called 'consolidation policy', and incomes policy initiatives in several countries (for example to suspend or change wage indexation conventions).

Real convergence and market integration

It is an old proposition of economics that if you open markets for goods, services, labour and capital you will increase efficiency, put downward pressure on prices, improve the volume versus price mix in nominal GDP, and tend to achieve an upward equalisation of the productivity of the factors of production, – which is the Community objective of 'real convergence'. It is a new experience that Europe has seen its volume versus price mix develop poorly, especially relative to the US which has seen its mix evolve recently in a very favourable way. Is this due in some degree to the more open and flexible US economy, with possibly a new structural effect of recent deregulation and supply side measures? Alongside its justified grumbling about US macro policy, Europe seems to be concluding that there is a lesson here for European market rigidities (national and cross-country). A new momentum in favour of internal (EC) market liberalisation for goods, services and capital markets, together with national reforms of labour market law, social regulations etc. appears to be building up. In order actually to deliver internal market liberalisation, you certainly need more than coordinated action – you are in the business of EC legislation, which in turn becomes a matter of voting rules and behaviour in the Council of Ministers. Here too there are signs that political leaders in the EC are prepared to look again at the rules of majority versus unanimity voting in areas of clear Community jurisdiction. So there is a possible model here of synergy between cooperative macro-economic policy moves. They can support each other, and indeed either could be difficult to advance without the other.

Redistribution

Even the strongest enthusiasts for open markets know that in reality there will be problems of speed, smoothness and evenness of distribution of the gains from market liberalisation. This problem is obviously of concern to Ireland, the south of Italy, parts of the United Kingdom, Greece and even more for Portugal and Spain to come. There are also therefore triangular links in the policy system between monetary stabilisation, liberalisation of markets and regional transfer questions. The European Community budget has various financial mechanisms aimed at these problems. For example Italy and Ireland's adhesion to the European Monetary System was conditioned on a five-year package of investment subsidies and loans from the Community, and these have been implemented.

Coordination around the US–Japan–Europe triangle

Macroeconomic coordination is not very impressive between these regions at the moment. The question here is whether we are likely to return to a situation in which the gains for coordination appear to be big enough to justify coordinated policy initiatives. I will argue that the answer could become 'yes', at least for some episodes in economic cycles, and possibly even 'yes' to the point of inducing more systematic changes in the rules of the game – the main candidate here being the exchange rate.

I will illustrate my point with some remarks on the prospects for 1985 or 1986, in particular the risk that the process of correcting the US financial policy mix could lead to a dangerous situation for the world economy, such that the US would look for supportive action in the rest of the industrialised world alongside its own policy adjustments.

There must be at least a possibility that the US could make a rough job of its policy adjustments in 1985 or 1986, in the sense of suffering for a period a rather sharp stop to growth and imports while real interest rates remain very high. With sluggish growth in Europe and Japan, there could be very serious problems again with the world indebtedness problem. The exchange rate of the dollar could also become highly unstable at some stage with a large fall potentially causing serious inflation problems in the US. In this case, notably in the event that the US might embark upon a significant fiscal contraction, the US might well need to look to Europe and Japan to support world trade demand and possibly the dollar's exchange rate also.

It would well be then that Europe and Japan should respond. There could in fact be a special problem to look after here in the triangular relationship, which is on the balance of payments side. Someone will have to take over a part of the present US deficit, but Europe is unlikely to be the major volunteer, because the present imbalance is largely a Pacific affair. This obviously means that there would have to be an explicit differentiation between the European and Japanese policy reactions, presumably using the exchange rate as well as domestic financial variables for this purpose.

In short, there could well be future episodes for achieving a substantially better outcome from a coordinated solution; maybe, to hazard a guess, as much as 2–4% of world GDP as the difference between an unsuccessful non-cooperative versus successful cooperative management of a given cyclical episode. The case for episodic cooperation from time to time is not so difficult to identify, even outside Europe.

Finally on systems and targeting principles, and speaking quite personally, I would want to encourage the efforts of Professors McKinnon, Meade and Williamson to define principles for soft exchange rate policy between US-Japan-Europe combined with domestic policy management rules. These may seem long-shots as of today, but the capacity of purely discretionary policy convergence and surveillance to deliver results is not so impressive. There is a choice, then, between episodic cooperation 'on' and 'off' for specific moves in given situations, and these other ideas for rules. There should be a future for one or the other. A permanently non-cooperative system in macroeconomic affairs is likely to inflict heavy costs on all parties.

LOUKA T. KATSELI

Thank you Mr Chairman,

I would like first to focus on some issues that concern 'spillover effects', and especially on the point raised by Matt Canzoneri regarding the sign and symmetry of spillover effects. Secondly, I would like to talk about some aspects of coordination which we haven't touched in this conference.

Regarding asymmetries in spillover effects, it's important to recognize that there exist asymmetries not only of the effects but also of the origin of specific shocks. More importantly there also exist asymmetries regarding the monitoring of outcomes and policy design.

During the last decade most of the shocks in the international economy had to do with input prices. Partly as a result of the increasing strength of unions, we experienced sharp increases in labour prices especially in Europe. The 70s were also characterized by sharp increases in the oil price. More recently we have seen high nominal and real interest rates largely connected with US policy. Shocks that are 'demand shocks' for some countries become 'supply shocks' for others, since countries are linked both through trade in final and intermediate products and through financial transactions. It would be interesting to study if in fact disturbances exhibit systematic properties as to their origin and if not what type of insurance scheme could protect a country from random external disturbances. For example recent proposals in international debt negotiations to put a cap on interest rates could be analysed as an effort by borrowing countries to insure themselves against future fiscal or monetary policy by their creditors.

The origin of the shocks is important even if shocks are in fact internal. Whether a shock originates from a country's government, from its labour unions, from its exporters, or from its asset-holders, has important implications as to the likely response and reaction of governments as well as to the likely success of efforts to coordinate economic policy.

Moving now on to the effects, it is widely known that there are asymmetric effects of policies across countries as a result of differences in labour market structure, differences in the composition of trade, differences in financial market behaviour and finally differences in institutional factors. As this is an area of extensive and well publicized research I'm not going to dwell on this point.

The third area of asymmetries concerns monitoring. We talked yesterday about time-consistency in policy. It should be noted that there exist both regional and functional inconsistencies in the monitoring of policies. For example an institution like the IMF applies different rules for monitoring LDC debt and their fiscal and monetary policies, as opposed to industrial countries facing similar domestic or external imbalances. It is interesting to quote a small passage from the recent report of the UN's Committee of Development Planning. It writes, 'improved international cooperation requires effective surveillance of national policies. They must not be inconsistent with accepted common objectives nor have negative repercussions on other countries.' It then goes on to say that the seal of approval, which is provided by the IMF and which is decisive for other resource flows to developing countries makes such surveillance even more intense and controversial. 'The surveillance of surplus or reserve currencies which is also stipulated for the Fund is at present neglected which makes the situation asymmetrical, unbalanced, and inequitable'. One should look more carefully at what is the source of these regional inconsistencies.

I would also stress 'functional' inconsistencies, that is between lending or borrowing countries or between labour and capital within a given country. I've seen many discussions on rigidities of wages, but little has been said about rigidity of profits.

Looking now at the institutional apparatus for coordination, one notes hierarchical structures of decision making which might be inappropriate for the outcomes that are sought. Within these hierarchical structures there exists a compartmentalization of decision making both within and between groups. Each of the important international committees such as the G-10 or G-20 etc. maintains almost complete control over specific areas and issues. Furthermore the existence of a hierarchical structure for decision making creates incentives for the delegation of authority to other groups higher up the scale. When players know that there exists another forum which is likely to make decisions that suit better their own interest, they are prone to delegate that decision to that forum and to block its resolution within the existing one.

Let me give you an example. Four days after the Contadora resolution, in an important committee of the EC there was no talk whatsoever about the possibility of debt repudiation by these countries and the desirable response by the EC community. When these issues were raised, the response from more than one participant was that these issues are discussed in G-10 and not within the EC. At the same time, everybody agreed that such discussion would be both interesting and beneficial to the promotion of EC interests. The delegation of decision-making to other groups in order to ensure particular outcomes is quite usual and could be appropriately modelled as a 'game'.

Apart from decision-making there also exists compartmentalization of issues. There is a lot of pressure for example to limit UNCTAD's activities to particular trade issues as opposed to financial or monetary conditions which are resolved in the IMF.

In conclusion, it seems to me that there exist basic asymmetries not only in structures but also in policy prescriptions, in monitoring and decision making. In my view these asymmetries are connected with the international institutional framework and the way it was originally set up.

Speaking now about coordination per se it is important to provide an answer for at least three questions. First, who are the agents who come together? Secondly, why do they choose to coordinate their activities? Thirdly, what are the likely outcomes?

When we talk about coordination it is important to make distinctions between governments, central bankers, labour, industry etc. The characteristics of games and outcomes will differ quite substantially depending on the group and the time profile in which it is operating. The time consistency of policy actions will be different if you talk about governments, bankers or other agents. One could look for criteria that would determine 'optimum coordination areas', as we do with criteria for 'optimum currency areas'. These could include political, economic or functional characteristics. My guess is that the type and the likely outcome of the game we set-up in our theoretical approaches will be largely influenced by these criteria.

Why now do actors come together? Apart from the reasons that have already been expounded by Dick Cooper, i.e. the public good and the externalities aspects of coordination, there are four other important reasons which should be considered. These include: (a) the legitimization of public policy at home especially where there is internal opposition to specific policy measures, (b) enforcement of a national position to a larger set of players which becomes feasible if there is asymmetric market power among them, (c) enforcement of a group position on individual actors (reparation payments, debt rescheduling etc.) and finally (d) reduction of uncertainty which might have to do with the sharing of information, or the development of common policy objectives as a form of mutual insurance.

The underlying reason(s) why actors come together, is an important determinant of the likely outcome. It will determine for example the probability of a minimum consensus scenario, or of outcomes with a specific national, regional or ideological bias. There is probably a mapping between the composition of a group of actors, the ultimate purpose of their coordinating efforts and the likely outcome of this process.

In conclusion it seems to me that there are two important aspects of coordination. The first has to do with the feasibility and optimality of different coalitions and the second with the appropriateness of the institutional structure for the promotion of common objectives.

STEPHEN MARRIS

During most of my previous incarnation as an OECD official I used to be rather critical of my academic friends because they did not seem to be working much on what was our primary concern – the international coordination of macropolicies (it's called 'cooperation' in official circles). I was therefore delighted to find, when I left the official world a year ago, that quite a number of academics – most of whom are gathered here – had developed a keen interest in the subject.

After listening to the proceedings over the last two days I have somewhat more mixed feelings. I had assumed that this renewed interest in the subject had been stimulated by the fact that over the last few years we have been witnessing a marvellous (un?)controlled experiment in *uncoordinated* macropolicies. I now find, however, that another reason for this academic interest is that technological advances have made it possible to make empirical use of the elegant tools of game theory and control theory quite cheaply and quickly – and that this is a subject to which they seem to apply rather nicely.

At the technical level, I am not qualified to judge whether the use of these tools has yielded new insights. Coming from the world of policymaking I was encouraged to find that such concepts as Nash and Pareto optima and time consistency are definitely very relevant to the problems of real world policymaking. But looking at the results of attempts to apply them systematically and empirically most of the substantive results achieved so far seem to me to be either rather obvious or rather obvious nonsense.

One main thread that runs through the substantive results is the Prisoner and his Dilemma. Following the 'weak currency crises' of the Lira, the French Franc and Sterling in 1975–76, the phenomenon of overshooting was formalized by the academic profession. It had two implications for international macropolicy. Any country wanting to expand was, with flexible rates, confronted with a significantly worsened split between increased output and increased inflation, especially in the case of monetary expansion. Equally, any country wanting to reduce inflation had a strong incentive to do so through monetary contraction. Thus a prevailing theme in the literature, much in evidence over the last few days, has been the danger that, with flexible rates, rational behavior by individual countries could impart a deflationary bias into the system as a whole.

My own feeling on this is that events have now moved on. First, as far as the late 1970s and early 1980s are concerned, I would tend to accept Ken Rogoff's point that since there was probably an inflationary bias in domestic monetary and fiscal policies, this international deflationary bias may, at the time, have been a good thing. Indeed, there was more to it than this. I would argue that after the second oil crisis economic cooperation actually itself introduced a deflationary bias into the system. What happened was that the major powers became convinced – in my view rightly – that they had to do something decisive about inflation. So whenever they met together they tried to bolster each other's courage to do it. It was not that they were Prisoner Dilemmaed, they were deliberately and collectively summoning up the courage to put us through the worst post-war recession – and most (but not all) of them knew what they were doing. So if we want to analyze this period with our nice new tools one should introduce a shift variable for this change in the major powers' preference function – which they then effectively imposed on the rest of the world.

It becomes more complicated if we try to carry on using this same model to bring the story up to date. As the major countries moved successfully down their steepened anti-inflationary preference curve we might have expected the Prisoner's Dilemma to re-emerge. And indeed the French government provided a vivid reminder of how adverse the trade-offs had become for an individual (socialist) country which wanted to expand. It was not obvious that we would have found another expansionary candidate had it not been for the apparently accidental combination of two remarkable people, Ronald Reagan and Paul Volcker.

What happened next may not have been entirely the result of an historical accident. Most of our models tell us that the United States is the one country that can obtain a distinctly favorable combination of expansion and low inflation through a combination of expansionary fiscal and contractionary monetary policies. More generally, it was perhaps inevitable that as the whole world was put through the wringer of disinflation, it would turn out to be the most powerful and creditworthy country which took the expansionary lead because it was the only one which could get away with it.

Thus Oudiz and Sachs, in their Brookings paper (1984), made an extremely ingenious effort to show that the present concatenation of divergent fiscal and monetary policy can be explained in terms of rational behavior by governments with different preference functions working within a common framework of understanding about how the world works. The fact is, however, that there is a much more plausible explanation of what has happened, namely that the major countries are now basing their policies on quite *different* models of how the world works.[1] What I find so frustrating is that, as set out in my Graham Lecture,[2] it should be obvious to all reasonable economists that there is something profoundly wrong with the national and international mix of monetary and fiscal policies currently being followed by the major industrial economies. And yet – despite the renewed academic interest in macropolicy coordination – the work done so far seems to have confused the issues as much as it has clarified them.

Where does this leave us as far as the application of our nice new tools? My feeling is that it should lead us back to having a further look at the models themselves. There is really not much point in playing around with optimization techniques when, as Matt Canzoneri pointed out, both academics and governments disagree not only about the magnitude but also often about the signs of the spillover effects of different policy actions in multi-country models.

Three quick points about the models. First, they are still not tracking exchange rates at all well over the time horizon relevant to macropolicy making. Moreover, I suspect that the potential for stabilizing speculation with respect to the sort of 3–5 year cycles we are seeing is diminishing. If so, it follows that exchange rates are likely to move more in response to given changes in monetary and fiscal policies than in the past – and hence by more than suggested by our models.

Second, the models need to deal more explicitly and empirically with debt accumulation, both national and international. How far can a government pile up debt domestically before this puts upward pressure on real interest rates? How far can a country pile up external debt before this exerts downward pressure on the exchange rate? In many cases, e.g. the United States, we tend to assume that these causalities lie outside the time horizon of the policy simulations. But although this may be true in the sense that the lags are long, it is surely unwise to ignore them in exercises directed toward the optimization of national and international macropolicies.

Third, I am suspicious of models which suggest that it can pay off for a country to export inflation now through an over-valued exchange rate and then later re-import it when the rate has to come back down to its equilibrium level. I strongly believe that this underestimates the irreversible damage done to the structure and dynamics of the economy concerned by prolonged periods of misalignment.

Apart from improving the models, what else could be done? It might be fun to play around with a system in which different countries are basing their policies on *different* models, and then see what happens to each country's welfare according to its own preferences depending on which model turned out to be right. Second, it might be useful to extend Sachs' work on countries' revealed preferences to test how time consistent they are and what is the minimum necessary level of international consistency (all countries cannot have a shadow price for foreign exchange above one – at least not for long). Work along these lines might at least help to demonstrate how inherently unstable the present constellation of policies really is. But surely the longer term objective should be to develop more realistic models of how the world works, to impose on them a sensible preference function in terms of shadow prices for growth, inflation and foreign exchange (allowing for differences in national tastes so long as they are internationally consistent) and *then* use optimization tools to show that there are important gains to be obtained from macropolicy coordination.

This may sound implausible, but I am less gloomy than Dick Cooper – for a rather gloomy reason. My own reading of the future is that, to use his analogy – we are headed for a rather serious epidemic of economic cholera. If I am right, this could mean that the work we are doing could turn out to have much more practical relevance than seems likely at the moment. The United States is headed for trouble, and is going to discover that it is much more dependent on the rest of the world than it presently realizes.

And history teaches us that it is only when the United States becomes convinced that there is something wrong with the international economic system that things actually begin to happen.

NOTES

1 See my comments on Oudiz & Sachs (1984), 68–71.
2 See Marris (1984).

REFERENCES

Oudiz G. and J. Sachs (1984). 'Macroeconomic Policy Coordination Among the Industrial Economies', *Brookings Papers on Economic Activity*, 1, 1–64.
Marris, Stephen (1984). *Managing the World Economy: Will we ever Learn?*, Princeton Essays in International Finance No. 155.

Index

Numbers in italics indicate a reference to figures